ARCHITECTURAL
MODELING AND RENDERING
WITH AUTOCAD® R13 AND R14

ARCHITECTURAL
MODELING AND RENDERING
WITH AUTOCAD® R13 AND R14

Branko Kolarevic

John Wiley & Sons, Inc.

New York ▪ Chichester ▪ Weinheim ▪ Brisbane ▪ Singapore ▪ Toronto

This publication is designed to provide accurate and authoritative information in regard to the subject matter covered. It is sold with the understanding that the publisher is not engaged in rendering professional services. If professional advice or other expert assistance is required, the services of a competent professional person should be sought.

AutoCAD is a registered trademark of Autodesk, Inc.

Library of Congress Cataloging-in-Publication Date:

Kolarevic, Branko, 1963–
    Architectural modeling and rendering with AutoCAD R14 / Branko Kolarevic.
        p.   cm.
    Includes index.
    ISBN 0-471-19418-2 (pbk. : alk. paper)
    1. Architectural rendering—Programmed instruction.   2. Computer graphics.   3. AutoCAD (computer file)   I. Title.
    NA2728.K66   1998
    720'.28'40285—dc21   98-16457
                                                                 CIP

Printed in the United States of America.

10   9   8   7   6   5   4   3

To Wade Hokoda

CONTENTS

In the more than eight years I have taught 3D computer graphics to architecture students, I often have been frustrated by the lack of an appropriate textbook. The reference manuals and user's guides that came with the software were of little use in the class. The books that I was able to find in the bookstores or that I received from publishers either covered the theoretical concepts or the mechanics of such and such program. The theoretical books lacked the practical tutorials that students could use to learn by doing; the practical books lacked the explanation of theoretical concepts, which were necessary for developing a true understanding of how computer graphics work and how they can be creatively applied in architectural design.

As a result, I developed a set of short tutorial exercises to complement the lectures in which I introduced the basic concepts and demonstrated how they were implemented in particular software. I used Andrea Palladio's Villa Rotonda as a building that students would model and render, and used AutoCAD (because of its ubiquity in schools and offices) as a software through which basic concepts could be demonstrated and learned. Thanks to the exercises, students were able to quickly acquire the necessary knowledge and to develop skills in using the software with little effort, and those are exactly the aims of this book.

In writing this book, I have relied extensively on my previous teaching experience of first introducing the theoretical concepts and then providing an opportunity to better understand them through learning by doing. That is how the book is structured. By reading the theoretical chapters, you will develop an understanding of fundamental principles, which are illustrated by numerous examples. By completing the tutorial exercises, you will gradually become acquainted with AutoCAD and its most important 3D modeling and rendering commands and features. (The enclosed CD-ROM contains files for each of the seven tutorial exercises, so that you can start almost at any point. The files are also provided in case you make a mistake that you can't correct.)

Note that this book won't teach you all of the AutoCAD commands and options; it will, however, teach you how to effectively use AutoCAD's modeling and rendering features to explore and represent the building's geometry, form, and spatial qualities.

ACKNOWLEDGMENTS

I thank with the deepest gratitude Professor William J. Mitchell, who taught me the secrets of geometric modeling during my studies in the late 1980s at Harvard University Graduate School of Design, and Mr. Wade Hokoda, Prof. Mitchell's assistant and a digital artist *par excellance,* who demonstrated so skillfully the magic of computer graphics (and to whom this book is dedicated).

I thank Harvard University Graduate School of Design for providing an exceptional environment for learning and research in design computation and computer graphics. I also thank the University of Belgrade Faculty of Architecture for inspiring me in my early professional and academic endeavors.

Special thanks are reserved for my former students in Boston, Los Angeles, Miami, and now in Hong Kong, who helped me with their critical insights and constructive suggestions to improve the quality of the teaching materials and methods I used. Their hard work, unending quest for new knowledge, and exceptional quality of their projects were a source of constant inspiration. Ricardo Castro, Cheung Wai Man, Javier Cordova, Bjorn Green, Alex King, Benson Lee Chi Kit, Clive Lonstein, Robert Mayo, Marc Peter, Philip Smith, and Gary Wunderlich kindly provided images from their projects for this book.

This book was produced as I was teaching design and computing-related subjects at the Department of Architecture at the University of Hong Kong. I thank Marc Aurel Schnabel, my colleague, for producing some of the images in this book.

I also thank Janet Feeney, associate editor at John Wiley & Sons, Inc., for her enthusiastic support of this project, and Amanda Miller, editor, for her understanding as deadlines kept passing by.

Last, but not least, I thank my parents, Milka and Radomir, and Vera Parlac, my wife and colleague, for their support and constant concern as I was working on this book.

1

INTRODUCTION

The field of computer graphics comprises the art and science of creating images of three-dimensional objects. It blends computer programming, descriptive and analytical geometry, linear algebra, physics, traditional art and presentation techniques, and creative innovation. It is a diverse discipline that is still rapidly changing and evolving.

The term *computer graphics* means different things in different disciplines. To a scientist, it denotes ways to visualize complex scientific data; to a doctor, it provides ways to see inside a patient's body; to an engineer, it means efficient ways to analyze the behavior and appearance of objects; to an artist, it opens new possibilities to explore color, shape, and three-dimensional form; to an architect, computer graphics provides new ways to efficiently generate a building's layout and form, to visualize its exterior, and to analyze spatial qualities of its interior spaces.

In architecture, and in engineering and manufacturing, computer graphics introduced *computer-aided design (CAD)*, a new electronic medium for creating drawings and images of envisioned designs. Computer-aided design changed the way in which architects worked—the drafting tables, pencils, and rulers were replaced by computer monitors, workstations, and CAD software. Instead of drawing a line with pencil and ruler, an architect picks two points on a computer screen; to create a "paper" drawing, an architect prints a computer drawing onto paper using an ink-jet plotter.

The introduction of new digital media was met with outright hostility by some architects, which resulted not so much from true opposition to the idea but from the lack of understanding of the computer graphics concepts and new opportunities that opened up. Bit by bit, old myths gave way to new possibilities that computer graphics offers for creative exploration and expression of design ideas.

A BRIEF HISTORY OF COMPUTER GRAPHICS AND COMPUTER-AIDED DESIGN

The field of computer graphics was born in the early the 1960s, shortly after computers became part of the modern society. Then, as now, computers were used as powerful electronic number crunchers that could perform millions of mathematical calculations in a very short period of time, much faster than a human could. In the beginning, computers were used almost exclusively for scientific and military purposes, and to automate data processing in some large business operations. With the advent of computer graphics, computers found a new use: to simulate the physical world in which we live by using *computationally synthesized images.*

Back in the 1950s, in the early days of computing, computer-aided design was *imaginable.* The computers were a commercial reality. As soon as there were computers, engineers started to envision design machines. In 1956, *Fortune* magazine published a fairly accurate depiction of a computer-aided design workstation, complete with graphic input devices and a multi window display showing different views of a 3D object (Figure 1.1). Shortly after that article appeared, the first *vacuum-tube* computer capable of drawing lines electronically was developed at MIT; that very first computer graphics machine was called Whirlwind. In July 1962, in Moscow's *Pravda*, Professor Sinyakov asked, "Can a machine create a design?" Shortly thereafter, in 1963, Steven Coons outlined functions of a future CAD system in considerable detail in his seminal paper, "Outline of the Requirements for a Computer Aided Design System."

The real breakthrough occurred in 1963, when Ivan Sutherland demonstrated a sketching program called Sketchpad, developed for the TX-2 computer as part of his doctoral work at MIT

1.1 One of the early visions of a CAD system, published in the July 1956 issue of Fortune *magazine.*

Lincoln Laboratory (Figure 1.2). Sketchpad was a truly original thesis that introduced many ideas that are still widely used in computer graphics and CAD software. Sketchpad allowed engineers for the first time to generate drawings by using an interactive graphics terminal, and to manipulate them by using a light pen and a keyboard. Sutherland's pioneering work clearly demonstrated that CAD is *possible*.

1.2 Ivan Sutherland demonstrating Sketchpad.

(Reprinted with permission of Lincoln Laboratory, Lexington, MA)

In the following years, the field of computer graphics developed very rapidly. Numerous prototypes were introduced. In the mid-1960s, the first generation of CAD systems appeared, based on *mainframe* computers and *refreshed vector displays*. In 1966, IBM introduced an elaborate system known as DAC-1 (Design Augmented by Computer) for use by General Motors in automobile design. By the end of the 1960s, CAD systems were employed in various aspects of mechanical, civil, electrical, chemical, and industrial engineering.

In those early days, application of CAD in architecture lagged considerably behind applications in engineering. Architects did become interested, but there was general hostility to the idea and considerable ignorance of the potential benefits offered by computer technology. The fundamental reasons for that apparent lack of interest were mainly economic, since in those days CAD required investments of several hundred thousand or even millions of dollars. CAD was then a very expensive endeavor.

In 1963, Timothy Johnson of MIT's department of architecture created the first 3D modeling program by extending Sketchpad to 3D. At the same time, a number of interactive computer-aided design systems appeared, including COPLANNER by Souder and Clark (1964) and the well-known URBAN5 by Negroponte and Groisser (1970). During the 1960s, the first practical applications were mostly in the areas of structural and mechanical calculations, cost estimation and economic analysis, and specifications production; none of them involved any elaborate graphics.

Various articles and papers by Dawson, Eberhard, Souder, and Clark appeared in the early 1960s, discussing the potential of CAD in architecture. In 1964, Christopher Alexander published his book *Notes on the Synthesis of Form*, in which he discussed the use of systematic computer-based methods in architectural design. In 1964, a conference called "Architecture and the Computer" was held at Boston Architectural Center, attracting some 600 attendees. In 1968, Murray Milne organized at Yale University a major conference on computer graphics in architecture and design.

The invention of *solid state integrated circuits, time sharing,* and *remote terminals* brought in the mid-1960s a third generation of computer systems. As a result of advances in computer hardware and software algorithms, ComputerVision Corporation released in 1969 the first general purpose CAD system. By the end of 1969, there were a few CAD systems in practical use in large architectural offices.

In the 1970s, CAD became *available.* The fourth generation of computer systems based on VLSI (Very Large Scale Integration) circuit chips reached the market; the so-called minicomputers, such as DEC PDP-11, were introduced. As a result, the second generation of CAD systems emerged. Several corporations, such as ComputerVision, Applicon, Autotrol, and Calma, were marketing the so-called turnkey CAD systems. Autotrol became the first drafting system produced for and marketed exclusively to AEC (Architecture/Engineering/Construction) professionals. In the United Kingdom, there were large-scale CAD systems developed for use in public sector system-building programs (CEDAR, HARNESS, OXSYS, CARBS, SSHA, etc.).

The introduction of the first *microprocessors* (complete processors on a single chip) resulted in further miniaturization, further decreases in cost, and substantial increases in performance. In 1971, Intel Corporation introduced its famous 4004 microprocessor. MITS Altair 8800 became the first *personal computer* introduced on the market.

In addition to advances in hardware design and production, active research in the late 1960s and early 1970s resulted in the development of several important algorithms in computer graphics and artificial intelligence. In 1968, Ivan Sutherland invented the first *head-mounted display* based on a pair of cathode-ray tubes, the early predecessor of present-day virtual reality (VR) systems (Figure 1.3). Henry Gouraud, a researcher at the University of Utah, introduced in 1971 a *smooth shading* technique based on simple interpolation techniques (Figure 1.4). Bui Tuong Phong further improved Gouraud's shading algorithms and created what is nowadays one of the most used rendering techniques.

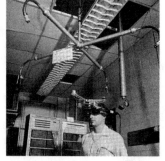

1.3 The predecessor of the VR system: Ivan Sutherland's head-mounted display (1968).

Academic institutions in the United States took the lead in computer-aided architectural design (CAAD) research. The Institute of Physical Planning at Carnegie-Mellon University became well known for its research on building description and space planning issues, and the Architecture Machine Group at MIT, led by Nicholas Negroponte, boldly ventured into the application of artificial intelligence in architecture and urban design.

1.4 *Flat and smooth shading.*

Architecture researchers have also made important contributions to the development of computer graphics. Charles Eastman and Chris Yessios (then at Carnegie-Mellon University) were among the pioneers of solid modeling. Donald Greenberg and his Computer Graphics Laboratory at Cornell University were on the forefront of computer graphics research in the 1970s and 1980s. William Mitchell and his students at UCLA were exploring the leading edge in the application of computer graphics in design. Nicholas Negroponte founded the Media Lab at MIT.

With the rapid developments in computer graphics, architects became interested in exploiting the capacity of computer graphics systems to simulate movement through architectural environments. In 1968 at UCLA, Peter Kamnitzer created the first architectural animation, called *Cityscape*, which was produced using General Electric's spacecraft landing simulation. In 1974, Donald Greenberg from Cornell University demonstrated a famous animation simulating the movement through the university campus.

Particularly important, from an architectural point of view, was the introduction of *desktop* computer graphics systems in 1975 by DEC and Tektronix Corporation. At the same time, inexpensive 8-bit personal computers were marketed by Apple Computer and Commodore. By the late 1970s, the idea of *personal computing* was established; the revolution, however, began with the introduction of the IBM PC (*personal computer*) in 1981. In 1982, a company called Autodesk introduced the first CAD program for the IBM PC, called AutoCAD (Figure 1.5). The CAD finally became *affordable*.

By the mid 1980s, a number of companies, such as Sun Microsystems, Apollo, and Tektronix, were marketing powerful 32-bit *workstations* for computer graphics and computer-aided design (the third generation of CAD systems). In 1984, IBM introduced PC AT (Advanced Technology) and publicly released its

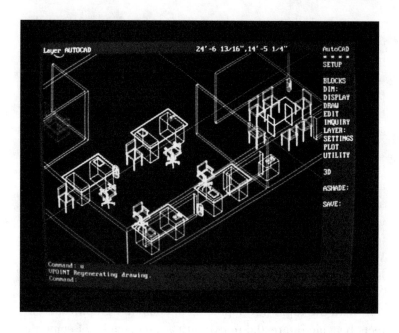

1.5 The early AutoCAD.

specifications; as a result, a number of less expensive "clones" appeared, among which Compaq dominated. Apple Computer released in 1984 a personal computer that featured its revolutionary Graphical User Interface (GUI), based on a *desktop* metaphor, first developed at Xerox PARC (Palo Alto Research Center). That first GUI introduced "icons," "menus," and "windows" as elements of computer-user interaction (Figure 1.6). Microsoft Corporation, the maker of Disk Operating System (DOS) for IBM PCs and clones, licensed Apple's innovative operating system and created its own version called Windows.

By the mid 1980s, the fourth generation of CAD systems was reality. Inexpensive 16-bit personal computers running simple CAD software became commonplace in architectural offices and schools. By the late 1980s, inexpensive 3D modeling and rendering programs appeared for personal computers.

In summary, since the early days of the 1960s, computer graphics has evolved from crude wire-frame images to photorealistic renderings (Figure 1.7), which can now be produced on inexpensive personal computers.

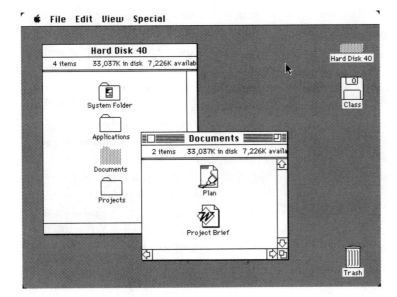

1.6 The elements of a Graphical User Interface: "icons," "menus," and "windows."

A BRIEF DESCRIPTION OF HOW CAD WORKS

Computer drawings and images are created using computer *hardware* and *software*, that is, various *devices* and *programs* used to store and process graphic information in drawings and images.

The computer hardware of a typical CAD workstation consists of *input, processing,* and *output* devices (Figure 1.8). A keyboard and some *pointing* device, a mouse or a digitizing tablet, are used to *input* data, such as commands or point locations, into the computer system. The processing unit, a computer itself, consists of a very fast *processor chip* (or multiple chips), often referred to as the *CPU* (short for *Central Processing Unit*); fast-working memory called *RAM* (*Random Access Memory*), used to store information while the system is in use; large-capacity *hard disk(s)*, used to "permanently" store data; and other devices, such as graphic accelerator, network, and modem cards. All these components are mounted on, or connected to, the *motherboard,* a plastic board with an embedded network of data channels called a *bus,* which binds all these components together into one operating unit (Figure 1.9). After the graphic information is processed by the processing unit, it is *output,* or displayed, on a computer monitor or some other output device, such as a printer or a plotter.

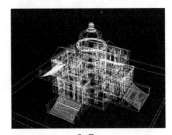

1.7a

1.7b

1.7 From wire-frame to photorealistic images.

1.8 A typical CAD worksta-tion.

1.9 Inside a computer system.

The computer system relies on *operating system software,* such as Microsoft Windows, to carry out its duties. Through Graphical User Interface (GUI), a user *interacts* with the system, that is, issues the commands, and enters the necessary informa-tion. To make computer use easier, all modern GUIs rely on a *desktop* metaphor, featuring *icons, windows,* and *menus* (Figure 1.10). *Icons* are used to represent *files,* which hold data; *applica-tions* (or *programs*), which are used to do something useful, such as write a memo or a create a drawing; *folders,* used to store and organize files and applications; and various *storage devices,* such as floppy and hard disks and CD-ROMs. *Windows* are used to display the *contents* of a file, hard disk, etc.

CAD *applications,* such as *AutoCAD* (Figure 1.11), are used to create drawings and models, and render images. The user interface typically consists of icon toolbars, pull-down menus, and graphics and command windows. To draw a line, a user can point and click on the appropriate icon (Figure 1.12), choose an item from a pull-down menu (Figure 1.13), or enter LINE in the command window (Figure 1.14). Once the command is issued, the system will request that additional information be provided, such as the location of the line's endpoints. The user then points and clicks at appropriate locations in the graphics window to specify points, or enters numeric coordinates at the command

1.10 The Graphical User Interface of the Microsoft Win-dows operating system.

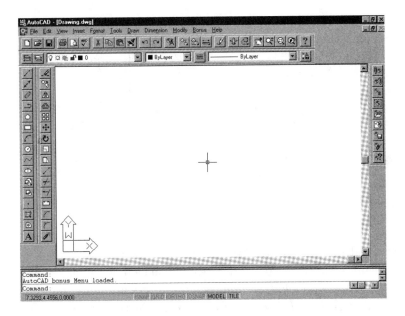

1.11 *AutoCAD's interface.*

1.12 *The* line *icon.*

prompt (Figure 1.15). Other 2D objects, such as arcs, circles, and rectangles, are drawn in similar fashion. Various *editing* operations and transformations can be applied to drawn objects—they can be moved, rotated, scaled, mirrored, trimmed, extended, stretched, offset, arrayed, copied, etc.

In CAD systems, a line is described by the x, y, and z coordinates of its endpoints (Figure 1.16). For each line in the drawing, CAD software stores a *database record* that describes its properties, such as endpoint coordinates, color, and thickness. To create an image of the drawing within the graphics window, the CAD software reads the database records and draws each object by converting its three-dimensional coordinates into two-dimensional coordinates of the computer screen.

3D objects are constructed by *extruding* or *revolving* 2D shapes (Figure 1.17). For example, to extrude a 2D shape, the user first selects the appropriate "tool" by pointing and clicking on its icon, then selects the shape to be extruded, and specifies the height of extrusion. Various 3D objects are available as "primitives," that is, they are predefined in the software and can be instantiated anywhere in the model space. The 3D objects can also be manipulated in many different ways; they too can be moved, rotated, scaled, mirrored, trimmed, extended, stretched, added, intersected, subtracted, etc. The created 3D objects are

1.13 *Issuing the Line command by choosing an item from a pull-down menu.*

```
Command: LINE
From point:
To point:
6.0836, 3.1222,0.0000
```

1.14 *You can enter the desired command at the command prompt.*

1.15 *Point locations can be specified numerically or graphically.*

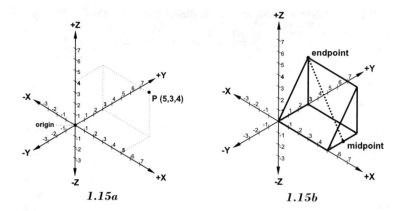

1.15a

1.15b

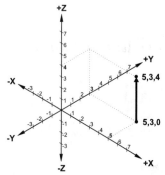

1.16 *Line endpoints are described by their x, y, and z coordinates.*

typically shown in *wire-frame* mode, that is, as if made of wire (Figure 1.18). To verify the results of the modeling operations, the user can create a *hidden-line* view by issuing a single command (HIDE). A *shaded* view can also be created in a single step.

If the CAD software supports *rendering*, an image of a 3D model can be computed with simulated illumination and surface

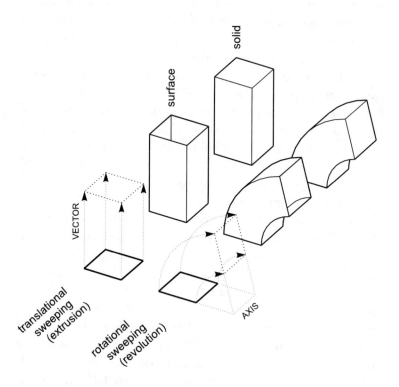

1.17 *3D objects can be constructed by extruding and revolving 2D shapes.*

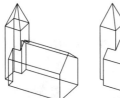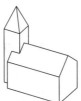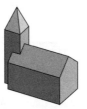

effects, such as transparency, reflection, and cast shadows (Figure 1.19). Light objects can be located in 3D space (Figure 1.20), and their properties defined (Figure 1.21). Material definitions (Figure 1.22) can be attached to 3D objects to render them realistically (Figure 1.23). The rendering software will compute an image based on the model's *geometry, lighting,* and *surface material* information, taking into account factors such as the angle and the intensity of the light incident on the surface, and the degree to which the surface reflects and transmits the light that hits it.

Finally, the produced drawing and images can be printed on paper using various output devices, such as printers and plotters, to create black-and-white, gray-scale, or color drawings. Computer-controlled milling machines, laser cutters, or stereolithography devices can be used to produce a physical scale model from 3D data.

Note that within the computer, drawings, 3D models, and rendered images are stored as nothing more than *strings of 0's and 1's,* which in turn become *off* and *on* states of various electronic and magnetic components of the computer system. Using *binary representation,* all text and graphic data are encoded as sequences of 0's and 1's. ASCII (American Standard Code for Information Interchange) standard defines how each alphanumeric character is encoded in binary format; for example, character A has a numeric code of 65, which is encoded as 01000001; lowercase C is encoded as 01100010. Each character is encoded as a string of 8 bits, or 1 *byte* (1 byte = 8 bits). Thus, a text containing 2,000 characters will require 2,000 bytes, that is, approximately 2 kilobytes (1 kilobyte = 1,024 bytes) of digital storage space. In a similar fashion, every decimal number has its binary counterpart (Figure 1.24). Therefore, numbers, which correspond to x, y, and z coordinates describing point locations, are encoded and stored as binary numbers.

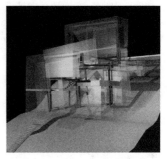

1.19 A computer-rendered image.

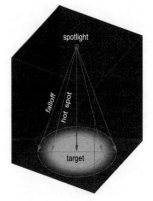

1.20 Light objects can be located anywhere in 3D space.

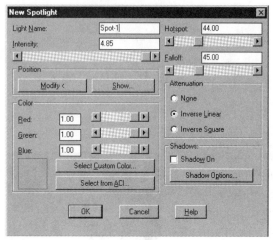

1.21

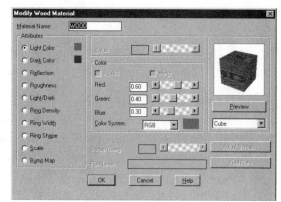

1.22

1.21 *Light properties can also be defined.*

1.22 *Material definitions can be attached to 3D objects . . .*

The computer 2D drawings and 3D models contain the so-called *vector* data (Figure 1.25), that is, records that are translated into *x* and *y* coordinates of line (vector) endpoints on the computer screen. Computer images, on the other hand, contain *raster* data (Figure 1.26), that is, a numeric description of light intensities for each picture element, or *pixel*. In computer images, pixels are organized in rows and columns, thus creating a raster—hence the name *raster graphics*. Each pixel has an associated numeric value, which corresponds to the light intensity. These intensities are also encoded as strings of 0's and 1's (Figure 1.27).

In summary, everything in the digital world is represented as strings of 0's and 1's, whether it is a text, a drawing, or an image. This very simple representation technique has very powerful implications—imagine Le Corbusier's *Villa Savoye* encoded as

1.23 *. . . to render them realistically.*

strings of 0's and 1's! The distinction between the digital worlds of bits and our physical reality comprised of atoms becomes increasingly blurred.

ABOUT THIS BOOK

As your read through this book, you will learn how to *draw* 2D shapes that depict various building elements (Figure 1.28), how to *model* 3D objects from 2D shapes (Figure 1.29), how to illuminate 3D objects to *render* images that simulate realistic effects such as shadow casting and material textures (Figure 1.30), and finally, how to create *animations* by adding a fourth dimension, *time,* to computer models (Figure 1.31).

Accordingly, the book is divided into four major sections covering *2D drawing, 3D modeling, rendering,* and *animation.* Each section has a chapter that introduces basic theoretical concepts, followed by tutorial exercises in AutoCAD, the CAD program used in most architectural firms and schools around the world. This approach should allow you not only to become acquainted with basic concepts of computer graphics but also to see how these concepts are actually implemented in software and how they can be used in architectural modeling and rendering.

AutoCAD was chosen as a software platform for tutorial exercises not because it is the best CAD program available on the market today but because of its rich, powerful features and functionality, and most important, because of its dominant position in the professional and academic markets worldwide. By most estimates, AutoCAD today commands two-thirds of the world market (in other words, a lion's share). Thus, it is very likely that a reader of this book will have an opportunity to use AutoCAD someplace and practice the modeling and rendering concepts introduced in this book.

AutoCAD is a program with a relatively long history. It was introduced in 1982 by a small company called Autodesk, Inc., located in the San Francisco metropolitan area. It was the first drafting program created and marketed for IBM's revolutionary personal computer (PC), introduced a year earlier, in 1981. The introduction of the IBM PC made computing affordable, and when AutoCAD was introduced a year later, even the smallest of architectural offices were able to use CAD in everyday work.

0	0
1	1
2	10
3	11
4	100
5	101
6	110
7	111
8	1000
9	1001
10	1010
11	1011
12	1100
13	1101
14	1110
15	1111
16	10000
17	10001
18	10010
19	10011
20	10100

1.24 Binary representation of decimal numbers.

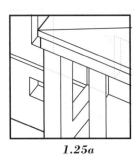

1.25a

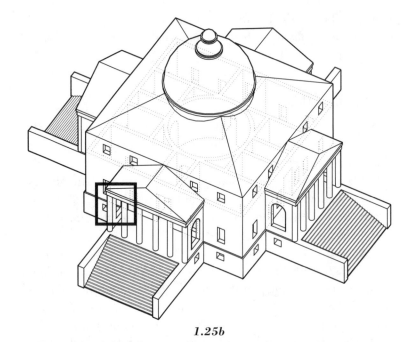

1.25 Vector graphics.

1.26 Raster graphics.

1.25b

1.26a

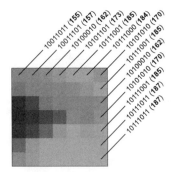

1.27 Binary representation of
digital images.

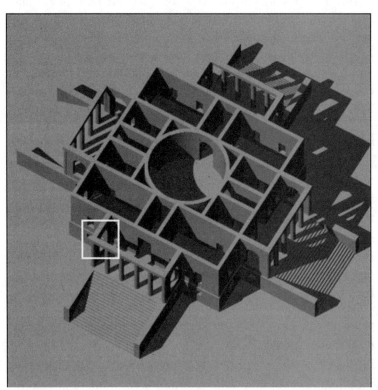

1.26b

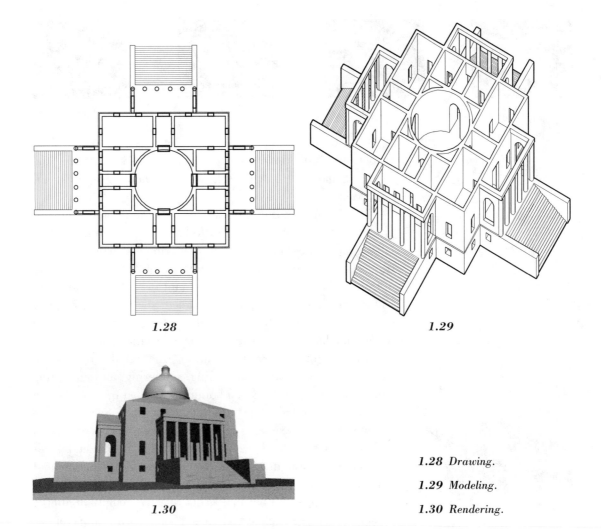

1.28

1.29

1.30

1.28 *Drawing.*

1.29 *Modeling.*

1.30 *Rendering.*

The early AutoCAD was very modest in its features; it was basically a two-dimensional drafting program. By the mid-eighties, three-dimensional entities, such as 3DLINE and 3DFACE, were introduced—AutoCAD was given a third dimension. *Surface modeling* became a standard part of AutoCAD with Release 9. In Release 10, *solid modeling* was introduced as an add-on program called AME (Advanced Modeling Extension). With Release 12, solid modeling was standard, and Autodesk introduced an add-on rendering program called AutoVision. AutoCAD became fully object oriented in Release 13; its inner structure was completely redesigned. The current release, R14,

| 1.31a | 1.31b | 1.31c | 1.31d |

1.31 Animation.

represents a further improvement in AutoCAD's functionality; the rendering module (formerly AutoVision) is now part of the standard package.

By completing the tutorial exercises in the book, you will gradually become acquainted with AutoCAD's interface and its most important 3D modeling and rendering commands and features. The book doesn't cover all the AutoCAD commands and options, and is by no means an attempt to replace AutoCAD's Reference Guide. It will, however, teach you how to effectively use AutoCAD's modeling and rendering features to explore and represent a building's geometry, form, and spatial qualities.

Each tutorial exercise contains illustrated step-by-step instructions for drawing, modeling, rendering, and animating Villa Rotonda (Figure 1.32), a building designed by Renaissance architect Andrea Palladio. Villa Rotonda was chosen as the subject of the tutorial exercises not only because of its historical and architectural value but because its geometry and form lend themselves nicely to the demonstration of many concepts associated with 3D computer modeling and rendering described in this book. It was selected because of its relative layout simplicity, numerous symmetries, and presence of both rectilinear and circular shapes and volumes in its geometry.

1.32 Villa Rotonda.

VILLA ROTONDA

Andrea Palladio, the villa's designer, was a Renaissance architect famous for his treatise *I Quatro Libri dell'Architettura* (*The Four Books of Architecture*) and the countryside villas, city palaces, and churches he designed in the sixteenth century in northern Italy. Villa Almerico (Villa Rotonda or La Rotonda as it is often referred to) is probably his best-known building (Figure 1.33). It was built in the mid-sixteenth century (1565/6–69) on a hill outside Vicenza as a country residence for Paolo Almerico, a papal prelate. Construction of the villa was incomplete when Palladio died (1580), and Scamozzi supervised the remaining work, mainly on the dome and the exterior stairs.

Villa Rotonda is unique in Palladio's opus—it is the only centralized pavilion villa he designed. It is situated on top of a hill, commanding views of the countryside on all four sides. Its bisymmetrical centralized layout and openness on all four sides result from its location and the owner's social position. Palladio

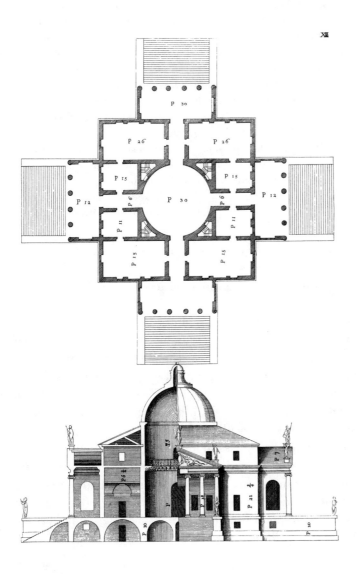

1.33 Plan and elevation drawings of Villa Rotonda from Palladio's Book II.

described the villa's site as a "theater," and to take advanta...
the beautiful views, he repeated the entry portico on all fou...
sides. According to Palladio:

> The site is as pleasant and as delightful as can be found;
> because it is upon a small hill, of very easy access, and is
> watered on one side by *Bacchiglione*, a navigable river; and
> on the other it is encompassed with most pleasant risings,
> which look like a very great theatre, and are all cultivated,
> and abound with most excellent fruits, and most exquisite
> vines: and therefore, as it enjoys from every part most beauti-
> ful views, some of which are limited, some more extended,
> and others that terminate with the horizon; there are loggias
> made in all the four fronts; under the floor of which, and of the
> hall, are the rooms for the conveniency and use of the family.
> The hall is in the middle, is round, and receives its light from
> above. The small rooms are divided off. Over the great rooms
> (the vaults of which are according to the first method) there is
> a place to walk around the hall, fifteen foot and a half wide. In
> the extremity of the pedestals, that form a support to the stairs
> of the loggias, there are statues made by the hands of Messer
> Lorenzo Vicentino, a very excellent sculptor.
>
> (excerpted from *Book II;*
> English translation by Isaac Ware, 1735)

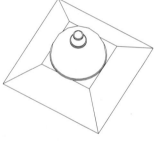

1.34 *An unlikely design of the villa's dome as depicted in* Book II.

The central *sala,* the domed, cylindrical space in the center of the building, also dominates the exterior massing of the building. The *sala* has direct access to all four porticoes and is surrounded by rectangular secondary rooms.

Note that the dome depicted in *Book II* was never executed; the built version differs considerably from Palladio's design, which has left some ambiguities. The elevation drawing (Figure 1.33) depicts the dome as if placed on a flat platform (Figure 1.34), an unlikely design; an accurate rendition should show the intersection of the dome's cylindrical drum and the flat planes of the slanted roof as ellipsoidal forms (Figure 1.35).

In the tutorial exercises in this book, various approximations of the villa's geometry were made (Figure 1.36). The interior and exterior dimensions were rounded to 6-in. (15-cm) increments. The columns were crudely streamlined as cylinders, without bases and capitals. Cornices were not modeled, nor were the vaulted ceilings. Statues were also eliminated. Other crude

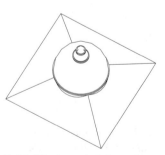

1.35 *The intended design?*

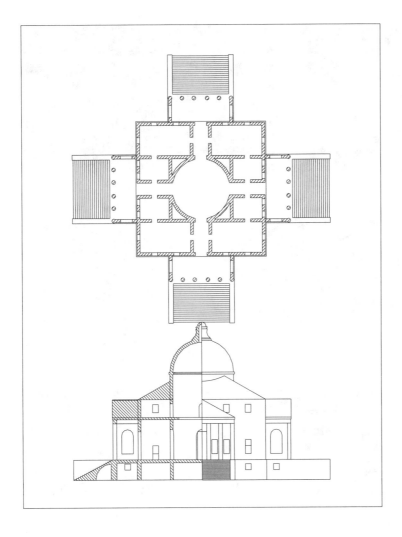

1.36 The crude "copy" of the original shown in Figure 1.33.

approximations were made to simplify the modeling task. Note that the aim was not to create an accurate model of Villa Rotonda but to use the villa as a unifying theme for the tutorials.

EXAMPLES

The following *analytical* and *experiential* images illustrate how computer graphics can be used to effectively communicate design ideas and spatial qualities. The images were created by students at the University of Miami School of Architecture.

1.37a

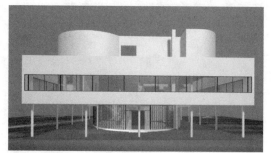

1.37b

1.37 Villa Savoye by Le Corbusier, 3D computer model and rendering by Marc Peter.

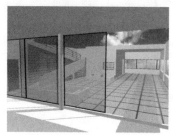

1.37c

1.37d

1.37e

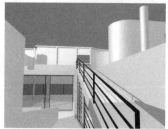

1.37f

1.38a

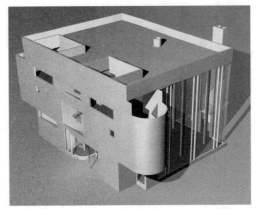

1.38b

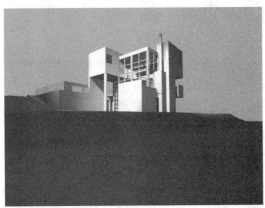

1.39a

1.39b

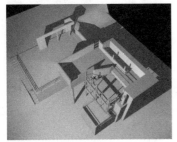

1.39c

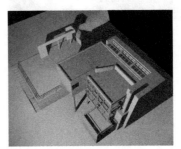

1.39d

1.38 *House in Pound Ridge by Richard Meier; 3D computer model and rendering by Gary Wunderlich.*

1.39 *Giovanniti House by Richard Meier; 3D computer model and rendering by Clive Lonstein.*

1.40a

1.40b

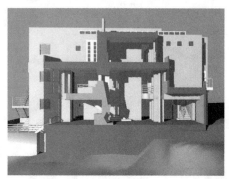

1.40c

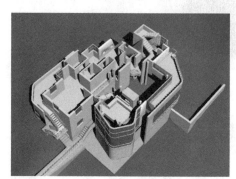

1.40d

1.40 *Westchester house by Richard Meier; 3D computer model and rendering by Javier Cordova and Alex King.*

1.41 *Guardiola House by Peter Eisenman; 3D computer model and rendering by Philip Smith.*

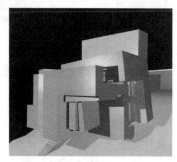

1.41a

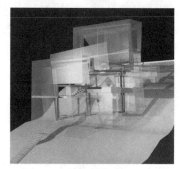

1.41b

1.42a

1.42b

1.42 *Folie No. 47 by Bernard Tschumi; 3D computer model and rendering by Ricardo Castro.*

1.43a

1.43b

1.43 *Villa Emo by Andrea Palladio; 3D computer model and rendering by Robert Mayo.*

1.44a

1.44b

1.44 *St. Ivo della Sapienza by Francesco Borromini; 3D computer model and rendering by Bjorn Green.*

2

BASIC CONCEPTS: 2D DRAWING

2D GRAPHIC OBJECTS

Architectural drawings are highly structured collections of graphic objects, such as straight lines, circular arcs, circles, and closed polygons, and various annotations, such as notes and dimensions, all of which are nothing more than traces of lead or ink on paper. In manual drafting these graphic objects are drawn precisely using instruments (tools), such as straightedges and compasses. The instrument that is being used determines the kind of object to be drawn. A designer generates straight lines using a straightedge, and circular arcs using a compass. The available drafting tools limit the kind of objects that can be drawn, i.e., the instruments determine the repertoire of graphic objects that can be drawn.

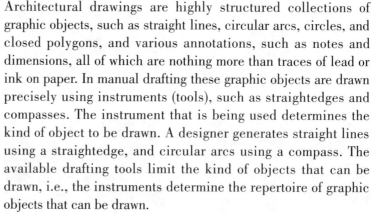
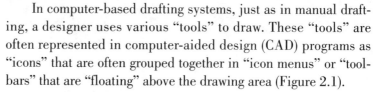

2.1 Iconic toolbars.

In computer-based drafting systems, just as in manual drafting, a designer uses various "tools" to draw. These "tools" are often represented in computer-aided design (CAD) programs as "icons" that are often grouped together in "icon menus" or "toolbars" that are "floating" above the drawing area (Figure 2.1).

As in hand drafting, these "tools" determine what can be drawn. A designer can draw straight lines using the "line" tool, or rectangles using the "rectangle" tool. This is where similarities between traditional, manual drafting tools and their computer-based counterparts end. In manual drafting, to draw a straight line, a designer continuously moves a pencil or ink pen along a straightedge from one point to another. In CAD systems, all that is needed to draw a straight line is to *select two points;* once the points are selected, the program automatically *draws* the line.

In fact, all drawing in CAD systems is accomplished through *point specification.* By selecting two points only, a designer can draw a line, a rectangle, or a circle (Figure 2.2).

Whereas in manual drafting a circle is drawn by first finding a center, and then determining the radius, in CAD systems a circle can be graphically drawn in at least three different ways: (a) by specifying two points where one defines the center and the other one defines the length of the radius, (b) by specifying two points that define the circle's diameter (the center is the midpoint between the two selected points), and (c) by specifying three points that lie on the circle's perimeter (Figure 2.3). In similar fashion, a circular arc can be specified in many different ways. Note that with CAD systems, a designer has no difficulty drawing arcs of large radius, which is often difficult in manual drafting.

In addition to "tools" to draw straight lines, circular arcs, and circles, CAD systems offer "tools" to draw ellipses, rectangles, squares, and other equilateral polygons (pentagons, octagons, etc.). Many systems also support *spline curves* and *polylines.* A spline curve, much like the pinned wooden splines used in manual drafting, are specified by control points, i.e., the points that control the curvature, which may or may not lie on the curve (Figure 2.4). *Polylines* are connected sequences (chains) of short line and arc segments that can form open or closed shapes, which are treated as single objects (Figure 2.5). *Closed polylines* are of particular interest, since they can form the base shapes of three-dimensional solid forms.

Each of the graphic objects can be assigned attributes such as color, line width, or line type. Polylines can also be assigned solid fills (Figure 2.6).

One important attribute of two-dimensional graphic objects is their display order. By default, the order in which the objects are displayed is the same in which they were drawn—a new

To draw a line, choose the Line tool from the Draw toolbar, or enter LINE or L at the command prompt, specify points, and press Enter or Return, or the right mouse button, when done.

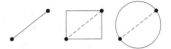

2.2 By specifying two points, a designer can draw a line, a rectangle, or a circle.

To draw an arc, choose the Arc tool from the Draw toolbar, or enter ARC or A at the command prompt, and follow the instructions. Similarly, to draw a circle, choose the Circle tool, or enter CIRCLE or C at the command prompt, and follow the instructions.

2.3 Specifying a circle.

2.4 Spline curves.

2.5 Closed polylines.

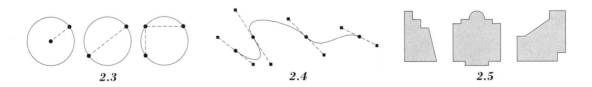

2.3 *2.4* *2.5*

To draw a spline curve, choose the Spline tool from the Draw toolbar, specify points, press Enter, Return, or the right mouse button when done, and specify the start and end tangent.

To draw a polyline, choose the Polyline tool from the Draw toolbar or enter PLINE at the command prompt, specify points, and press Enter, Return, or the right mouse button when done, or press C (i.e., close) followed by Enter, Return, or the right mouse button to create a closed shape. To draw circular arcs as part of a polyline, enter A when prompted for a point.

To assign line widths, use the Polyline tool to draw lines and arcs, and enter W (width) when prompted for the first point to set the polyline width. To create solid-filled shapes in R13, use the Solid tool. In R14 solid fills can be applied to any closed shape.

object will appear on top of the previously drawn ones. The display order can be changed by moving objects to the front or the back of the display list (Figure 2.7).

2D COORDINATE SYSTEMS AND POINT SPECIFICATION

In manual drafting, lines and other graphic objects are drawn on a sheet of paper, a two-dimensional rectangular surface of definite size. The precise location of graphic objects is often measured from the edges of the drawing surface or in relationship to the existing ones. In CAD systems, a designer draws on a two-dimensional surface of infinite size, which has its "origin" and two perpendicular axes, labeled x and y, which are used to determine the location of points in relation to the origin. This concept of an origin and two perpendicular axes defines a *two-dimensional Cartesian coordinate system*, a concept that is the basis of all CAD

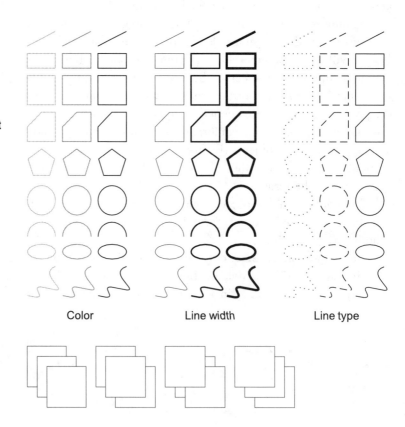

Color   Line width   Line type

2.6 Two-dimensional objects and graphic attributes.

2.7 Display order.

software. Within such a system, points are specified by their x and y coordinates, pairs of numbers that correspond to distances from a point to each of the two axes, i.e., distances from the origin in x and y direction (Figure 2.8). All graphic objects are drawn by specifying point locations within this rectangular coordinate system. Consequently, object descriptions, i.e., records in the drawing database, consist of x and y coordinate pairs that correspond to the specified points (Figure 2.9).

A designer can draw graphic objects by entering x and y coordinates of the specific points. For example, to draw a square with a side of 2 units, located 4 units in x direction and 2 units in y direction from the origin, a designer can enter the following coordinate pairs (in counterclockwise fashion) for each of the four corners: (4,2), (6,2), (6,4), (4,4) (Figure 2.10).

It is, however, a rather tedious and time-consuming process to draw objects in this fashion. Instead of using *absolute* coordinates, that is, coordinates in reference to the origin, a designer can use *relative* coordinates, in reference to a previously specified point. So the same square can be drawn by entering the following coordinate pairs: (4,2), (@2,0), (@0,2), (@−2,0). The symbol @ (pronounced "at") indicates relative coordinates, that is, relative distances in x and y direction from a previously specified point (Figure 2.11).

To draw a rectangle, choose the Rectangle tool from the Draw toolbar, or enter RECTANG at the command prompt, and specify two points that represent the opposite corners. To draw an ellipse, choose the Ellipse tool, or enter ELLIPSE at the command prompt, and follow the instructions. To draw a square or any other regular polygon, select the Polygon tool, or enter POLYGON at the command prompt, specify the number of sides, and follow the prompts.

2.8 Cartesian coordinate system.

2.9 A line in a Cartesian coordinate system.

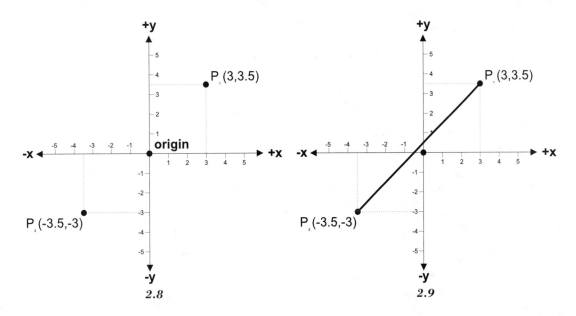

2.8

2.9

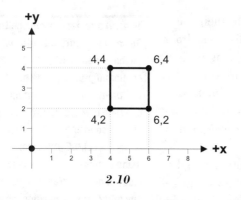

2.10

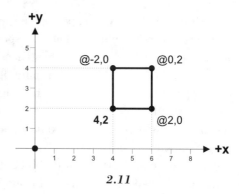

2.11

2.10 *Drawing a square by explicitly specifying the coordinate pairs for each of the four corners.*

2.11 *Using absolute and relative Cartesian coordinates to draw a square.*

In addition to the Cartesian coordinate system, many CAD systems provide point specification using *polar* coordinates. In a polar coordinate system, a point location is described by its *distance* from the origin and an *angle* that the connecting line forms with the axis, whose direction often coincides with the *x* axis of the Cartesian coordinate system (Figure 2.12).

Alternatively, a designer can draw a square by using both Cartesian and polar, and absolute and relative, coordinates, as illustrated in Figure 2.13. Note that all angles are measured from the *x* axis (often called the horizontal axis).

2.12 *Polar coordinate system.*

2.13 *Cartesian and polar, and absolute and relative, coordinates.*

GEOMETRIC AND VISUAL AIDS

Designers, however, usually do not think in terms of Cartesian or polar coordinates. In addition to specifying points *numerically*, designers can also indicate point locations *graphically* by directly

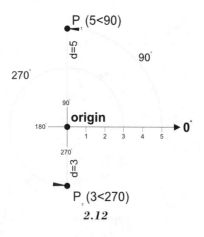

2.12

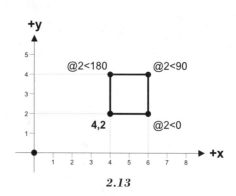

2.13

"picking" points in the drawing display area. Most CAD systems use a *cursor* (either a small "cross" or a pair of "cross hairs") as a visual aid for point selection (Figure 2.14). The location of the cursor in the drawing display area is controlled by a "pointing device" (a mouse or a tablet). The act of picking a point (usually by clicking on the left mouse button) is often referred to as "digitizing," since a pair of coordinates is associated with the selected point location in the drawing display area.

Another visual aid provided in CAD systems is "rubber-banding" (Figure 2.15). For example, when drawing a line, after the first point is picked, the system will display a "rubber-band" line that will dynamically follow the cursor until the second point is selected. Many systems will also dynamically display other graphic objects in this fashion, such as arcs and circles, while the designer is selecting the points that define them.

To visually aid designers in selecting points at specific locations and in determining distances, CAD systems also feature *grids*, regular patterns of dots displayed across the drawing surface. Grids are modular, and can be square, rectangular, polar, rotated, or superimposed (Figure 2.16). As a visual aid, grids are not unique to CAD systems—modular grids are often used by architects in building layouts. Unlike grids in manual drafting, the grids in CAD systems are not fixed—the grid's module, origin, and orientation can be changed as needed during drawing.

Obviously, it is quicker and more convenient to select points graphically than to enter coordinates numerically. Drawing with the aid of grids, however, is imprecise; for example, when selecting a point that is visually located on top of a grid point at (4,2), a designer may actually choose a point located at (4.0367,1.9984).

2.14 The cursors for point selection.

2.15 "Rubber-banding."

2.16 Grids.

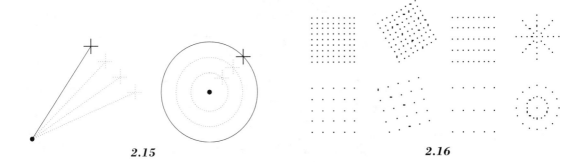

2.15

2.16

To specify grid and snap module, choose Drawing Aids from the Tools (R13 Options) menu, and enter the desired values into the appropriate fields in the dialog box (Figure 2.17). Alternatively, you can enter GRID or SNAP at the command prompt.

AutoCAD does not support polar grids. You can use a square or a rectangular grid and rotate it if needed using the SNAP command or by entering the rotation value in the Drawing Aids dialog box (Figure 2.17).

Press the F7 key or double click on the GRID button in the status bar to toggle on and off the grid display.

Press the F9 key or double click the SNAP button in the status bar to toggle the snap mode on and off. Use snapping whenever possible while drawing!

2.17 Setting grid and snap modules.

Such an outcome is often highly undesirable and, as will be demonstrated later, can lead to problematic results in dimensioning and in 3D modeling. That is why the *snap* feature is provided in CAD systems for accurate, precise drawing.

Conceptually, snap is a feature very similar to grid, but with a different purpose. While grid is a *visual* aid, *snap* is a geometric drawing aid that enables designers to draw precisely by choosing points from a small subset, which is defined as a modular pattern of points at specific intervals. Snap forces the cursor to "jump" in exact intervals on top of an invisible grid of points. A designer can specify different modules (intervals) for grid and snap, and that is often the case (Figure 2.17). For example, a grid interval may be set to 1 foot, and snap to 1 inch. (Sometimes grid pattern may be too dense to display. In such instances, a larger grid module should be set.)

A precise and fast way to draw the square shown in Figure 2.10 is to (1) set the grid module to 1 unit, (2) set the snap module to 1 unit too, and then (3), using grid as a reference, pick points that are two units apart.

It is of paramount importance to use snap whenever possible while drawing. Precision and accuracy are some of the key benefits that CAD systems offer, and to achieve them, one should almost constantly use snap. Note, however, that this imposition of precision can be detrimental in early stages of design, when the form and shape are still in flux.

In addition to the grid and snap modules, most CAD systems offer an *orthogonal mode* of drawing, where the movement of the

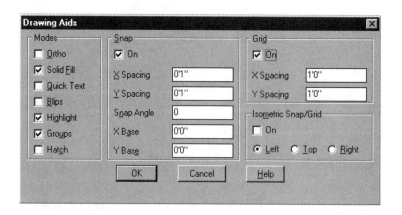

cursor is constrained to x and y (horizontal and vertical) direction. This feature is especially useful when a building's geometry is orthogonal—it permits a designer to very quickly draw horizontal and vertical lines, and to quickly and accurately align various objects in the drawing.

As the drawing develops, new objects can be drawn by *object snapping*, that is, by precisely selecting significant points on existing objects: endpoints or midpoints of lines and arcs, center points of circular objects, intersections, etc. (Figure 2.18).

Some of these significant points are explicitly represented in the drawing, and some are often only implied; an obvious example of the latter are apparent intersections of lines (see Figure 2.18); this feature is especially useful, since alignments are very common in architectural drawings. By snapping to apparent intersections, aligned objects can be drawn quickly and precisely (Figure 2.19).

In addition to explicit selection of significant points through object snap, many CAD systems can automatically display (*highlight*) these points in the vicinity of the cursor, and thus further speed the selection.

As will be demonstrated later in the tutorial exercises, *object snapping* provides a very quick and accurate way to locate points. By first drawing a skeleton of *construction lines* (a time-tested classical drafting technique), a designer can often eliminate the need for painstaking calculation of point locations and distances

Endpoint   Intersection   Tangent (to last point)   Center

Midpoint   Apparent intersection   Perpendicular (to last point)   Quadrant

To constrain drawing to "horizontal" and "vertical" direction only, check the Ortho box in the Drawing Aids dialog box (Figure 2.17). You can also press the F8 key on the keyboard to toggle Ortho mode on and off; you can also double click on the Ortho button in the status bar.

You can specify one of the object snapping modes whenever Auto-CAD prompts you to choose a point or to specify a displacement vector, a distance, or an angle. Enter END to specify the endpoint object snap mode, MID for midpoint, INT for intersection, PER for perpendicular, etc. It is sufficient to enter only the first three characters of the desired object snap mode.

2.18 Significant points that can be selected through object snapping.

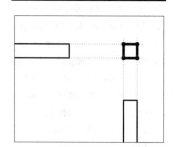

2.19 Drawing aligned objects by snapping to apparent inter-sections.

Use the XLINE command or choose the Construction Line tool to draw infinite skeleton lines.

AutoCAD will display a square box cursor whenever it expect objects to be selected. You can pick objects individually or enter W (window) or C (crossing) to choose objects by specifying a rectangular selection area. Enter A to add objects to the selection set, or R to remove them.

2.20 Using construction lines is an efficient way to precisely locate points in the drawing.

by simply snapping to significant points on the underlying lines (Figure 2.20).

BASIC OPERATIONS

In CAD systems, drawing objects can be *inserted selected,* and once selected, can be *deleted, transformed,* or *replicated.* Objects are inserted by selecting the appropriate drawing tool, such as *line, arc, circle,* and by locating points that define the object to be drawn, such as endpoints of a line.

An object must be *selected* before it can be deleted, repli-cated, or transformed. *Object selection,* as one of the most basic operations in CAD systems, can be performed in several ways: objects can be selected one by one, or as a group, by specifying a selection boundary (often a rectangle) and choosing objects that are *within, crossing,* and/or *outside* the specified boundary (Fig-ure 2.21). Selected objects form *selection sets,* which can be stored for future reference. Drawing objects can be added to or removed from the sets during the selection process.

Deletion of objects is performed by removing the correspond-ing records from the drawing database. Besides deletion, every CAD system should provide the four basic Euclidean transforma-tions of *translation, rotation, reflection,* and *scaling* (figure 2.22).

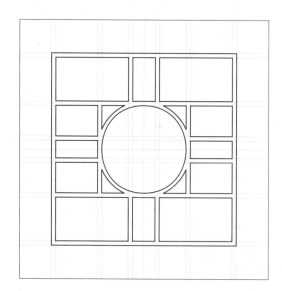

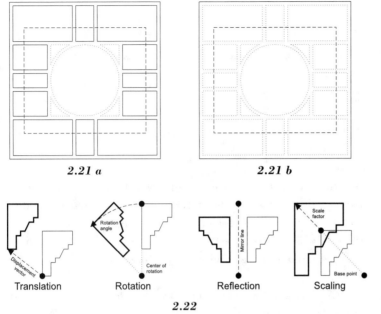

2.21 a   2.21 b   2.21 c

Translation   Rotation   Reflection   Scaling

2.22

2.21 *Selecting objects that are (a) within, (b) within and crossing, and (c) crossing the rectangular boundary.*

2.22 *Translation, rotation, reflection, and scaling transformations.*

Each of these transformations requires different parameters to be provided before they can be carried out by the system. *Translation* requires that a *displacement vector* be specified, usually by locating two points in the drawing. *Rotation* requires a *center point* and an *angle of rotation*. *Reflection* is based on an *axis*, a reflection line, to be specified by locating two points. *Scaling* requires a *base point* and a *scaling factor*, which can be specified either numerically or graphically. When one of these transformations is applied, a CAD system will typically display a *ghosted image* of the selected objects as they are dynamically transformed, thus providing visual feedback to the designer. (Note that none of the four Euclidean transformations alters the geometry of the selected objects.)

To lengthen a line or displace a corner of a rectangle, a designer can choose a specific point (a *grip*) and *drag* it to a new location. A designer can also *break, trim, extend, fillet, chamfer,* or *stretch* existing objects (Figure 2.23). *Trim* and *extend* operations require existing objects to be specified as boundaries for shortening and lengthening, respectively. The *fillet* operation inserts a circular arc that is *tangent* to selected objects, which are automatically trimmed or extended to meet the newly

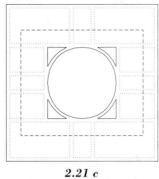

In AutoCAD, all operations and transformations are accessible through the Modify toolbar. You can also enter a desired command (DELETE, MOVE, ROTATE, etc.) at the command prompt.

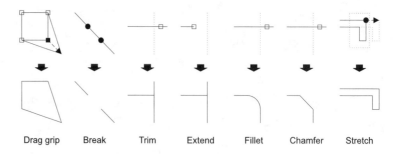

2.23 *Typical transformations.*

Drag grip   Break   Trim   Extend   Fillet   Chamfer   Stretch

Use the FILLET command with a radius of zero to trim or extend objects to a point. Since the radius is zero, AutoCAD cannot place an arc between the objects.

inserted arc at its endpoints. Similarly, the *chamfer* operation inserts a line segment between two objects. The *stretch* operation can also be used to shorten or lenghten objects. This operation is especially useful because it provides efficient modification of an entire group of objects, such as relocating a door opening within a wall.

Existing graphic objects can be *replicated* using *copy, array,* and *offset* operations (Figure 2.24). *Copy* is used to create exact duplicates of existing objects. *Array* replication creates *circular* (*polar*) and *rectangular* patterns of selected objects. *Offset,* as its name implies, creates at a specified *distance* a new object similar in shape to the original one. It is most often used to draw parallel polylines representing walls, roads, or pathways.

VIEWING

In traditional drafting, the size of a paper sheet and the drawing scale must be selected before drawing begins, and all graphic objects must be drawn in the selected scale. When drawing using CAD systems, *neither sheet size nor scale need to be determined in advance.* There is *no* drawing scale and no conversion of true, full-scale distances into their scaled counterparts while drawing.

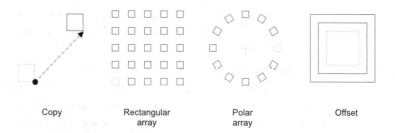

Copy   Rectangular array   Polar array   Offset

2.24 *Replication.*

All sizes and distances are specified using their full-scale values: for example, a 12 ft (3.60 m) long wall partition is drawn as a 12 ft (3.60 m) long rectangular shape. Sheet size and drawing scale are determined when *printing* or *plotting*, that is, when the drawing is output on paper.

This lack of the drawing scale and infinite drawing area often confuses new users confronted with the small, finite size of a computer display. The computer display provides a rectangular area within which a drawing can be displayed at *any* size. A designer can view an entire building layout within that area or just one room within a building. This is accomplished through a viewing operation called *zooming*, which is somewhat analogous to a photographer's use of lenses to *zoom in* on a subject to see it in more detail, or to *zoom out* to capture a wider context. Accordingly, to see the drawing in more detail, the designer should *zoom in* using one of the viewing operations (commands), and should *zoom out* to see more of the drawing displayed on the screen (Figure 2.25). Zooming in is often accomplished by specifying a rectangular area (a *window*) that should fill the display area.

Another viewing operation common in CAD systems is *panning,* analogous to panning in photography. To see another portion of the drawing using the same display scale, a designer *pans* to it by "moving" a rectangular display "window" (Figure 2.26). Another way to think of panning is to imagine "sliding" the drawing underneath a "fixed" rectangular window.

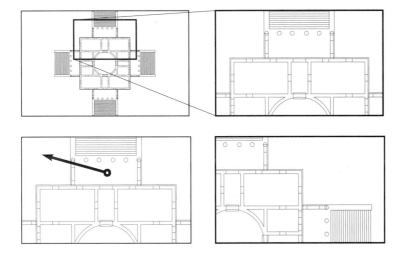

2.25 *Zooming.*

2.26 *Panning.*

Even though specifying the drawing scale is not required, most CAD systems require that *boundaries* or *limits* of the drawing area be specified to facilitate internal computation, creating another point of confusion for new users. To alleviate the problem, in many CAD systems, designers are asked to first specify the *sheet size* and the *drawing scale* when creating new drawings. These parameters are then used by the system to compute the drawing limits in "true" size. For example, when drawing a building that is 100 ft by 80 ft (30 by 24 m) big, another 10 ft (3 m) should be added on every side, thus resulting in the drawing limits of 120 ft by 100 ft (36 m by 30 m) (Figure 2.27).

STRUCTURE: LAYERS AND SYMBOLS

Drawings are highly structured representations of buildings, created according to time-tested drafting conventions and procedures. Different building systems, such as electric wiring or HVAC layout, are often drawn on separate *transparent* sheets of paper, which are often overlaid on one another to produce final drawings or to check for potential conflicts. In these drawings, *symbols* are used to denote components of various systems.

CAD systems use analogous concepts to structure drawings. Instead of transparent sheets of paper used in traditional drafting, CAD systems use *layers*, *named* parts of a drawing with similar

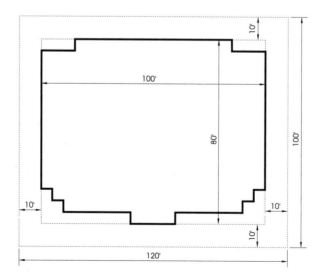

2.27 *Drawing boundaries (limits).*

content. A single drawing can contain numerous layers; one drawing file can contain graphic information for all floors of the building, whereby each floor layout is drawn on a separate layer. For example, graphic objects representing wall elements of the first floor can be *assigned* to a layer named 1-WALLS, whereby 1 denotes the first floor, and WALLS describes the content; graphic objects representing window openings on the first floor can be stored on layer 1-OPENINGS, and so on (Figure 2.28).

Specific layers can be displayed or not, depending on what information is needed. As an example, consider a single drawing file (database) that contains layers named LAYOUT, HVAC, and LIGHTING. To view the layout of ventilation ducts, a designer can display layers LAYOUT and HVAC, and not LIGHTING. Similarly, to view the lighting layout, a designer can display layers LAYOUT and LIGHTING, and not HVAC.

In summary, layers facilitate the organization and display of graphic information pertaining to a building. CAD systems provide

AutoCAD provides a virtually unlimited number of layers. To set up layers, or to change layer properties, choose Layers from the Tools menu (R13 Options). You can also enter LAYER or LA at the command prompt.

2.28 Layers.

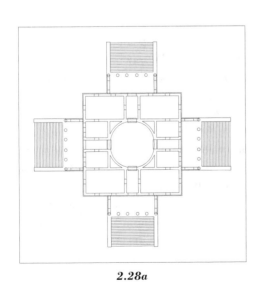

2.28a

2.28b

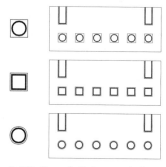

2.29 By redefining symbol definitions, many alternatives can be quickly explored.

Use the BLOCK command to create symbol definitions, and use the INSERT command to create instances of symbols. You can redefine a symbol, draw new objects, and create a symbol (block) with the same name. Note how all the symbol instances are automatically updated to reflect the change.

Use colors to assign pen thickness when plotting or printing. For example, all the objects that are yellow can be printed (or plotted) using line thickness of 0.35 mm; all red objects can be printed using line thickness of 0.25 mm, etc. If you decide that some objects should be printed using a different pen thickness, simply change their color (or layer assignment).

ways to create and name layers, to assign graphic objects to specific layers, to shift objects from one layer to another, and to control the display of layers for drawing viewing, editing, or printing.

Symbols, or *blocks*, are repeatable shapes that provide another way to structure drawings and as will be demonstrated, offer additional advantages. To define a symbol, a designer first creates its "master" definition that contains graphic objects and a reference point that is used to place instances of the symbol within a drawing. Such mechanism is very similar to the use of stencils in traditional drafting. The stencil contains cutouts, "master" definitions of symbols, and instances are created by tracing the stencil cutouts. Unlike their stencil counterparts, symbols defined in CAD systems can have different scales and, most important, can be easily redefined, whereby instances of the original definition are automatically updated to reflect the change (Figure 2.29).

In addition to using layers and symbols, a drawing can also be structured by *grouping* objects into hierarchies and by using *external references*. External references are especially useful for complex drawings where small file sizes are important. Separate drawing files can be externally referenced, i.e., displayed without increasing the size of the drawing file where they are placed.

PRINTING AND PLOTTING

Until the world is truly paperless, architectural drawings will continue to be produced on paper. *Printers* and *plotters* are hardware devices used to "transfer" CAD drawings onto paper by using *lead* (as in pencils), *ink* (as in ink pens), or *toner* (as in photocopy machines). Regardless of what kind of device is being used, the output procedure is very similar.

As already mentioned, CAD drawings are created using true, full-scale values for coordinates and dimensions; paper size and drawing scale are specified only when *printing* or *plotting*. Typically, the user has to specify the size and orientation (Figure 2.30) of the paper medium to be used and indicate the printing scale (for example, $\frac{1}{16}$" = 1' or 1:200). Often, "pen" numbers (if pen plotters are used) or specific line widths and line types must be associated with *specific colors* used in the drawing to achieve the desired output (Figure 2.31).

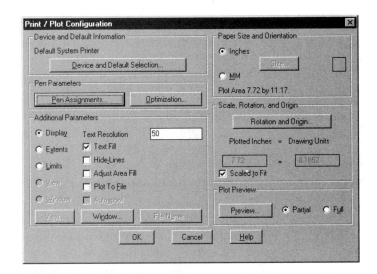

2.30 *AutoCAD's printing dialog box.*

2.31 *The Pen Assignments dialog box.*

Many options can be quickly explored when printing or plotting. The same CAD drawing can be output at different scales. Different line widths can be assigned to colors. Different layers can be displayed to create different drawings.

DRAWING STRATEGIES

Drawing should be set up first before anything is drawn. The first step is to specify *units* to be used—English (feet and inches) or metric—and choose the units display format. Once the units are chosen, drawing *limits* (boundaries) should be specified taking into account the building's full-scale size. Drawing *layers* should be defined next. An appropriate *grid* module for visual reference and a *snap* module for accurate drawing should be specified, and finally, the entire drawing area should be displayed.

After the initial drawing setup, a skeleton of construction or grid lines is typically drawn as an organizational device and a visual guide for drawing. This approach corresponds to a well-established manual drawing practice of first laying out the pencil construction lines and using them later to draw in more detail. The skeleton lines can be used to snap new graphic objects quickly into place, and then these new objects can be used as a geometric reference for further drawing until the entire drawing is completed (Figure 2.32).

Often an existing hand-drafted drawing has to be either redrawn using a CAD system or used as a basis for a new drawing. There are four methods a designer can employ to enter a hand-drafted drawing: *tracing, scaling, scanning,* and *hybrid scanning.*

Tracing or *digitizing* requires a tablet or digitizer, a special hardware device for point specification. An existing hand-drafted

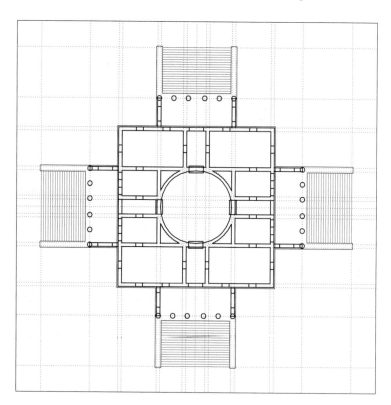

2.32 Using construction lines in drawing.

drawing is attached to the tablet's surface, and points are selected by *tracing* the drawn objects. As a drawing method, tracing is not very accurate and is commonly used to draw contour lines. It is probably the easiest of the four methods, but it requires extensive corrections if dimensional accuracy is important. *Scaling* is the most accurate of the four methods if the drawing contains dimensional information. It often involves reading the dimensions of the drawing by using a scale rule (hence the name). *Scanning* involves, as its name implies, scanning the drawing into a digital image, which is then processed by the conversion software and converted into a CAD drawing. Scanning requires special hardware (a scanner) and conversion software, and often produces drawings that require extensive editing. An alternative method is *hybrid scanning*, where the scanned image is used as an underlay in CAD software, and graphic objects are drawn on top of the scanned image (Figure 2.33).

The drawing strategy to be employed depends largely on what kind of drawing is to be created. Obviously, a fully anno-

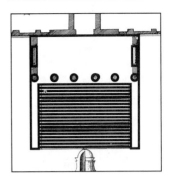

2.33 Hybrid scanning: A scanned image of the drawing is used as an underlay on top of which new objects are drawn.

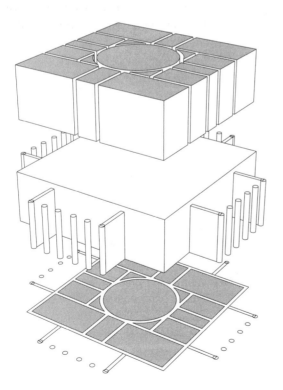

2.34 3D solid modeling requires closed 2D shapes for the construction of 3D forms.

2.35 A "plan" drawing of Andrea Palladio's Villa Rotonda that contains 2D shapes that correspond to the building's first-floor solids and voids.

tated construction drawing is different from a drawing to be used as a basis for 3D modeling. Often a construction drawing will require considerable editing to be suitable for 3D modeling work, because three-dimensional modeling requires *closed two-dimensional shapes* to construct 3D forms (Figure 2.34). These closed shapes will often be redundant and overlapping, resulting in 2D drawings that are *structurally* and visually very different from drawings commonly produced in architectural practice (these differences will be obvious after the first 3D modeling tutorial).

Therefore, when creating a 3D computer model of a building from existing hand-drafted drawings, a designer should first create a 2D drawing that contains *closed* shapes that correspond to *solid* and *void* building elements (Figure 2.35). The drawing must be set up first by specifying *units, drawing limits, grid* and *snap* modules, and *layers.* An appropriate method should be used to enter a hand-drafted drawing, typically either *scaling* (by reading the dimensions of an existing drawing using a scale) or *hybrid scanning* (by tracing the underlying scanned image of an existing drawing). A skeleton (grid) of construction lines should be drawn next as a visual and geometric reference for drawing specific building elements.

TUTORIAL 1: DRAWING SETUP

In this tutorial exercise you will be introduced to the elements of AutoCAD's interface: the graphics window, pull-down menus, toolbars, flyouts, dialog boxes, and command prompts. You will also learn how to set up a drawing in AutoCAD and how to create a skeleton of construction lines that will be used later to draw the floor plans of Andrea Palladio's Villa Rotonda (Figure 3.0).

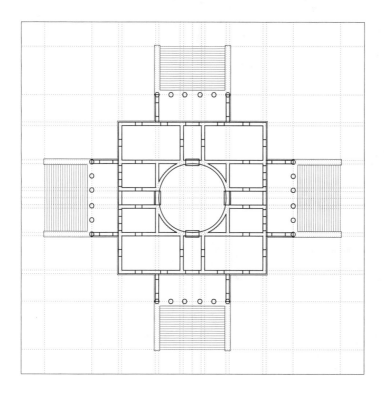

3.0 The "plan" drawing of Andrea Palladio's Villa Rotonda with a skeleton of underlying construction lines.

3.1 AutoCAD R13 and R14 program icons.

AUTOCAD'S USER INTERFACE

1 Start AutoCAD by double-clicking its icon (Figure 3.1). After a few seconds, a new drawing window will appear.

2 Notice how AutoCAD's application window consists of several elements (Figures 3.2a and 3.2b). On the top is the *menu bar,* which contains *pull-down menus* with commands. Below the menu bar (and elsewhere on the screen) are *toolbars* that contain *icons* ("tools") representing various commands. The *graphics window* (the actual drawing area) fills most of the screen. The *command window* and the *status bar* are at the bottom. The command window is where you enter commands by typing and where Auto-CAD displays prompts and messages. The *status bar* shows the *cursor coordinates* and the status (on or off) of the various drawing and visual aids (modes) such as *grid, snap,* and *ortho.*

   Notice in the lower left corner of the graphics window a pair of arrows labeled *x* and *y*—they are the coordinate system icons

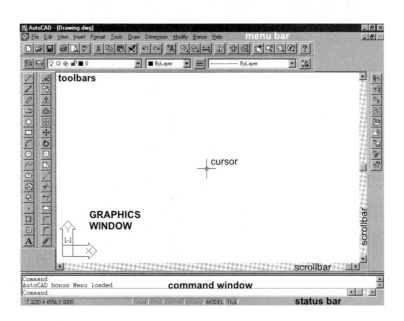

3.2a AutoCAD R14 application window.

indicating the direction of positive *x* and *y* axes (Figure 3.2c). AutoCAD uses a fixed Cartesian coordinate system called *World Coordinate System* (WCS), with a fixed *origin* (where axes meet)

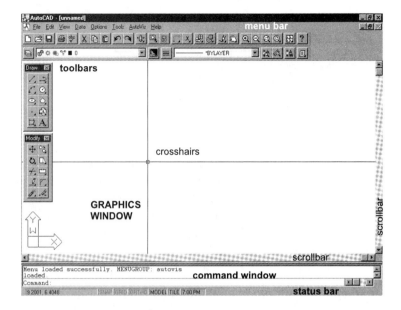

3.2b *AutoCAD R13 application window.*

Both *x* and *y* coordinates of the World Coordinate System origin equal zero.

at a point whose coordinates are 0,0. The origin point is located at the very lower left corner of the graphics windows by default.

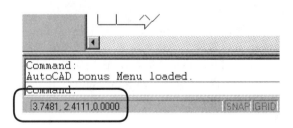

3.2c *The WCS icon.*

3.2d *Coordinate display in the status bar.*

Move the mouse (your pointing device) across the graphics window and notice how AutoCAD dynamically displays the underlying cursor coordinates in the status bar (Figure 3.2d).

3 You can execute an AutoCAD command by selecting a corresponding *tool icon* on one of the toolbars, by choosing an item from one of the pull-down menus, or by typing the command at the command prompt.

Type LINE at the command prompt, and then press the *Enter* or *Return* key. AutoCAD will prompt you for the first point by displaying the message "*From point:*" in the command window (Figure 3.3).

You can start any command by entering it at the command prompt. Note that after entering the commands or responses to prompts, you must press Enter, Return, or the space bar key, or press the right mouse button. All command window input instructions in this book assume this step from now on.

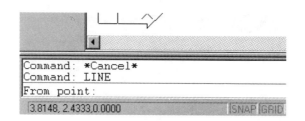

```
Command: *Cancel*
Command: LINE
From point:
3.8148, 2.4333,0.0000                    SNAP GRID
```

3.4a *R13 and R14* Draw *tool-bars.*

3.4b *The* Draw *tool with a* ToolTip *displayed.*

Click somewhere within the graphics window (if you are using a mouse, press the left button to click). AutoCAD will prompt you for the next point by displaying the message *"To point:"* in the command window. Notice the *rubber-band* line that follows the cursor as you move it across the graphics window. Again, click somewhere in the graphics windows to pick a point. AutoCAD will draw a line and will again prompt you for a point, in case you want to continue drawing lines. To end the command, press *Enter, Return,* or the *space bar* key, or click the right mouse button (or the Return button on your pointing device) in response to the command prompt message.

4 This time you will draw a line by selecting the *Line* tool on the *Draw* toolbar (Figure 3.4a). First make sure that the *Draw* toolbar is visible on screen. If it isn't, from the *View* (R13 *Tools*) menu, choose *Toolbars,* and then choose *Draw.*

Place the cursor over the *Line* tool icon on the toolbar (don't click, just position the cursor). A *ToolTip* with the command name (*Line*) will appear below the cursor (Figure 3.4b).

To execute the LINE command, position the cursor on the *Line* tool, and click once. Notice that the same prompt as in the previous step will appear in the command window. Select two points in the graphics window to draw a line, and then end the LINE command.

Notice that some tools in toolbars have a small black triangle in the lower right corner, an indication that a tool contains a *fly-out,* that is, a pop-up toolbar with additional commands. To display the flyout, place the cursor on top of the tool, and hold down the pick button (the left button on the mouse) until the flyout appears (Figure 3.4c).

5 You can *dock, float, resize, reposition,* or *close* any toolbar (Figure 3.5a).

To undock a toolbar, place the tip of the cursor arrow over one of the toolbar's edges, hold down the pick button, and while holding down the pick button, *drag* (move) it away from the dock region until it has a thick outline (Figure 3.5b). Release the pick button.

3.4c R13 Line *tool flyout.*

Some toolbars, such as Standard, Object Properties, Draw, and Modify, are visible by default. To display additional toolbars on screen, from the View [R13 Tools] menu choose Toolbars, and then choose the toolbar you want to show.

When you move a cursor (represented as an arrow) over any tool icon, a ToolTip below the cursor will display the name of the tool.

Tools with a small black triangle in the lower right corner contain flyouts with additional commands. To display a flyout, place the cursor on top of the tool icon and hold down the pick button until the flyout appears. To start a command, click a tool on the flyout.

To close a toolbar, click on the close box in the upper right corner.

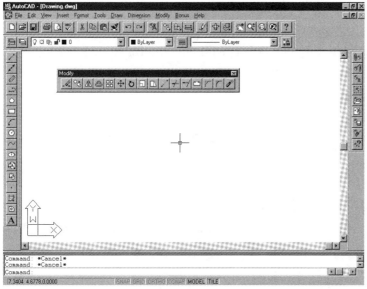

3.5a

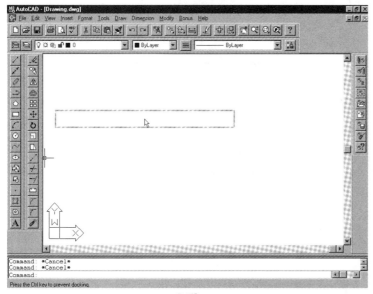

3.5b

3.5a A docked Draw *toolbar and a floating* Modify *toolbar.*

3.5b Undocking a toolbar.

Choose AutoCAD Help Topics
(R13 Contents) from the Help
menu to learn the basic facts
about a specific command or
procedure. You can also choose
Quick Tour for a quick overview
of AutoCAD's features.

The floating toolbar can be placed anywhere on screen, and it can be resized. To relocate a floating toolbar, place the tip of the cursor over the toolbar's caption, and press (hold down) the pick button. A thick outline of the toolbar will appear—drag it to another location, and release the pick button.

6 As you select commands, AutoCAD displays a *dialog box* or a set of options. From the *Tools* [R13 *Options*] menu, choose *Drawing Aids*. AutoCAD will display the *Drawing Aids* dialog box (Figure 3.6), in which you can specify snap and grid spacing and other options.

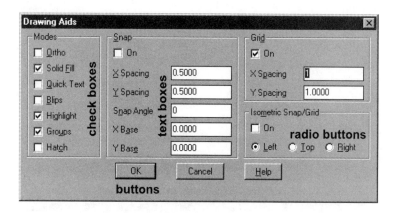

3.6 The Drawing Aids *dialog box.*

Grid is a pattern of dots that
helps you draw and align objects
and visually determine distances
between them. It is analogous to
placing a sheet of grid paper
under a drawing. Double-click
the GRID button in the status bar,
or press F7 or Ctrl-G to turn grid
on or off at any time.

This dialog box contains *buttons, check boxes, radio buttons,* and *text (numeric) fields* (Figure 3.6). Double-click the text box (the numeric field) labeled *X Spacing* in the *Grid* section of the dialog box, and enter 1 once the existing value is highlighted. Press the *Tab* key on the keyboard, and notice how the number in the box labeled *Y Spacing* has changed automatically to *1.0000*, the value you have entered previously. Click inside the check box labeled *On* in the *Grid* section to display a grid of dots in the graphics window. Finally, click on the *OK* button. A pattern of dots (called *grid*), spaced one unit apart, will appear in the graphics window. (Notice also that the GRID button in the status bar is "turned on.")

7 Not all AutoCAD commands display dialog boxes. Often, *command options* will be displayed as a prompt message in the command window. Enter CIRCLE in the command window. Notice the resulting prompt in the command window:

```
2P/3P/TTR/<Center point>:
```

At this point, you can pick a center point of the circle, which is the *default* option indicated by angle brackets (<>), or choose one of the three options. Enter 3P to choose the *3P (three points)* option, and draw a circle by specifying three points that lie on its perimeter. Notice how AutoCAD dynamically displays a ghosted image of the circle after you select the second point.

3.8a *The* Erase *tool.*

8 You can respond to some of the command prompts using several options, none of which will be displayed in the command window. For example, whenever you have to select an existing object that was already drawn, you will see the "Select objects:" prompt, to which you can respond in one of the several ways. You can pick objects *one by one,* or you can enter W to specify a *rectangular selection window,* A to *add,* or R to *remove* objects from the selection set, or another object selection option (for a full description, see AutoCAD User's Guide).

Select the *Erase* tool (Figure 3.8a) on the *Modify* toolbar. (If you don't see the *Modify* toolbar, from the *View* (R13 *Tools*) menu, choose *Toolbars,* and then choose *Modify.*)

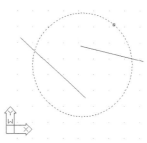

3.8b *The highlighted circle.*

AutoCAD will display the "*Select objects:*" prompt message in the command window. Notice how the cursor has changed into a small square box (the "pickbox"). Click on the circle to select it. The circle will become *highlighted,* a visual indication that it is selected (Figure 3.8b).

Next enter W at the command prompt to choose additional objects by specifying a rectangular selection boundary around them. AutoCAD will prompt you for two points that correspond to opposite corners of the rectangular box (Figure 3.8c).

Make sure that the two lines are completely within the selection box. Notice how AutoCAD dynamically displays the rectangular selection box as you move the cursor across the graphics window. Once the selection window is specified, AutoCAD will inform you how many objects are selected and will again display the "*Select objects:*" prompt. To complete object selection, press *Enter, Return,* or the *space bar* key on the keyboard, or press the

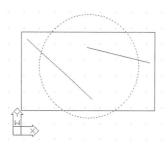

3.8c *The rectangular selection box around two lines.*

right mouse button (the return button on your pointing device). AutoCAD will erase the selected objects from the graphics window (and the corresponding records in the drawing database).

9 Choose the *Redraw View* tool from the *Standard* toolbar (use *ToolTips* to locate it) to refresh the drawing display, i.e., to remove the temporary point markers called *blips* (that look like small crosses) if there are any left on the screen.

10 Now select the *Line* tool and draw a 2 × 2 square using the displayed grid as a reference, and try to be as precise as possible. As you pick points, notice that the coordinate values of the selected points are fractional (for example, 3.9768,4.027).

11 Choose *Undo* from the *Edit* menu to undo the *Line* command. This time draw the same 2 × 2 square precisely using *absolute* coordinates (Figure 3.11). Again select the *Line* tool, and enter 4,2 as coordinates of the first point. These coordinates will locate the point that is 4 units along *x* axis, and 2 units along the *y* axis. Enter 6,2 as coordinates for the second point, 6,4 for the third point, and 4,4 for the fourth point. To close (complete) the square shape, enter c at the "*To point:*" prompt.

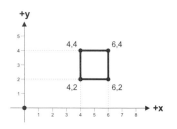

3.11 A 2 × 2 square with absolute coordinates of its corners.

12 The square can also be precisely drawn using *relative* point coordinates (Figure 3.12). Choose *Undo* from the *Edit* menu to undo the *Line* command. Instead of selecting the *Line* tool from the *Draw* toolbar, enter L (short for LINE) at the command prompt (followed by the *Enter* or *Return* key) to start the Line command. Enter the same absolute coordinates (4,2) for the first point. When asked for the next point, enter @2,0 to locate a point that is 2 units along *x* axis and 0 units along the *y* axis from the previously selected point. (The symbol @, pronounced "at," indicates that you are using *relative* coordinates to specify the point location.) Continue to specify the locations of the square's corners by entering @0,2 as coordinates for the third point, and @−2,0 (notice the minus sign for the *x* coordinate) for the fourth point. As in the previous step, use the c (close) option to complete the square shape.

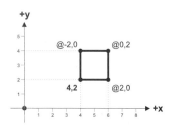

3.12 A 2 × 2 square with relative coordinates of its corners.

13 You can draw the same square shape using *relative polar* coordinates (figure 3.13a). Undo the Line command previously executed. This time draw another square shape using the *Polyline* tool (figure 3.13b). This tool on the *Draw* toolbar, as its name implies, is used to create a *polyline,* a connected sequence of line or arc segments that form a *single object.* The square shapes you have drawn previously were composed of four line objects. The square shape you will draw now is a single object, even though it looks exactly like the previous ones.

Enter the same coordinates for the first point (4,2). When asked for the next point, enter @2<0 to locate a point that is at a distance of 2 units from the previous point at an angle of 0 degrees (which coincides with the positive *x* axis). Specify the other two points by entering @2<90 and @2<180, respectively. (In AutoCAD, angles increase counterclockwise and decrease clockwise.) Notice that you could have entered @–2<0 for the last specified point (@2<180). To close the square shape, enter c at the command prompt.

14 If the distances (lengths) are known, it is definitely easier to draw shapes using relative coordinates. Even though your drawing will be precise, it is often tedious to draw in that fashion. A more efficient way is to use *snapping* to specify points. The *snap* mode restricts cursor movements to specific intervals (*spacing*), which you can define.

Choose *Drawing Aids* from the *Tools* (R13 *Options*) menu (Figure 3.14). Enter 0.5 for *x* and *y* spacing in the *Snap* section, and place the check mark in the check box labeled *On* to turn on the snapping. Notice that *snap* and *grid* spacings are different

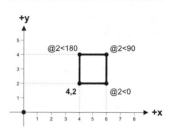

3.13a *A 2 × 2 square with* relative polar *coordinates of its* corners.

3.13b *The* Polyline *tool.*

Use the SNAP button in the status bar, or press the F9 key or Ctrl-B to turn snap on and off.

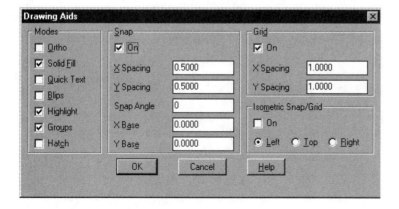

3.14 *The* Drawing Aids *dialog box.*

(they are set to 0.5 and 1.0, respectively). Click on the *OK* button
to continue.

Draw another 2×2 square next to the exiting one using grid
points as a reference. Notice how the cursor "jumps," i.e., moves
across the graphics window in precise increments, which equal
0.5 unit. Note that you don't have to count the grid points or cursor "jumps" to determine distances. You can use the coordinate
display in the status bar to read the distances as you draw (see
note in margin).

15 You can see another part of the drawing by *scrolling* or *panning*. To *scroll* a drawing, use the horizontal and vertical scroll
bars in the graphics window. You can scroll using scroll bar
arrows or the "thumbwheel" (Figure 3.15a).

Click on the "down" arrow in the vertical scroll bar to move
the drawing view down. Click on the "left" arrow in the horizontal
scroll bar to move the drawing view to the left (Figure 3.15b).

You can also move the drawing view in any direction by *panning*.

[R14] To pan across the drawing, choose the *Pan Realtime*
tool from the *Standard* toolbar (use the *ToolTips* to locate the tool).
Notice how the cursor changes from an arrow to a "hand." Hold
down the left mouse button (the pick button on your pointing
device), and move the cursor in the desired direction. Notice how
the drawing view follows the movement of the cursor. Release the

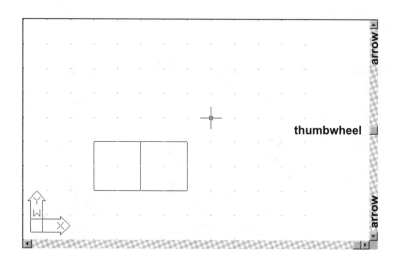

*3.15a The scroll bar with
arrows and the thumbwheel.*

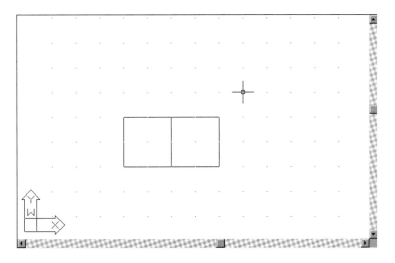

3.15b *The graphics window after scrolling.*

button once the view is at the desired position. Press the *Escape* (*Esc*) key or *Enter* to exit the command.

[R13] To pan across the drawing, you must specify a displacement, either numerically or by selecting two points. Choose the *Pan Point* tool from the *Standard* toolbar and pan to the right by selecting two points. At the "*Displacement:*" prompt, select the first point on the right side of the drawing. At the "*Second point:*" prompt, select a point on the left side. The drawing view will move to the right.

You can invoke the zoom command by entering Z or ZOOM at the command prompt.

16 You can also change the drawing magnification by *zooming in* or *out* (figures 3.16a and b). First choose the *Zoom All* tool in the *Standard* toolbar to return the drawing view to its original position.

Then choose the *Zoom Out* tool to, as its name implies, zoom out. The drawing will be reduced by 50% (Figure 3.16c).

Next choose the *Zoom In* tool and observe how the drawing "enlarges" by 200% (i.e., the previous zoom will be reversed). Choose the *Zoom Out* tool twice, and observe how the drawing "shrinks" with each zoom. Then choose *Zoom Window*, and specify the rectangular area around the two drawn squares as an area of the drawing to be "enlarged." When prompted to choose the first corner, pick a point below and to the left of the first square. Choose the other corner by selecting a point above and to the right of the second square. The selected area will be magnified to fill the graphics window (Figure 3.16d and 3.16e).

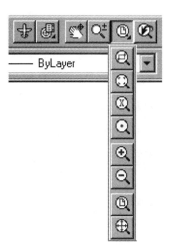

3.16a *R14 zooming tools.*

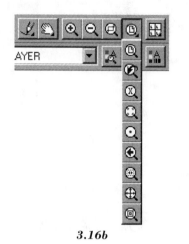

3.16b

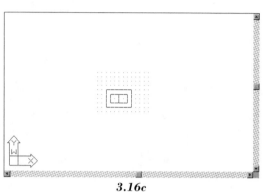

3.16c

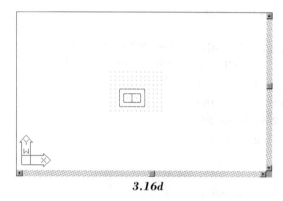

3.16d

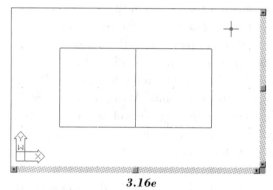

3.16e

3.16b R13 zooming tools.

3.16c Zooming out by 50%.

3.16d Selecting the rectangular area (window) to zoom in.

3.16e The graphics window after zooming in.

[R14] You can also zoom in and out in *realtime*. Choose the *Zoom Realtime* tool, click somewhere in the graphics window, and move the cursor in and out of the graphics window. Notice how the magnification of the drawing changes dynamically. Press the *Escape* (*Esc*) or *Enter* key to exit the command.

[R13] There is no support for realtime zoom in R13.

SETTING UP A DRAWING

17 Through the previous steps you have mastered some of the basic concepts related to computer-based drawing. In this section

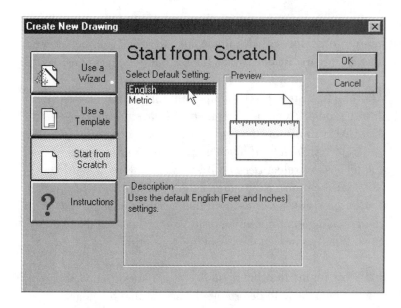

3.17a *The* Save Drawing *dialog box.*

3.17b R14 Create New Drawing *dialog box.*

you will learn how to set up a drawing that will contain the floor plans of Andrea Palladio's Villa Rotonda.

Start a new drawing. Choose *New* from the *File* menu. Since there is already a drawing displayed on the screen, AutoCAD will ask whether you want to save it. Click on the *No* button (Figure 3.17a). Next AutoCAD will display the *Create New Drawing* dialog box (Figures 3.17b and c).

[R14] Click on the *Start from Scratch* button, and select the *English* default setting to use feet and inches, or *Metric* to use metric units. Click on the *OK* button to continue.

In the tutorial exercises, both English (feet and inches) and metric values will be provided whenever coordinates or distances need to be specified. Metric values will always be given in meters and will be displayed within brackets.

If you make a mistake while executing any of the AutoCAD commands, press the Escape (Esc) key to cancel the command execution, or if the command is completed, use the UNDO command (from the Edit menu, choose Undo, or enter U at the command prompt) to return the drawing to its previous state, before the command was executed.

3.17c R13 Create New Drawing *dialog box.*

3.18 *The* Units Control *dialog box.*

3.19a *Determining the drawing limits.*

3.19b *Setting the drawing limits.*

[R13] Note that AutoCAD gives you an option to name this new drawing. You will give it a name later when you save it to the disk for the first time. Click on the *OK* button to continue.

18 The first step in setting up a new drawing is to choose the drawing units. From the *Format* (R13 *Data*) menu, choose *Units*. AutoCAD will display the *Units Control* dialog box (Figure 3.18).

Select *Architectural* if you want to work in English units (feet and inches), or select *Decimal* if you want to work in metric units. Click on the numeric box under the heading labeled *Precision*, and in the resulting drop-down list, set the precision to *0′-0″* if you are using imperial units, or to *0.000* if you are using metric units. Finally, click on the *OK* button to continue.

19 Next set the drawing limits, i.e., the drawing's invisible rectangular boundary. To determine the size of that boundary, calculate the size of the rectangle that bounds the building's "foot-print" and add ⅕ or less on each side. The bounding box for Palladio's Villa Rotonda is 133′ × 133′ [41.7 × 41.7]. Therefore, the size of the drawing's boundary should be 160′ × 160′ [48 × 48] (Figure 3.19a).

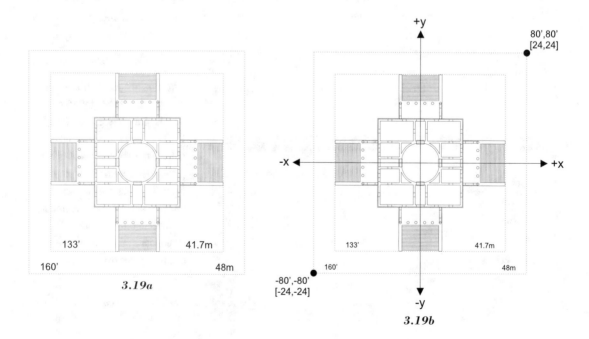

3.19a

3.19b

Drawings limits are specified by two points that correspond to the lower left and upper right corners of the boundary. Since the building is bisymmetrical, it is appropriate to place the building's "center" into the origin of the coordinate system, where the two axes intersect. The lower left corner of the limits, therefore, should be placed at −80′,−80′ [−24,−24], and the upper right corner at 80′,80′ [24,24] (Figure 3.19b).

To set the limits, choose *Drawing Limits* from the *Format* (R13 *Data*) menu, and enter −80′,−80′ [−24,−24] for the coordinates of the lower left corner, and 80′,80′ [24,24] for the coordinates of the upper right corner (Figure 3.19c).

You can always change the limits if the drawing extends beyond its originally set boundary.

```
Reset Model space limits:
ON/OFF/<Lower left corner> <0'-0",0'-0">: -80',-80'
Upper right corner <1'-0",0'-9">: 80',80'
   0'-4", 0'-6",0'-0"                    SNAP GRID ORTHO OSNAP MODEL TILE
```

3.19c Entering the drawing limits in the command window.

20 Next set the drawing grid and snap modules. From the *Tools* (R13 *Options*) menu choose *Drawing Aids*. In the *Drawing Aids* dialog box (Figure 3.20) enter 1′ [0.3] for x and y *Spacing* (module) in the *Snap* section. (Double-click into the appropriate numeric field and type the values; press the *Tab* key to move to the next field.) Enter 5′ [1.5] for x and y *Spacing* in the *Grid* section. Click inside the check box labeled *Ortho* in the *Modes* section to constrain the drawing to x and y direction only. Click the check box labeled *On* in the *Snap* section to turn the snapping on, i.e., to make snapping to module active. Next click inside the check box labeled *On* in the *Grid* section to display the modular grid. (Each of these three check boxes should display a *check mark* inside the box.) Finally, click on the *OK* button to continue.

You can toggle the grid display (i.e., turn it on or off) by pressing the F7 key or by double-clicking on the button labeled Grid in the status bar on the bottom of the window. Similarly, to turn ortho on or off, press the F8 key, or double-click the ORTHO button. To turn snap on or off, press the F9 key, or double-click the SNAP button.

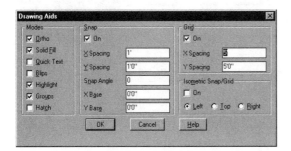

3.20 Specifying the grid and snap modules.

3.21a *The* Zoom All *tool icon.*

21 Display the entire drawing area. From the *View* menu, choose *Zoom,* and then *All,* or click on the *Zoom All* icon in the *Standard* toolbar (Figure 3.21a). Notice that the drawing area is square in shape and that the grid dots are spaced 5′ [1.5m] apart (Figure 3.21b).

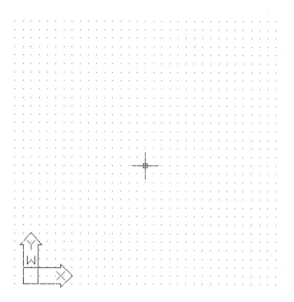

3.21b *The graphics windows after drawing setup.*

22 It is time to save what was done so far. To save the drawing to a file, choose *Save* from the *File* menu. In the *Save Drawing As* dialog box, enter *Rotonda* as the drawing name, and if necessary choose the directory (folder) where it should be saved (Figure 3.22). Then click on the *OK* button to continue.

3.22 *R14 and R13* Save Drawing As *dialog boxes.*

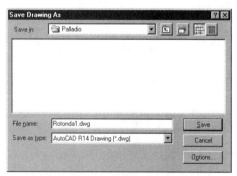

3.22a

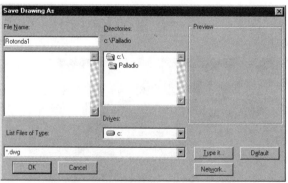

3.22b

DRAWING A SKELETON OF CONSTRUCTION LINES

23 In this section you will draw a skeleton of construction lines, a set of precisely placed infinite lines. These lines will be used as a visual and geometric reference for creating shapes that depict solid and void elements of Villa Rotonda (Figure 3.23a).

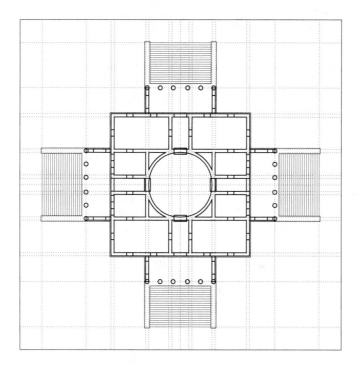

Save your drawing frequently as you work on it. It is a good habit to develop. Otherwise you may lose hours of work if the program or computer "crashes" or "freezes" unexpectedly, or if the computer loses power.

3.23a Villa Rotonda's construction lines.

In AutoCAD you always draw on some *layer*. As described in the previous chapter, *layers* are analogous to transparent overlays on which you place and organize drawing objects that are related in some way. Each layer has an associated *name, color,* and *line type,* which help to differentiate among various layers and objects in the drawing. Layers are, therefore, one of the principal ways of organizing and managing information in drawings.

You will draw the construction lines on a *layer* named GRID. To create this layer, choose *Layer* (R13 *Layers*) from the *Format* (R13 *Data*) menu.

[R14] Click on the *New* button in the *Layer & Linetype Properties* dialog box (Figure 3.23b).

The number of layers in the drawing and the number of objects per layer are unlimited in AutoCAD.

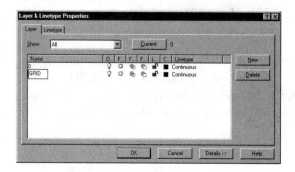

3.23b *R14* Layer & Linetype
Properties *dialog box.*

A new layer (*Layer1*) will be added to the list. Type GRID to assign a new name to this layer. Notice that there is already one layer in the list, named *0* (zero). This is the default layer in Auto-CAD, and it can't be deleted or renamed.

Assign the yellow color to layer GRID. First click on the *Details>>* button to display additional information about layers. Make sure that layer GRID is selected (highlighted) in the list, and then click on the box labeled *Color,* displaying *White* as the layer's color. Choose yellow color in the drop-down list (Figure 3.23c). The assigned color is displayed in the layer list box.

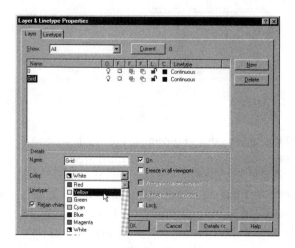

3.23c *Specifying the layer color (R14).*

The last step is to set layer GRID as the *current* drawing layer. Only one layer can be current. Make sure that GRID is selected (highlighted) in the layers list, and click on the *Current* button. Click *OK* to close the dialog box. The current layer will be displayed in the *Object Properties* toolbar (figure 3.23d).

[R13] Type GRID and click on the *New* button in the *Layer Control* dialog box (Figure 3.23e). A new layer named GRID will be added to the list. Notice that there is already one layer in the list, named *0* (zero). This is the default layer in AutoCAD, and it can't be deleted or renamed.

3.23d *The current layer is displayed in the* Object Properties *toolbar.*

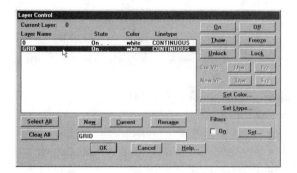

3.23e *R13* Layer Control *dialog box.*

Assign the yellow color to layer GRID. First click on the layer's name in the list, and then click on the *Set Color* button. Choose yellow color in the *Standard Colors* palette in the top section of the *Select Color* dialog box (Figure 3.23f). Click on the *OK* button. The assigned color is displayed in the layer list box.

The last step is to set layer GRID as the *current* drawing layer. Only one layer can be current. Make sure that GRID is selected (highlighted) in the list, and click on the *Current* button. The *Current Layer* area in the top left corner of the dialog box should list GRID as the current layer. Click *OK* to close the *Layer Control* dialog box. The current layer will be displayed in the *Object Properties* toolbar (Figure 3.23g).

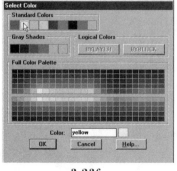

3.23f

3.23g

3.23f *Specifying the layer color (R13).*

3.23g *The current layer is displayed in the* Object Properties *toolbar.*

3.24a The Construction Line *tool.*

3.24b Specifying an option at the command prompt.

24 You will first draw the main horizontal and vertical axes. Choose *Construction Line* tool (Figure 3.24a) on the *Draw* toolbox. Select option V (vertical) when prompted for a point, i.e., enter V at the command prompt (Figure 3.24b).

Draw a vertical construction line through the origin (0,0)

```
Command:
Command:
Command: _xline Hor/Ver/Ang/Bisect/Offset/<From point>: v
```
59'-0", -28'-0",0'-0"   SNAP GRID ORTHO OSNAP MODEL TILE

point. Enter 0,0 when prompted for a point. Right click (press the right mouse button or the return button if you are using some other pointing device) or press the *Enter* or *Return* key when prompted for another *through point* to complete the command.

In AutoCAD you can right click or press *Enter* to repeat the last executed command. Right click or press *Enter* to repeat the *Construction Line* (*XLINE*) command, and draw the horizontal axis. Enter H (*Horizontal*) when prompted for a point, and enter 0,0 as coordinates of the *through point*. Right click or press *Enter* to complete the command (figure 3.24c).

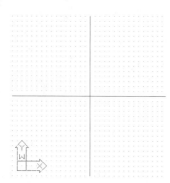

3.24c A vertical and a horizontal construction line.

25 Next use the *Offset* tool (figure 3.25a) on the *Modify* toolbox to draw construction lines on both sides of the main axes.

Select the *Offset* tool, and enter 15′ [4.5] as *offset distance*. Offset both the vertical and horizontal axes on both sides (Figure 3.25b). Select one of the axes, offset it on one side, select it again, and offset it on the other side. Do the same with the other axis. (When done, right click or press *Enter* to complete the offset com-

3.25a The Offset *tool.*

3.25b Offsetting construction lines.

3.25a

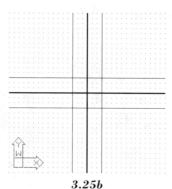

3.25b

mand.)

26 Offset the four construction lines created in the previous step for 1′6″ [0.45] to define the wall thickness (Figure 3.26). Right click or press *Enter* to reissue the offset command and enter 1′6″ [0.45] as offset distance.

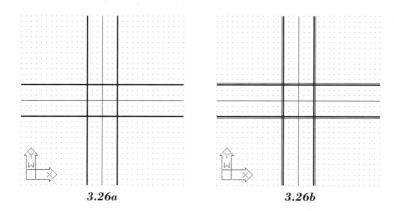

3.26a   3.26b

3.26 Offsetting the construction lines to define the wall thickness.

27 Draw the construction lines that delineate outer walls. Choose the *Offset* tool and set the offset distance to 15′ [4.5]. Offset the four *outer* lines that frame the central space (Figure 3.27). Reissue the offset command, set the offset distance to 1′6 [0.45], and offset the four new lines (Figure 3.27).

When specifying English units (feet and inches), you don't have to enter the quotation mark character (″) for inches, but you must enter the apostrophe character (′) for feet.

If you make a mistake, press the Escape (Esc) key to cancel any command in progress. To correct a mistake after the command is completed, choose Undo from the Edit menu.

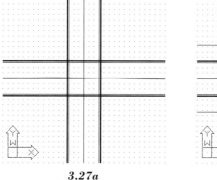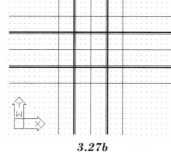

3.27a   3.27b

3.27 Offsetting the construction lines for outer walls.

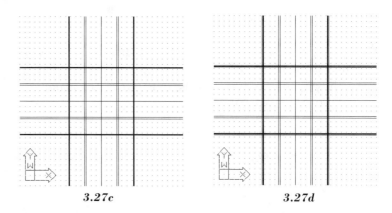

3.27c   3.27d

28 Create the construction lines at the end of the portico stairs. Set the offset distance to 33′ [9.9] and offset the four construction lines that delimit the villa's main volume (Figure 3.28).

3.28 Offsetting the construction lines for portico stairs.

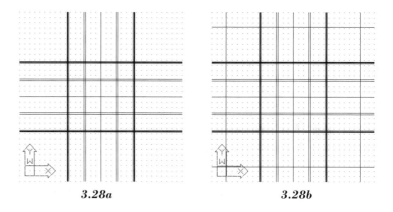

3.28a   3.28b

29 Draw a circle that corresponds to the central *sala* space. Choose the *Circle* tool, enter 0,0 for the center point, and enter 15′ [4.5] for the radius. Offset the circle for 1′6 [0.45] to define the wall thickness (Figure 3.29).

30 Next draw the construction lines for corridor walls. Offset the vertical axis on both sides for 4′ [1.2]. Offset the horizontal axis on both sides for 3′ [0.9]. Finally, offset these four new lines for 1′6 [0.45] to define the wall thickness (Figure 3.30).

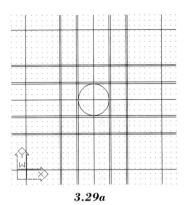

3.29a

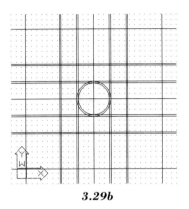

3.29b

3.29 *Defining the central* sala *space.*

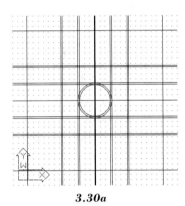

3.30a

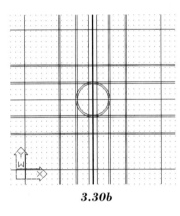

3.30b

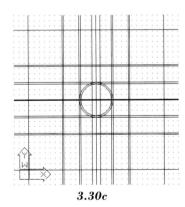

3.30c

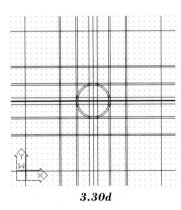

3.30d

3.30 *Offsetting the construction lines for corridor walls.*

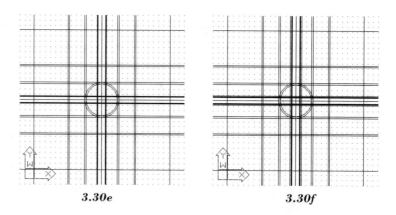

3.30e   3.30f

31 Finally, create the construction lines (the "center" lines) for the portico columns. Offset the outermost construction lines by 21′ [6.3] toward the center of the villa (Figure 3.31).

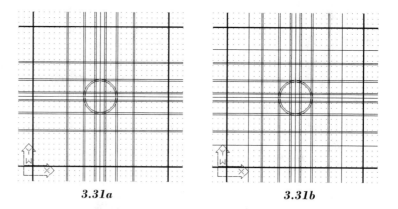

3.31 Offsetting the construction lines for portico columns.

3.31a   3.31b

3.32 The Save *tool.*

32 Save your drawing. Choose *Save* from the *File* menu, or click on the *Save* tool on the *Standard* toolbar (Figure 3.32). If you do not want to continue at this point, choose *Exit* from the *File* menu to exit AutoCAD.

You have completed the first tutorial exercise. You have drawn a skeleton of construction lines for Villa Rotonda. In the next tutorial exercise, you will draw the shapes that correspond to the villa's solids and voids by using this skeleton as a visual and geometric reference.

TUTORIAL 2: DRAWING SHAPES

In this tutorial exercise you will draw the shapes that correspond to solid and void volumes in Andrea Palladio's Villa Rotonda. You will first draw the volume outlines of the main (first) level, followed by the base (zero), and the second level. At the end of the exercise you will create a printout of the main-level "plan."

VOLUME (SPACE) OUTLINES OF THE MAIN VOLUME

1 Start AutoCAD, and open the previously saved drawing (Rotonda.dwg). If you are continuing from the last exercise, skip this step.

2 Before you draw anything, change the grid and snap spacing. Choose *Drawing Aids* from the *Tools* (R13 *Options*) menu. Set the grid spacing to 1' [0.3], and snap to 1" [0.01]. Turn off the grid display by removing the check mark in the *Grid* check box (Figure 4.2).

3 Create a new layer for the main- (first-) level volume outlines. Choose *Layer* (R13 *Layers*) from the *Format* (R13 *Data*) menu, or click on the *Layers* tool icon on the *Standard* toolbar (Figure 4.3). Create a new layer named 1-WALLS, assign red color to it, and make it the current layer. Its name should be displayed in the *Layer Control* field on the *Standard* toolbar.

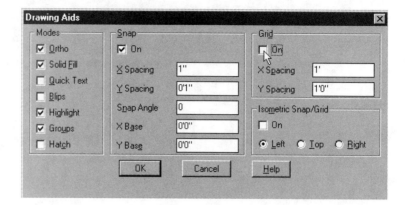

4.3 The Layers *tool icon.*

To disable the running object snap modes, click on the *Clear All* button.

You can also enter the OSNAP command at the command prompt to set the running object snap modes.

It is important to learn the time-saving features, such as drawing the rectangular shapes using the RECTANG instead of PLINE command, or pressing the *Return* key (or the right mouse button) to reissue the commands.

4 You will snap to the intersections of the underlying construction lines to draw the shapes that correspond to outlines of the main-level solid and void volumes. Instead of repeatedly choosing the *intersection object snap mode,* use the *running* object snap. This feature enables the desired object snap mode to be in effect whenever you have to select a point (until you change it). Choose *Object Snap Settings* (R13 *Running Object Snap*) from the *Tools* (R13 *Options*) menu, and select the *Intersection* mode by placing the check mark in the appropriate box (Figures 4.4a and b). Click on the *OK* button to continue.

5 You are now ready to begin drawing. To draw the circular shape in the center of the building (Figure 4.5), choose the *Circle* tool, or enter C at the command prompt, and pick the intersection of the two axial construction lines as the center point. Enter 15′ [4.5] as the radius, or click on one of the intersections of the underlying inner circle with construction lines. Note that the circle's color is red—that is because the color of the current layer (1-WALLS).

6 You will first draw the shapes in one quarter of the building's layout and will later use the MIRROR command to replicate the rest. Select the *Polyline* tool (Figure 4.6a) on the *Draw* toolbar and draw the volume outlines as shown in Figure 4.6c. To form closed polylines, enter C (close) at the command prompt to draw the last segment of each shape. Alternatively, you can use the *Rectangle* tool (Figure 4.6b) on the *Draw* toolbar to create the rectangular shapes—that way there are two fewer points to spec-

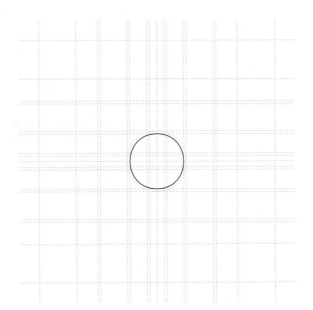

4.4a *The* Osnap Settings *dialog box in R14.*

4.4b *The* Running Object Snap *dialog box in R13.*

4.5 *The central circular volume (*sala*).*

ify, that is, you can draw these shapes twice as fast. Zoom in if necessary as you draw.

4.6a *The* Polyline *tool.*

4.6b *The* Rectangle *tool.*

4.6c *The closed polyline (rectangular) shapes.*

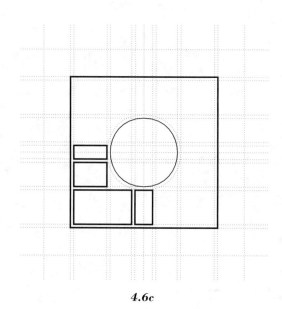

4.6c

7 Create a closed shape for the stairwell volume, which is next to the central space. First draw the L shape using the *Polyline* tool (Figure 4.7a). (To exit the PLINE command, press *Return* when done.) To draw the arc segment, select the *Arc* tool, and specify the *center* option (enter C). Place the center of the arc at the intersection of the axial construction lines (that is, at the center of the building). Then pick the start and end points (Figure 4.7b).

To join the previously drawn polyline and arc objects into a *single closed polyline shape,* use the PEDIT command or the *Edit Polyline* tool. When prompted to select a polyline, enter L (last) followed by *Return* to select the previously drawn arc object. Since that arc object is not a polyline, AutoCAD will ask whether you want to turn it into one. Since the default answer to this prompt is Y (yes), press *Return* to continue. Choose the join option—enter J at the command prompt followed by *Return.* When prompted to select objects, hold down the *Ctrl* (control) key and pick the L polyline shape to start the so-called cycle mode, which permits you to choose one of the overlapping objects. Auto-CAD will display the *<Cycle on>* message in the command win-

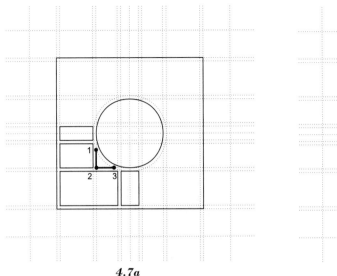

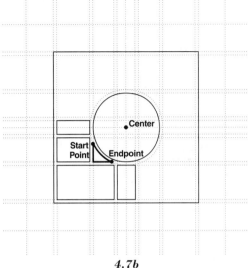

4.7a

4.7b

4.7a *Drawing the L shape.*

4.7b *Completing the stairwell volume outline.*

dow. Continue to click on the L shape until it is selected (high-lighted), and then press *Return* to exit the cycle mode. Press *Return* again to exit the object selection mode. Notice that the first option in the PEDIT command prompt is *Open*, which indicates that the polyline is now closed. Press *Return* one more time to exit the command.

8 Replicate the drawn volume outlines in the remaining part of the building layout using the *Mirror* tool (Figure 4.8a) in the *Modify* toolbar, or the MIRROR command. Select the objects to be mirrored by window selection (enter W when prompted to select objects, then pick two points as shown in Figures 4.8b and c). Use axial construction lines as mirror lines (Figures 4.8b and c). When prompted to delete old objects, enter N (No), or press *Return* (or *Enter*), since N is the default choice.

Use the PEDIT (Polyline Edit) command whenever you want to remove or add vertices to a polyline (Edit Vertex option), turn it into a curve, or join several objects into a single polyline.

4.8a *The* Mirror *tool.*

9 Save the drawing file. Choose *Save* from the *File* menu, or click on the *Save* tool on the *Standard* toolbar.

SOLID VOLUMES OF THE ENTRY PORTICO

10 Using the *Rectangle* tool, draw the front portico's left side wall (Figure 4.10).

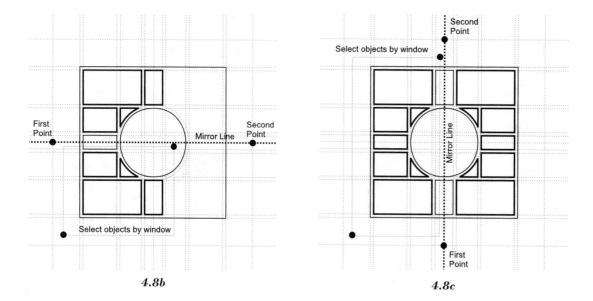

4.8b

4.8c

4.8b *The first mirroring.*

4.8c *The second mirroring.*

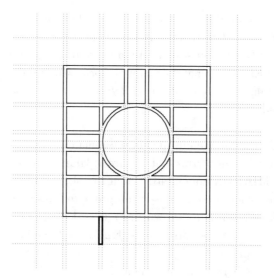

4.10 *The front portico's left side wall.*

11 Clear the running object snap modes. Choose *Object Snap Settings* (R13 *Running Object Snap*) from the *Tools* (R13 *Options*) menu, and click on the *Clear All* button (Figures 4.4a and b). Click on the *OK* button to continue.

12 Turn off the GRID layer. Click on the down arrow next to the *Layer Control* box in the *Object Properties* toolbar (Figures 4.12a and b). A list of layers and their properties will be displayed. Click on the lightbulb (R13 sun) symbol to *turn off* the GRID layer (Figures 4.12c and d). Click anywhere in the drawing window to continue. Make sure that 1-WALLS is still the current layer—its name should be displayed in the *Layer Control* field.

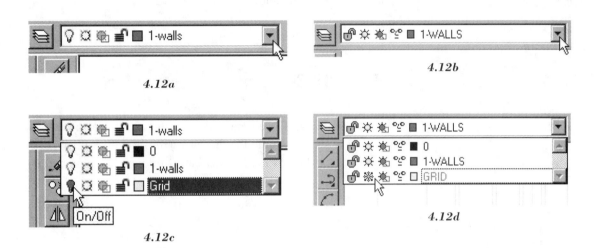

4.12a

4.12b

4.12c

4.12d

13 Draw a circular column centered at the end of the portico's left wall (figure 4.13a), i.e., its midpoint. Choose *Toolbars* from the *View* (R13 *Tools*) menu, and select the *Object Snap* toolbar (Figures 4.13b and c). Choose the *Circle* tool, then the *Midpoint* object snap mode on the *Object Snap* toolbar, and pick the front edge of the portico's wall. Set the radius to 1′ [0.3].

14 Use the rectangular ARRAY command to create the next two columns (Figure 4.14a). Choose the *Array* tool (Figure 4.14b), or enter ARRAY at the command prompt. When prompted to select objects, enter L (last) to select the last drawn object, the circular column. Press *Return* or *Enter* to complete the object selection. Choose rectangular array—enter R, the default choice. The array should have 1 row and 3 columns. Set the spacing between columns to 6′2″ [1.85].

15 Use the *Mirror* tool or the MIRROR command to create the right side of the portico. Select through window selection the wall

4.12a R14 Layer Control *box.*

4.12b R13 Layer Control *box.*

4.12c R14 Layer Control *list.*

4.12d R13 Layer Control *list.*

You can also enter at the command prompt the first three characters of the object snap mode, followed by *Return* or *Enter.* Enter END for endpoint, MID for midpoint, INT for intersection, PER for perpendicular, etc.

In R14 hold down the *Ctrl* (control) key and press the right mouse button (*Return* button on your pointing device) to display the *Object Snap* pop-up list (Figure 4.13d).

4.13a A circular column centered at the end of the portico's wall.

4.13b R14 Object Snap *toolbar.*

4.13c R13 Object Snap *toolbar.*

4.13d R14 Object Snap *pop-up list.*

object and three columns as objects to be mirrored, and pick two *midpoints* as shown in Figure 4.15 as points on the mirror line.

The porticoes on the other three sides are identical to the one you have just completed. Once a 3D model of one portico is completed, the other three will be created through replication by polar ARRAY command.

16 Save the drawing file.

THE VILLA'S BASE

17 All of the base's volume outlines will be created on layer 0-WALLS, where 0 stands for the base (zero) level, and WALLS describes the layer's content. Create this new layer named 0-

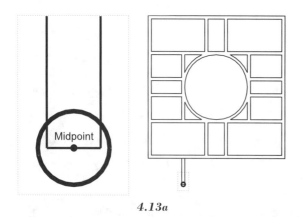

4.13a

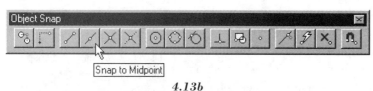

4.13b

4.13c

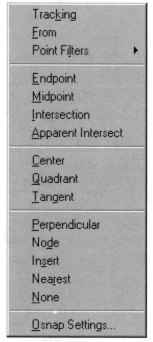

4.13d

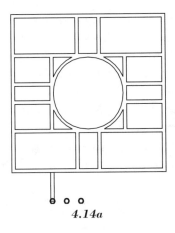

4.14a

4.14b

4.14a The column array.

4.14b The Array tool.

WALLS, assign the green color to it, and make it the current layer. Make sure that the GRID layer is off.

18 Create the main volume at the base level by offsetting the outer volume outline at the main level by 6″ [0.15] (Figure 4.18a). Choose the *Offset* tool (Figure 4.18b) on the *Modify* toolbar. Enter 6″ [0.15] as the offset distance and select the main volume outline as the object to offset (see Figure 4.18a). Pick a point anywhere outside the main volume as the side to offset. Press *Return* or *Enter* to exit the offset command when prompted again to choose an object to offset.

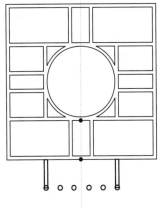

4.15 Completing the portico by mirroring.

You can also enter LAYER or LA at the command prompt to manipulate layers.

New outline

Outline to offset

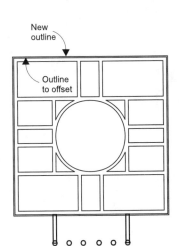

4.18a

4.18b

4.18a Offsetting the main volume outline.

4.18b The Offset tool.

4.19a *The* Properties *tool.*

19 The newly drawn volume outline (polyline) is created on layer 1-WALLS, as indicated by its red color. To place the new polyline on the appropriate layer (0-WALLS), choose the *Properties* tool (Figure 4.19a) on the *Object Properties* toolbar, and enter L (last) when prompted to select objects. Click on the *Layer* button in the *Modify Polyline* dialog box (figure 4.19b), and select the 0-WALLS layer from the list (Figure 4.19c). Click on the *OK* button in both dialog boxes to continue. The polyline is assigned to layer 0-WALLS, as indicated by its green color (the color of the 0-WALLS layer).

20 Turn on the GRID layer. Click on the down arrow next to the *Layer Control* box on the *Standard* toolbar. A list of layers and

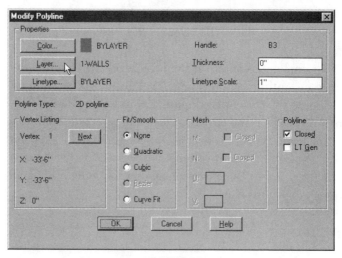

4.19b *The* Modify Polyline *dialog box.*

4.19b

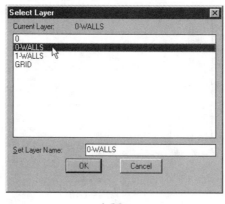

4.19c *The* Select Layer *dialog box.*

4.19c

their properties will be displayed. Click on the lightbulb (R13 sun) symbol to turn on the GRID layer (Figures 4.20a and b). Click anywhere in the drawing window to continue. Make sure that 0-WALLS is still the current layer—its name should be displayed in the *Layer Control* box.

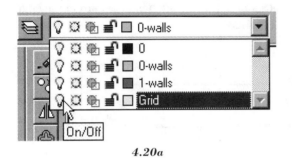

4.20a

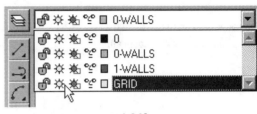

4.20b

21 Zoom into the portico stairs area. Choose the *Zoom Window* tool (figure 4.21a) on the *Standard* toolbar, and select a rectangular area as shown in figure 4.21b.

4.20a R14 Layer Control *list.*

4.20b R13 Layer Control *list.*

You can also enter the CHPROP command to change the object properties. In R14 you can use the abbreviated CH command, which displays a dialog box to change the properties.

You can also choose *Zoom,* then *Window,* in the *View* menu to zoom in by window.

4.21a

4.21a The Zoom Window tool.

4.21b The portico stairs area.

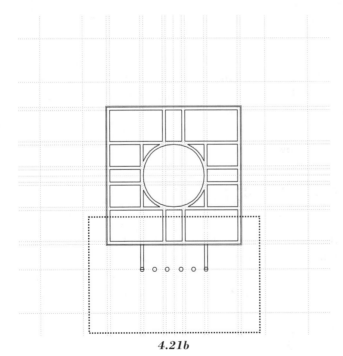

4.21b

You can enter the SNAP command at the command prompt and type the new value for the snap spacing.

22 Set the snap module to 6″ [0.15].

23 Draw the U-shaped portico base using the *Polyline* tool (or enter the PLINE command at the command prompt). The polyline should be drawn at the distance of 6″ [0.15] (1 snap module) from the construction lines and 1′ [0.3] (2 snap modules) from the edge of the columns (Figure 4.23).

You can enter Z at the command prompt followed by A to zoom all.

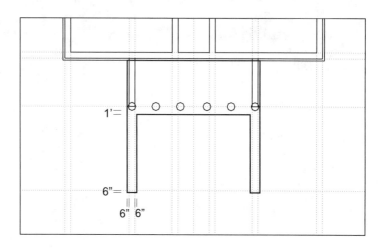

4.23 The U-shaped portico base.

4.24 The Zoom All *tool.*

24 Zoom to the drawing limits. Choose *Zoom*, then *All*, from the *View* menu or click on the *Zoom All* tool on the *Standard* toolbar (Figure 4.24).

25 Save the drawing file.

OPENINGS—DOORS AND WINDOWS

26 In this part of the exercise you will draw openings—doors and windows—on the main (first) level. Create a layer named 1-OPENINGS, assign the cyan color to it, and make it the current layer. Turn off layers GRID and 0-WALLS.

27 Set the snap spacing to 1″ [0.05].

28 Draw the openings using the *Rectangle* tool (or RECTANG command) in one quarter of the building (Figure 4.28a), and use the *Mirror* and *Copy* tools to replicate them in the remaining part of the building (Figures 4.28b and c).

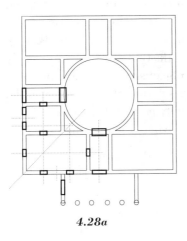

4.28a

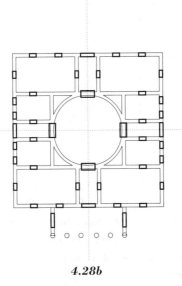

4.28b

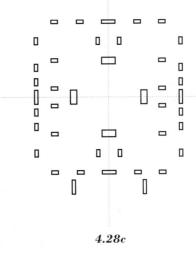

4.28c

4.28a *Drawing openings in the main level.*

4.28b *Main level with door and window openings.*

4.28c *Layer 1-OPENINGS— main-level door and window openings.*

All windows and interior doors are 3′ [0.9] wide. Exterior doors are 6′ [1.8] wide. The openings should have the same thickness as the main level walls—1′6″ [0.45]. The only exceptions are the doors to the *sala* (the central circular space); their thick-

4.28d The Move *tool.*

You do not need to enter the leading zero when specifying decimal values. For example, instead of 0.45 you can enter .45.

Use the *Snap From* tool (or enter FROM) whenever you need to specify a point relative to some existing point. Don't forget to enter the relative coordinates symbol (@) when specifying distances, and enter both relative *x* and *y* distances.

ness should be 2'10" [0.85] or so. The *sala* door openings should protrude on both sides of the wall.

You can draw the openings using exact dimensions anywhere in the drawing, and place them in the correct location using the *Move* tool (Figure 4.28d) on the *Modify* toolbar. For example, use the *Rectangle* tool, pick a point somewhere in the drawing, and enter the relative coordinates of the opposite corner (for a 3' × 1'6" [0.9 × 0.45] horizontal opening, enter @3',1'6 [@.9,.45]). Choose the *Move* tool, and enter L (last) to select the previously drawn polyline. Specify *midpoint* object snap mode, and pick one of the horizontal edges to select its midpoint in response to the "*From point:*" prompt. Again specify *midpoint* object snap, and select the appropriate "wall" edge where the opening is located (Figure 4.28e).

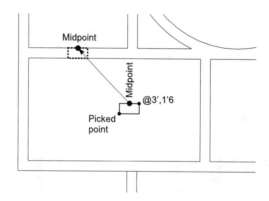

4.28e You can draw the shape first, and move it into the appropriate location using object snap.

4.28f The Snap From *tool.*

You can draw the same shape in its correct location using the *Snap From* tool. Choose the *Rectangle* tool, and when prompted for the first point, choose the *Snap From* tool (Figure 4.28f) on the *Object Snap* toolbar. Choose *Midpoint* object snap mode when prompted for the *base point*, and select the midpoint of the wall's edge (Figure 4.28g). Enter @-1'6,0 [@-.45,0] as the offset distance from the midpoint. Then enter @3',-1'6 [@.9,-.45] as the relative coordinates of the opposite corner.

29 Save the drawing.

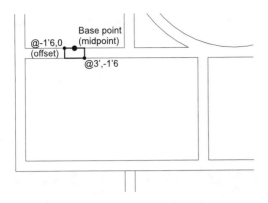

Base point
(midpoint)

@-1'6,0
(offset)

@3',-1'6

4.28g Drawing the opening's shape using relative coordinates.

PLOTTING THE DRAWING ON A PRINTER

30 Display (turn on) all layers but the GRID layer (Figure 4.30a). Print this drawing even though it is not complete (you will draw the entry stairs and array the porticoes later in 3D exercises). If you want, you can add the stairs (they are 1' [0.3] wide) and replicate the porticoes (Figure 4.30b), but don't use that drawing for the following exercise.

4.30a Incomplete 2D drawing of the Villa Rotonda.

4.30b Complete 2D drawing of the Villa Rotonda.

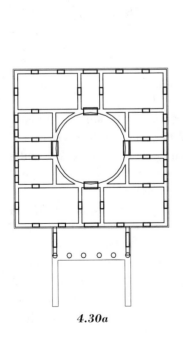

4.30a

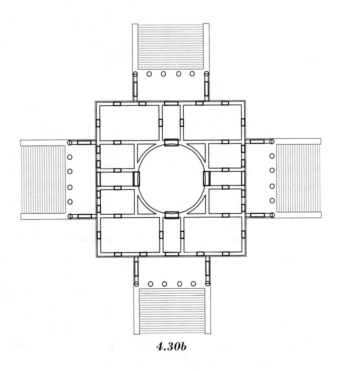

4.30b

31 Choose *Print* from the *File* menu. Choose *Extents* in the *Additional Parameters* section (Figure 4.31a) as the area to print. Remove the check mark in the *Scaled to Fit* check box (click inside), and set the printing scale to 1″ = 32′ (384 inches, i.e., drawing units) [2.5 mm = 1 m (i.e., drawing units)], which corresponds to ¹⁄₃₂″ = 1′ [1:400] scale (Figure 4.31a).

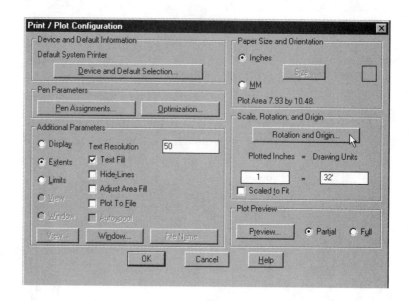

4.31a The Print/Plot Config-uration *dialog box.*

Before you can print to a printer or a plotter, you must *configure* it, i.e., you have to indicate to AutoCAD that a specific output device is present, and install the driver for it. To learn how to con-figure printers or plotters, con-sult the *AutoCAD Configuration Guide* or the manufacturer's doc-umentation.

If you are using a pen plotter, assign *pen numbers* (from the pen carousel) instead of line widths to AutoCAD colors.

Click on the *Plot Origin and Rotation* button to center the drawing on paper (letter [A4] size). Set *Plot Rotation* to 0 degrees, *X Origin* to 3.0 [75 mm] and *Y Origin* to 4.0 inches [100 mm] (Figure 4.31b). Choose the *Full* button in the *Plot Preview* sec-tion, and click on the *Preview* button to see the full preview of the printed drawing (Figure 4.31c). Press the *Esc* or *Enter* key to con-tinue, i.e., to return to the print dialog box.

Click on the *Pen Assignments* button to assign line widths to specific colors. Select color number 1 (red) and set the width of 0.2 for it (Figure 4.31d). If you recall, red color was assigned to layer 1-WALLS. All objects on this layer, i.e., those objects that are red, will be printed using this line thickness. Click on color 3 (green) and assign the width of 0.1 to it (all green objects, i.e., those on layer 0-WALLS, will be printed using this line width).

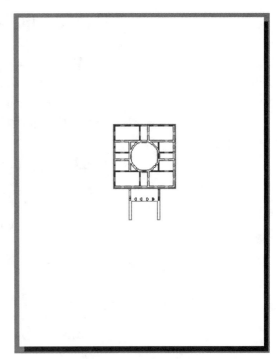

Plot Rotation and Origin ☒

┌─ Plot Rotation ──────────────────────────┐
│ ⊙ 0   ○ 90   ○ 180   ○ 270   │
└───┘

┌─ Plot Origin ─────────────────────────────┐
│ X Origin: [3.00]   Y Origin: [4.00 ⌶] │
└───┘

       [OK]   [Cancel]

4.31b

4.31c

Then click on color 4 (cyan) and assign the width of 0.3 to it. When done, click on the *OK* button. Finally, click on the *OK* button in the print dialog box to complete the printing. AutoCAD will show the printing progress, and shortly thereafter the drawing will be printed.

4.31b The Plot Rotation and Origin *dialog box.*

4.31c Plot preview.

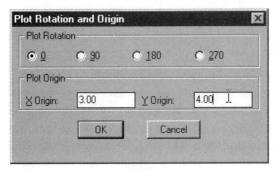

Pen Assignments ☒

Color	Pen No.	Linetype	Speed	Pen Width
1	1	0		0.010
2	2	0		0.010
3	3	0		0.010
4	4	0		0.010
5	5	0		0.010
6	6	0		0.010
7	7	0		0.010
8	8	0		0.010
9	9	0		0.010
10	10	0		0.010
11	11	0		0.010

┌─ Modify Values ──────┐
│ Color: [   ]   │
│ 1 (red)   │
│ Pen: [1]   │
│ Ltype: [0]   │
│ Speed: [   ]   │
│ Width: [0.2]   │
└──────────────────────┘

[Feature Legend...]   Pen Width [   ]

       [OK]   [Cancel]

4.31d Assigning the line widths to colors.

VOIDS IN THE BASE LEVEL

32 At the base level, you have drawn only the outline of the main volume and the portico's U-shaped base. In this section you will add the outlines of voids within the main volume.

Before you start drawing, set the snap spacing to 6″ [0.15].

33 Create the following layers and assign colors as desired:

0-OPENINGS (for openings at the base level)
2-SLAB (for the second-level slab)
2-WALLS (for the second-level walls)
2-OPENINGS (for the second-level openings)

Set layer 0-WALLS as the current layer, and turn off all other layers except 1-WALLS. You should see only the shapes of the layer 1-WALLS. Double-check that 0-WALLS is the current layer.

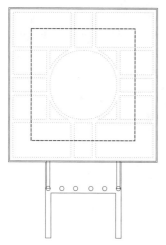

4.34a Selecting the room (void) outlines to copy.

4.34b The Properties *tool.*

34 The room (void) outlines at the base (zero) level are identical to those at the main (first) level. Therefore, you will make a copy of the existing room outlines, and assign the copied outlines to layer 0-WALLS. Choose the *Copy* tool on the *Modify* toolbar, and select the room (void volume) outlines using the C (crossing) object selection mode (Figure 4.34a). Enter 0,0 when prompted for the *base point or displacement.* Press *Enter* when prompted for the *second point of displacement.* As a result, two identical overlapping copies of the room shapes will exist on layer 1-WALLS.

Choose the *Properties* tool (Figure 4.34b) on the *Object Properties* toolbar to assign one copy of the room outlines to 0-WALLS layer. When prompted to select objects, enter P (previous) to choose the *previously* selected objects, i.e., objects selected in the previous copy operation. The "original" set of objects will be highlighted. Press *Enter* to complete object selection. In the *Change Properties* dialog box (Figure 4.34c) click on the *Layer* button, and choose layer 0-WALLS from the list (Figure 4.34d). Click on the *OK* button to continue. The color of the selected objects will change to green, an indication that they are assigned to layer 0-WALLS (whose color is green).

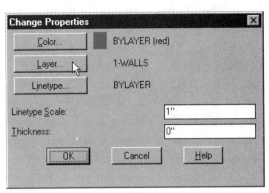

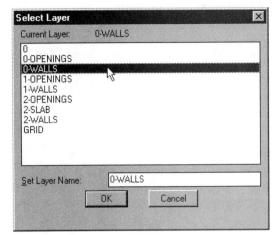

4.34c

4.34d

35 Choose the *Rectangle* tool to add a void volume outline under the portico (figure 4.35).

4.34c The Change Properties *dialog box.*

4.34d The layer list.

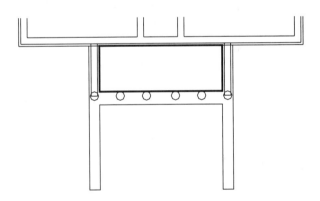

4.35 Adding a void volume under the portico.

THE BASE-LEVEL OPENINGS

36 In this section you will draw the openings at the base level. Turn on layer 0-OPENINGS and make it the current layer. Turn off all other layers except 1-OPENINGS and 0-WALLS.

37 Turn off the *ortho* mode. Press the *F8* key, or double-click the *Ortho* button on the status bar.

38 Draw two 3'-[0.9-] wide openings near the corner, and draw a 3'- [0.9-] wide window opening on the left side of the portico (Figure 4.38a). Turn off layer 1-OPENINGS and use the *Mirror* tool to replicate these openings on the other three corners of the building (Figure 4.38b).

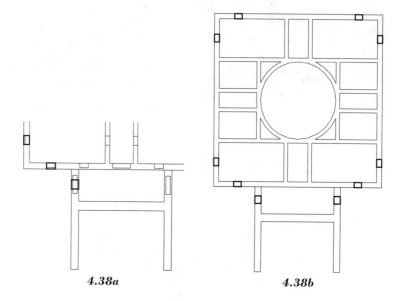

4.38a Drawing the openings at the base level.

4.38b The openings at the base level.

4.38a   4.38b

39 Save the drawing.

THE SECOND-LEVEL VOLUMES

40 In this section you will create the second-level volume outlines. Turn on layer 2-WALLS. Set the current layer to 2-WALLS and turn off all other layers except 1-WALLS.

41 Create a copy of the main volume and all room outlines (Figure 4.41) with the displacement of 0,0, and assign one set of the outlines to layer 2-WALLS.

42 Turn off layer 1-WALLS. Only the current layer 2-WALLS should be visible.

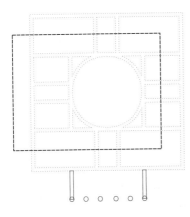

4.41 *Selecting the main and room outlines to copy.*

43 Using the *Rectangle* tool draw one large square on the inner side of the main volume (Figure 4.43a) by snapping to the corners of the rooms (use *endpoint* or *intersection* object snap). Draw another square on the outer side of the stairwells (Figure 4.43b). Delete most of the copied room outlines as shown in Figure 4.43c. Refer to Figure 4.43d for the final layout of the second level.

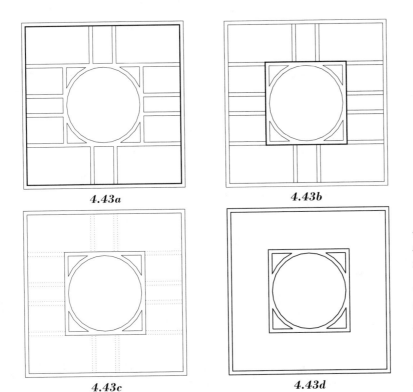

4.43a

4.43b

4.43c

4.43d

4.43a *Drawing a large square on the inner side of the main volume.*

4.43b *Drawing another square around the stairwells.*

4.43c *Deleting some of the copied room outlines.*

4.43d *Final layout of the second level.*

44 Save the drawing.

THE SECOND-LEVEL SLAB

45 Turn on layer 2-SLAB and make it the current layer. Layer 2-WALLS should remain visible.

46 Make a copy of the main volume, central circle, and stair-well outlines with the displacement of 0,0 (Figure 4.46). Assign the copied outlines to layer 2-SLAB.

47 Turn off layer 2-WALLS. Only the current layer (2-SLAB) should be visible.

48 Offset the circle inside by 3′ [0.9]. Delete the original circle. Refer to Figure 4.48 for the final slab layout.

4.46 Copying the outlines.

4.48 Second-level slab.

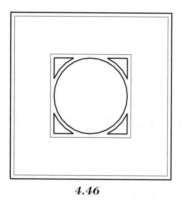

4.46

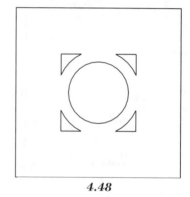

4.48

49 Save the drawing.

THE SECOND-LEVEL OPENINGS

50 Turn on layers 1-OPENINGS and 2-OPENINGS, and make 2-OPENINGS the current layer. Turn off all other layers.

51 Copy the outlines of the openings near the corners, as shown in Figure 4.51, with the displacement of 0,0. Assign the copied outlines to layer 2-OPENINGS.

52 Using the *Rectangle* tool draw 3'- [0.9-] wide door openings to the cylindrical space (Figure 4.52).

53 Turn off layer 1-OPENINGS to verify the openings layout (refer to Figure 4.53 for comparison).

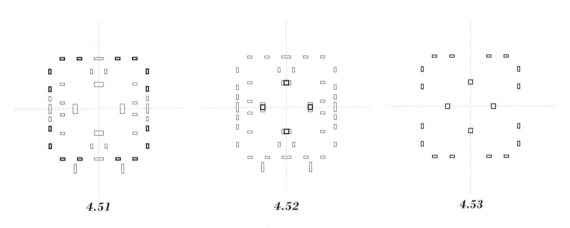

| 4.51 | 4.52 | 4.53 |

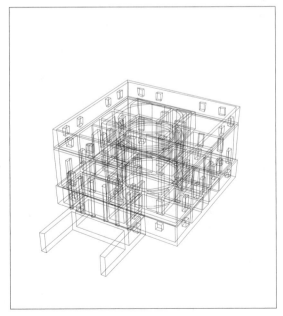

4.51 Copying the openings.

4.52 Door openings to the cylindrical space.

4.53 Openings on the second level.

4.55 2D shapes extruded into 3D solid objects.

54 Save the drawing. If you do not want to continue at this point, choose *Exit* from the *File* menu to exit AutoCAD.

In this tutorial exercise you have created most of the closed shapes, outlines of the building's solid and void volumes. In the next exercise you will *extrude* these two-dimensional shapes into three-dimensional *solid* objects and place them at the appropriate locations in space (Figure 4.55).

5

BASIC CONCEPTS: 3D MODELING

In traditional architectural practice, the use of various physical scale models in design adds powerful ways to explore and represent ideas beyond the flat realm of sketches and drawings. *Massing models* are often created to study and convey volumetric composition and relationships of the building and its context. *Building models* are more detailed and include various building elements such as walls, columns, windows, and doors. *Detail models* are studies of a particular interior space, a specific building element, or a construction assembly, and are often created in later phases of design development.

Typically, such physical scale models are assemblies of elements cut from thin materials, such as cardboard, balsa wood, Plexiglas, or metal sheets, or from solid materials, such as wood or solid foam blocks. Three-dimensional *computer models* are produced in analogous fashion—by constructing and assembling *surface* and *solid* objects in 3D space.

3D COORDINATE SYSTEMS

Three-dimensional geometric modelers extend the capabilities of two-dimensional drafting systems by providing a rich set of features to *construct, transform,* and *project* 3D geometric forms as collections of *lines, surfaces,* and *volumes* in space. In modeling systems, such geometric objects are typically constructed within a three-dimensional Cartesian coordinate system, a straightfor-

All AutoCAD 2D object snap modes (*endpoint, midpoint, center, perpendicular, intersection,* etc.) are available in 3D as well.

ward extension of the two-dimensional version introduced in the second chapter. Point locations are described by *x, y, z* coordinate triplets (Figure 5.1). As in two-dimensional drawing systems, points can be specified *numerically,* by entering either *absolute* or *relative* coordinates (Figure 5.2), or *graphically,* either by object snapping (Figure 5.3) or by snapping to grid points defined by snap spacing.

Depending on the direction of the positive *z* axis, there are so-called *right-hand* and *left-hand* Cartesian coordinate systems. The definition of both systems relies on an analogy with the hand fingers: the thumb indicates positive direction of the *x* axis, the index finger positive direction of the *y* axis, and the middle finger the positive *z* axis (Figure 5.4). If we assume that the *x* and *y* axes have the orientation as in Figure 5.1, then in the "right-hand" coordinate system (Figure 5.4), the positive *z* axis points "up,"

AutoCAD employs the "right-hand" 3D Cartesian coordinate system.

and in the "left-hand" system, it points "down." Since not all modeling systems visually indicate the direction of the positive *z* axis, it is often convenient to use the middle finger of the right or left hand (depending on the implemented coordinate system) to determine the correct direction when constructing or manipulating the geometric objects in "virtual" 3D space of computer modeling systems.

Another "right-hand" rule becomes handy when *rotating* objects in 3D space. In most 2D drafting systems, positive rotation is in counterclockwise direction. In 3D space, however, rotation takes place about one of the coordinate axes, and metaphors of clockwise or counterclockwise rotation are no longer applicable.

5.1 Three-dimensional coordinate system.

5.2 Absolute and relative 3D coordinates.

5.3 Object snapping in 3D space.

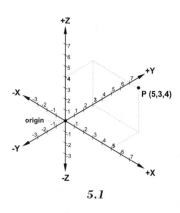

5.1

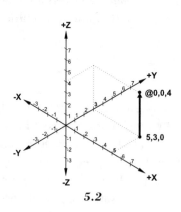

5.2

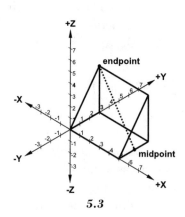

5.3

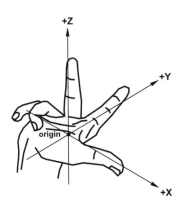

5.4 *The "right-hand" coordinate systems.*

The *right-hand* rule identifies the direction of the positive rotation in the following fashion: If you align the *thumb* of your right hand with the positive direction of an axis, the *curl* of your fingers will indicate the positive rotation about that axis (Figure 5.5).

In addition to Cartesian coordinates, some modeling systems also provide point specification in *cylindrical* and *spherical* coordinate systems, which stem from the *polar* 2D coordinate system described in the second chapter. In a *cylindrical* coordinate system, point location is described by three parameters: *distance* from the origin, *angle* from the x axis in the horizontal plane (often referred to as the xy plane), and *distance* from the horizontal plane (Figure 5.6). In a *spherical* coordinate system, the third parameter is different—the *angle* from the horizontal plane is used instead of distance (Figure 5.7). Both systems are rarely used in architectural 3D modeling.

AutoCAD supports all three coordinate systems: *3D Cartesian, cylindrical,* and *spherical.* 3D Cartesian coordinates are specified as *x,y,z* triplets. Cylindrical coordinates are specified using the following convention: *Distance<Angle,Height (z)* (for example, *5<45,4*). Spherical coordinates are specified as *Distance< Angle in xy Plane<Angle from xy Plane* (for example, *5<45<60*). Relative 3D coordinates are preceded by the @ (pronounced "at") symbol (for example, *@5,4,2*).

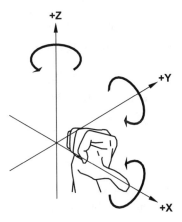

5.5 *Positive rotation about axes.*

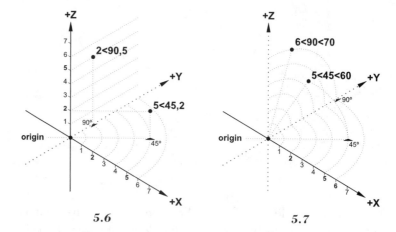

5.6 *Cylindrical coordinate system.*

5.7 *Spherical coordinate system.*

5.6

5.7

CONSTRUCTION PLANES

A typical problem that confronts new users of modeling systems is how to draw 2D shapes or construct 3D forms on vertical or slanted planes in space. The solution is simple—before such objects can be drawn, new *reference* or *construction planes* must be defined.

In most 3D modeling systems, there is a "global" or "world" coordinate system, defined by origin point and *x, y,* and *z* axes. Additional "local" coordinate systems, often referred to as reference or construction planes, can be defined by giving coordinates of three points that lie on it, or by rotating about one of the coordinate axes. A *three-point* definition is a standard method in most modelers to specify a local coordinate system: the first selected point defines its *origin,* the second point specifies the *positive direction of the x axis,* and the third point defines the *xy plane* (Figure 5.8). Using these and other methods of definition, a new construction plane can be created to coincide with any surface in the model (Figure 5.9).

Note that in most modelers, a newly defined construction plane can be saved under a specific name (such as FRONT_FACADE or SECOND_FLOOR) and recalled later.

3D GEOMETRIC PRIMITIVES

In *Vers une architecture,* Le Corbusier wrote that "Egyptian, Greek, or Roman architecture is an architecture of prisms, cubes

In AutoCAD, the user defined reference or construction plane is called the *User Coordinate System* or *UCS.*

and cylinders, pyramids or spheres." Indeed, buildings are often conceived and abstracted as compositions of such simple geometric forms, or *primitives.*

Many 3D modeling systems provide a "standard" vocabulary of 3D geometric primitives very similar to the one mentioned by Le Corbusier. Typically, a modeling vocabulary includes *boxes* (with *cubes* as a subset), *wedges, pyramids, cylinders, cones,* and *spheres* (Figure 5.10). Additional 3D geometric primitives can also be constructed from 2D shapes by *sweeping* or *skinning operations,* described in the next two sections.

Each of the above-mentioned primitives can be created as a *wire-frame, surface,* or *solid (volumetric)* object. *Wire-frame* objects are composed of curvilinear elements, lines and curves in space, and appear as if composed of "wires" (Figure 5.11). *Sur-*

To define a construction plane (*User Coordinate System*), enter the UCS command and select one of the options, or choose *UCS* (R13 *Set UCS*) from the *Tools* (R13 *Options*) menu. A UCS can be specified by three points in space, rotation about *x, y,* or *z* axis, alignment with an object, translation of the origin, direction of the positive *z* axis, or alignment with the current view (projection) plane. Use the *Save* option to store UCS definitions, and use the *Restore* option to reuse them. Note that UCSs can be *deleted* or *redefined* as well.

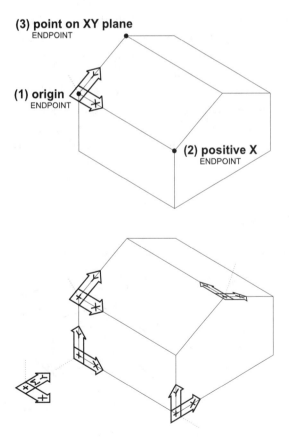

(3) point on XY plane
ENDPOINT

(1) origin
ENDPOINT

(2) positive X
ENDPOINT

5.8 Three-point definition of the construction plane.

5.9 Construction planes.

In many systems, solid objects look just like wire-frame or surface ones in the *wire-frame* display mode, but the underlying database representation is very different.

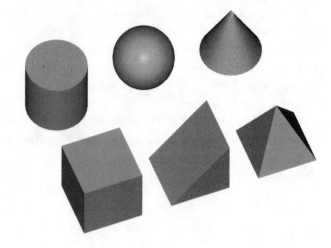

5.10 *"Standard" 3D geometric primitives.*

AutoCAD can create all three types of 3D primitives: *wire frame, surface,* and *solid.* *Wire-frame* primitives are all 2D objects previously introduced (*line, rectangle, polyline, arc, circle, ellipse,* etc.) and *3D polyline.* *Surface* primitives are *box, wedge, pyramid, cone, sphere, dome, dish, torus, 3D face, 3D mesh,* and *extruded, revolved, ruled,* and *edge surfaces.* Solid primitives are *box, sphere, cylinder, cone, wedge, torus,* and *extruded* and *revolved* solids. All these primitives can be selected from appropriate toolbars— *Draw, surface,* and *Solid,* respectively.

5.11 *Cube and half-cube as wire-frame, surface,* and *solid objects. Note that the surface cube lacks volume—it is hollow.*

face objects are composed, as their name implies, of surfaces *without thickness. Solid* objects are volumetric, i.e., they have volume (mass) and are completely enclosed. (Note that *closed* surface objects lack volume, i.e., they are hollow.)

The distinction between wire-frame, surface, and solid (volumetric) objects is an important one. Whether an object is a surface or a solid will determine what can be done with it. For example, there are powerful editing and data extraction operations applicable only to solid objects. In addition, since the tech-

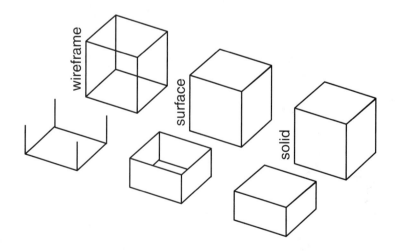

niques of surface and solid modeling are different, the development of building models can often evolve in different ways depending on the technique that was applied.

SWEEPING OPERATIONS

As mentioned in the previous section, additional 3D geometric primitives can be constructed from 2D shapes through *sweeping operations.* A 2D profile (shape) can be translated along a linear path (*translational sweeping*), rotated around an axis (*rotational sweeping*), or swept *along an arbitrary path* from its construction plane to form a 3D object, a *surface* or *solid* object (Figure 5.12). For example, a cone can be created by rotational sweeping of an inclined line, a sphere by rotational sweeping of a semicircle, etc. (In fact, all the primitives previously mentioned can be constructed by sweeping.) Note that in some modelers, the translational sweeping is referred to as *extrusion,* and rotational sweeping as *revolution.* 3D objects generated by translational sweeping are in some modeling systems called *tabulated* or

AutoCAD supports both *translational* and *rotational sweeping,* and *sweeping along an arbitrary path.* Translational sweeping is referred to as *extrusion,* and rotational sweeping as *revolution.* Sweeping along a path is available as an option of the EXTRUDE command. Additional 3D construction operations are provided by add-on modules, such as *AutoSURF* (surface modeler) and *Designer* (parametric solid modeler).

Classical molding can easily be constructed by drawing the molding's profile and the path along which the profile is swept.

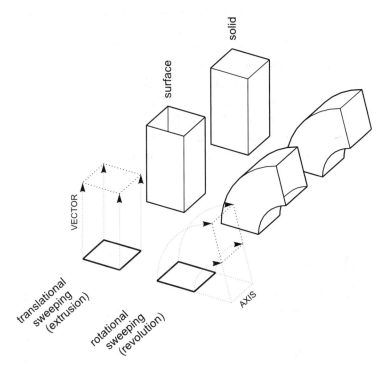

5.12 Constructing 3D objects from 2D shapes by sweeping.

extruded, and objects created by rotational sweeping are often referred to as *revolved* (surfaces or solids).

Some 3D modelers provide simultaneous translational and rotational sweeping to construct *helical* objects. For example, a spiral ramp can be constructed in this fashion by translating and rotating a line through space at the same time (Figure 5.13). In some modelers, the base profile can be *scaled* as it is swept through space. For example, a truncated cone can be created by scaled translational sweeping of a circle; likewise, a truncated pyramid can be created by scaled sweeping of a square (Figure 5.14).

In some surface modelers, *ruled surfaces* can be created by sweeping two ends of a line along different paths (Figure 5.15). By sweeping two ends of an inclined straight line along circles, a *hyperboloid* can be created (Figure 5.16). Another well-known ruled surface, a *hyperbolic paraboloid,* can be constructed by sweeping along two nonplanar straight lines (Figure 5.17).

SKINNING OPERATIONS

3D objects can also be created by drawing a sequence of profiles (2D sections) over which a 3D object (surface or solid) can be created (Figure 5.18). This technique, called *skinning,* is particularly useful in modeling some complex, "organic" forms in architecture, such as columns in Antonio Gaudi's Sagrada Familia.

There are two skinning methods: *ruled* and *lofted* (Figure 5.18). In ruled skinning, 2D profiles are connected with ruled surfaces, whereby continuity is disregarded, i.e., sharp transitions can exist between surfaces. In lofted skinning, continuity is main-

Ruled surfaces are supported by AutoCAD.

Ruled skinning is done in Auto-CAD by separate insertions of ruled surfaces (RULESURF) between profiles. **Lofted skinning** is not supported in the standard AutoCAD package. **Covering** is provided through *edge surfaces* (EDGESURF), which can be created between four bounding curves in space. Note that *Auto-SURF,* an AutoCAD add-on module provided separately by Autodesk, provides extensive surface modeling and editing operations.

5.13 *Constructing helical objects by simultaneous translational and rotational sweeping.*

5.14 *The base profile can be scaled as it is swept through space.*

5.13

5.14

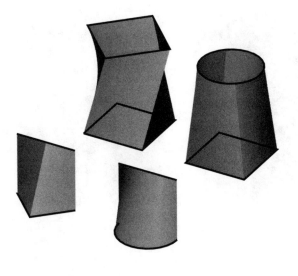

5.15 Ruled surfaces.

5.16

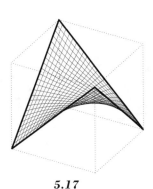

5.17

5.16 Hyperboloid, an example of a ruled surface.

5.17 Hyperbolic paraboloid,
another example of a ruled
surface object.

tained—the resulting surface will be smooth, without sharp edges
or corners.

Another skinning technique available in some modelers is
covering (Figure 5.19). This technique creates a smooth surface
between curves that represent its boundaries. Some modelers
limit the number of bounding curves (typically between two and
six), and some will refuse to *cover* curves that don't touch at endpoints.

Skinning is also used in terrain modeling. In some modeling
programs, contour lines are used as 2D profiles over which a surface mesh is created (Figure 5.20).

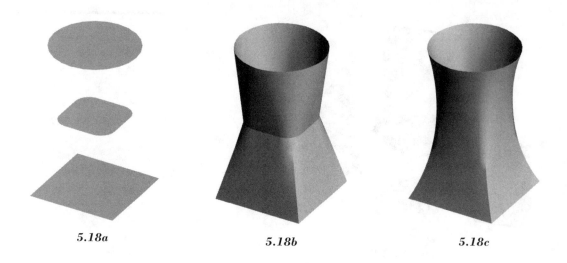

5.18a   **5.18b**   **5.18c**

5.18 Ruled and lofted skin-ning over 2D profiles.

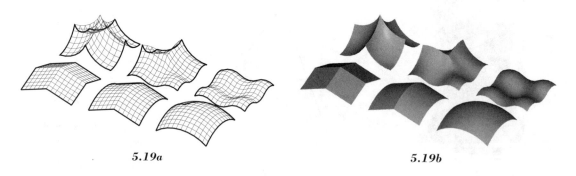

5.19a   **5.19b**

5.19 Covering.

BOOLEAN OPERATIONS

In the nineteenth century, mathematician George Boole invented the *theory of sets* and defined the set operations of *union, intersection,* and *subtraction,* later named after him as *Boolean.* Since 3D geometric objects created by 3D modelers are nothing more than *sets* of interrelated points in space, the Boolean operations are also provided by some modelers to create *composite* surfaces and volumes (Figures 5.21 and 5.22).

When a *union* operation is applied to two surfaces (closed shapes, such as square A and circle B as in Figure 5.21), the

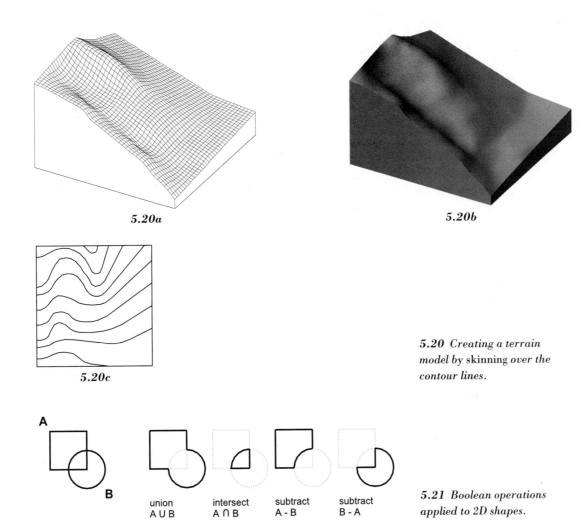

5.20a

5.20b

5.20c

5.20 Creating a terrain model by skinning over the contour lines.

A

B

union
A ∪ B

intersect
A ∩ B

subtract
A - B

subtract
B - A

5.21 Boolean operations applied to 2D shapes.

resulting shape is created by computing the new boundary that encloses both shapes. *Intersection* computes a closed area common to both shapes. *Subtraction* can be applied to shapes A and B in two ways: Either shape B is subtracted from shape A (A - B), or shape A is subtracted from shape B (B - A).

Applying Boolean operations to closed, well-formed 3D objects is a straightforward extension of the previous example (Figure 5.22). *Union* creates an object that encloses both objects (cube A and cylinder B). *Intersection* computes a closed volume common to both objects. Finally, *subtraction,* as in 2D, can be

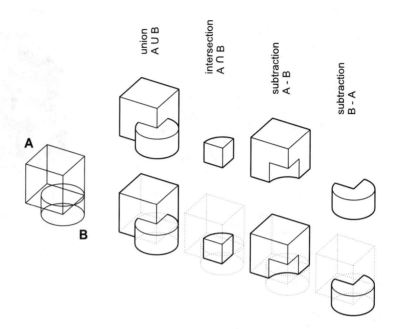

union
A ∪ B

intersection
A ∩ B

subtraction
A - B

subtraction
B - A

A

B

5.22 *Applying Boolean opera-*
tions to 3D forms.

AutoCAD supports all three
Boolean operations: *union, inter-*
section, **and** *subtraction.* **3D solid**
objects can also be created by
slicing.

applied in two ways: Cylinder B can be subtracted from cube A, and vice versa.

Note that 3D objects (either closed-surface or volumetric forms) must overlap spatially or have overlapping surfaces for Boolean operations to be carried out. (In some modelers, the second condition is not applicable.) Also, note that 3D objects must be *completely closed* ("watertight") and must be *well formed*—self-intersecting objects will be rejected (Figure 5.23).

Applying Boolean operations to simple 3D geometric primitives can easily create some rather complex 3D forms. For example, the pendentive in Figure 5.24 can be constructed by first subtracting a smaller sphere from a larger one, and then intersecting the resulting object with a box (Figure 5.26). By applying Boolean operations to two overlapping boxes, complex 3D objects can be created in one step, as illustrated by Figure 5.25.

Some solid modelers maintain a hierarchical description of composite objects, called a *Constructive Solid Geometry Tree* (or *CSG tree,* in abbreviated version), which stores a geometric description of all primitives and applied Boolean operations in an inverted treelike structure. For example, Figure 5.26 shows a CSG tree for the pendentive composite solid object depicted in Figure 5.24. The "leaf" nodes are the primitives used to create

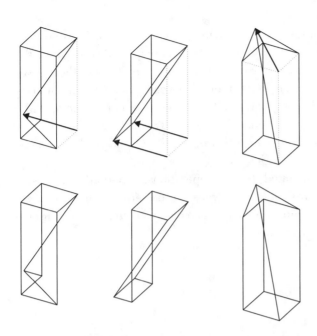

5.23 *Boolean operations cannot be applied to self-intersecting objects.*

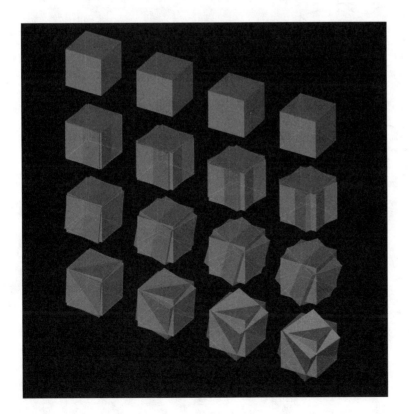

5.24 *Constructing a* pendentive *from simple geometric primitives.*

5.25 *Another example of constructing complex forms from 3D primitives.*

composite solids using Boolean operations, which are shown at higher nodes. At the "root" node is a completed solid form. By changing the parameters associated with primitives or their position and orientation, many alternatives can quickly be explored— a modeler that supports CSG tree editing can automatically compute the consequences of changes (Figure 5.27). Some modelers even support *substitution* of primitives and Boolean operations in a CSG tree (Figure 5.28).

As demonstrated, Boolean operations, variation, and substitution of primitives in CSG trees are powerful tools for design exploration. Complex 3D forms can easily be created and various options quickly explored.

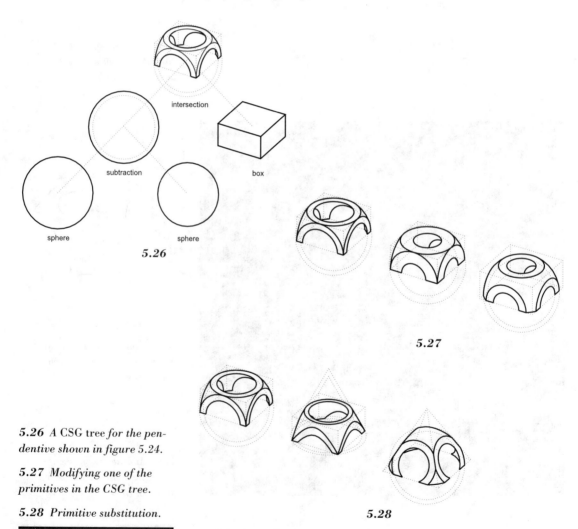

intersection

subtraction

box

sphere

sphere

5.26

5.27

5.26 *A CSG tree for the pendentive shown in figure 5.24.*

5.27 *Modifying one of the primitives in the CSG tree.*

5.28 *Primitive substitution.*

5.28

BASIC 3D OPERATIONS

As in drafting systems, 3D objects can be *inserted* and *selected,* and once selected, can be *deleted, transformed,* or *replicated.* A 3D object is inserted by selecting the appropriate modeling tool, such as *box, cylinder, or extrude,* and by locating points and assigning values to parameters that define it.

As in 2D drawing, an object must be *selected* before it can be deleted, replicated, or transformed. In 3D systems, object selection is accomplished in the same ways as in 2D: objects can be selected one by one or as a group by specifying the selection boundary and choosing objects that are *within, crossing,* and/or *outside* the specified boundary (Figure 5.29). Selected objects form *selection sets,* and objects can be *added* or *removed* from the sets during the selection process.

3D objects can be *translated, rotated, reflected,* or *scaled.* These four Euclidean transformations are carried out in almost identical fashion as in 2D systems (Figure 5.30). Translation requires a *displacement vector,* which can be specified by locating two points in 3D space. Rotation can take place about one of the axes, and reflection can take place across a plane instead of a line as in 2D (Figure 5.31).

Some systems offer an *attach* operation to facilitate positioning of objects in desired relationships. For example, an object can be placed on top of another one, and rotated so that their "front" faces are coplanar. Instead of performing two operations (translation and then rotation), those two objects can be *attached* in one step, often by *pairing* the corresponding points (Figure 5.32). Technically, the *attach* operation is simply a combination of translation and rotation, as illustrated by this example.

In some modeling systems, *trim, extend, fillet, chamfer,* and *stretch* operations can also be applied to 3D objects. A 3D object can be trimmed by or extended to a construction plane or some other surface object (Figure 5.33). 3D objects can also be *stretched* (Figure 5.33). Edges can be *filleted* or *chamfered* (Figure 5.34).

AutoCAD versions R13 and R14 do not support *CSG tree editing* (an older version, R12, *does* provide CSG tree editing!). In fact, this is one of the main shortcomings of AutoCAD's solid modeler. Furthermore, there aren't any commands to alter the parameters associated with created solid *primitives.* For example, you can't change the height of an extruded cylinder—to make the cylinder object higher or shorter, you must first make a duplicate, place it in space above the original cylinder at the appropriate distance, and apply the *union* (to make the cylinder higher) or *subtraction* operation (to make the cylinder shorter).

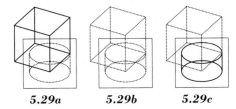

5.29a   5.29b   5.29c

5.29 Selecting objects in 3D space that are (a) within, (b) within and crossing, and (c) crossing the rectangular boundary.

In AutoCAD, 3D objects can be *moved, rotated, mirrored,* and *scaled* in 3D space. The standard 2D *rotate* and *mirror* commands have 3D complements: *3D Rotate* and *3D Mirror. 2D Rotate* performs rotation about a point in the *xy* plane of the current UCS, and *3D Rotate* performs rotation about an axis in 3D space. *2D Mirror* performs mirroring about an axis in the *xy* plane, and *3D Mirror* about a plane in space.

AutoCAD provides *attaching* of objects through the *ALIGN* command. 3D objects can be aligned by a *point, edge,* or *face.* In all three cases, corresponding *pairs of points* must be specified: *one* pair for *point* alignment, *two* pairs for *edge* alignment, and *three* pairs for *face* alignment.

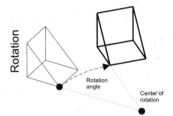

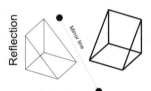

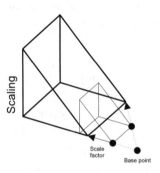

5.30 Translation, rotation, reflection, and scaling in 3D.

5.31 Reflection across a plane and rotation about an axis.

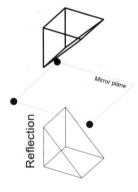

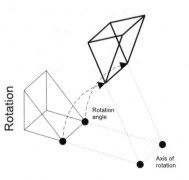

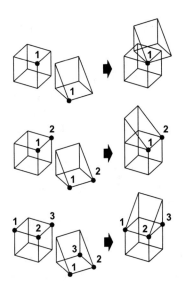

In AutoCAD, *trim, extend, fillet, chamfer,* and *stretch* operations have limited application to 3D objects. Surface objects *cannot* be trimmed, extended, filleted, or chamfered—they can be stretched, however. Solid objects can be trimmed by *slicing* but can't be extended or stretched; they can be filleted or chamfered.

5.32 Attaching objects by performing translation and rotation in one step.

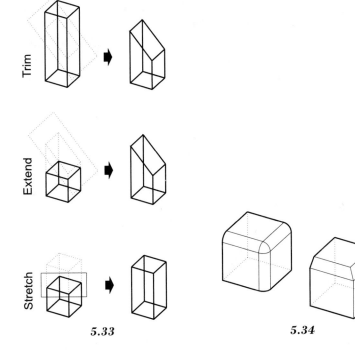

Trim

Extend

Stretch

5.33

5.34

5.33 Geometric transformations of 3D objects.

5.34 Filleted and chamfered edges.

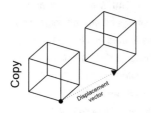

Copy

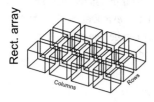

Rect. array

Columns · Rows

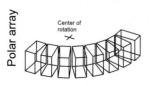

Polar array

Center of rotation

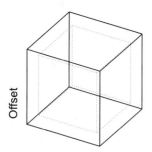

Offset

5.35 Replication.

In AutoCAD, 3D objects can be *copied* or *arrayed* anywhere in 3D space. You cannot, however, *offset* 3D objects.

3D objects can also be *replicated* using *copy, array,* and *offset* operations (Figure 5.35). As in 2D, *copy* creates exact duplicates of existing objects. *Array* replication creates circular (polar) and rectangular patterns of selected objects on a 2D plane, or cylindrical and prismatic patterns in 3D space. *Offset* creates at a specified distance or through a selected point a new object similar in form to the original. The offset operation is mostly used to create *shells,* i.e., thin objects.

Many modelers approximate curved surfaces for display and editing purposes as *meshes of four-sided patches* (Figure 5.36), analogous to approximation of curves by short line segments in some drafting systems. The curvature of surface meshes can be changed by manipulating the control points in space (Figure 5.37), in a fashion similar to the editing of 2D spline curves. Note that curved surfaces can be defined as various kinds of interpolated surfaces, such as *bicubic, Bezier, B-spline,* or *NURBS (Non-Uniform Rational B-Spline),* and that different curves respond differently to the manipulation of control points.

TOPOLOGICAL EDITING

In most modeling programs the description of an object's spatial boundary is stored as indexed lists of *vertices (points), edges,* and *faces.* The first list is an indexed list of points containing x, y, and z coordinates of each vertex. The second list is an indexed list of edges with pointers, i.e., indexes to endpoint records. The third

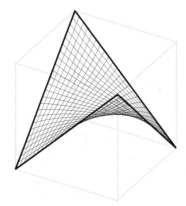

5.36 Surface mesh.

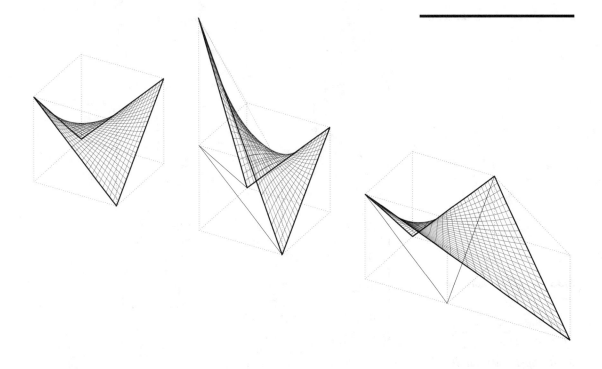

list is a list of bounding faces with indexes to edges bounding each face (Figure 5.38). Since these records describe an object's boundary, such database representation is accordingly referred to as *boundary representation,* or *B-Rep* for short.

Boundary representation accurately describes an object's *topology*—the dependencies between its various geometric components, such as vertices, edges, and faces. Through *topological editing* (or *tweaking,* as it is sometimes called), translation, rotation, and scaling operations can be applied to various elements of an object's topology. Vertices, edges, and faces, individually or in groups, can be translated, rotated, or scaled (Figure 5.39). Objects can be bent, twisted, slanted, or made longer, shorter, higher, etc. Figure 5.40 shows some possible transformations of simple 3D objects through topological editing.

Note that it is fairly easy to *deform* an object's geometry during topological editing. Most modelers require that objects be carefully edited to avoid the creation of *self-intersecting* objects (Figure 5.41) or the transformation of planar faces in solids into *nonplanar* ones (Figure 5.42).

5.37 Changing the curvature of surface meshes by manipulating the control points.

Meshed surface objects can be modified in AutoCAD by manipulating *grips,* located at mesh vertices. To display grips, click on one of the surface objects in 3D space.

AutoCAD supports *topological editing* of surface but *not* solid objects. Vertices, edges, and facets of *surface meshes* can be manipulated, i.e., translated, rotated, etc.

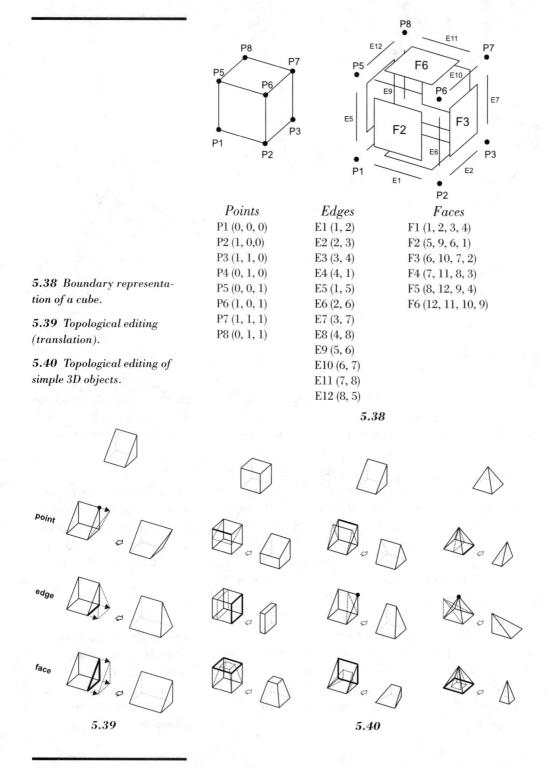

5.38 *Boundary representation of a cube.*

5.39 *Topological editing (translation).*

5.40 *Topological editing of simple 3D objects.*

Points	Edges	Faces
P1 (0, 0, 0)	E1 (1, 2)	F1 (1, 2, 3, 4)
P2 (1, 0,0)	E2 (2, 3)	F2 (5, 9, 6, 1)
P3 (1, 1, 0)	E3 (3, 4)	F3 (6, 10, 7, 2)
P4 (0, 1, 0)	E4 (4, 1)	F4 (7, 11, 8, 3)
P5 (0, 0, 1)	E5 (1, 5)	F5 (8, 12, 9, 4)
P6 (1, 0, 1)	E6 (2, 6)	F6 (12, 11, 10, 9)
P7 (1, 1, 1)	E7 (3, 7)	
P8 (0, 1, 1)	E8 (4, 8)	
	E9 (5, 6)	
	E10 (6, 7)	
	E11 (7, 8)	
	E12 (8, 5)	

5.38

5.39

5.40

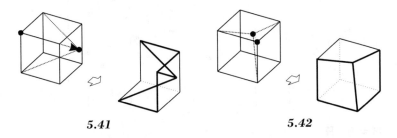

5.41

5.42

5.41 Self-intersecting object.

5.42 Nonplanar faces.

PARAMETRIC VARIATION

Instead of being assigned fixed values, parameters that define 3D objects (such as height or radius) can also be stored as *variables* or *formulas*. For example, a cylinder's height and diameter can be defined as variables. By assigning different values to the variables, different cylinders can easily be created (Figure 5.43). Modeling programs that support *parametric variation* are called *parametric modelers*.

A variable can *depend* on values assigned to other variables; thus, variables can be *dependent* or *independent* (there are also *constant* variables). For example, a column's height may be a *function* of its diameter—whenever the diameter changes, the height changes as well (Figure 5.44). Note that variables associated with one object can depend on variables associated with other objects.

The standard AutoCAD modeler does *not* support parametric variation. Autodesk's *Designer*, an add-on module for AutoCAD, provides fully featured parametric modeling.

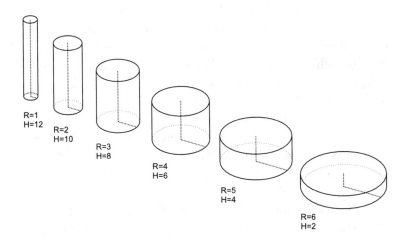

R=1
H=12

R=2
H=10

R=3
H=8

R=4
H=6

R=5
H=4

R=6
H=2

5.43 Parametric variation of a cylinder's parameters.

H = 5 * R

5.44 *Dependent variables.*

Parameters associated with the *position* and *orientation* of objects can also be defined as variables or formulas. That way, interdependencies between objects can be established, and the model's *behavior under transformations* defined. Different configurations of 3D objects can be explored by changing the values of variables (Figure 5.45).

STRUCTURING 3D MODELS

The concepts associated with the structuring of 2D drawings, such as *symbols, layers, groups,* and *external references,* are applicable to 3D models as well. 3D symbols can be defined, and their instances placed in space. Symbol definitions can easily be changed, their instances automatically updated, and consequently, different formal alternatives explored (Figure 5.46).

The concept of "layers" is somewhat less clear when applied to 3D models. The metaphor of layers as transparent sheets is no longer appropriate, because the contents of layers can intertwine in 3D space (Figure 5.47). Therefore, the layers in 3D modeling can best be described as named parts of the model that contain objects with similar content. For example, the layer named 1-WALLS can contain 3D objects that represent the first-floor walls, layer 1-WINDOWS objects that represent window openings, etc. It is very important to structure, i.e., divide the 3D model into a set of appropriately named layers. A carefully "layered" model can greatly facilitate modeling and creation of various 3D drawings and images that show, for example, a building's interior (Figure 5.48).

As in 2D drawing, 3D models can also be structured by *grouping* objects into *hierarchies,* and by using *external refer-*

5.45 *Creating different 3D configurations by* parametric variation.

ences. Since modeling files can be quite large, and therefore require a considerable amount of working memory to store and display geometric information, it is often convenient to subdivide a large model into smaller files that are then *externally referenced* as needed. For example, each floor of a building can be stored in a separate file, whereby files containing other floors are externally referenced for 3D construction and display purposes.

MODELING STRATEGIES

In most cases, *volumetric (solid) modeling* is the most suitable technique to create 3D models of buildings, since most buildings are often best abstracted as collections of solid and void volumes. Typically, both *additive* and *subtractive* modeling methods will be applied to create a building's 3D model. In additive modeling, all objects are modeled as *solid volumes* and are incrementally *added* to the composition, step by step. In subtractive modeling, most objects are conceived as *void volumes* that are then *subtracted* from the solid ones. Which of the two methods will be applied depends on the building's *spatial organization* and the way each

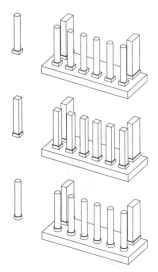

5.46 *Different alternatives can quickly be explored by redefining 3D symbols.*

5.47 *Layers in 3D space.*

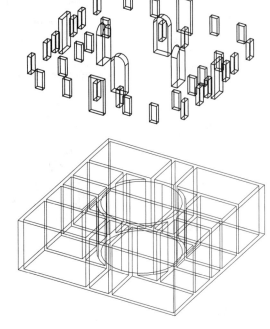

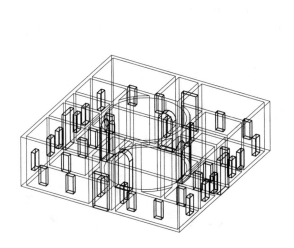

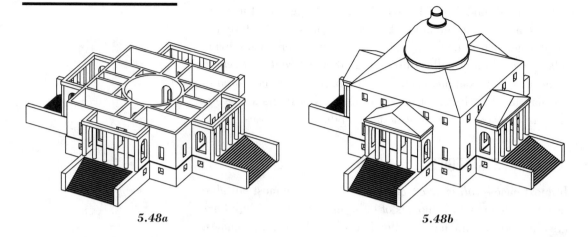

5.48a   5.48b

5.48 By turning off certain layers, different drawings and images can easily be created.

designer *abstracts* the buildings. For example, a simple rectangular enclosed space can be modeled as four solid prismatic volumes (boxes) that are then *added* together by a *union* operation (Figure 5.49). Another approach is to model two rectangular boxes, one representing the solid outer volume, and the other one the void inner volume, and then *subtract* the inner volume from the outer one (Figure 5.49).

A window opening in a single rectangular wall can be created by modeling four wall segments as solids added by union into a single one, or as the opening's void volume subtracted from the wall's solid volume (Figure 5.50).

As already mentioned, which of the two solid modeling methods will be applied depends largely on the building's spatial organization. For example, most of Le Corbusier's villas can be modeled in large part by additive modeling, since most of them

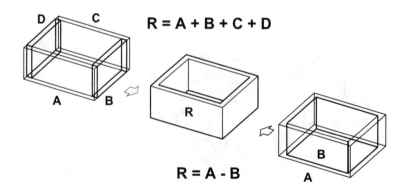

5.49 Additive *and* subtractive modeling.

$$R = A + B + C + D$$

$$R = A - B$$

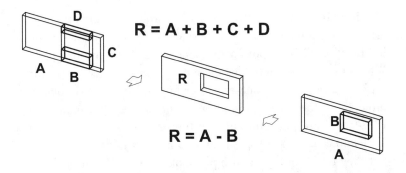

$$R = A + B + C + D$$

$$R = A - B$$

5.50 Creating a window opening by additive and subtractive modeling.

feature "stacked" floors, whereby slab, wall, and opening volumes can easily be separated. Adolf Loos's houses are almost impossible to model by additive modeling, since most of the inner spaces are intertwined and located at different levels. His *Raum Plan* mandates that each inner space be modeled as a void that is then subtracted from the overall solid volume of the building.

VIEWING

Geometric models are created in a "virtual" 3D space that is then *projected* to a 2D surface of the computer monitor. Using one of the projection methods—*orthographic, axonometric, oblique*, or *perspective*—3D coordinates of points in space are converted into *xy* coordinate pairs in the two-dimensional plane of the computer screen.

As in other professions, tradition and conventions guide the use of specific projection methods in architecture. *Orthographic* projections, such as plans and elevations, have been used by architects and builders for a long time (the earliest recorded use of a building plan was in 2150 B.C.—more than 4,000 years ago—during the reign of King Gudea of Lagash). Today plans, sections, and elevations are standard in any architectural presentation. *Oblique* projections became popular in the nineteenth century thanks to August Choisy and were widely used by modernist architects in the early twentieth century. *Axonometric* projection, especially *isometric*, was widely used as engineering and technical professions were developed. Alberti was the first to formulate the principal rules of creating a *perspective* projection, which fascinated many creative minds of the sixteenth and seventeenth centuries.

In traditional projective geometry, projections are created by establishing a picture plane somewhere in space and casting projection "rays" from points in space toward the picture plane. Where those "rays" intersect the picture plane, the corresponding projected points are located. In orthographic and axonometric projections, the projection rays are *parallel* (i.e., they do not converge) and are perpendicular to the projection plane (Figures 5.51 and 5.52). In oblique projection, the rays are parallel too, but they intersect the picture plane at an angle (Figure 5.53). In perspective projection, however, the projection rays *converge* toward the viewer's eye, and the picture plane is perpendicular to the principal line of sight (Figure 5.54).

In computer graphics, projections are created by mathematical procedures, which are applied to *xyz* coordinate triplets. For

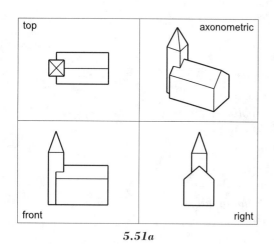

5.51a

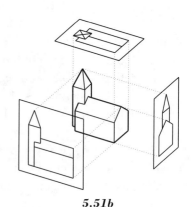

5.51b

5.51 *Orthographic projections: Projection rays are* parallel *and* perpendicular *to the picture plane.*

5.52 *Axonometric projection: Projection rays are* parallel *and* perpendicular *to the picture plane.*

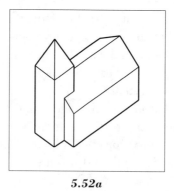

5.52a

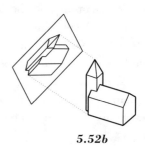

5.52b

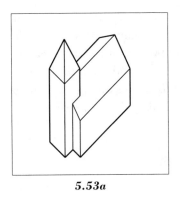

5.53a

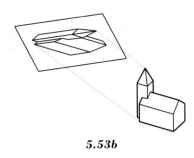

5.53b

5.53 Oblique projection: Projection rays are parallel and oblique to the picture plane.

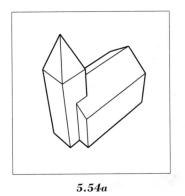

5.54a

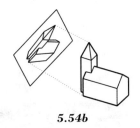

5.54b

5.54 Perspective projection: Projection rays are converging, and the line of sight is perpendicular to the picture plane.

example, orthographic projections are created by discarding one of the 3D coordinates. Plan projection is created by discarding the z coordinate, "front" elevation by discarding the y coordinate, etc. In perspective projection, the x and y coordinates are divided by depth, the z coordinate, multiplied by a constant related to the view angle: $x = x / (c * z)$, $y = y / (c * z)$. Similar mathematical procedures are used to compute xy screen coordinate pairs for axonometric and oblique projections.

Each projection method requires that certain viewing parameters be specified. *Orthographic* projections are the simplest— often all that has to be chosen is a menu option that specifies the viewing direction or the location of the picture plane (Figure 5.55). In most modelers, *axonometric* projection is specified by two parameters associated with the viewing vector: its angle in xy plane, and its angle *from xy* plane (Figure 5.56). These two parameters are often referred to, respectively, as *azimuth* and *altitude*.

AutoCAD does *not* support *oblique* projection. You cannot create *plan-oblique* or *facade-oblique* projections in AutoCAD. The other three projection methods (*orthographic, axonometric,* and *perspective*) are fully supported.

Note that orthographic projections can be specified in this fashion as well: the plan projection can be generated by setting the azimuth to 270° and the altitude to 90°; front elevation can be produced by setting the azimuth to 270° and the altitude to 0° (Figure 5.57). In fact, orthographic projections are *special cases* of axonometric projection, as demonstrated by these two examples.

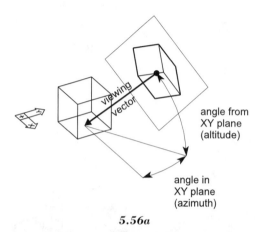

5.56a

5.55 *Choosing an orthographic projection.*

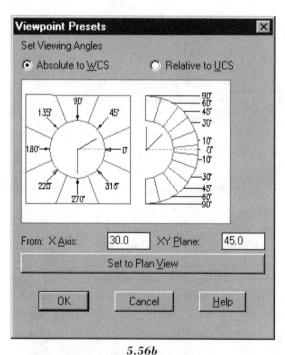

5.56b

5.56 *Axonometric projection parameters.*

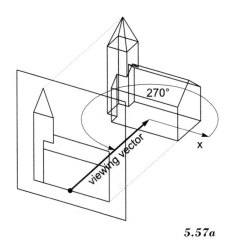

5.57a

5.57b

From: X Axis: 270.0   XY Plane: 0.0

5.57 *Orthographic projections are special cases of axonometric projection.*

In some modeling programs, *isometric* axonometric projections can be created by choosing one of the menu options (Figure 5.58) or by setting the azimuth to 45° (NE), 135° (NW), 225° (SW), or 315° (SE), and the altitude to 35.3° (Figure 5.59). These projections are fairly common in architecture presentations because they are not that difficult to draw manually: all three *foreshortening ratios* (in *x, y,* and *z* direction) are *equal,* and if the building's geometry is orthogonal, all lines are at 60°, 90°, or 120° from the horizontal straight edge (Figure 5.60).

Oblique projections are supported by very few modelers, which is surprising, considering that they are fairly easy to com-

5.58

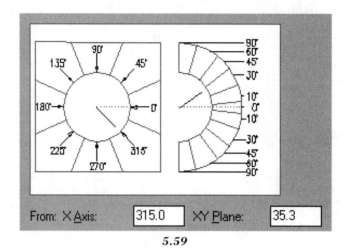

5.59

5.58 *Choosing an isometric projection from a menu.*

5.59 *Setting up an isometric projection (SE) by azimuth and altitude.*

5.60 *Cube in isometric projection.*

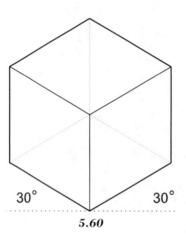

30°   30°

5.60

pute. Typically, the inclination angles of *x* and *y* axes are specified to compute the corresponding oblique projection. For example, the *45° facade oblique* projection can be produced by setting the inclination angles of *x* and *y* axes to 0° and 45°, respectively (Figure 5.61). The *60° plan oblique* projection can be generated by setting the inclination angles to −30° and 60° (Figure 5.62).

In some modeling programs, the creation of a perspective projection simply involves choosing the *perspective* option in one of the menus; perspective projection is instantly computed from the parameters of an existing orthographic or axonometric projection. Often, however, if a specific perspective is wanted, from a particular viewpoint, the setup requires that several parameters

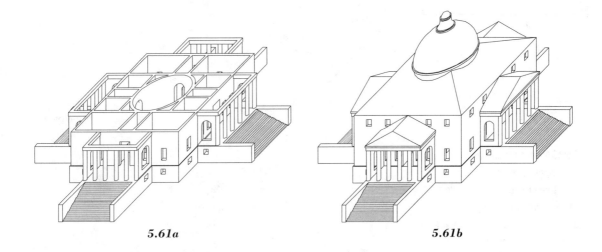

5.61a   5.61b

be provided: (1) location of the *viewpoint*, in some programs referred to as *eye* or *camera*, (2) location of the *target point*, (3) *viewing angle*, called *lens length* or simply *zoom* in some programs that use the camera metaphor, and (4) location of the *front* (or *hither*) and *back* (or *yon*) clipping planes (Figure 5.63). The view (eye) and target points define the *line of sight*, which, with the viewing angle, defines the *cone of vision* or, as it is often

5.61 *The 45° facade oblique projection.*

5.62 *The 60° plan oblique projection.*

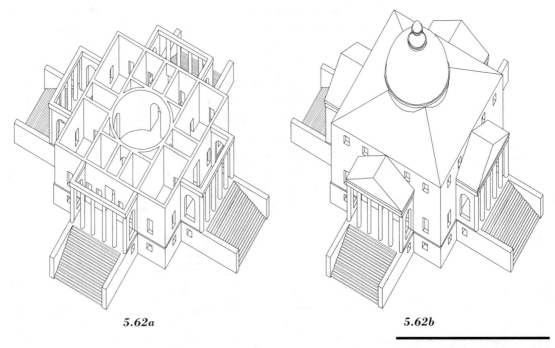

5.62a   5.62b

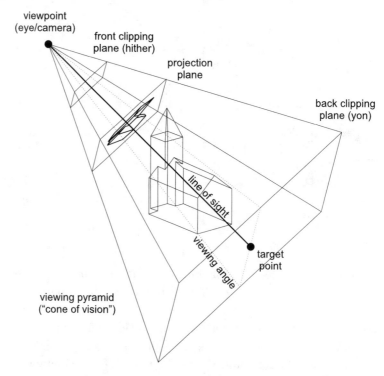

viewpoint
(eye/camera)

front clipping
plane (hither)

projection
plane

back clipping
plane (yon)

line of sight

viewing angle

target
point

viewing pyramid
("cone of vision")

AutoCAD uses a *camera* metaphor in setting up a perspective projection. To change the *viewing angle,* adjust the *zoom lens length.* Note that you can also *twist* the camera, and *pan* as well.

5.63 *Perspective projection.*

called, the *viewing pyramid* (a more appropriate metaphor, since the picture plane has a rectangular shape).

The location of view and target points is defined by 3D coordinates, either numerically or graphically. Conventional *one-point, two-point,* and *three-point* perspective can be created by careful positioning of the view and target points (Figure 5.64). For example, if the building's geometry is orthogonal, a *one-point* perspective can be created by specifying a line of sight perpendicular to the "front" facade. For a *two-point* perspective, the line of sight should be specified at an angle. In both cases, view and target points should be positioned at the same height, i.e., they should have the same *z* coordinate; if the heights are different, a *three-point* perspective is generated (Figure 5.65).

5.64 *One-, two-, and three-point perspective.*

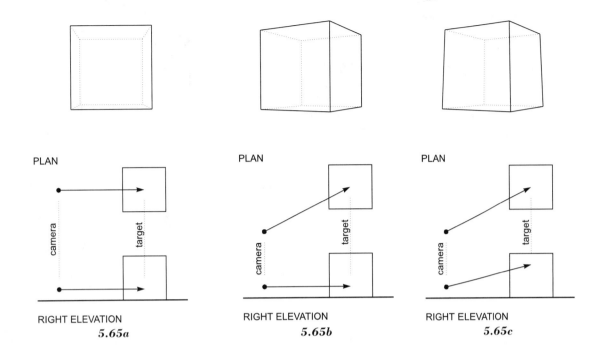

PLAN   PLAN   PLAN

camera   target   camera   target   camera   target

RIGHT ELEVATION   RIGHT ELEVATION   RIGHT ELEVATION

5.65a   *5.65b*   *5.65c*

The viewing angle is typically set to 45°, which corresponds to normal human vision. In programs that support the *camera* metaphor, this viewing angle is attained by specifying a 50-mm lens length. Another standard setting is 60°, or 35 mm, for a wider view of the 3D scene (Figure 5.66). Wide view angles (values greater than 60°, i.e., values smaller than 35 mm) should generally be avoided, since they can result in distorted perspective projections and can therefore create a deceiving perception of the represented space—this is especially true for perspectives of interior spaces (Figure 5.67). Sometimes, however, wide-angle perspective can be used to emphasize some elements of the building's geometry (Figure 5.68). Wide angles (75°–90°) can also be used to generate *plan* perspective, for better readability (Figure 5.69).

Some modeling programs offer *depth clipping* to eliminate from the scene those objects that lie in front or in back of the viewing pyramid. This is accomplished by specifying the distance of the front (hither) and back (yon) clipping planes from the viewpoint. *Sectional perspectives,* for example, can be created by placing the front clipping plane inside the building (Figure 5.70).

5.65 Setting up a one-point, two-point, and three-point perspective of a cube.

To create a one-point perspective, two coordinates (x and z or y and z) should be the same for the view and target points, i.e., $x_{view} = x_{target}$ or $y_{view} = y_{target}$, and $z_{view} = z_{target}$. For a two-point perspective, only the z coordinate should be the same ($z_{view} = z_{target}$). To obtain a three-point perspective, all three coordinates should be different for both points.

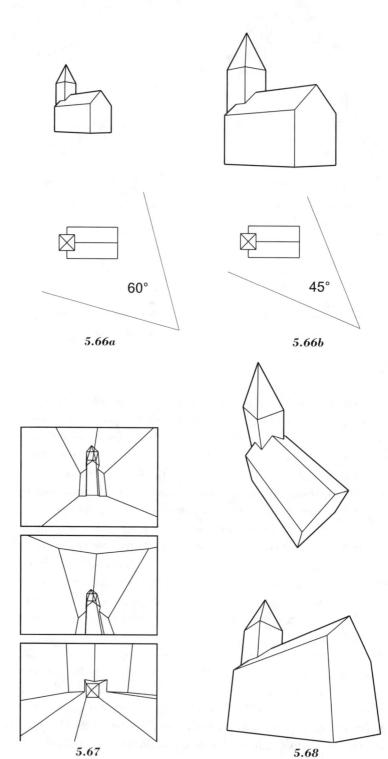

5.66 *View angle.*

5.66a

5.66b

60°

45°

5.67 *A wide viewing angle (120°) can create a distorted representation of interior spaces.*

5.68 *Wide-angle (90°) perspective can be used to emphasize the building's geometry.*

5.67

5.68

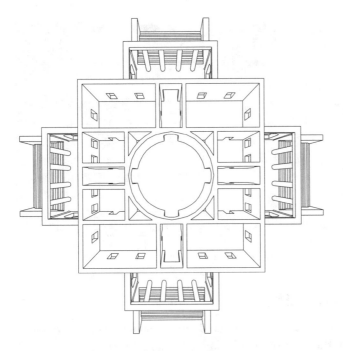

5.69 Plan perspective specified using wide viewing angle (90°).

Most modelers can simultaneously display more than one projection. Typically, the program's window is subdivided into four *viewports*, each displaying a different projection: top, front, right, and axonometric or perspective (Figure 5.71). In some programs, the number and configuration of viewports can be changed freely, as well as their content (Figure 5.72). Note that projections displayed in viewports are automatically updated as the model is changed.

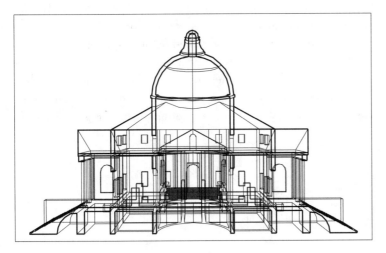

5.70 Sectional perspective created by depth clipping.

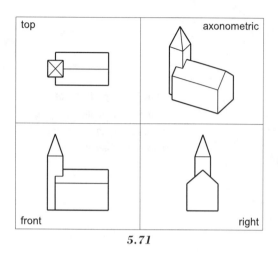

top   axonometric

front   right

5.71

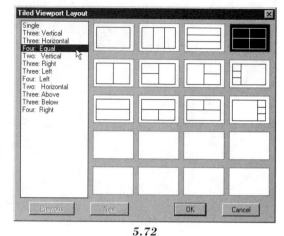

5.72

5.71 Viewports.

*5.72 The number and config-
uration of viewports can be
changed in most modelers.*

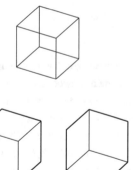

*5.73 Two readings of a cube
displayed in wire-frame mode.*

*5.74 Display conventions for
relieving spatial ambiguities.*

HIDDEN-LINE REMOVAL

A common problem encountered during modeling is *spatial ambi-
guity* of the wire-frame display. For example, an axonometric of
the cube shown in Figure 5.73 can be understood in two different
ways. One reading is that the viewpoint is *above* the cube, and the
other *underneath* the cube. To relieve such ambiguities, some
systems employ display conventions such as varied line weight,
line type, color, or intensity to indicate depth (Figure 5.74).

A far better approach is to generate a *hidden-line* or *shaded*
view of the model (Figure 5.75). The *hidden-line* procedure computes which edges are cut or hidden by opaque surfaces. In most
modelers, this is a fairly quick process that produces fairly ade-
quate representations of the model's geometry.

Hidden-line drawings produced by modeling programs, however, often need to be corrected and improved to achieve acceptable *graphic quality*. A rather common problem in most modelers
is that hidden-line algorithms do not create new edges implied by
the model's geometry, as in intersecting objects (Figure 5.76). To

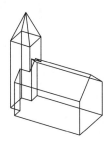 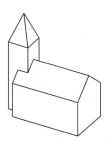 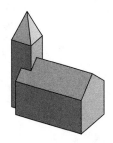

5.75 Wire-frame, hidden-line, *and* shaded *views*.

correct such display problems, avoid the intersecting objects, or, if that is not possible, add missing lines later by editing the 2D projection drawing.

Another common problem is the hidden-line display of curved surfaces, such as cylinders or spheres, which are often faceted and can produce areas of considerable *graphic density* (Figure 5.77). Often, extraneous lines must be deleted to create drawings with an acceptable level of graphic uniformity (Figure 5.78).

Often some edges, such as the outline of the building's volume or its openings, need to be emphasized by a thicker line width for visual clarity (Figure 5.79). This and other traditional

In AutoCAD R14 hidden-line and shaded views of the model can be created by choosing *Hide* or *Shade* (and one of the four shading modes) from the *View* menu. In R13 enter the HIDE or SHADE command; use the SHADEDGE command to specify one of the four shading modes (0–*256 colors*, 1–*256 colors with edges*, 2–*16-color hidden line*, 3–*16-color filled*).

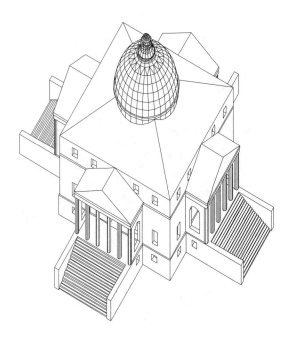

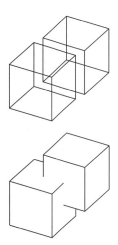

5.76 *A typical hidden-line display of intersecting objects.*

5.77 *Faceted appearance of curved surfaces.*

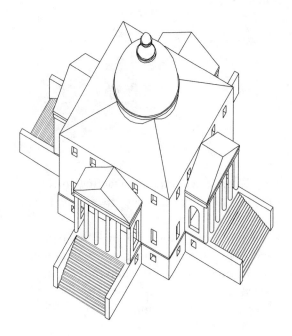

5.78 *The same drawing after extraneous lines were deleted.*

5.79 *Visual emphasis in hidden-line drawings.*

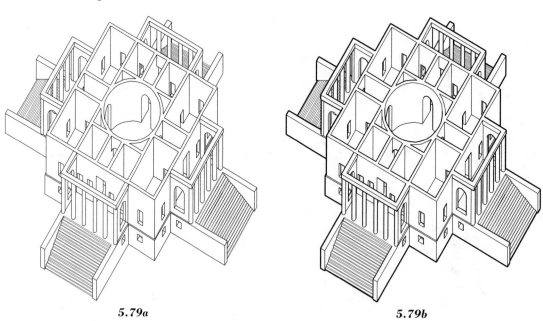

5.79a   **5.79b**

graphic conventions often require tedious editing of hidden-line drawings. In addition, graphic elements, such as foliage or human figures, are sometimes added to "soften" the drawings and add a sense of *scale*.

To facilitate graphic improvement of hidden-line projections, most modelers provide procedures for the conversion of 3D projections into 2D drawings that can later be modified. Such hidden-line drawings can be imported into illustration programs and further enhanced by creating closed polygonal shapes to which various *tonal values* and *patterns* can be applied (Figure 5.80). Another possibility is to process hidden-line drawings by special graphic utilities into drawings that look like sketches or freehand drawings.

POST-PROCESSING

Hidden-line removal, i.e., visible surfaces and edges computation, is the simplest available technique to *visualize* 3D forms created by modelers. Once a building model is created in modeling software, its geometry can be *rendered realistically* in color, with correct tonal values and textures (Figure 5.81). There are several rendering techniques, such as *cosine, Gouraud* and *Phong shad-*

Use the *Solid Profile* (SOLPROF) command in AutoCAD to generate hidden-line views *without* the faceted appearance of curved solid objects. Note that this command requires the *paper space* mode of operation.

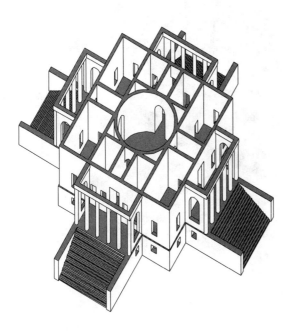

5.80 Hidden-line drawings can be further enhanced in illustration programs.

The standard AutoCAD R13 program package includes only the simplest rendering techniques. It offers *smooth* shading of curved surfaces and limited definition and assignment of material properties. *Autovision,* the visualization add-on module for AutoCAD R13, offers advanced rendering techniques, such as *ray tracing,* with *shadow casting* and *texture mapping.* In R14, the AutoVision module is an integral part of the standard package.

ing, *ray-tracing,* and *radiosity,* which are implemented in currently available visualization programs. Those techniques are introduced in detail in Chapter 10.

Physical scale models can be produced from computer models. An inexpensive technique is to "flatten" the 3D model into a 2D drawing that contains all its facets (Figure 5.82), print or plot such a drawing, mount (glue) the printouts onto cardboard or some other material, cut the individual facets, and glue them together. Instead of cutting the facets by hand, *laser cutters* can be used. The drawing is simply "plotted" on a laser cutter—the drawing geometry guides the laser, which accurately cuts the facets from the material. In fact, most professional model shops use laser cutters to cut the pieces needed to assemble architectural models.

Other *CAM (Computer-Aided Manufacturing)* techniques are available as well. *Numerically controlled (NC) milling machines* can be used to create 3D topographic models, or some simple massing models. *Stereolithography* is probably the most versatile technique (and one of the most expensive). A typical stereo litho-

In R14, solid objects can be *exported* in STL (stereolithography) format. Choose *Export* in the *File* menu, and select *Lithography* (.*stl*) from the list of supported file formats.

AutoCAD does not support the "flattening" of solid objects. Solid objects can be *exploded,* i.e., broken into outlines of the bounding surfaces, and those outlines can be laid out one by one on a 2D drawing plane.

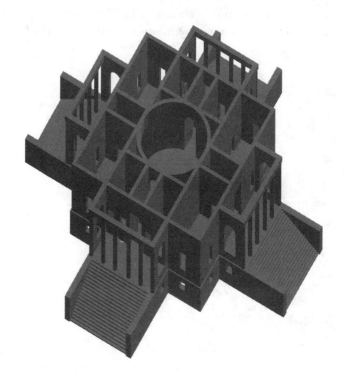

5.81 Computer rendering.

graphy system employs a laser that solidifies a liquid polymer in a layer-by-layer fashion until the entire model is solidified. Most modern modelers support the STL (stereo lithography) file output format. Model files saved in this format can be electronically sent to service bureaus, which can then produce and ship back a plastic physical scale model of the building.

3D solid models can also be used for *structural analysis*. Volume and other mass properties, such as centroid and moments and products of inertia, can automatically be computed for each solid object. Furthermore, the model can be subdivided into *finite elements*, small triangular patches, which are used by *FEA* (*Finite Element Analysis*) programs to compute structural and thermal properties.

Solid models can have other uses as well. Quantities of materials can automatically be computed. Interior volumes can be used in acoustical analysis, and so on.

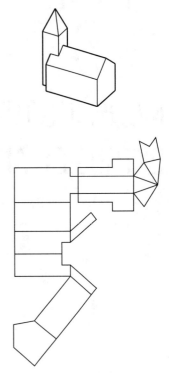

5.82 A "flattened" 3D model for cutting and assembling by hand.

CHAPTER

6

MODELING TUTORIAL 1: EXTRUSION AND VIEWING

In this exercise you will extrude the previously created two-dimensional volume outlines into three-dimensional volumes (solids) and position them correctly in space. You will also learn how to create various views of the model, such as orthographic (plan and elevations), axonometric, and perspective. You will also set up multiple viewports and create hidden-line and shaded views.

3D EXTRUSION: THE BASE LEVEL

1 In this section you will create 3D volumes (solids) at the base level. Start AutoCAD, and open the previously saved drawing (Rotonda.dwg). If you are continuing from the last exercise, skip this step.

2 Turn on and set layer O-WALLS as the current layer, and turn off layer 2-OPENINGS. Make sure that all other layers, except O-WALLS, are turned off. You should see only the shapes of the layer O-WALLS (Figure 6.2). Double-check that O-WALLS is the current layer—its name should be displayed in the *Layer Control* box in the *Object Properties* toolbar.

3 You should set up an axonometric view of the 3D modeling space before you begin extruding 2D shapes into 3D volumes.

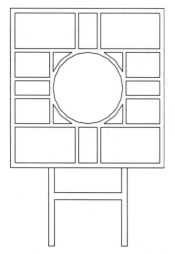

6.2 2D shapes of the layer O-WALLS.

From the *View* menu, choose *3D Viewpoint*, then *Select* (R13 *Rotate*). In the resulting *Viewpoint Presets* dialog box enter 300 as the angle *from x axis* and 30 as the angle *from xy plane* (Figure 6.3a), and click on the *OK* button to continue. The two-dimensional shapes of the layer O-WALLS will appear in an axonometric view (Figure 6.3b).

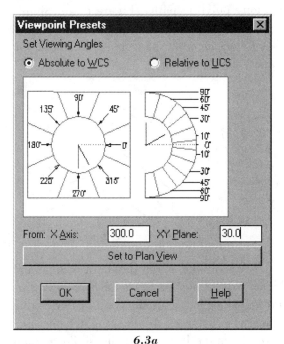

6.3a Setting the parameters of the axonometric view.

6.3b Axonometric view of the 2D drawing.

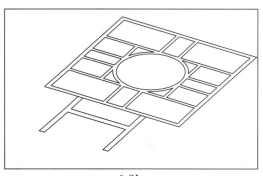

6.3a

6.3b

4 You can extrude 2D closed shapes by choosing the *Extrude* tool on the *Solids* toolbar (Figure 6.4a) or by entering EXTRUDE at the command prompt. To display the *Solids* toolbar, choose *Toolbars*, then *Solids* from the *View* (R13 *Tools*) menu.

When prompted for the *height of extrusion,* you can either enter a numerical value or pick two points in the model space that will define the extrusion distance.

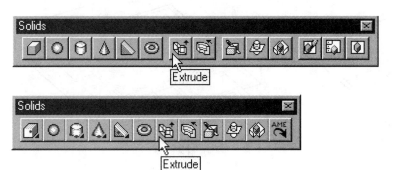

6.4a The Solids *toolbar in R14 and R13.*

Before you proceed, note that AutoCAD will refuse to extrude *open* 2D polyline shapes. If necessary use the PEDIT command to close open polylines. Also note that you can specify the *tapering angle* to create objects with uniformly slanted side surfaces (Figure 6.4b). Note that AutoCAD will not execute extrusion that results in a self-intersecting tapered solid. You can also sweep 2D shapes along polyline paths (Figure 6.4c). Simply choose the *Path* option when prompted to specify the extrusion height—the path should not lie on the same plane as profile, nor should it have the areas of high curvature.

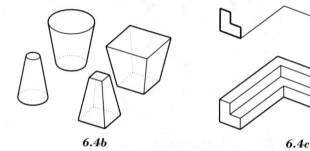

6.4b *Tapered extruded solids.*

6.4c *Extruding (sweeping) a profile along a path.*

6.4b   6.4c

Choose the *Extrude* tool, and select the main volume and portico outlines (Figure 6.4d). Enter 10′ [3] as the *height of extrusion.* Press *Enter* or the *Return* button on the pointing device (the right button if you are using a mouse) to select the default value (0) for the *taper angle.* From the *View* menu, choose *Zoom*, then *All* (or choose the *Zoom All* tool on the *Standard* toolbar) to display the entire 3D model (Figure 6.4e).

6.4d *Selecting the main volume and portico outlines for extrusion.*

6.4e *The extruded volumes (solids).*

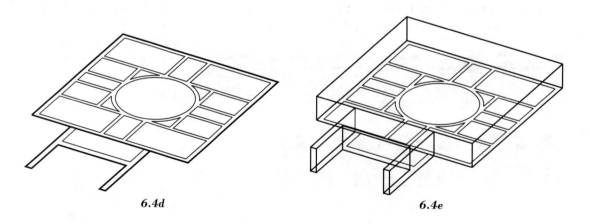

6.4d   6.4e

5 Extrude the remaining outlines (Figure 6.5a) by 8'6" [2.55].
Note that these AutoCAD solid objects correspond to *void volumes* or *rooms* within the base level (Figure 6.5b). These volumes
will later be subtracted from the two volumes created in the previous step.

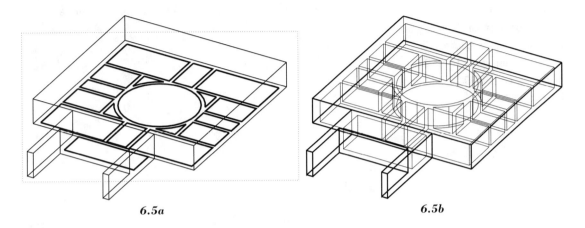

6.5a

6.5b

6 Turn on and set the layer O-OPENINGS as the current layer,
and turn off the layer O-WALLS. Make sure that all other layers,
except O-OPENINGS, are turned off—you should see only the
shapes of the layer O-OPENINGS (Figure 6.6).

*6.5a Selecting the remaining
outlines using the* window (w)
*option. Note that the two previously extruded volumes are
partially outside the rectangular selection area, and
therefore won't be selected.*

6.5b The void volumes *or*
rooms *within the base level.*

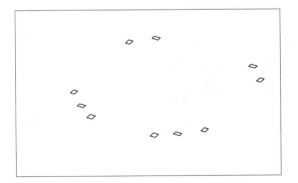

*6.6 Outlines of the openings
at the base level.*

7 Extrude the openings outlines by 3' [0.9]. Note that the openings volumes are located on the "ground," i.e., they are not at the
correct position. You will translate (*move*) them 5' [1.5 m] up in
space, in the direction of the positive *z* axis. Choose the *Move* tool

In addition to the MOVE command, you can apply to 3D objects almost all of the editing command mentioned so far, such as ROTATE, MIRROR, SCALE, etc. There are also 3D version of some commands, such as ROTATE3D for rotation in three-dimensional space, i.e., for rotation that is not limited to the 2D plane, and MIRROR3D, for mirroring in 3D space.

(Figure 6.7a) on the *Modify* toolbar, select the openings volumes, and enter 0,0,5′ [0,0,1.5] when prompted for the *base point or displacement*—you are instructing AutoCAD to displace the openings by 0 unit along the *x* axis, 0 unit along the *y* axis, and 5′ [1.5 m] along the *z* axis. Press *Enter* when prompted for the *second point of displacement*, since the displacement was already specified. Notice that the volumes will shift up in space (Figure 6.7b).

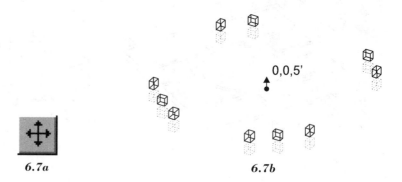

6.7a The Move *tool.*

6.7b *Translating openings volumes up in space.*

6.7a   **6.7b**

8 Turn on the layer O-WALLS to verify that the openings are properly positioned (Figure 6.8). Save your model—click on the *Save* tool on the *Standard* toolbar.

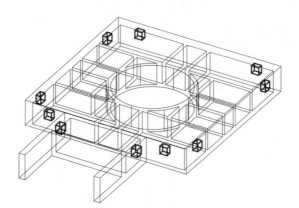

6.8 *The base-level volume outlines.*

9 Since a wire-frame view can be misleading, it is often desirable to generate a *hidden-line* view of the model. Choose *Hide* from the *View* menu (R13 has no menu choice), or select the *Hide* tool from the *Render* toolbar (Figure 6.9a). You can also enter

HIDE at the command prompt. After a few seconds AutoCAD will display a hidden-line view of the model (Figure 6.9b).

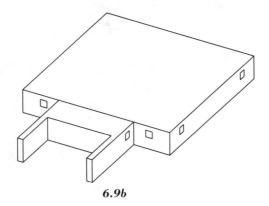

6.9a   **6.9b**

6.9a The Hide *tool.*

6.9b The hidden-line *view of the model.*

SETTING UP MULTIPLE VIEWPORTS

10 So far you have been working in a single view (or *viewport*) of the model space. You can actually split the graphics area to display several *tiled viewports* simultaneously (Figures 6.10a and 6.12), each showing different projections (plan, front and right elevation, axonometric, perspective, etc.). As you work on the model, changes you make in one viewport are instantly reflected in the others. For example, if you move an object in a plan view, you can see the effects of that transformation in other views automatically. Or if you have both full and detail views visible, you can observe the effects of detailed editing on the entire model.

You can display tiled viewports in different configurations (Figure 6.10a). In this exercise you will subdivide the graphics area into three viewports. Each of these three viewports will show a different projection of the model: the upper left one will display a plan view, the lower left a front view, and the right one an axonometric view (Figure 6.12).

From the *View* menu, choose *Tiled Viewports*, then *Layout*. In the resulting dialog box select viewport configuration *Three: Right* or click on its icon tile (Figure 6.10a). The graphics area will be divided into three tiled viewports, as shown in Figure 6.10b.

Note that only one viewport is active (current) at a time; you can switch among viewports at any time, even in the middle of a command. In each tiled viewport, you can pan, zoom, and set snap and grid modes. You can draw from one viewport to another when executing a command, and name a viewport combination so you can reuse it later.

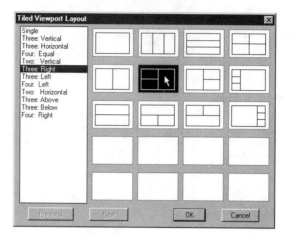

6.10a *Selecting a viewport configuration.*

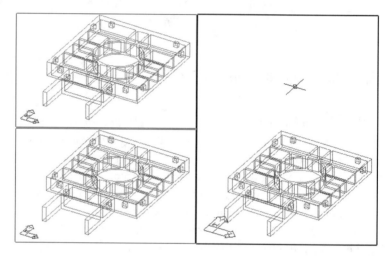

6.10b *The graphics area divided into three viewports.*

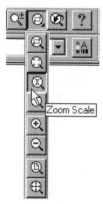

6.11a *The* Zoom Scale *tool.*

11 Click inside the upper left viewport to make it active (*current*). From the *View* menu, choose *3D Viewport* (R13 *3D Viewpoint Presets*), then *Top*, to set up a plan view in this viewport. Select the *Zoom Scale* tool from the *Zoom* flyout (Figure 6.11a) to zoom with a specified scale factor. Enter .8x at the command prompt to display the plan view at 80% of its current size (Figure 6.11b).

12 Click inside the lower left viewport to make it active. From the *View* menu, choose *3D Viewpoint* (R13 *3D Viewpoint Presets*), then *Front*, to set up a front view in this viewport, then zoom out by 80% (figure 6.12).

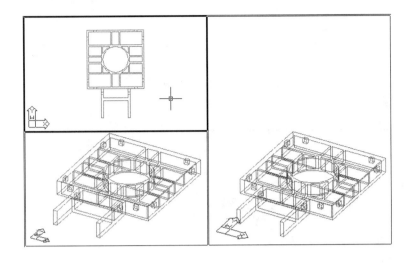

6.11b *The plan view displayed at 80% of its previous size.*

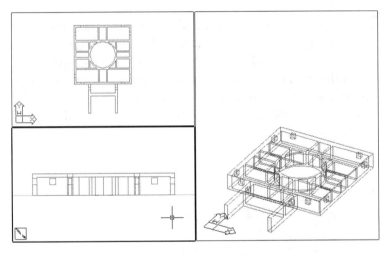

6.12 *Three tiled viewports showing different views (projections) of the model: plan, front, and axonometric.*

3D EXTRUSION: THE FIRST LEVEL

13 Turn on and set the layer 1-WALLS as the current layer, and turn off all other layers. You should see only the shapes of the layer 1-WALLS (Figure 6.13). (Double-check that 1-WALLS is the current layer—its name should be displayed in the *Layer Control* box in the *Object Properties* toolbar.)

14 For faster selection of objects, work in the plan view. Make the plan viewport active—click anywhere inside it.

Note that the viewport must be active before you can apply viewing operations, such as *zoom* **and** *pan.*

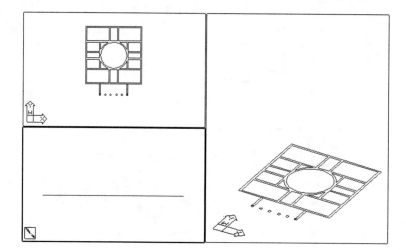

6.13 *2D shapes of the layer 1-WALLS.*

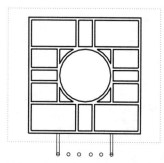

6.15a *Selecting the main volume and room outlines for extrusion.*

15 Choose the *Extrude* tool, and select the main volume and room outlines (Figure 6.15a). Enter 20′ [6] as the *height of extrusion*. Press *Enter* to select the default value (0) for the *taper angle*. The outlines will be extruded upward (Figure 6.15b). (Note that extruded solid objects that correspond to the rooms should be treated as *void volumes,* which will later be subtracted from the main volume.)

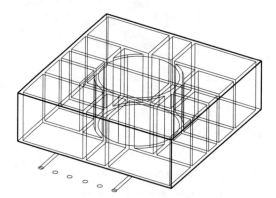

6.15b *The extruded volumes (solids).*

16 Select portico elements, i.e., its side walls and columns (Figure 6.16a), and extrude them by 18′ [5.4] (Figure 6.16b).

17 Turn on and set the layer 1-OPENINGS as the current layer, and turn off the 1-WALLS layer. You should see only the

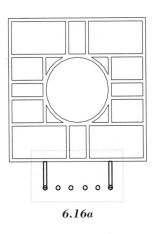

6.16a

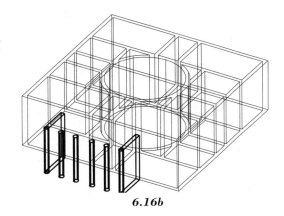

6.16b

shapes of the layer 1-OPENINGS (Figure 6.17). (Double-check that 1-OPENINGS is the current layer—its name should be displayed in the *Layer Control* box in the *Object Properties* toolbar.)

6.16a *Selecting the portico outlines for extrusion.*

6.16b *Extruded portico side walls and columns.*

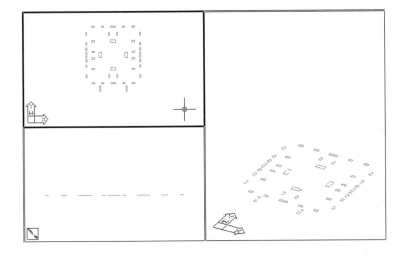

6.17 *2D shapes of the layer 1-OPENINGS.*

You can select 3D objects just as you would the 2D ones. You can use any of the object selection modes provided by AutoCAD, such as individual, *window* (W), *crossing* (C), *polygonal window* (WP), *fence* (F) selection, etc. You can also *add* (A) and *remove* (R) objects from the selection sets.

18 Select only the window openings (Figure 6.18a) and extrude them by 7′ [2.1] (Figure 6.18b). Move the extruded volumes up in space by 3′ [0.9], which is the height of the parapet wall. (Enter the displacement of 0,0,3′ [0,0,0.9].)

19 Select the door openings between rooms (Figure 6.19a) and extrude them by 7′ [2.1] (Figure 6.19b).

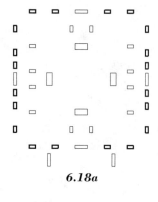

6.18a

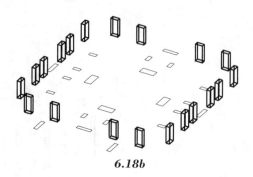

6.18b

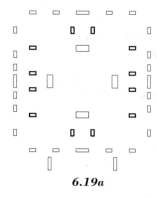

6.19a

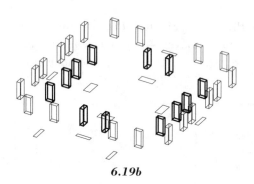

6.19b

6.18a Selecting the window openings for extrusion.

6.18b Extruded window openings.

6.19a Selecting the door openings between rooms for extrusion.

6.19b Extruded door openings between rooms.

20 Select the door openings to the central volume (Figure 6.20a) and extrude them by 12′ [3.6] (Figure 6.20b).

21 Select the entrance door openings (Figure 6.21a) and extrude them by 14′ [4.2] (Figure 6.21b).

22 Select the portico openings (Figure 6.22a) and extrude them by 9′ [2.7]. Move the extruded volumes up in space by 3′ [0.9] (Figure 6.22b). (Enter the displacement of 0,0,3′ [0,0,0.9].)

23 The solid objects that belong to the first level (layers 1-WALLS and 1-OPENINGS) should be moved up in space by 10′ [3], which is the height of the base level underneath. Therefore, turn on the layer 1-WALLS. (Both 1-OPENINGS and 1-WALLS layers should be displayed.)

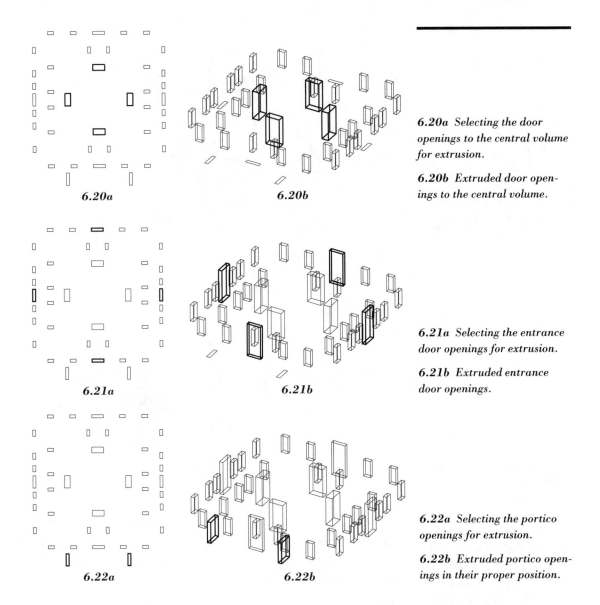

6.20a Selecting the door openings to the central volume for extrusion.

6.20b Extruded door openings to the central volume.

6.20a

6.20b

6.21a Selecting the entrance door openings for extrusion.

6.21b Extruded entrance door openings.

6.21a

6.21b

6.22a Selecting the portico openings for extrusion.

6.22b Extruded portico openings in their proper position.

6.22a

6.22b

24 Move the elements of the first level up in space by 10′ [3] (Figure 6.24). (Enter the displacement of 0,0,10′ [0,0,3].)

25 Now, in addition to the first-level layers, display (turn on) both base-level layers (0-WALLS and 0-OPENINGS). The graphics area should look like Figure 6.25.

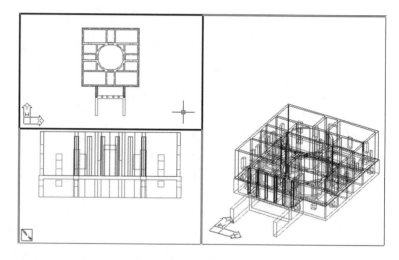

6.24 *Translating the solid objects of the first level up in space.*

0,0,10'

6.25 *The first two levels of the building.*

Note that in hidden-line views the curved surfaces of 3D objects are faceted, that is, approximated by rectangular and triangular facets. You can change the number of generated facets through the FACETRES (FACET RESolution) command. The default value of the FACETRES variable is 0.5; typically, a value of 2.0 will generate satisfactory approximations (10 is the maximum value).

26 Click inside the front viewport to make it active, and create a hidden-line view. Next click inside the axonometric viewport, and create another hidden-line view of the model. Notice how the columns are *faceted* (Figure 6.26).

27 Save your model.

3D EXTRUSION: THE SECOND LEVEL

28 Turn on and set the layer 2-SLAB as the current layer, and turn off all other layers. You should see only the shapes of the layer 2-SLAB (Figure 6.28).

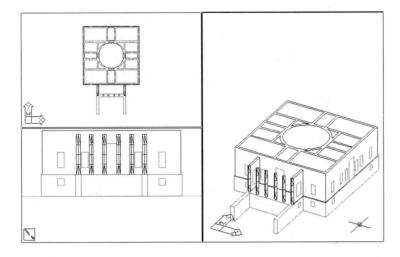

6.26 *The hidden-line views of the first two building levels.*

29 For the faster selection of objects, work in the plan view. Make the plan viewport active—click somewhere inside it. Extrude all outlines by 1′ [0.3] (Figure 6.29).

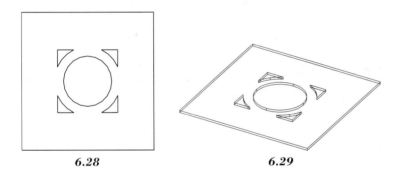

6.28   6.29

6.28 *2D shapes of the layer 2-SLAB.*

6.29 *Extruded volumes of the second-level slab.*

30 Turn on and set the layer 2-WALLS as the current layer, and turn off the layer 2-SLAB. You should see only the shapes of the layer 2-WALLS (Figure 6.30).

31 Extrude all volume outlines by 9′ [2.7] (Figure 6.31).

32 Turn on and set the layer 2-OPENINGS as the current layer, and turn off the layer 2-WALLS. You should see only the shapes of the layer 2-OPENINGS.

6.30 *2D shapes of the layer 2-WALLS.*

6.31 *Extruded volumes of the layer 2-WALLS.*

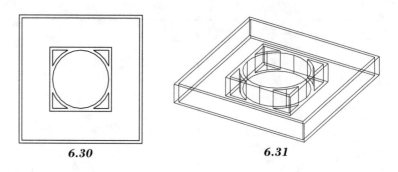

6.30

6.31

33 Extrude the window openings (Figure 6.33a) by 4′ [1.2] and move them up in space by 2′6″ [0.75] (Figure 6.33b).

6.33a *Selecting the window openings for extrusion.*

6.33b *Second-level window openings.*

6.33a

6.33b

34 Extrude the door openings to the central space (Figure 6.34a) by 5′6″ [1.65] (Figure 6.34b).

6.34a *Selecting the door openings for extrusion.*

6.34b *Extruded door openings.*

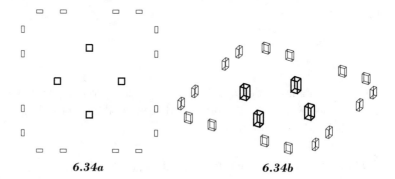

6.34a

6.34b

35 Solid objects that belong to the second level (layers 2-SLAB, 2-WALLS, and 2-OPENINGS) should be moved up in space by

30′ [9], which is the total height of the base and first levels under-neath. You should, however, first move up by 1′ [0.3] all objects on layers 2-WALLS and 2-OPENINGS, because there is a 1′- [0.3-] thick slab underneath them. Therefore, turn on the layer 2-WALLS. Both 2-OPENINGS and 2-WALLS layers should be displayed (Figure 6.35).

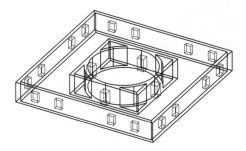

6.35 Solid objects on the layers 2-WALLS and 2-OPENINGS.

36 Move all the objects on layers 2-WALLS and 2-OPENINGS up in space by 1′ [0.3]. (Enter the displacement of 0,0,1′ [0,0,0.3].)

37 Now turn on the layer 2-SLAB. Move all the second-level objects up in space by 30′ [9] (Figure 6.37). (Enter the displacement of 0,0,30′ [0,0,9].)

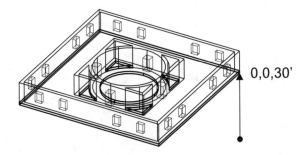

0,0,30′

6.37 Translating solid objects of the second level up in space.

38 Let's take a look at what has been accomplished so far. Turn on the layers for all three levels. The levels should be stacked up in space, as shown in Figure 6.38.

It is often difficult to "read" the wire-frame model views and to perform efficient selection and editing when too many objects are displayed. As demonstrated in this exercise so far, a carefully structured model can greatly facilitate modeling and editing work.

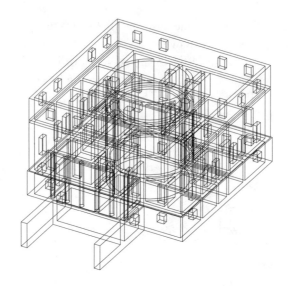

6.38 A wire-frame view of what has been modeled so far.

39 Make the front viewport active. Choose the *Zoom All* tool to display the model in its entirety, and then zoom out by 80% (choose the *Zoom Scale* tool, and enter 0.8x as the scale factor).

40 Create a hidden-line view in the front viewport. Next click inside the axonometric viewport, and create another hidden-line view of the model (Figure 6.40).

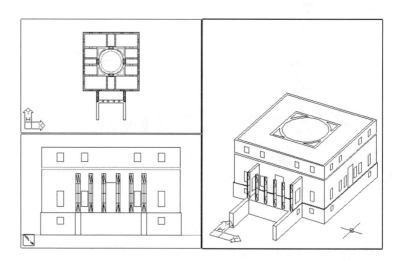

6.40 The hidden-line views of the model.

41 Save the model file.

PERSPECTIVE VIEWING

42 In AutoCAD, axonometric (or orthographic) projections can easily be transformed into perspectives. The perspective's *line of sight* will correspond to the existing viewing vector; the user has to adjust the camera's location only, i.e., its distance from the target point, which is often too small.

To create a perspective view, first click inside the axonometric viewport to make it active (if it isn't already). Next choose *3D Dynamic View* from the *View* menu, and select the entire model when prompted to select objects (AutoCAD requires that some objects be selected as a reference for perspective setup). Enter D (the *Distance* option) when perspective options are displayed in the command window (Figure 6.42a). Enter 300′ [90] as the distance between camera and target points. A temporary perspective view will be displayed in the viewport (Figure 6.42b). Use the *Pan* option (enter PA at the command prompt) to center the perspective in the viewport. Pick a point close to the model's center when prompted for a *displacement base point*. Notice how the perspective view changes *dynamically* (hence the name) as you move the pointer to select a second point. When the perspective view is correctly set up, enter X (the *eXit* option) to complete the command.

You can also enter DVIEW at the command prompt to perform the *dynamic viewing*, i.e., dynamic setup of axonometric (parallel) and perspective projections.

As you can see, there are several options that control the setup of perspective views. Almost all of them provide dynamic feedback. Use the *POints* (PO) option to pick camera and target points in model space. The *CAmera* (CA) option controls the location of the camera point; accordingly, the *TArget* (TA) option changes the location of the target point. To change the viewing angle (field of view), use the *Zoom* (Z) option, and enter the desired "lens length." Use the *TWist* (TW) option to tilt the camera. The *CLip* (CL) option controls the location of the clipping planes.

6.42a The DVIEW (3D Dynamic View) command options.

```
Select objects: Other corner: 132 found
Select objects:
CAmera/TArget/Distance/POints/PAn/Zoom/TWist/CLip/Hide/Off/Undo/<eXit>:
27'-4",-54'-8",0-0"          SNAP GRID ORTHO OSNAP  MODEL TILE
```

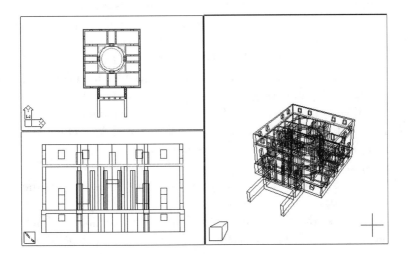

6.42b Setting up a perspective view.

43 Create a hidden-line view in the perspective viewport (Figure 6.43).

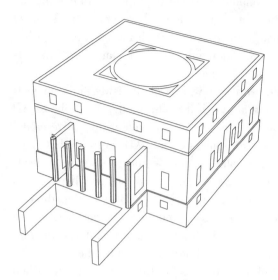

6.43 A hidden-line perspective view of the model.

44 Save the model file.

45 If you wish, make a printout of the hidden-line perspective view, even though the model is not complete. (If you want, you can array the portico objects about the origin—but don't use that drawing for the following exercise.)

First make sure that you have a printer configured for use with your system. We will assume that there is a letter-size (or A4-size) laser or ink-jet printer connected to your computer, and that such a printer is set up as the *default system printer*.

Choose *Print* from the *File* menu. Choose *Display* (i.e., the perspective viewport, *not* the entire display) in the *Additional Parameters* section (Figure 6.45a) as the area to print. Place the check mark in the *Scaled to Fit* check box so that the perspective is scaled to fit the extents of the printable area. Also check the *Hide Lines* box—this step is very important; otherwise you will print a wire-frame view.

Click on the *Plot Origin and Rotation* button, and set the *Plot Rotation* to 0 degree, and both *X Origin* and *Y Origin* to 0. Next choose the *Full* button in the *Plot Preview* section and click on the *Preview* button to see the full preview of the printed draw-

Refer to the *Windows* documentation on how to configure printers for use with your computer system. Refer to the *AutoCAD Installation Guide* for instructions on how to configure printers for use with AutoCAD.

If you do not see the *Print/Plot Configuration* dialog box, set the CMDDIA system variable to 1—enter the CMDDIA command, and enter 1 as the new value.

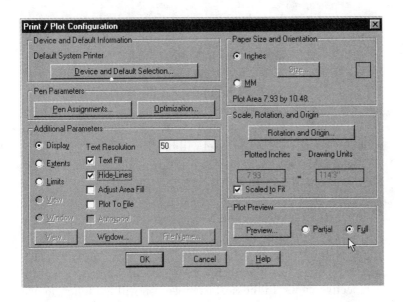

6.45a The Print *dialog box.*

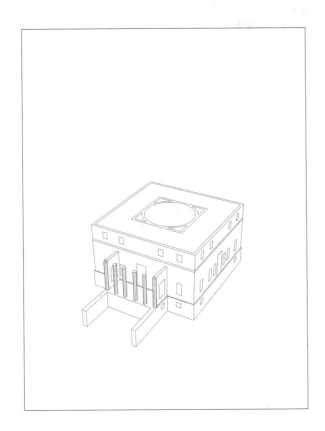

*6.45b The perspective
printed on letter-size paper.*

ing. Press *Esc* or *Enter* key to continue, i.e., to return to the print dialog box.

Before you click on the *OK* button, click on the *Pen Assignments* button to assign the same line width (0.2) to all colors. When done, click on the *OK* button. Finally, click on the *OK* button in the print dialog box to complete the printing. AutoCAD will show the printing progress, and shortly thereafter the drawing with a perspective of your model will be printed (Figure 6.45b).

If you do not want to continue at this point, choose *Exit* from the *File* menu to exit AutoCAD.

In this tutorial exercise you have extruded the outlines of the building's solid and void volumes and have learned how to manipulate 3D objects in the model space. You have also learned how to set up multiple viewports and how to generate perspective views. In the next exercise you will learn how to use *User Coordinate Systems* (construction planes) to construct additional building elements, such as portico stairs, pediments, and arched openings. You will also learn how to set up a two-point perspective.

MODELING TUTORIAL 2: CONSTRUCTION PLANES

In this exercise you will learn how to set up and use *User Coordinate Systems* (construction planes) to construct additional building elements, such as portico stairs, pediments, and arched openings. You will also learn how to *save named views* and how to set up a *two-point perspective*.

SAVING THE VIEWS

1 In this section you will learn how to save views so that you can restore them later. Start AutoCAD, and open the previously saved drawing (Rotonda.dwg). If you are continuing from the last exercise, skip this step.

2 Make active the lower left viewport showing the front view of the model. *Save* that view (you will need it later), and then set up the *right* elevation view in that viewport. Choose *Named Views* from the *View* menu. Click on the *New* button in the *View Control* dialog box (Figure 7.2a), enter FRONT as the view name, and click on the *Save View* button (Figure 7.2b). The view name will appear in the view list (Figure 7.2c). Click on the *OK* button to continue.

3 To set up the right elevation view in the lower left viewport, from the *View* menu choose *3D Viewpoint* (R13 *3D Viewpoint Pre-*

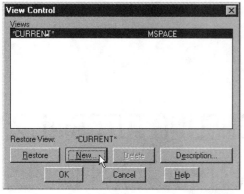

7.2a

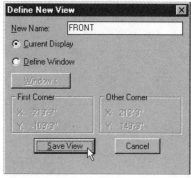

7.2b

7.2a The View Control *dialog box.*

7.2b *Saving the front view.*

7.2c *The list of saved views.*

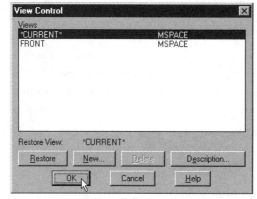

7.2c

sets), then *Right.* Select the *Zoom Scale* tool from the *Zoom* flyout, and enter .9x at the command prompt to display the view at 90% of its current size (Figure 7.3).

4 Click inside the right viewport (showing a perspective) to make it active, and save it for later use. As in the previous step, choose *Named Views* from the *View* menu, and name this view BIRDS_EYE_PERSPECTIVE (don't forget to enter the *underscore* characters, because AutoCAD doesn't allow blank spaces in view names!).

5 In the same (right) viewport set up an axonometric view with angles of 330 degrees *from x axis* and 30 degrees *from xy plane.* From the *View* menu choose *3D Viewpoint,* then *Select* (R13 *Rotate*), and enter these values into appropriate boxes.

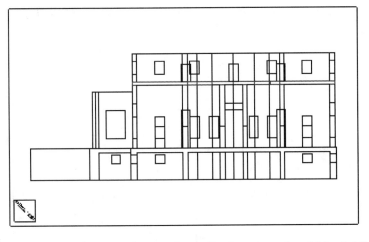

7.3 The right view displayed at 90% of its previous size.

After this step, the graphics display area should look like Figure 7.5.

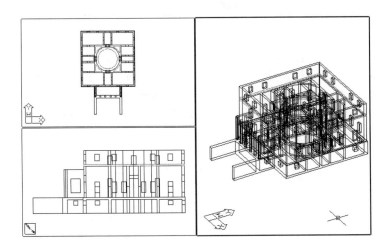

7.5 Three tiled viewports showing the plan, right, and axonometric views of the model.

MODELING THE PORTICO STAIRS

6 In this section you will model the portico stairs at the base level (Figure 7.6a). You will first set up a vertical *UCS (User Coordinate System)*, i.e., a construction plane aligned with the right stair wall, and then draw a closed 2D polyline shape that will be extruded to create the stairs volume.

Create a new layer named 0-STAIRS, assign blue color to it, and make it the current layer. Turn off all other layers except the

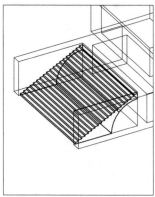

7.6a *The portico stairs.*

7.6b *3D volumes of the layer 0-WALLS.*

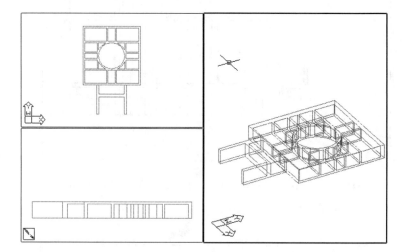

layer 0-WALLS. You should see only the 3D volumes of the layer 0-WALLS (Figure 7.6b).

7 The 2D polyline shape of the portico stairs (Figure 7.7a) should be drawn on a vertical construction plane, parallel to the right side of the model. To make the drawing process easier, that construction plane should be aligned with the inner side of the stair wall (Figure 7.7b).

7.7a *The closed 2D polyline shape of the portico stairs.*

7.7b *Aligning the construction plane with the inner side of the stair wall.*

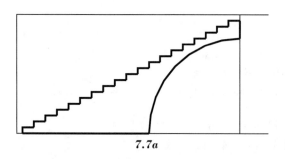

7.7a

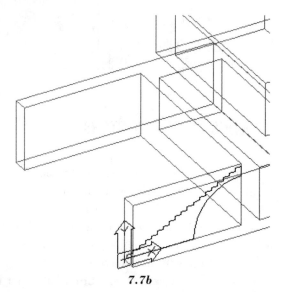

7.7b

As was already mentioned, in AutoCAD a user-defined construction plane is referred to as a *User Coordinate System*, or *UCS* for short. You define a UCS to change the location of the current *xy* plane, its origin point, and the *z* axis. You can locate a UCS anywhere in 3D space, and you can define several User Coordinate Systems, each having a different origin location and *xy* plane orientation. To indicate the origin and orientation of the UCS's *xy* plane, you can display the *UCS icon* (Figure 7.7c) at the UCS origin point. Note that a *"broken pencil" icon* (Figure 7.7d) appears in the view when the *xy* plane of the UCS is perpendicular to the viewing plane.

You can define a UCS in several ways. You can specify a *new origin,* a *new xy plane,* or a *new z axis; align* the UCS with an existing object; *align* the new UCS with the viewing plane; *rotate* the UCS about any of the axes; or select a *preset* UCS from a set that AutoCAD provides. All these options are available in the *UCS* (R13 *Set UCS*) section of the *Tools* (R13 *View*) menu (Figure 7.7e) or in the *UCS* flyout on the *Standard* toolbar (Figure 7.7f).

The global Cartesian coordinate system is referred to in AutoCAD as the *World Coordinate System,* or *WCS* for short. If you ever "get lost" in 3D space while defining a new UCS, you can always return to the WCS by choosing *UCS* (R13 *Set UCS*), then *World,* from the *Tools* (R13 *View*) menu.

7.7c The UCS icon.

7.7d The "broken pencil" icon.

Note that in AutoCAD the input and display of coordinates are *relative* to the currently used User Coordinate System. The 3D extrusion is also relative to the current UCS. You can save and restore as many UCSs as needed.

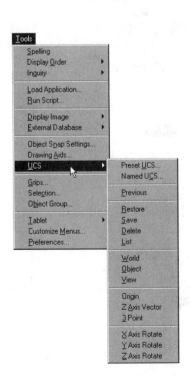

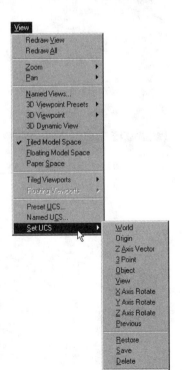

7.7e The UCS options available in the menu (R14 and R13).

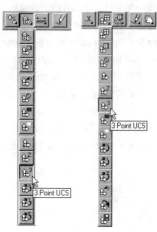

In this tutorial you will define a UCS either by selecting a *preset* one or by selecting *three points* that define the origin, the direction of the positive *x* axis, and the direction of the positive *y* axis.

Make sure that the axonometric viewport is active. Begin by placing the UCS icon at the origin point. In R14, from the *View* menu choose *Display,* then *UCS Icon,* and then *Origin* (Figure 7.7g). In R13, from the *Options* menu choose *UCS,* then *Icon Origin.* Notice how the icon shifts to the center of the building, where the origin point (0,0,0) is located (Figure 7.7h).

7.7f *The* UCS *flyout on the* Standard *toolbar (R14 and R13).*

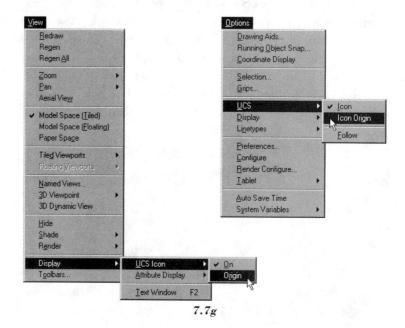

7.7g

7.7g *Placing the UCS icon at the origin point (in R14 and R13).*

7.7h *The UCS icon displayed at the origin point.*

7.7h

Note that AutoCAD displays the UCS icon in the lower left corner of the viewport if the origin point is outside of the current view. This is a default location of the UCS icon.

8 So far you have been working on a *World Coordinate System (WCS)*, i.e., AutoCAD's "global" Cartesian coordinate system. To draw a closed 2D polyline shape of the portico stairs, set up a vertical UCS parallel to the right side of the model. In R14 from the *Tools* menu, choose *UCS*, then *Preset UCS*. In R13, from the *View* menu choose *UCS Presets*. In the resulting *UCS Orientation* dialog box, choose the *Right* icon tile (Figure 7.8a), and click on the *OK* button. The UCS icon will change its orientation (Figure 7.8b). The UCS you have just defined is vertical and parallel to the right side of the model.

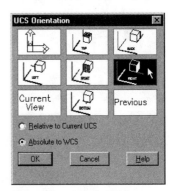

7.8a Choosing the Right preset UCS.

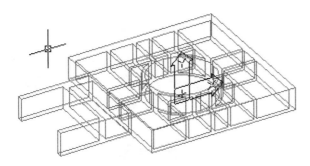

7.8b The new orientation of the UCS icon.

9 The vertical UCS you have just defined passes through the middle of the model (bisects it). You need to define a UCS that is parallel to the one you have, with the origin located at the lower left corner of the right stair wall (Figure 7.10b).

First zoom in to the portico area on the left side of the axonometric view—choose the *Zoom Window* tool from the *Zoom* flyout, and specify a rectangular area as shown in Figure 7.9.

10 Define a new UCS by moving the origin to the corner of the stair wall (Figure 7.10b). From the *Tools* (R13 *View*) menu choose *UCS* (R13 *Set UCS*), then *Origin*. When prompted for the new location of the origin point, first select the *Endpoint* object snap mode from the *Object Snap* flyout (Figure 7.10a) on the *Standard* toolbar (or enter END at the command prompt), and pick the

An alternative way to set up this UCS is to use the *3 Point* option. You pick three points that correspond to the origin, a point on the positive *x* axis, and a point where the positive *xy* quadrant should be located (i.e., the direction of the positive *y* axis). You can pick the lower left corner of the right stair wall as the UCS origin, the inner lower corner as a point on the positive *x* axis, and the upper left corner (above the origin) as the point on the positive *y* axis.

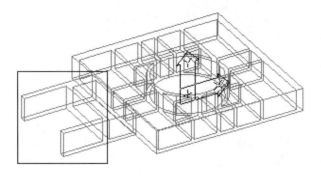

7.9 *Zooming in to the portico area.*

lower left corner of the right stair wall, as shown in Figure 7.10b. The UCS icon will be displayed at the new location of the origin point (Figure 7.10b).

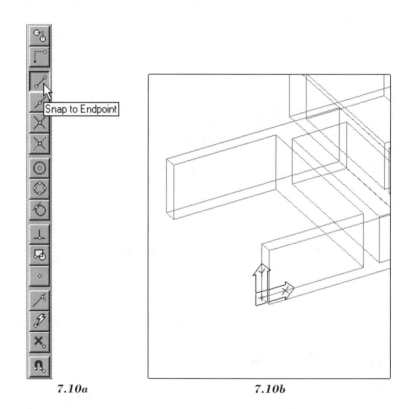

7.10a *Choosing the* Endpoint *object snap mode.*

7.10b *The UCS icon displayed at the lower left corner of the right stair wall.*

7.10a   7.10b

11 You will draw the 2D outline of the stairs in the lower left viewport showing the right elevation of the model. Click inside that viewport to make it active, then zoom in to the portico area on the left side of the viewport, as shown in Figure 7.11.

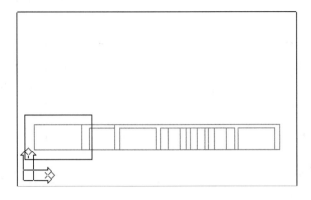

7.11 Zooming in to the portico area.

12 Display the UCS icon at the origin point in this view (Figure 7.12). In R14, from the *View* menu choose *Display*, then *UCS*, and then *Origin*. In R13, from the *Options* menu choose *UCS*, then *Icon Origin*.

Before you perform a zoom operation in a viewport, first make that viewport active (current) by clicking inside it.

You can also use the UCSICON command to specify how the UCS icon is displayed in the viewport.

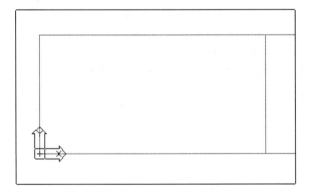

7.12 The UCS icon displayed at the origin point.

13 Before you begin to draw, verify that the snap spacing is set to 6″ [0.15] (from the *Tools* menu choose *Drawing Aids*), and that the snap mode is on. Also, verify that the running object snap modes are disabled (from the *Tools* [R13 *Options*] menu choose *Object Snap Settings* [R13 *Running Object Snap*], and click on the *Clear All* button).

14 Select the *Polyline* tool and draw the first step at 6″ [0.15] from the wall's end (refer to Figure 7.14). The step's riser is 6″ [0.15] high, and the tread is 1′ [0.3] wide (Figure 7.14).

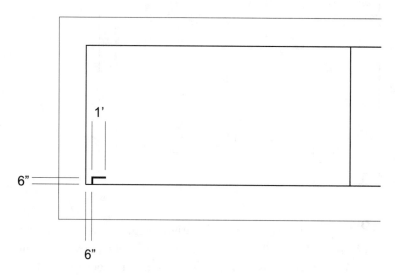

1'

6"

6"

7.14 Drawing the first step.

You can display *grid* as a visual reference while drawing. Choose *Drawing Aids* from the *Tools* menu, and set the desired grid spacing. You can also enter GRID at the command prompt.

Alternatively, you could have continued to draw the steps using the *Polyline* tool. Copying, however, is a faster method to draw the stairs shape.

15 Next make additional copies of the previously drawn step, and join them into a single polyline (Figure 7.15). Select the *Copy* tool, enter L to select the last drawn object (the step's polyline), and press the *Enter* key to complete the object selection. When prompted for the *base point,* choose the *Multiple* copy option: enter M at the command prompt. Pick the riser's bottom point as the *base point,* and make copies of the step until you reach the top. Press the *Escape* key to stop the copy command. (Notice how the step polylines are simultaneously displayed in the axonometric view as you copy.)

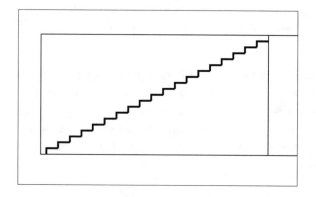

7.15 Copying the step's polyline.

16 To join the step polylines into a single object, use the *Polyline Edit* tool on the *Modify* toolbar (or enter PEDIT at the command prompt). Select the first step as a polyline to edit, enter J (the *Join* option) at the next prompt, and using the crossing (c) or window (w) selection mode select the remaining polylines. Enter X to exit the PEDIT command. (Note that AutoCAD will refuse to join the polylines if their endpoints do not meet, i.e., if they are not coincident.)

17 You will draw the remaining part of the stairs outline (Figure 7.17) in several steps. Use the *Line* tool (or enter L at the command prompt), and draw a 1′6″- [0.45-] long vertical line (*Line 1* in Figure 7.17) down from the endpoint of the last step. Pick the first point of that line at the endpoint of the last step. Either pick the second point graphically or enter its relative coordinates of @0,–1′6 [@0,–.45].

You do not have to enter the inches symbol (″) nor leading zeros in decimal numbers (as in 0.45) when entering coordinates.

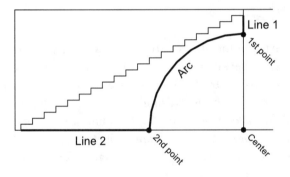

7.17 Drawing the remaining part of the stairs outline.

Use the *Arc* tool to draw the arc segment underneath the steps (refer to Figure 7.17). Select the center (c) option, and place the center at the corner of the stair wall, pick the bottom endpoint of the previously drawn line as the arc's first point, and pick the second point at the bottom edge of the stair wall. Draw the remaining line segment (*Line 2* in Figure 7.17) that connects the arc to the first step.

18 Finally, use the *Polyline Edit* tool (or enter PEDIT at the command prompt) to join the steps polyline with the previously created line and arc segments. To verify that the resulting polyline is closed after joining, make sure that the first option displayed in the PEDIT command prompt is *Open* (you can't create solid objects from open polyline shapes). Enter X to exit the PEDIT command.

Refer to the axonometric view (Figure 7.18) to verify that the stairs polyline is properly drawn.

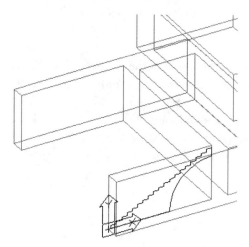

7.18 *The 2D polyline outline of the portico stairs in the axonometric view.*

19 Before you extrude the stairs outline into a solid volume, measure the distance between the stair walls to determine the height (length) of extrusion. In R14 choose the *Distance* tool from the *Inquiry* flyout on the *Standard* toolbar (Figure 7.19a), or choose *Inquiry,* then *Distance,* from the *Tools* menu. In R13 enter DIST at the command prompt. Use *endpoint* object snap to select two endpoints on the stair walls as shown in Figure 7.19b. The measured distance should be 29′ [8.7] (Figure 7.19c].

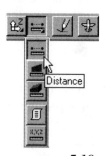

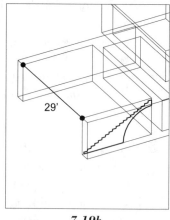

7.19a *The* Inquiry *flyout on the* Standard *toolbar (R14).*

7.19b *Measuring the distance between stair walls.*

7.19a

7.19b

```
Distance = 29'-0",   Angle in XY Plane = 0,   Angle from XY Plane = 270
Delta X = 0'-0",   Delta Y = 0'-0",    Delta Z = -29'-0"
Command:
-11'6",18'-0",0'-0"                    SNAP GRID ORTHO OSNAP MODEL TILE
```

7.19c *The display of the measuring results.*

20 Use the *right-hand rule* to determine the direction of the positive *z* axis before extrusion. The positive *z* axis points toward you, i.e., away from the stairs. The height of extrusion, therefore, should be −29′ [−8.7]—notice the negative sign. The extrusion will be performed in the direction of the negative *z* axis.

Choose the *Extrude* tool from the *Solids* toolbar and extrude the stairs outline (Figure 7.20).

21 Display the front view in the lower left viewport. Apply the *Zoom All* tool in both the front and axonometric views. (Make each viewport active before you apply the zoom command.) Zoom out by 90% (.9x) in both views. The graphic display area should look like Figure 7.21.

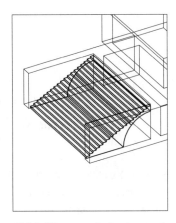

7.20 *The extruded volume of the portico stairs.*

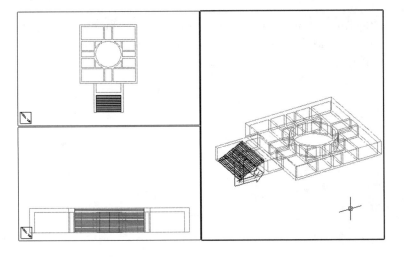

Note that the extrusion is *relative* to the current UCS. Shapes are extruded in the positive or negative direction of the local *z* axis.

7.21 *The portico stairs in all three views.*

22 Save the model file.

MODELING THE ARCHITRAVE AND THE CORNICE

23 In this section you will model a U-shaped volume that represents the portico's architrave. You will also create a cornice volume as a rectangular solid that also acts as a slab above the portico (Figure 7.23).

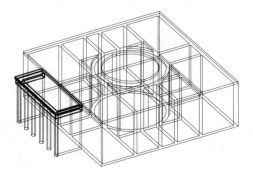

7.23 The architrave and cornice volumes.

Return to the World Coordinate System (WCS). From the *Tools* (R13 *View*) menu choose *UCS* (R13 *Set UCS*), then *World*. Notice how the UCS icon changes its position and orientation in all three views. There is a *broken pencil* icon in the front view because the WCS is perpendicular to that view.

24 Turn on and set the layer 1-WALLS as the current layer. Turn off all other layers. You should see only the 3D volumes of the layer 1-WALLS (Figure 7.24).

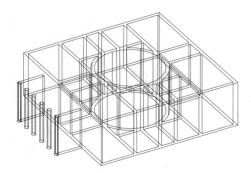

7.24 3D volumes of the layer 1-WALLS.

25 Make the plan viewport active, and zoom in to the portico area, as shown in Figure 7.25.

26 You will draw the architrave's U shape at its correct location in space, which is 28′ [8.4] above the "ground" WCS plane. To do that, you will move the construction plane 28′ [8.4] up in space,

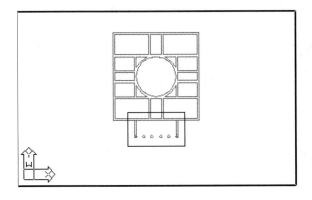

that is, you will define a new UCS, parallel to the WCS, by moving the *origin* point to 0,0,28′ [0,0,8.4].

First make sure that none of the object snap modes are
active, and then define a new UCS. From the *Tools* (R13 *View*)
menu choose *UCS* (R13 *Set UCS*), then *Origin*. When prompted
for the new location of the origin point, enter 0,0,28′ [0,0,8.4].
Notice in the axonometric view how the UCS icon is displayed at
the new location of the origin point.

27 Set the *snap spacing* to 3″ [0.075], and make sure that the
snap is *on*.

28 In the plan view draw a single U-shaped polyline outline of
the architrave. The polyline is offset 3″ [0.075] from the side
walls, but it touches the columns (refer to Figure 7.28).

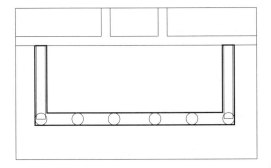

7.28 *Drawing the U-shaped*
outline of the architrave.

29 Extrude the architrave's outline by 2′ [0.6]. The architrave's
solid volume should be located above the portico columns and
side walls (Figure 7.29).

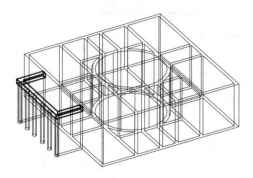

7.29 The architrave's volume.

30 The rectangular cornice volume belongs to the layer 2-SLAB. Turn on this layer and set it as the current layer.

31 The cornice outline should be drawn on top of the architrave's volume, that is, on a construction plane (UCS) that is 2′ [0.6] above the current one. As in step 26, move the origin of the current UCS up in space by 2′ [0.6]. From the *Tools* (R13 *View*) menu choose *UCS* (R13 *Set UCS*), then *Origin*. When prompted for the new location of the origin point, enter 0,0,2′ [0,0,0.6].

32 Draw the outline of the cornice volume as a rectangular shape that touches the second-level slab and extends 3″ [0.075], i.e., one snap module, over the architrave on the other three sides (Figure 7.32).

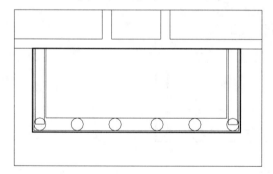

7.32 The rectangular shape of the cornice volume.

33 Extrude that rectangular outline by 1′ [0.3]. The cornice's solid volume should be located above the architrave (Figure 7.33).

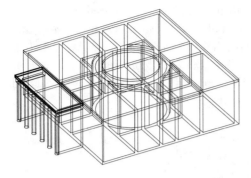

7.33 The cornice's volume.

34 Save the model file.

MODELING THE PEDIMENT

35 In this section you will create the pediment's triangular volume, located above the portico (Figure 7.35a).

Turn on and set the layer 2-WALLS as the current layer. Turn off the layer 1-WALLS, but leave the layer 2-SLAB on (displayed on the screen). You should see only the 3D volumes of layers 2-SLAB and 2-WALLS (Figure 7.35b). Make sure that the layer 2-WALLS is the current layer.

7.35a The pediment's triangular volume.

7.35b The 3D volumes of layers 2-SLAB and 2-WALLS.

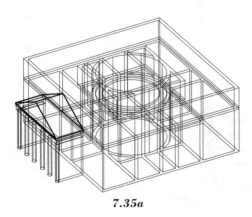

7.35a

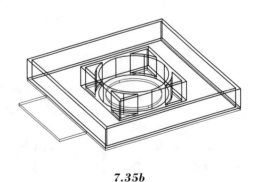

7.35b

36 To draw the pediment's triangular shape, you will set up a UCS parallel to the *front* side of the model, and locate its origin at the *midpoint* of the cornice's front edge (Figure 7.37).

An alternative way to set up this UCS is to rotate the current, horizontal UCS about its *x* axis by 90 degrees (choose the *Rotate X* option in the menu). That will make it vertical and parallel to the front of the model. Next move the UCS origin to a new location.

In R14 from the *Tools* menu, choose *UCS*, then *Preset UCS*. In R13 from the *View* menu choose *UCS Presets*. In the resulting *UCS Orientation* dialog box, choose the *Front* icon tile, and click on the *OK* button. Notice how the UCS icon changes its orientation (Figure 7.36). The UCS you have just defined is vertical and parallel to the front side of the model.

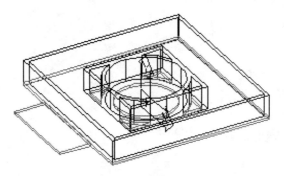

7.36 *A front UCS passing through the middle of the building.*

37 Move the origin of the UCS to align it with the front side of the cornice volume. From the *Tools* (R13 *View*) menu choose *UCS* (R13 *Set UCS*), then *Origin.* When prompted for the new location of the origin point, select the *Midpoint* object snap mode from the *Object Snap* flyout on the *Standard* toolbar (or enter MID at the command prompt), and pick the midpoint of the cornice's top front edge in the axonometric view, as shown in Figure 7.37. The UCS icon will be displayed at the new location of the origin point (Figure 7.37).

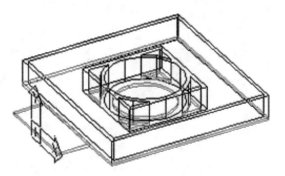

7.37 *The UCS origin at the midpoint of the cornice's top front edge.*

38 To draw with more precision, zoom in to the area around the cornice in the front view, as shown in Figure 7.38.

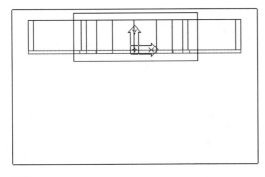

39 Set the snap spacing to 6″ [0.15]. Make sure that the snap is on.

40 Use the *Polyline* tool and draw the pediment's triangular outline, as shown in Figure 7.40. The pediment should reach the ends of the cornice on both sides and should touch the top of the second-level walls. (Pick points without using the object snap.)

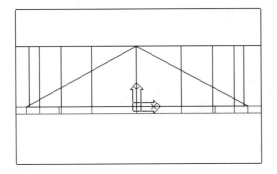

7.40 The pediment's triangular outline.

41 Before you extrude the pediment's outline, determine the height of extrusion by measuring the width of the cornice's volume, i.e., the distance between its front and back sides. Use the *Distance* tool from the *Inquiry* flyout (in R14), or enter DIST at the command prompt, and pick two endpoints on the cornice's volume using object snapping. The measured distance should be 13′3″ [3.975].

42 Extrude the pediment's outline by −13′3″ [−3.975] (notice the negative sign). The resulting volume should appear on top of the cornice and should touch the front wall of the second level (Figure 7.42).

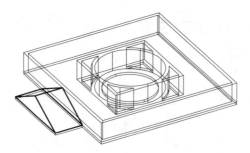

7.42 *The pediment's volume.*

43 Save the model file.

MODELING THE PORTICO'S ARCHED OPENINGS

44 In this part of the tutorial you will draw the arched openings in the portico's side walls (Figure 7.44). Turn on and set the layer 1-OPENINGS as the current layer, and turn off all other layers. You should see only the opening volumes of the first level.

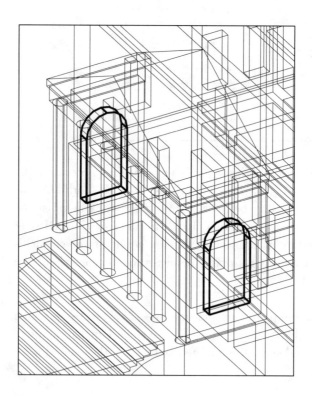

7.44 *The arched openings in the portico's side walls.*

45 Display the *right* view in the lower left viewport. The graphics area should look like Figure 7.45.

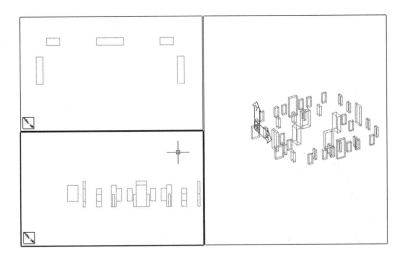

7.45 The opening volumes of the first level.

46 To draw the outline of the arched opening, you need to set up a UCS parallel to the *right* side of the model, with the origin point at the lower left corner of the existing portico opening (Figure 7.47).

First set up a UCS parallel to the right side of the model. In R14, from the *Tools* menu choose *UCS*, then *Preset UCS*. In R13, from the *View* menu choose *UCS Presets*. In the resulting *UCS Orientation* dialog box, choose the *Right* icon tile (Figure 7.46a), select *Absolute to WCS* option, and click on the *OK* button. The UCS you just defined is vertical and parallel to the right side of the model (Figure 7.46b).

A UCS can be set up *relative to the current UCS* or *absolute to the WCS*. It is often better to use the second option to avoid a confusing outcome.

7.46a Setting up a right UCS absolute to the WCS.

7.46b A vertical UCS parallel to the right side of the model.

7.46a

7.46b

47 Change the origin of the UCS. Using the *endpoint* object snap option, snap onto the lower left corner of the portico's opening (Figure 7.47).

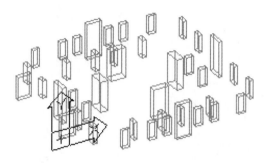

7.47 Snapping the origin of the UCS to the lower left corner of the portico's side wall opening.

48 In the right elevation viewport, zoom in to an area around the existing rectangular opening in the portico (Figure 7.48).

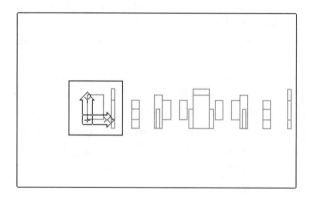

7.48 Zooming in to an area around the existing opening.

49 Use the *Polyline* tool (or enter PLINE at the command prompt) to draw the arched opening (Figure 7.49). (Check that the snap spacing is set to 6″ [0.15] and that the snap is on.) Use the existing rectangular opening as a reference. Begin to draw at the lower left corner (without using the object snap). Next pick the upper left corner, and switch to the *arc* mode (enter A at the polyline command prompt). Pick the upper right corner as the arc's second endpoint, and switch back to the *line* mode (enter L at the polyline command prompt). Pick the lower right corner as the next point and close the polyline shape (enter C).

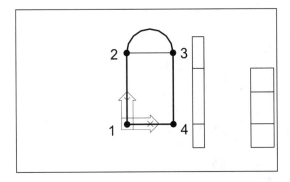

50 Extrude the arched outline by −1′6″ [−0.45] (notice the negative sign). The new opening volume should overlap in space with the old one.

51 Zoom in to the portico area in the axonometric view, and *copy* the new arched opening to the other side of the portico. Use *endpoint* object snapping to pick the displacement points (Figure 7.51).

52 Use the *Erase* tool and delete the old rectangular openings.

53 Save the model file.

MODELING THE ARCHED OPENINGS IN THE *SALA*

54 In this section you will model the arched door openings to the central cylindrical volume, called *sala* (Figure 7.54a). You will create these openings on both the first and the second levels.

Choose the *Zoom All* tool to display all the openings in all three viewports. Then zoom in to the *sala* area in each of the three viewports. After you perform these zoom operations, the graphics display area should look like Figure 7.54b.

55 To draw the arched opening outline, place the UCS origin at the lower left corner of the door opening on the left side of the building (see Figure 7.55). Use *endpoint* object snap to locate this point.

7.51 Copying the new arched opening to the other side of the portico.

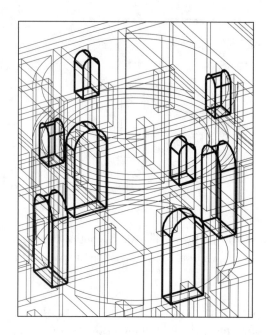

7.54a Arched door openings to the sala.

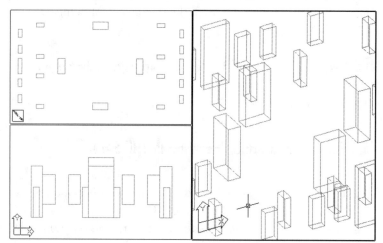

7.54b The openings on the first level.

56 Using the *Polyline* tool draw the opening's arched outline by picking the corner points of the existing rectangular opening (just as you did in step 49). You can draw in either the right or the axonometric viewport (Figure 7.56).

57 Extrude the newly drawn outline by −2′10″ [−0.85] (notice the negative sign).

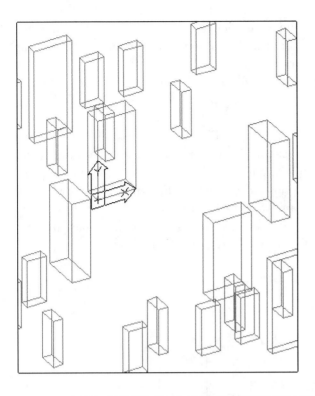

7.55 *Placing the UCS origin at the new location.*

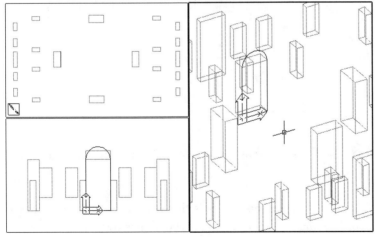

7.56 *The outline of the arched opening.*

58 Notice that you need four identical instances of the arched door opening around the *sala*'s perimeter. You will use the *Array* tool (Figure 7.58) from the *Modify* toolbar and create a *polar* (rotational) array of openings. Before you execute the array com-

7.58 *The Array tool.*

AutoCAD also provides a three-dimensional version of the ARRAY command called ARRAY3D. In addition to specifying the number of *rows* and *columns,* you can also specify the number of *levels.*

mand, you should set up the World Coordinate System, i.e., you should create an array in the horizontal plane; otherwise, the doors will be arrayed vertically.

From the *Tools* (R13 *View*) menu choose *UCS* (R13 *Set UCS*), then *World.*

59 Choose the *Array* tool (Figure 7.58), and select the arched opening volume as the object to array. Specify *Polar* array (enter P). Enter 0,0 (the origin's coordinates) as the *center point of array.* Enter 4 as the *number of items* in the array. Enter 360 as the *angle to fill.* Finally enter Y (*Yes*) when prompted whether to *rotate objects as they are copied.* The four arched door openings should appear in the model (Figure 7.59).

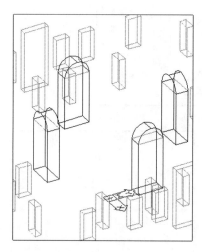

7.59 *The four arched door openings to the* sala.

60 Use the *Erase* tool and delete the four old rectangular openings.

Develop a habit of saving your work often (every 15 to 20 minutes). That way you won't lose hours of work if something unexpected happens, such as a power outage, or if your system "freezes." (Unfortunately, most people learn this lesson the hard way!)

61 Now perform more or less the same steps to create arched door openings to the *sala* on the second level (Figure 7.61).

Turn on and set the layer 2-OPENINGS as the current layer, and turn off all other layers. You should see only the opening volumes of the second level.

Repeat steps 54 to 60 and create the arched openings on the second level in a similar way. The result should look like figure 7.61. (Don't forget to erase the old rectangular openings.)

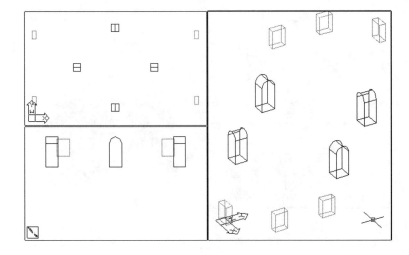

7.61 *Arched door openings to
the* sala *on the second level.*

62 Save the model file.

CREATING A TWO-POINT PERSPECTIVE

63 In this section you will array the portico solids around the
building. Then you will create hidden-line axonometric and perspective views of the model.

Turn on all the layers except the layer GRID, and set the
layer 0 (zero) as the current layer. Select the *world* coordinate
system. Choose the *Zoom All* tool to display the model in its
entirety in all three viewports.

64 To complete the geometry of the first three levels, array the
portico objects around the building so that the porticoes appear
on the remaining three sides.

Choose the *Array* tool, and select in the plan view all the
objects that compose the portico. Use the *crossing* option to make
the selection (Figure 7.64a). Specify *Polar* (enter P) array. Enter
0,0 (the origin's coordinates) as the *center point of array*. Enter 4
as the *number of items* in the array. Enter 360 as the *angle to fill*.
Finally enter Y (*Yes*) when prompted whether to *rotate objects as
they are copied*. The additional porticoes should appear on the
remaining three sides of the model (Figure 7.64b).

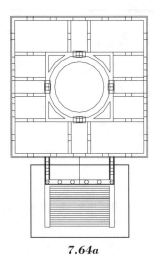

7.64a

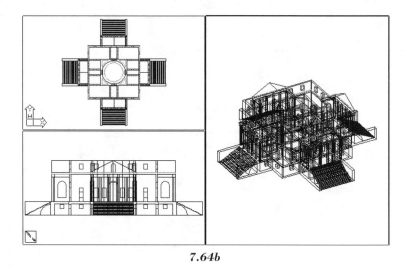

7.64b

7.64a *Selecting the objects that compose the portico.*

7.64b *The volumes of the first three levels.*

Choose the *Zoom All* tool to display the model in its entirety in all three viewports. Zoom in if necessary. The graphics area should look like Figure 7.64b.

Congratulations! You have modeled *all* the volumes on the first three levels! (You will complete the model in the next tutorial exercise.)

65 Create hidden-line axonometric and right elevation views of the model and compare the results to figure 7.65.

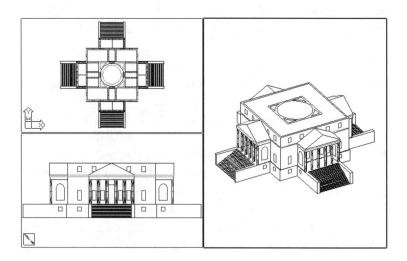

7.65 *The hidden-line views of the model.*

66 To set up a two-point perspective in the right viewport, make that viewport active, and choose *3D Dynamic View* from the *View* menu (or enter DVIEW at the command prompt). Select all the objects. When the DVIEW command prompt is displayed, enter PO (the *POints* option) to enter the coordinates of the camera and target points. Enter the coordinates of 0,0,5′6″ [0,0,1.65] for the target point, and 90′,−180′,5′6″ [27,−54,1.65] for the camera point location (note the same z coordinate for both points). Next enter D (the *Distance* option) and press the *Enter* key to accept the default distance value; a temporary perspective view is generated. Then enter Z (the *Zoom* option) and enter 35 for the lens length (which corresponds to a 60° viewing angle); note how the perspective changes. Finally, enter X (the *eXit* option) to exit the DVIEW command.

You can also specify a two-point perspective by picking points in the plan view. Use the *.XY filters* feature to preserve the *x* and *y* coordinates of the picked points and provide the *z* coordinate numerically. Simply enter .XY (followed by *Enter*) before you pick a point. AutoCAD will prompt you for the *z* coordinate. (Remember that the *z* coordinate must be the same for both camera and target points in order to generate a two-point perspective.)

67 Create a hidden-line perspective view (Figure 7.67).

7.67 A hidden-line two-point perspective view of the model.

68 Save the perspective view under the name TWO_POINT_ PERSPECTIVE (do not forget to enter the *underscore* characters). Choose *Named Views* from the *View* menu, click on the *New* button, enter the new view name, and click on the *Save View* button. Click on the *OK* button to continue.

69 Save the model file.

If you do not want to continue at this point, choose *Exit* from the *File* menu to exit AutoCAD.

In this tutorial exercise you have learned how to set up and use the *User Coordinate System* to construct additional building elements, such as portico stairs, pediments, and arched openings.

You have also learned how to *save named views* and how to set up a *two-point perspective*.

In the next exercise you will complete the building model. You will model the *roof* and *dome* objects, and apply the *Boolean operations* of *union, intersection,* and *subtraction* to the building's volumes to create its *solid elements* and *void spaces*.

MODELING TUTORIAL 3: BOOLEAN OPERATIONS

I n this exercise you will complete the building model. You will first model the *roof* and create the *dome* object as a *revolved solid.* You will then apply *Boolean operations* of *union, intersection,* and *subtraction* to existing volumes to create the building's *solid elements* and *void spaces.*

MODELING THE ROOF

1 In this section you will use *Boolean operations* of *intersection* and *subtraction* to create the roof's form. First you will create two triangular prismatic volumes (Figure 8.1a) and then *intersect* them to produce a square, pyramidal solid object (Figure 8.1b). Then you will create the central cylinder (Figure 8.1c) and *subtract* it from the pyramid (Figure 8.1d).

If you exited AutoCAD at the end of the previous exercise, start it again, and open the model file (Rotonda.dwg).

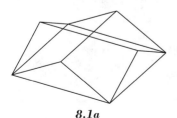

8.1a

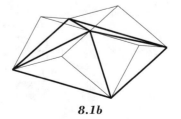

8.1b

8.1a Creating the roof: two overlapping triangular prisms.

8.1b The pyramidal object produced by intersecting the prisms.

8.1c *The central cylindrical volume.*

8.1d *The roof's volume produced by subtracting the cylinder from the pyramid.*

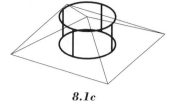

8.1c

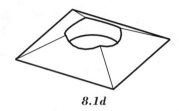

8.1d

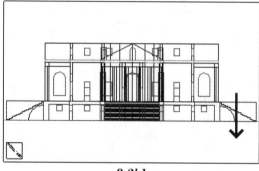

8.2a *The* Pan *tool.*

2 Set up a front view in the lower left viewport. From the *View* menu choose *3D Viewpoint* (R13 *3D Viewpoint Presets*), then *Front*. Use the *Pan* tool (Figure 8.2a) on the *Standard* toolbar and "slide" the view toward the bottom edge (Figure 8.2b).

8.2b1

8.2b2

8.2b Panning *in the front view.*

3 Make the right viewport active (click anywhere within it), and set up an axonometric view. Set the angle *from x axis* to 300, and set the angle *from xy plane* to 30 degrees (Figure 8.3).

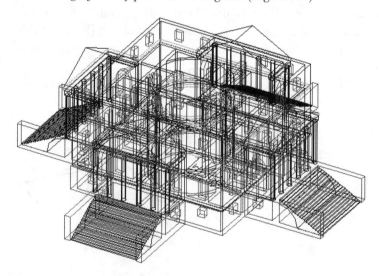

8.3 *An axonometric view of the model.*

4 You will use the solid objects on the layer 2-WALLS as a geometric reference to construct the triangular prismatic volumes.

Create a new layer named ROOF, assign some color (magenta) to it, and make it the current layer. Turn off all other layers except 2-WALLS. You should see only the volumes of the layer 2-WALLS. (Make sure that the layer ROOF is the current layer.)

5 In the axonometric view zoom in to the immediate area surrounding the solid objects of the layer 2-WALLS (Figure 8.5).

Note that in R14 you can use the *Zoom Realtime* tool to zoom in and out dynamically (in real time).

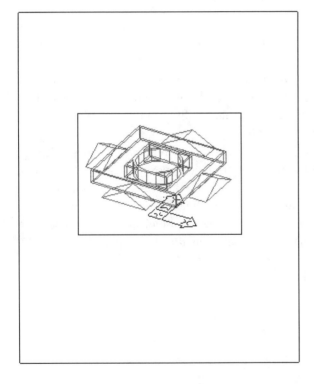

8.5 Zooming in to the solid objects of the layer 2-WALLS.

6 Use the *3 Point* option to set up a UCS aligned with the front face of the main volume (Figure 8.6b). From the *Tools* (R13 *View*) menu choose *UCS* (R13 *Set UCS*), then *3 Point*. When prompted for the *origin point,* use *endpoint* object snap and select the lower left corner of the front wall (see Figure 8.6a). Pick the lower right corner point as a *point on positive portion of the x axis* (use *endpoint* object snap). Finally pick the upper left corner as a *point on positive y portion of the UCS xy plane* (use *endpoint* object snap).

You could have used the *front preset UCS* and moved its origin to a correct location to set up this UCS. You should, however, learn how to use the *3 Point* option since it offers a quick way to set up *any* UCS (for example, on a slanted surface).

The UCS should be aligned with the front face of the main volume, as shown in Figure 8.6b.

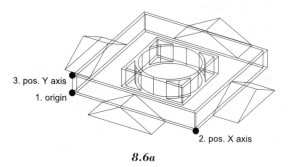

3. pos. Y axis

1. origin

2. pos. X axis

8.6a

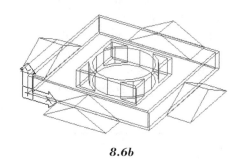

8.6b

8.6a *Setting up a UCS using the* 3 Point *option.*

8.6b *The UCS should be aligned with the front face of the main volume.*

Use the *Snap From* tool whenever you have to pick a point at some distance from existing objects. It is one of the most useful geometric drawing aids in AutoCAD.

7 Use the *Polyline* tool and draw in the axonometric view a triangular roof outline (Figure 8.7b). It should have the same slope as the pediment; therefore, its height should be 18′ [5.4].

Use the *Endpoint* object snap tool and pick the first polyline point at the upper left corner of the front wall (Figure 8.7b). To pick the second point, the triangle's apex, choose the *Snap From* object snap tool (Figure 8.7a) on the *Object Snap* toolbar, and then pick the endpoint of the pediment's ridge when prompted for the *base point* (use the *endpoint* object snap). Enter @0,18′ [@0,5.4] (*relative* coordinates) as *offset* distance (Figure 8.7b). Pick the next point at the upper right corner of the front wall, and close the polyline shape.

8.7a *The* Snap From *tool.*

8.7b *Drawing the roof's triangular outline.*

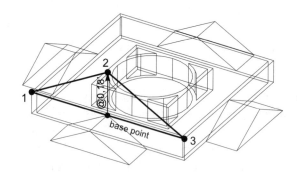

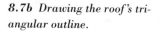

base point

8 Measure the width of the main volume using the DIST command. The width, i.e., the distance, should be 66′ [19.8].

9 Extrude the triangular outline by −66′ [−19.8] (note the negative height of extrusion). The resulting triangular prismatic volume should fit precisely over the main volume (Figure 8.9).

Note that in AutoCAD, the *extrusion* is always *relative* to the current UCS.

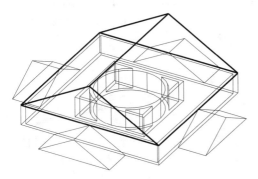

8.9 The extruded triangular prismatic volume.

10 To create the intermediate pyramidal volume of the roof, you will need another instance of the triangular volume that was just created, but rotated by 90 degrees (Figure 8.12).

Use the *Copy* tool to create an identical triangular volume. Specify the displacement of 0,0 when copying.

11 Before you rotate the copied volume, return to the World Coordinate System. (Otherwise, the rotation would be executed in the vertical UCS.) From the *Tools* (R13 *View*) menu choose *UCS* (R13 *Set UCS*), then *World*.

12 To rotate the copied volume, choose the *Rotate* tool, enter L (*Last*) to pick the last created object (the copied volume), enter 0,0 as coordinates of the *base point,* and enter 90 as the *rotation angle.* As a result, there should be two triangular volumes perpendicular to each other (Figure 8.12).

You can use the ROTATE3D command to perform rotation in 3D space, i.e., out of the *xy* plane of the current UCS. Instead of the *base point,* you specify a *rotation axis* either by picking two points in space or by choosing rotation about one of the UCS axes (*x, y,* or *z*).

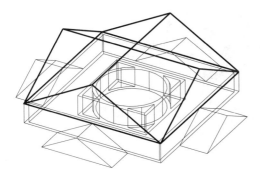

8.12 Two triangular volumes perpendicular to each other.

13 Intersect the two triangular volumes. In R14, from the *Modify* menu choose *Boolean,* then *Intersect,* or choose the *Intersect* tool on the *Modify II* toolbar. In R13, choose the *Intersect* tool from the *Explode* flyout (Figure 8.13a) on the *Modify* toolbar. Select the two solids that were created previously. The resulting object is a *pyramid* (Figure 8.13b).

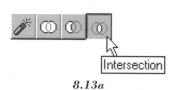

8.13a

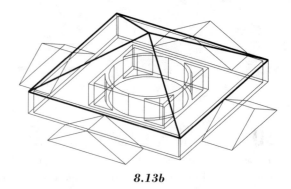

8.13b

8.13a The Intersect *tool (R13).*

8.13b The resulting pyramid *solid.*

Boolean operations of union, intersection, and subtraction can also be applied to *regions,* two-dimensional closed areas that can be created from closed shapes, such as circles or closed poly-lines. You can create *composite* regions by subtracting, combining, or finding intersections of regions. You can then *extrude* or *revolve* composite regions to create 3D solid objects.

8.14 The UCS set up at the bottom of the roof's pyramid.

14 Next you will create a central cylindrical volume, which will be subtracted from the pyramid (Figures 8.15b and 8.16b).

First set up a horizontal UCS at the bottom of the roof's pyramid, i.e., at the top of the second level, at 40' [12] from the "ground" (the World Coordinate System). Since this UCS is parallel to the World Coordinate System, all you have to do is locate a new origin. From the *Tools* (R13 *View*) menu choose *UCS* (R13 *Set UCS*), then *Origin,* and place the origin point at 0,0,40' [0,0,12] (Figure 8.14).

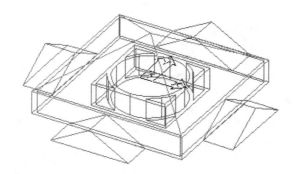

15 Choose the *Cylinder* tool from the *Solids* toolbar (Figure 8.15a) to create the central cylindrical volume (Figure 8.15b). Enter 0,0,0 as coordinates of the *center point*, 16′6″ [4.95] as the *radius*, and 18′ [5.4] as the *height*.

In addition to *cylinder,* other solid primitives available in AutoCAD are: *box, sphere, cone, wedge,* and *torus* ("doughnut").

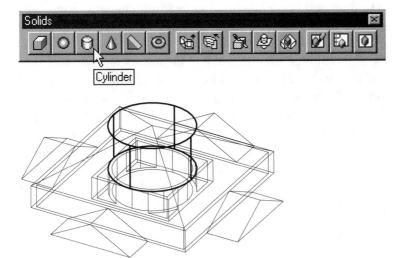

8.15a The Cylinder *tool in the* Solids *toolbar.*

8.15b The central cylindrical volume.

16 Subtract the cylinder from the pyramid. In R14, from the *Modify* menu choose *Boolean,* then *Subtract.* In R13, choose the *Subtract* tool in the *Explode* flyout on the *Modify* toolbar (Figure 8.16a). Select the pyramid as a *solid object to subtract from,* press *Enter,* and then select the cylinder as a *solid object to subtract.*

The roof's solid volume is now constructed (Figure 8.16b). Note the complex outline of the roof's top, composed of four elliptical arcs.

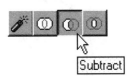

8.16a The Subtract *tool in the* Explode *flyout (R13 only).*

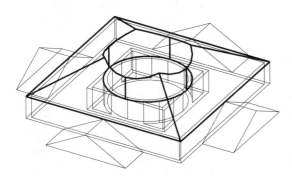

8.16b The resulting solid volume of the roof.

17 Save the model file.

MODELING THE DOME

18 You will model the remaining volume—the dome—by *revolving* one-half of its cross-section profile around a vertical axis to create a solid object (Figure 8.18a).

You will first draw one-half of the dome's cross-section profile as a closed 2D polyline shape. To draw this shape, you will set up a vertical UCS parallel to the front side of the model. In R14, from the *Tools* menu choose *UCS*, then *Preset UCS* (in R13 from the *View* menu choose *UCS Presets*). In the resulting *UCS Orientation* dialog box, choose the *Front* icon tile, select *Relative to Current UCS* option, and click on the *OK* button. The UCS you have just defined is parallel to the front side of the model, and it passes through its middle (Figure 8.18b).

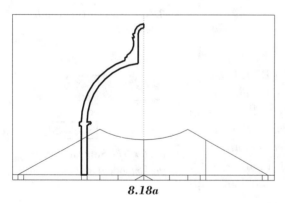

8.18a

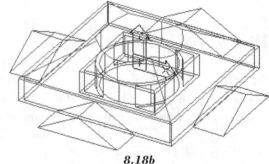

8.18b

8.18a Constructing the dome by revolving a 2D profile around a vertical axis.

8.18b Setting up a front UCS relative to the current UCS.

19 Create a new layer named DOME, assign some color (yellow) to it, and make it the current layer. Leave the layers 2-WALLS and ROOF displayed on the screen. (Make sure that the layer DOME is the current layer.)

20 You will use the front view to draw a fairly complex 2D cross-section profile of the dome. However, the viewport, where the plan view is displayed, is fairly small. To avoid numerous zoom operations, you should display the plan view as a *single viewport* that will cover the entire graphics area.

First save the existing viewport configuration so that you can restore it afterward. From the *View* menu choose *Tiled Viewports*, then *Save.* At the command prompt enter THREE_RIGHT as the *name* for the existing viewport configuration.

Next make the lower left viewport, where the front view is displayed, active. Then from the *View* menu choose *Tiled Viewports*, then *1 Viewport.* The front view will fill the entire graphics area.

21 Zoom in to the area where the cross-section profile will be drawn (see Figure 8.21).

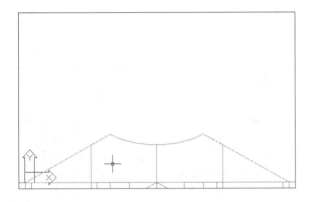

22 Make sure that the snap spacing is set to 6″ [0.15] and that the snap is on.

You will draw one-half of the dome's cross section using several polylines, trim them if necessary, and join them into a single polyline (using the *Polyline Edit* tool or PEDIT command). Use Figures 8.22b, c, and d as a reference, and follow the instructions below.

Use the *dynamic display of coordinates* in the *status bar* (Figure 8.22a) to determine distances as you draw. The coordinates will be displayed as *relative polar* distances from the previously selected point, in this format: *distance < angle.* Enter COORDS at the command prompt, and specify 2 as the new value of this system variable. Then, as you draw, read the distances in the status bar.

Dynamic display of coordinates in the status bar can be used as a *ruler* in AutoCAD to measure distance as you draw. There are three display modes for coordinates. The *static* display (COORDS = 0) updates only when you pick a point. The *dynamic* display (COORDS = 1) changes as you move the cursor. The third mode is the *dynamic* display mode in the form of *distance < angle* (COORDS = 2). Note that you can *toggle,* i.e., change the display modes by pressing the *F6* key or the *Ctrl-D* key combination on the keyboard.

8.21 Zooming in to the area where the cross-section profile will be drawn.

8.22a Dynamic display of coordinates.

| 12′-6″< 90   ,0′-0″ | | | SNAP | GRID | ORTHO | OSNAP | MODEL | TILE |

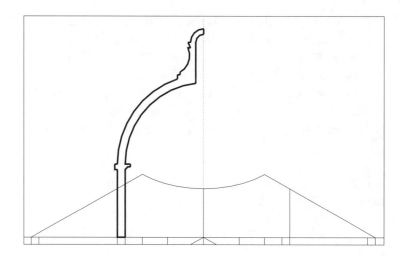

8.22b One-half of the dome's cross-section profile.

Figure 8.22c shows a possible strategy for drawing the profile. (1) Begin by drawing a single polyline object. (Use the dynamic coordinate display to determine distances.) (2) Draw the second polyline. (3) Draw a horizontal and a vertical line, and (4) use them as a reference to draw two arcs. (5) Draw the top of the dome as a single polyline object (see the next paragraph for instructions). Use the *Trim* tool in the *Modify* toolbar to trim arcs and lines; (6) select both arcs and the polyline shape above them as *cutting edges*, press *Enter*, and (7) pick the parts of *objects to be cut* as shown in Figure 8.22c. (8) Delete the two remaining lines, created in step 3. Finally, use the *Polyline Edit* tool (or enter PEDIT at the command prompt) to join these various objects into a single closed polyline shape.

Draw the shape on top of the dome as a single polyline—use Figure 8.22d as a reference. After you draw the first line segment (points 1 and 2), enter A to switch to the *arc* mode, and pick point 3 to draw the arc segment. Then enter L to switch back to the line mode, and pick point 4 to draw the next line segment. To draw the arc segment that follows, enter A (*Arc* mode), followed by D (*Direction*) to set the direction of the arc's tangent, and pick point 5; pick point 6 as the arc's endpoint. Enter L to switch back to the line mode, and pick points 7, 8, and 9 to draw the line segments that follow. Then switch again to the arc mode (enter A), and specify the arc's tangent direction (enter D) by picking point 10. Pick point 11 as the arc's endpoint, switch to the line mode, and

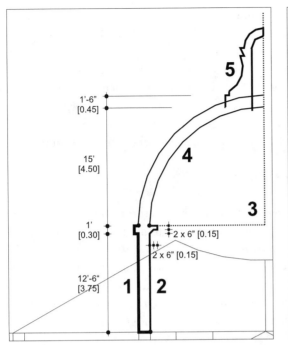

1'-6"
[0.45]

15'
[4.50]

1'
[0.30]

2 x 6" [0.15]

2 x 6" [0.15]

12'-6"
[3.75]

5

4

3

1 2

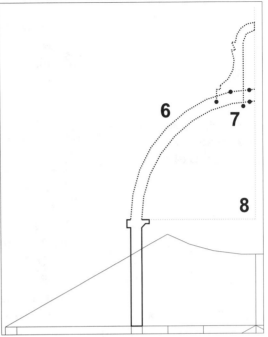

6 7

8

8.22c *A possible drawing strategy for drawing the dome's profile.*

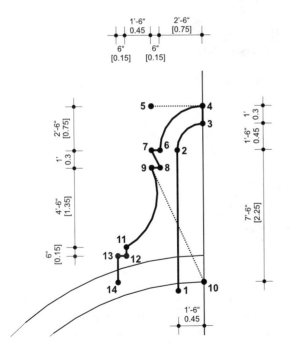

1'-6"
0.45

2'-6"
[0.75]

6"
[0.15]

6"
[0.15]

2'-6"
[0.75]

1'
0.3

4'-6"
[1.35]

6"
[0.15]

5   4

3

7 6   2

9 8

11

13 12

14   1   10

1'-6"
0.45

1'-6" 1'
0.45   0.3

7'-6"
[2.25]

8.22d *Drawing the top of the dome as a single polyline.*

pick points 12, 13, and 14 to draw the remaining line segments. Enter X to end, i.e., to exit the PLINE command.

23 You will now revolve this closed shape around the central vertical axis of the villa to create the solid object for the dome.

Restore the previously saved viewport configuration. From the *View* menu, choose *Tiled Viewports,* then *Restore.* Enter THREE_RIGHT as the name of the configuration to restore.

24 Set the current UCS to *World.*

Note that it is not necessary to set the current UCS to *world* to create revolved solids.

25 From the *Solids* toolbar choose the *Revolve* tool (Figure 8.25a). Select the dome's half-profile as the object to revolve. Enter 0,0 as the *start point of axis* of revolution, and 0,0,1 as the *end point of axis* (note that these two points define a vertical line—a central vertical axis of the villa). Press *Enter* to choose the default angle of revolution (*full circle*). As a result, AutoCAD will produce a solid object of the dome (Figure 8.25b).

8.25a The Revolve *tool.*

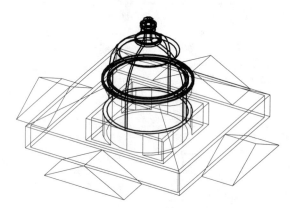

8.25b The revolved solid object of the dome.

26 Save the model file.

COMPLETING THE BASE LEVEL

27 In this section you will *subtract* the interior void volumes at the base level from the main volume, and then subtract the openings from the resulting solid. You will also *union* (add together) the solid volumes of the portico's base and stairs.

Turn on and set the layer 0-WALLS as the current layer. Turn off all other layers.

28 Use the *Subtract* tool from the *Solids* toolbar, and subtract all the interior voids from the main base volume. Select the main base volume in the plan view (Figure 8.28a) as the *solid object to subtract from,* and then press *Enter* to finish the first object selection step. Using the *crossing* selection method select all the interior voids as *solid objects to subtract* (Figure 8.28b).

Note that for *subtraction* you must perform two object selections. The first one defines a set of *solid objects to subtract from,* the second one specifies *solid objects to subtract.*

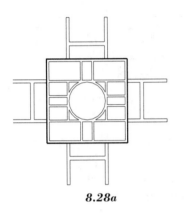

8.28a

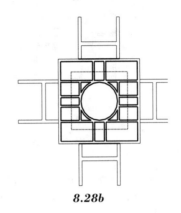

8.28b

8.28a Selecting the main volume as the solid object to subtract from.

8.28b Selecting the interior voids as solid objects to subtract.

29 Subtract the voids underneath the porticoes (Figure 8.29b) from the portico volumes (Figure 8.29a) *one at a time,* i.e., execute the subtraction separately for each portico.

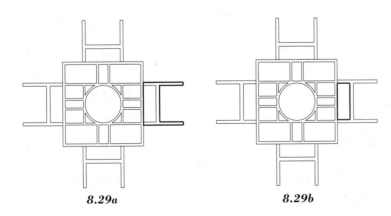

8.29a   8.29b

8.29a The portico's solid volume.

8.29b The void volume underneath the portico.

30 Next you will subtract the openings from the solid "walls." Turn on the layer 0-OPENINGS. (The layer 0-WALLS should remain as the current layer.)

31 First subtract the base openings from the base solid (Figures 8.31a and b).

8.31a *The main base solid as the solid object to subtract from.*

8.31b *The base openings as solid objects to subtract.*

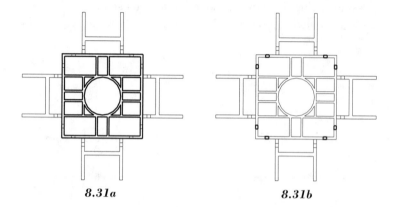

8.31a   *8.31b*

32 Subtract the two openings from the portico's solid object for each portico separately (Figures 8.32a and b).

8.32a *Solid object to subtract from (the portico solid).*

8.32b *Solid objects to sub-tract (openings).*

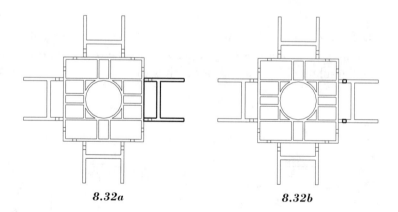

8.32a   *8.32b*

33 Last, you will add the stairs solid to the portico, which is the only remaining step before the base level is completed.
    Turn on the layer 0-STAIRS (the layer 0-WALLS is still the current layer).

34 In R14, from the *Modify* menu choose *Boolean*, then *Union*. In R13, choose the *Union* tool (Figure 8.34) on the *Solids* toolbar. Combine the two solid objects representing the stairs and the portico base into a single solid. Execute the *union* operation for each portico separately.

35 The base level is now completed.

At first, it may look as if nothing changed. Make the axonometric viewport active, and apply the *Zoom All* tool. Then issue the HIDE command.

As you can see, not all the visible lines are displayed. Even though objects, associated with layers that are *turned off*, are not displayed, they are still used by AutoCAD when computing the hidden-line views. To correct this problem, you should *freeze* all the layers that aren't visible.

When you *freeze* a layer, all the objects associated with it become *invisible*. By feezing layers, you also speed up *zoom, pan,* and *viewpoint* operations; improve *object selection* performance; and reduce *regeneration* time for complex drawings and models. Typically, you will freeze layers that you want to remain invisible for some time, or when you want to generate hidden-line views.

Thawing a layer is opposite from freezing. It makes the layer visible again. (Note that you still have to *turn on* a *thawed* layer to *display* its content on the screen; this may sound somewhat confusing, but that's how AutoCAD operates.)

To freeze a layer, click on the *sun* icon in the *Layer Control* drop-down list (Figure 8.35a) in the *Object Properties* toolbar. Note how the icon changes to a "grayed-out" version of the sun (the layer is not getting any "sunlight"—therefore it's frozen). Freeze all the layers that are turned off, and execute the HIDE command again.

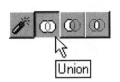

8.34 The Union *tool (R13).*

Instead of applying a subtraction operation to each of the four porticoes, you could model only one, delete the solid objects of the other three, and execute the *polar array* operation to create three additional instances.

In addition to being *turned on* or *off*, *frozen* or *thawed*, layers can also be *locked* or *unlocked*. When you *lock* a layer, you prevent any editing of objects associated with it. Lock the layers that shouldn't change to prevent accidental mistakes.

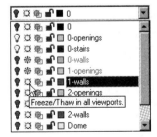

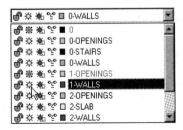

8.35a Freezing *the layers by clicking on the* sun *icons in R14 and R13.*

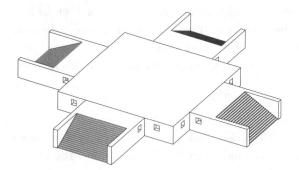

8.35b The "real" openings.

The openings now look like "real" openings (Figure 8.35b). (If you recall, all you got in the previous hidden-line views were rectangular outlines of the openings on the exterior.)

To clearly see the difference, set up a "worm's-eye" axonometric. First save the existing view as STANDARD_AXO (from the *View* menu choose *Named Views*, etc.). Then from the *View* menu choose *3D Viewpoint*, then *Select* (R13 *Rotate*). Enter 300 as *angle from x axis*, and –60 degrees (notice the negative sign) as *angle from xy plane*. Issue the HIDE command. Your viewpoint is underneath the building—note how you can clearly see the ceiling of

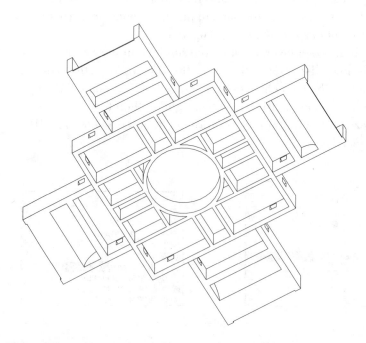

8.35c A "worm's-eye" axonometric of the villa's base.

each "room" (Figure 8.35c). Save this axonometric view as WORMS_EYE_AXO; do not enter the apostrophe character ('), because it's an "illegal" character to be used in layer or view names.

Restore the previously saved view STANDARD_AXO.

36 Save the model file.

COMPLETING THE FIRST LEVEL

37 As in the previous section, in this one you will also *subtract* the interior void volumes from the main volume, and subtract the openings from the resulting solid, but you will do that for the first level. You will also *union* (add together) the end columns and side walls in porticoes.

Thaw, turn on, and set the layer 1-WALLS as the current layer. Freeze all other layers. (There is no need to turn off layers when you freeze them.)

38 Subtract the void volumes from the main volume.

39 In each portico, union the end column and the side wall (Figure 8.39) for each side separately. Zoom in if necessary.

40 Thaw and turn on the layer 1-OPENINGS. (The layer 1-WALLS should remain as the current layer.)

41 First subtract the openings from the main solid (Figures 8.41a and b).

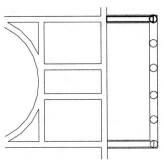

8.39 Combining the end column and the side wall into a single solid object.

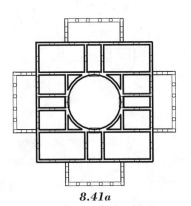

8.41a

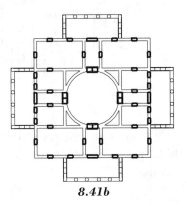

8.41b

8.41a The main solid as the solid object to subtract from.

8.41b Openings to be subtracted.

As in step 34, you could model only one portico, delete the solid objects of the other three, and execute the *polar array* operation to create three additional instances.

42 Subtract the arched opening from the portico's side wall for each side separately (Figures 8.42a and b).

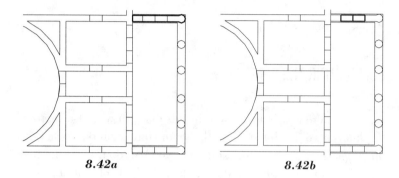

8.42a *Solid object to subtract from (the portico's side wall).*

8.42b *Solid object to subtract (the arched opening).*

8.42a   8.42b

43 The first level is now completed.

Make active the axonometric view and issue the HIDE command. Compare the result with Figure 8.43a (note that curved surfaces will be *faceted* in your view).

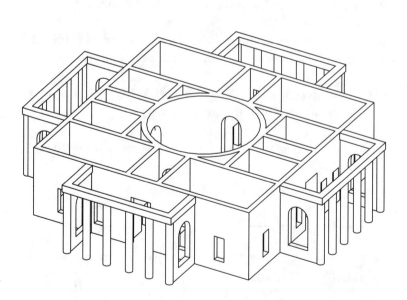

8.43a *The first level of the villa.*

Restore the view WORMS_EYE_AXO and create another hidden-line axonometric view. Compare the result with Figure 8.43b.

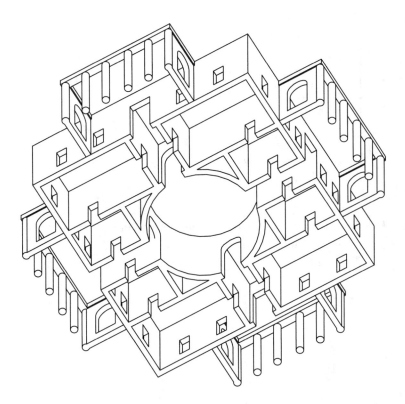

8.43b A worm's-eye view of the villa's first level.

Restore the view STANDARD_AXO.

44 Save the model file.

COMPLETING THE SECOND LEVEL

45 On the second level, you will first subtract voids in the slab, and then subtract interior void volumes and openings from the main volume.

Turn on, thaw, and set the layer 2-SLAB as the current layer. Freeze all other layers.

46 Subtract voids from the slab (Figures 8.46a and b). The slab is completed.

47 Turn on, thaw, and set the layer 2-WALLS as the current layer. Freeze all other layers.

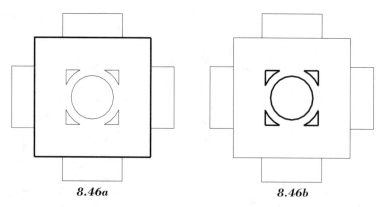

8.46a *Solid object to subtract from (the slab's solid volume).*

8.46b *Solid objects to subtract (the voids).*

8.46a   **8.46b**

48 First subtract the inner volume from the main volume to create the exterior wall (Figures 8.48a and b).

Then subtract the central cylindrical and stairwell volumes

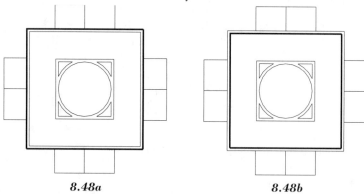

8.48a *Solid object to subtract from (the exterior volume).*

8.48b *Solid object to subtract (the inner void).*

8.48a   **8.48b**

from the inner volume bounding the central space (Figures 8.48c and d).

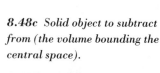

8.48c *Solid object to subtract from (the volume bounding the central space).*

8.48d *Solid objects to subtract (the cylindrical and stairwell volumes).*

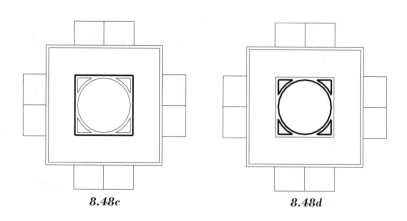

8.48c   **8.48d**

49 Turn on and thaw the layer 2-OPENINGS. (The layer 2-WALLS should still be set as the current layer.)

50 Subtract openings from the main solid (Figures 8.50a and b).

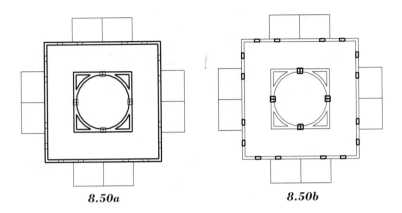

8.50a

8.50b

8.50a Solid object to subtract from (the main solid).

8.50b Solid objects to subtract (the openings).

51 The second level is now completed too—actually, the entire model is now finished!

Verify that everything was done as described in this section. Make the axonometric view active, and issue the HIDE command. Compare the result with Figure 8.51 (note that curved surfaces will be *faceted* in your view).

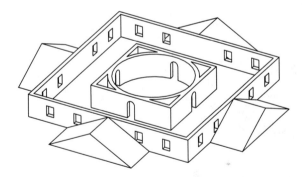

8.51 The second level of the villa.

52 Let's have a look at the entire model. Turn on and thaw all layers except the layer GRID, and set the layer 0 as the current layer.

Create a hidden-line elevation view in the lower left viewport, and compare the resulting image with Figure 8.52a. (Note that the curved surfaces will be *faceted* in your view.)

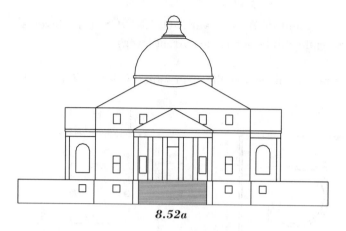

8.52a *The front elevation.*

8.52a

Also create a hidden-line axonometric view of the entire building, and compare it with Figure 8.52b.

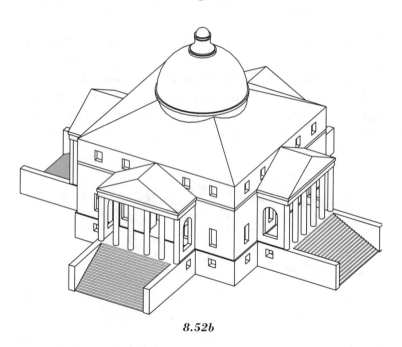

8.52b *A hidden-line axono-metric view of the completed model of Villa Rotonda.*

8.52b

53 Save the model file.

You can restore some of the views we have saved previously and create additional hidden-line images if you wish.

If you do not want to continue at this point, choose *Exit* from the *File* menu.

Now that the model is completed, you can generate different representations of the building's geometry, as you will do in the following exercise.

In the next chapter you will also learn how to "section" and "slice" a model, and how to create various representations of the building, such as "exploded" axonometric and perspective views.

9

MODELING TUTORIAL 4: VIEWING

In this tutorial exercise, you will generate different representations of the villa's geometry. You will learn how to turn 3D hidden-line views into 2D drawings you can edit, how to create "exploded" views, and how to "section" and "slice" the model.

CREATING A 2D DRAWING FROM AN AXONOMETRIC VIEW

1 In this section you will save a 3D hidden-line view as a 2D drawing that can be further edited. You will learn how to set up a "floating" viewport in "paper space" and how to use the SOL-PROF command to generate hidden-line profiles of solid objects.

   If you exited AutoCAD at the end of the previous exercise, start it again, and open the model file (Rotonda.dwg).

2 If the model consists of solid objects only, a far more effective way to generate hidden-line views in R13 is to use the SOLPROF command (or in R14 the *Setup Profile* tool on the *Solids* toolbar), which creates profile images of three-dimensional solid objects. Unlike the HIDE command, which *facets* curved surfaces of solid objects, this command displays only edges and silhouettes for the current view (see Figure 9.7b).

   Begin by making the right viewport active (the one with the axonometric view); from the *View* menu choose *Tiled Viewports*, then *1 Viewport*.

3 Before you can use the SOLPROF command, you have to set up a *floating viewport* in *paper space* (both of these concepts will be explained later). Choose *Model Space [Floating]* from the *View* menu, and enter F (*Fit* option) at the command prompt.

4 Change the axonometric views slightly. From the *View* menu choose *3D Viewpoint,* then *Select* (R13 *Rotate*). Enter 300 as *angle from x axis,* and 45 as *angle from xy plane.*

Zoom in so that the building fills the graphics area.

5 Set up a UCS that is aligned with the viewing plane. From the *Tools* (R13 *View*) menu choose *UCS* (R13 *Set UCS*), then *View.*

6 If you are using R14, choose the *Setup Profile* tool on the *Solids* toolbar (Figure 9.6a). If you are using R13, enter SOL-PROF at the command prompt.

9.6a The Setup Profile *tool (R14).*

Select all the displayed solid objects. Press *Enter* to select the default choice (Y—Yes) when prompted whether to *display hidden profile lines on separate layer* (if you enter N, AutoCAD treats all profile lines as visible, i.e., there will be no hidden lines). Press *Enter* again to select Y (Yes) when prompted whether to *project profile lines onto a plane* (if you enter N, AutoCAD will create profile lines with 3D instead of 2D objects). Finally, press *Enter* again to enter Y when prompted whether to *delete tangential edges* (a tangential edge is the transition line between two tangent faces).

The SOLPROF command will create two *blocks:* one for the visible lines and one for the hidden lines. Both blocks are placed on uniquely named layers using the following naming convention:

PV-*viewport handle* (e.g., PV-2A)	Visible profile layer
PH-*viewport handle* (e.g., PH-2A)	Hidden profile layer

A tangential edge is the imaginary edge at which two tangent faces meet. For example, if you fillet the edge of a solid box, tangential edges are created where the cylindrical face of the fillet blends into the planar faces of the box.

For example, if you create a profile in a viewport whose handle is 2A, the blocks containing the visible lines are placed on layer PV-2A, and the block containing the hidden lines (if requested) is inserted on layer PH-2A. (If these layers do not exist, the SOL-PROF command will create them. If they exist, the blocks will be added to the information that is already there.)

To see the results of the SOLPROF command, set the newly created layer PV-*xx* (where *xx* denotes the viewport handle) as the current layer, and turn off all other layers.

Notice how the curved surfaces (such as the dome and columns) are represented only by their silhouettes (Figure 9.6b). (You may want to turn off the display of the UCS icon.)

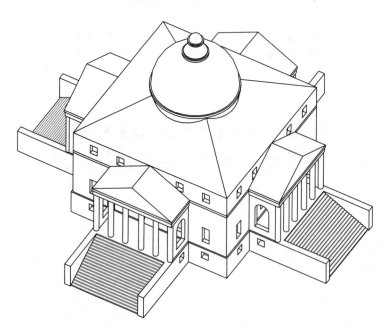

9.6b A hidden-line axonometric view generated by the SOLPROF command.

7 Since the SOLPROF command creates 2D objects, you can further edit them. You can delete unwanted lines, add additional elements, or make other changes.

Before you edit the objects, you must *explode* the block that contains all the visible lines. Choose the *Explode* tool (Figure 9.7a) on the *Modify* toolbar (or enter EXPLODE), and select any part of the displayed drawing. The EXPLODE command will decompose the block into individual 2D objects, such as lines or ellipses.

Choose the *Erase* tool on the *Modify* toolbar, and delete lines that represent the second-floor slab, and joint lines between porticoes and the base (see Figure 9.7b).

9.7a *The* Explode *tool.*

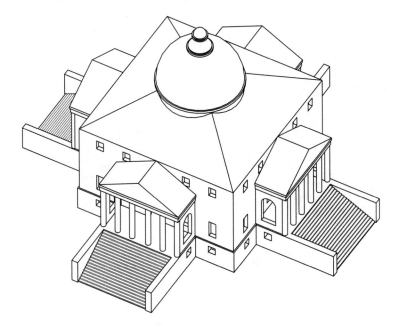

9.7b *The unwanted lines can be erased.*

You can further enhance the drawing by changing the color of selected lines or other 2D objects to plot or print them with different line widths. For example, the building's outline can be plotted with a thicker line, the steps with a thinner line, and so on (Figure 9.7c).

Select objects whose color you want to change. Choose the *Properties* tool (Figure 9.7d) on the *Object Properties* toolbar, click *Color,* and select the new color for the selected objects.

You can display additional information, such as plan layout, in an axonometric drawing (Figure 9.7e). For example, you can apply the SOLPROF command to a main volume solid on the first level (layer 1-WALLS), and change the line type of the resulting block object to dashed or dotted (another technique is to simply change the color and then plot that color with a different line type).

8 Save the model file under a different name, such as Temp.dwg; do not save it as Rotonda.dwg, because you will need that file unchanged for the rendering tutorial exercises.

Using the *Properties* tool, you can also change objects' line type. For example, you can assign *dotted* or *dashed* line type to hidden lines.

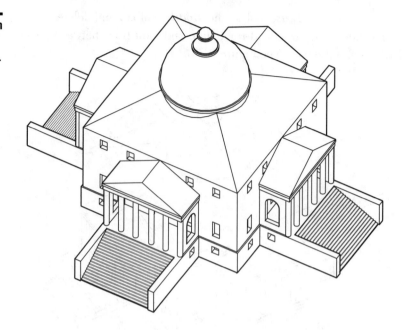

9.7c *The drawing can be further enhanced by changing the line widths of selected objects.*

9.7d *The* Properties *tool.*

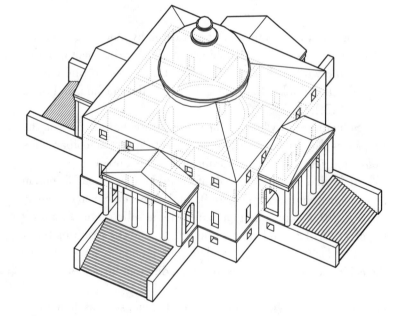

9.7e *Adding the plan layout of the first level to the axonometric drawing.*

CREATING A PLAN OBLIQUE VIEW OF THE MODEL

9 AutoCAD does not support the *oblique* projection. You can, however, create such views (Figure 9.11) from axonometric projections by *copying* 2D objects via *clipboard* to a new drawing file and *pasting* them with different x and y scale factors into a *new* drawing file.

From the *Edit* menu, choose *Copy,* and select all the 2D objects representing visible lines in the axonometric projection that was created previously.

The *clipboard* is a feature provided by the operating system software. It permits you to temporarily store a copy of selected objects before you paste them in another location or into another document.

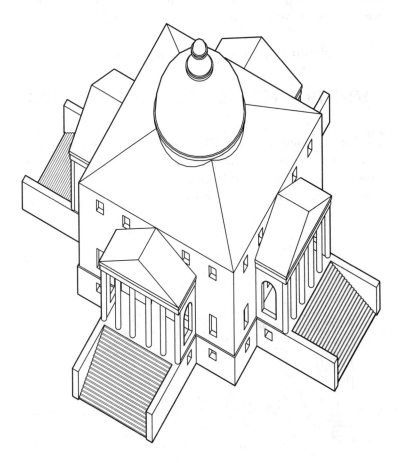

9.11 A plan oblique *view of the model.*

10 Create a new drawing file. From the *File* menu choose *New.* Don't save the changes to the existing file when AutoCAD prompts you to do so (click *No*).

11 *Paste* the previously copied objects into the new drawing. From the *Edit* menu choose *Paste*. Enter 0,0 when prompted for the *insertion point*. Enter 1 as *x scale factor,* and enter 1.41414141 as *y scale factor;* enter 0 as *rotation angle*.

The objects will be pasted as a single *block* object. Choose the *Zoom All* tool to display the *plan oblique* drawing in the graphic area (Figure 9.11).

This is a "true" plan oblique projection. The angle between the front and the right side of the building is 90 degrees; the angle between the horizontal lines of the front and right facades and the horizontal edge of the graphics area are 30 and 60 degrees, respectively.

12 Save the drawing file as Oblique.dwg.

CREATING 2D DRAWINGS FROM PERSPECTIVE PROJECTIONS

13 Unfortunately, the SOLPROF command cannot project visible and hidden lines onto the viewing plane in *perspective* projections. The best it can do is place 2D objects in 3D space as if you were creating an axonometric projection (Figure 9.13).

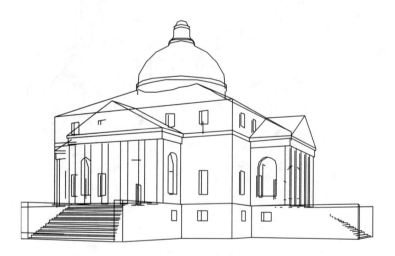

9.13 A hidden-line perspective view produced by the SOLPROF command.

There is a way, however, to produce 2D drawings from perspective projections. You can create a *plot file* of a hidden-line perspective view in the *Drawing Exchange Binary* (DXB) format and import that file into a new drawing file. Before you can actually perform that step, you will have to first configure AutoCAD to produce a DXB file when you print a drawing. This section will show you how to configure the *DXB file output,* how to plot to a DXB file, and how to import the created file back into AutoCAD.

Note that a 2D perspective drawing produced by this procedure will have one major shortcoming: all curved surfaces will be *faceted* and you will have to painstakingly delete the extraneous lines (see Figures 9.18 and 19).

Start by reopening the model file Rotonda.dwg.

14 First create a new "plotter" configuration that will define the *DXB file output.*

In R14:

1. From the *Tools* menu, choose *Preferences.*
2. In the *Preferences* dialog box, choose the *Printer* tab.
3. On the *Printer* tab, choose *New.*
4. Select *AutoCAD DXB file output format (pre-4.1)—by Autodesk, Inc.*
5. Enter a description—*DXB File Output*—in the *Add a Description* box. Then choose *OK.* The AutoCAD *text window* will appear, and several prompts will be displayed.

In R13, from the *Options* menu, choose *Configure.* The AutoCAD *text window* will appear.

1. Press *Enter* (or *Return*) to continue if instructed to do so by AutoCAD.
2. Enter 5 to select plotter configuration in the *Configuration Menu.*
3. Enter 1 to *add a plotter configuration.*
4. Enter 2 to select *AutoCAD file output formats (pre-4.1)—by Autodesk, Inc.*
5. Enter 2 to select *AutoCAD DXB file.*

The prompts that follow are identical for R14 and R13:

6. *Maximum horizontal (X) plot size in drawing units? <11.0000>:*—Enter 10.

You can also print to a file in *Postscript* format. However, this can often result in rather crude approximation of curves. The DXB file output produces better results.

7. *Plotter steps per drawing unit <1000.0000>:*—Press *Enter.*

8. *Maximum vertical (Y) plot size in drawing units? <8.5000>:*—Enter 10.

After you make these selections, AutoCAD will display the default settings for various plotting parameters, with the following prompt at the end:

9. *Do you want to change anything? (No/Yes/File) <N>—* Enter Y.

The default pen assignments will be displayed in the text window. Don't change any of those—therefore, at the prompt:

10. *Do you want to change any of the above parameters? <N>*—Press *Enter.*

11. *Would you like to calibrate your plotter? <N>*—Press *Enter.*

12. *Select degree of pen motion optimization, 0 or 1 <1>:*— Press *Enter.*

13. *Size units (Inches or Millimeters) <I>:*—Choose either, and enter I or M.

14. *Plot origin in Inches [or Millimeters] <0.00,0.00>:*— Press *Enter.*

Standard values for plotting sizes will be displayed next. At the prompt:

15. *Enter the Size or Width, Height (in Inches [or Millimeters]) <MAX>*—Press *Enter.*

16. *Rotate plot clockwise 0/90/180/270 degrees <0>:*—Press *Enter.*

17. *Adjust area fill boundaries for pen width? <N>*—Press *Enter.*

18. *Remove hidden lines? <N>*—Enter Y.

19. *Plotted Inches [or Millimeters] = Drawing Units or Fit or ? <F>:*—Press *Enter.*

20. If you are using R13, AutoCAD will ask you to *enter a description for this plotter.* Enter *DXB File Output.*

21. (R13) Enter 0 to *exit to configuration menu.*
22. (R13) Enter 0 to *exit to drawing editor.*
23. (R13) Press *Enter* to *keep configuration changes.*

The *DXB file output* plotter configuration is completed. (In R14, click *OK* to continue.)

15 Make the right viewport active (the one with the axonometric view), and restore a two-point perspective view (TWO_POINT_PERSPECTIVE), saved in one of the previous exercises. From the *View* menu choose *Named Views,* click TWO_POINT_PERSPECTIVE, click *Restore,* and click *OK* to continue.

16 Now print this perspective view to a DXB file. Choose *Print* from the *File* menu.

1. In the *Print/Plot Configuration* dialog box (Figure 9.16), click *Device and Default Selection,* and select the previously created configuration, the *DXB File Output.*

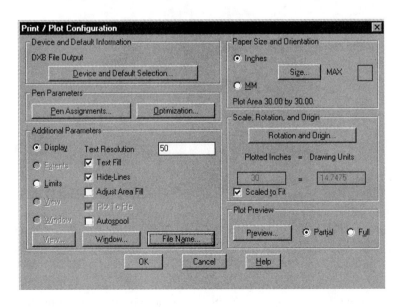

9.16 Entering the print parameters.

2. Select *Display* as the area to print.
3. Place a *check mark* in the box labeled *Hide-Lines* (if it is not already there).

4. Click on *File Name,* select a folder where the file should be saved, and enter the output file's name (for example, *2PtPersp.dxb*). Click *Save* to continue.
5. Place a *check mark* in the check box labeled *Scaled to Fit* (if it is not already there).
6. Click *OK* to complete. AutoCAD will create the specified file.

17 Open a new drawing file. Don't save the drawing changes when prompted to do so by AutoCAD.

18 Insert the previously saved DXB file into a new drawing. In R14, from the *Insert* menu choose *Drawing Exchange Binary;* in R13, enter DXBIN at the command prompt. In the *Select DXB File* dialog box, select the previously created DXB file. Click *Open.*

The hidden-line perspective view will be imported. Choose the *Zoom Extents* tool, or enter Z (*Zoom*) at the command prompt, followed by E (*Extents*), to see the entire drawing (Figure 9.18).

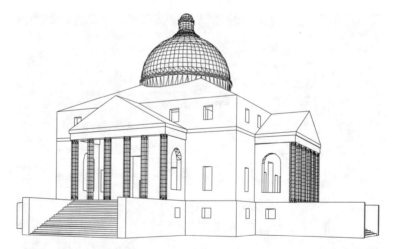

9.18 A hidden-line perspective view with faceted curved surfaces.

19 "Clean" the drawing. Use the *Erase* tool and delete the extraneous lines. Figure 9.19 shows the edited version of the drawing, without unneeded lines.

20 Save this drawing file as *2PtPersp.dwg.*

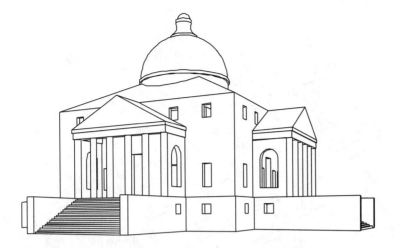

9.19 The "cleaned" version of the perspective.

CREATING AN EXPLODED VIEW

21 The model you have created was carefully structured. The various levels of the villa were subdivided into different layers, and the porticoes were not added to the main volume; that structure was in large part introduced to facilitate construction of the various elements of the building's geometry.

Such structure, however, was also introduced to facilitate manipulation of the completed model. For example, you can easily create hidden-line drawings showing the plan layout of the various building levels by simply turning off or freezing the appropriate layers (Figure 9.21). You can also create the so-called exploded views by moving various elements in space (see Figure 9.36). How you structure your model will in large part determine the kinds of representations you can generate.

Start by reopening the model file Rotonda.dwg.

22 First vertically split apart the various levels of the villa by moving objects on the corresponding layers up in space. Make the lower left viewport active, and display it as a single viewport in the graphics area.

23 Make sure that WCS (world) is the current UCS. Choose the *Move* tool on the *Modify* toolbar, and select solid objects on layers ROOF and DOME. Enter the displacement of 0,0,350′ [0,0,105]. The objects will shift up in space. Use the *Move* tool again, and

An appropriate model structure is particularly important for rendering. If different materials are to be applied to surfaces of a single object, that object should be split into separate objects *before* rendering.

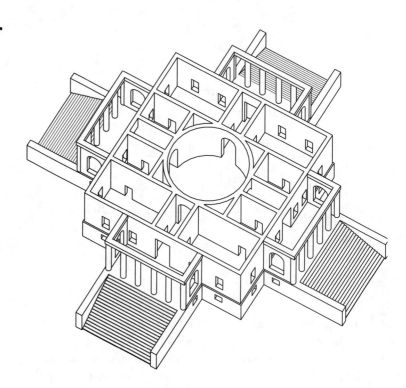

9.21 *The plan layout of Villa Rotonda.*

displace objects on the second level (layers 2-WALLS and 2-SLAB) by 0,0,180′ [0,0,54].

24 Now that you have displaced the objects, set up an axonometric view: Enter 300 as the angle *from x axis,* and enter 60 as the angle *from xy plane.*

25 As in step 3, you must set up a *floating viewport* in *paper space* before you can use the SOLPROF command. Choose *Model Space* [*Floating*] from the *View* menu, and enter F (*Fit* option) at the command prompt.

You can use the MVIEW command to set up multiple viewports in paper space.

26 Set a UCS aligned with the viewing plane. From the *Tools* (R13 *View*) menu choose *UCS* (R13 *Set UCS*), then *View.*

27 If you are using R14, choose the *Setup Profile* tool on the *Solids* toolbar. If you are using R13, enter SOLPROF at the command prompt. Select all the displayed solid objects. Press *Enter* at each prompt to select the default choices.

28 To see the results of the SOLPROF command, set the newly created layer PV-*xx*, which contains the visible lines, as the current layer, and turn off all other layers.

29 Save this hidden-line view as a separate drawing file.

First copy the visible lines to the clipboard. From the *Edit* menu, choose *Copy*, and select all the 2D objects representing the visible lines in the axonometric projection that was created previously.

30 Create a new drawing file. From the *File* menu choose *New*; don't save the changes to the existing file when AutoCAD prompts you to do so (click *No*).

31 *Paste* the previously copied objects into the new drawing. From the *Edit* menu choose *Paste*. Enter 0,0 when prompted for the *insertion point*. Enter 1 for both *x* and *y scale factors;* enter 0 as the rotation angle.

32 Choose the *Zoom All* tool to display the entire drawing in the graphics area.

33 Apply the *Explode* tool twice to the imported objects.

34 Using the *Line* tool add the "guide" lines, and trim them using the *Trim* tool where they are not visible (see Figure 9.36).

35 Assign a *dotted* line type to the "guide" lines. First load the *Dot* line type definition into the drawing: from the *Format* (R13 *Data*) menu, choose *Linetype*. Click *Load*, select *Dot* from the list, and click *OK*. Enter 100 [2.5] as the *object scale factor* (in R14, click on *Detail* first to specify this parameter), and click *OK*.

36 Select the *Properties* tool on the *Object Properties* toolbar, and select the "guide" lines. Click *Linetype*, select *Dot* from the list, and click *OK*. The guide lines should appear as dotted (Figure 9.36). If not, zoom in to one of them, and issue the REGEN command to regenerate the drawing display.

37 Save the drawing file as Exploded.dwg.

The SOLPROF command groups all visible lines into a single *block* object. When you use clipboard to *copy* and *paste*, AutoCAD creates another block from the selected entities. That's why you have to apply the *Explode* tool twice: the first time to explode the block created by the copy and paste procedure, and the second time to explode the block created by the SOLPROF command.

Use the LTSCALE command to adjust the *global scale factor* for the line type definitions.

You can create the same "exploded" view by generating three separate hidden-line drawings and combining them into a

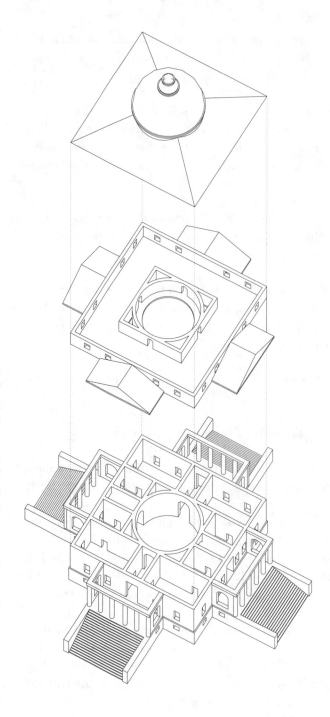

9.36 *An "exploded" hidden-line view of the villa.*

CREATING A 2D SECTION

38 In this part of the exercise you will learn how to create 2D sections through solid objects.

Start by reopening the model file Rotonda.dwg.

39 Create a new layer named SECTION, assign blue color to it, and make it the current layer.

40 Set the current UCS to a *front* UCS. In R14, from the *Tools* menu choose *UCS*, then *Preset UCS;* in R13, from the *View* menu choose *UCS Presets*. Choose the *Front* icon tile, and click *OK*. The UCS you have just defined is vertical, parallel to the front side of the model, and passes through the center of the villa.

41 To create a 2D section through the middle of the villa, use the *Section* tool (Figure 9.41a) on the *Solids* toolbar, or enter SECTION at the command prompt. This command uses the intersection of a selected plane and solid objects to create *regions* on the current layer; selecting several solids creates separate regions for each solid.

In the plan view, select solids along the "east-west" (right-left) axis using the *crossing* selection method (Figure 9.41b).

9.41a The Section *tool.*

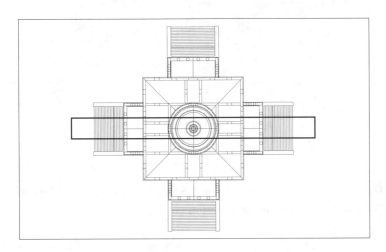

9.41b Selecting the solids for sectioning.

Enter *xy* when prompted for the section plane in order to use the *xy* plane of the current UCS. Press *Enter* to locate the sectioning plane at the origin of the UCS (0,0,0). AutoCAD will draw the 2D section outlines on that plane (Figure 9.41c).

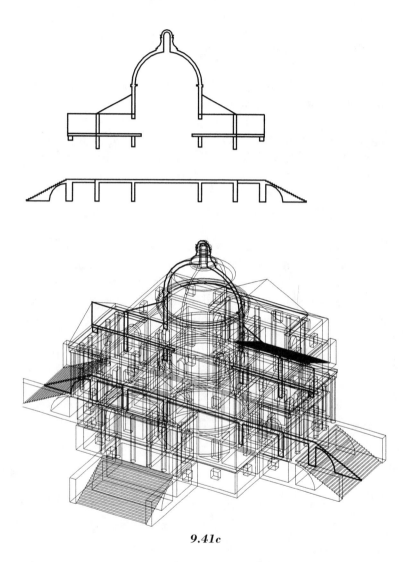

9.41c A 2D section through the middle of the villa.

9.41c

42 Turn off all the layers except SECTION (the current layer). You should see only the 2D section outlines.

43 You will now add a *hatch* pattern to the section outlines. Create a new layer named HATCH, assign cyan color to it, and set it as the current layer.

44 Choose the *Hatch* tool (Figure 9.44a) on the *Draw* toolbar. In the *Boundary Hatch* dialog box (Figure 9.44b) click *Pattern,* and select *ANSI31* from the list in the *Hatch Pattern Palette* dialog box (figure 9.44c) or from the drop-down list if you are using R13. Click *OK* to continue.

9.44a The Hatch *tool.*

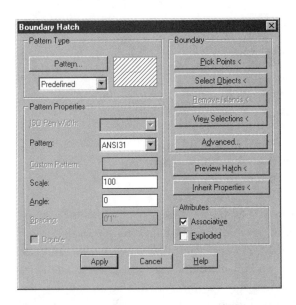

9.44b The Boundary Hatch *dialog box.*

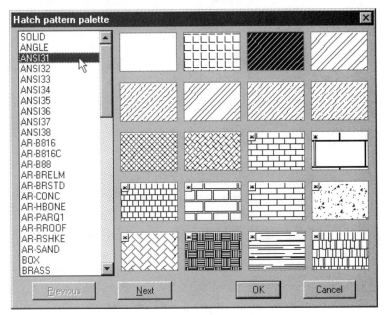

9.44c The Hatch Pattern Palette *dialog box (R14).*

Click *Select Objects,* and select all the section outlines. The dialog box will disappear so you can select the objects. It will reappear once you complete the object selection (Figure 9.44b). Enter 100 [2.5] as the *scale* factor, and click *Apply* to hatch the selected outlines (Figure 9.44d).

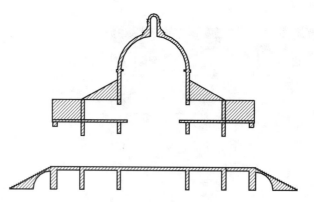

9.44d The hatched *section outlines.*

Note that according to the conventions of architectural drafting, you should also draw (display) what is visible in the cross-section view. To do that, you should *slice* the model into two halves, retain only one of them, and create a hidden-line front view. Then simply redisplay the cross-section layer, and the section drawing will be complete (see Figure 9.49). (You will learn how to *slice* a 3D model in the next section.)

45 Save this model file as Section.dwg.

CREATING A SECTIONAL PERSPECTIVE

46 In this section you will learn how to *slice* a 3D solid model, and how to create a *sectional perspective* view.

First turn on all layers, then turn off layers GRID, SECTION, and HATCH. Set the layer 0 as the current layer.

47 To slice the model, choose the *Slice* tool (Figure 9.47a) on the *Solids* toolbar, or enter SLICE at the command prompt. Select the entire model when prompted to select objects. Enter XY to use the *xy* plane of the current UCS as a *slicing plane,* and press *Enter* to select 0,0,0 as a point on the slicing plane.

As a result of the SLICE command, two solid objects will be created on each side of the slicing plane. You can retain both halves of the sliced solids or just the half you specify. (Note that sliced solids retain the layer and color properties of the original solid objects.)

You will retain only one half of the villa's model, so pick some point in the back of the building (for example, a corner of the roof), using *endpoint* object snap mode, to identify the half that should remain.

All the solid objects that intersect the *xy* plane of the current UCS will be sliced; those that don't will remain. Therefore, use the *Erase* tool to delete the remaining solid objects in the discarded half (use the plan view).

Save the model file, and then create a hidden-line axonometric view of the sliced model (Figure 9.47b), by using either HIDE or SOLPROF commands.

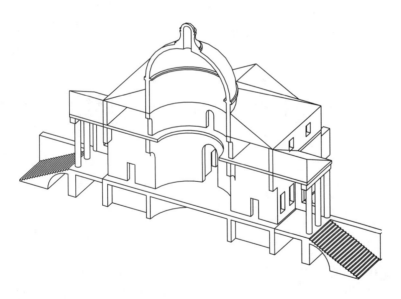

9.47a *The* Slice *tool.*

9.47b *The* sliced *model.*

48 Turn on layers SECTION and HATCH to further emphasize the sectioning of the model (Figure 9.48).

49 To create a "true" cross-section drawing of the model (Figure 9.49), select the front view, and reissue the HIDE or SOLPROF command.

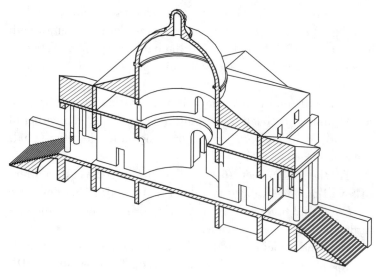

9.48 *A hatched sectional view
of the model.*

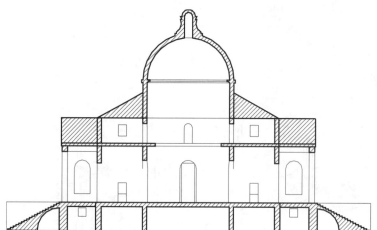

9.49 *The cross-section drawing of the villa.*

**You can create a hidden-line
view as one of the options of the
DVIEW command.**

50 Once the model is sliced, creating a sectional perspective is
a straightforward process. Make the right viewport active, showing the axonometric view, and use the DVIEW command, or
choose *3D Dynamic View* from the *View* menu, to set up a perspective. Select the entire model, and change the *distance* and
zoom parameters. Exit the DVIEW command, and issue the
HIDE command (Figure 9.50).

Alternatively, you can set up a frontal perspective view.
Make active the lower left viewport with a front view, and then set

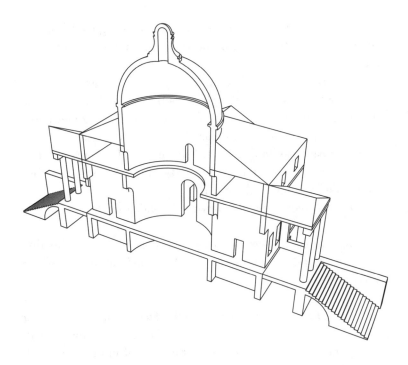

9.50 *A sectional perspective view.*

up a perspective view with appropriate parameters (distance, zoom, etc.).

LAYING OUT MULTIPLE VIEWS IN PAPER SPACE

51 AutoCAD provides two commands, SOLVIEW and SOL-DRAW, that automate the creation and layout of multiple hidden-line and sectional views. Specifically, SOLVIEW guides you through the process of creating orthographic and sectional views, and calculates and saves the view-specific information with each created viewport. That information is used by the SOLDRAW command to generate solid profiles and sections in the views. To use these commands, you must work in *paper space* (so far, you've worked exclusively in *model space*).

AutoCAD operates in either *model* or *paper* space. You work in paper space to lay out the drawing for printing. In paper space, you create *floating viewport objects* that contain different views of the model, i.e., the model space. (*Floating* viewports differ from *tiled* viewports, which split the screen into fixed model space

Note that because floating viewports are treated as objects, you cannot edit the model in paper space. To access the model in a floating viewport, you must toggle from paper to model space.

In *floating* viewports, the editing and view-changing capabilities are almost the same as in *tiled* viewports (the ones you have used so far). You have, however, more control over the individual views. For example, you can freeze or turn off layers in some viewports without affecting others. You can turn an entire viewport display on or off. You can also align views between viewports and scale the views relative to the overall layout.

views.) By switching from paper space to floating model space, you can still edit the model in the views within the floating viewports.

The first time you switch to paper space, the graphics area becomes a blank space that represents the "paper" on which you arrange multiple views of the model space as floating viewports. Floating viewports are treated as objects that you can move and resize to create a suitable layout. You can also draw objects, such as title blocks or annotations, directly in the paper space view without affecting the model itself.

Begin by reopening the drawing Rotonda.dwg.

52 You will set up the front elevation view in the first floating viewport. Therefore, set the current UCS to *Front* (use the *UCS presets*).

53 Switch to the *paper space*. From the *View* menu choose *Paper Space*. The graphics area will become blank, and AutoCAD will display the paper space UCS icon (Figure 9.53) in the lower left corner of the graphics area.

54 Set the limits of the paper space. From the *Format* (R13 *Data*) menu choose *Drawing Limits*. Press *Enter* to locate the lower left corner at 0,0. Enter 8.5″,11″ (letter size) [0.21,0.297 (A4 size)] as the coordinates of the upper left corner.

55 Set the grid spacing to 0.5″ [0.01], and snap spacing to 0.25″ [0.005]. Choose the *Zoom All* tool to see the entire paper space area.

56 In R14, choose the *Setup View* tool (Figure 9.56a) on the *Solids* toolbar, or if you are using R13, enter SOLVIEW at the command prompt.

The SOLVIEW command will prompt you to select one of its five options: *Ucs/Ortho/Auxiliary/Section/<eXit>*. Enter U (the *Ucs* option) to create a viewport that will contain a profile view relative to the user coordinate system currently active in the model space (which in this case is the *Front* UCS). The viewport projection will be created parallel to the *xy* plane of the UCS with the *x* axis pointing to the right and the *y* axis upward. The UCS

9.53 The paper space *UCS icon.*

You can switch between paper and model space by double-clicking the MSPACE or PSPACE box in the status bar. MSPACE will be displayed when you are working in paper space, and PSPACE.

9.56a The Setup View *tool.*

option will present four suboptions. Press *Enter* to select the *Current* option.

Enter 0.002 (1:500 scale) as the *view scale*. Enter 4.25″,1.75″ [0.105,0.05] as coordinates of the *view center*, and press *Enter* to confirm its location. (Note that you can relocate the view center; press *Enter* once you are satisfied with its location.) Set the viewport *clip corners* as shown in Figure 9.56b. Enter FRONT as *view name*.

If no viewports exist in your drawing, the UCS option is a good way to create an initial viewport from which other views can be created. All other SOLVIEW options require an existing viewport.

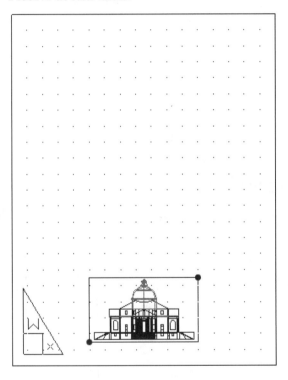

9.56b Setting up clip corners of the floating viewport showing the front elevation.

The SOLVIEW command prompt will reappear. This time enter S to select the *Section* option, and create a horizontal cross section (the plan view) through the model. Pick two points to specify the *cutting plane*, as shown in Figure 9.56c; use *Ortho* mode (press *F8*, or double-click *ORTHO* on the status bar) to specify a horizontal line. Make sure that the line cuts through all the openings. Pick a point near the top of the dome to specify *side to view from*. Enter 0.002 as *view scale*. Enter 4.25,4.5 [0.105,0.12] as coordinates of the *view center*, and press *Enter* to confirm its location. Pick the clip corners as shown in Figure 9.56d. Enter PLAN as *view name*.

9.56c *Setting up the horizontal cutting plane.*

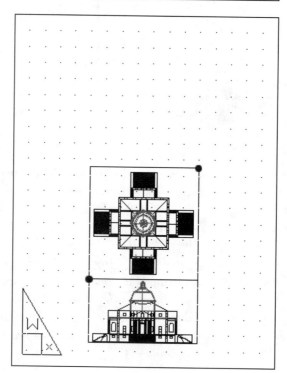

9.56d *Setting up clip corners of the floating viewport showing the plan view.*

The SOLVIEW command prompt will again reappear. This time enter O to select the *Ortho* option, and create a right-side elevation view. Pick the *midpoint* of the plan viewport's right side as the *side of viewport to project,* as shown in Figure 9.56e. Enter 7″,4.5″ [0.175,0.12] as coordinates of the *view center.* Set the clip corners as shown in Figure 9.56f. Enter RIGHT as *view name.*

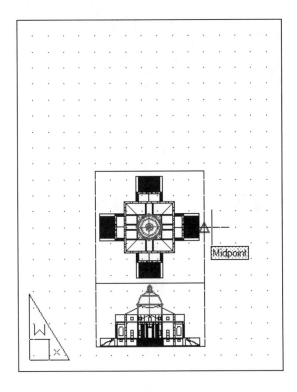

9.56e *Picking the right side of the viewport as the side to project.*

Again the SOLVIEW command prompt will appear. This time enter S to create a vertical cross section through the model. Click inside the plan viewport to make it active, and pick two points to specify the *cutting plane* through the middle of the building, as shown in Figure 9.56g. Use *Ortho* mode (press *F8*, or double-click *ORTHO* on the status bar) to specify a vertical line. Pick a point on the left side of the plan view to specify *side to view from.* Enter 0.002 as *view scale.* Enter 1.5,4.5 [0.035,0.12] as coordinates of the *view center,* and press *Enter* to confirm its location. Pick the clip corners as shown in Figure 9.56h. Enter SECTION as *view name.*

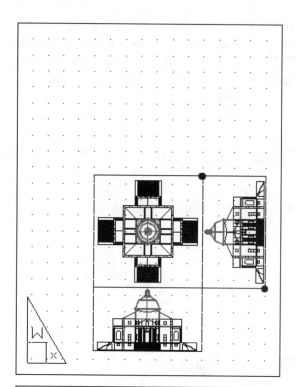

9.56f Setting up clip corners
of the floating viewport showing the right elevation.

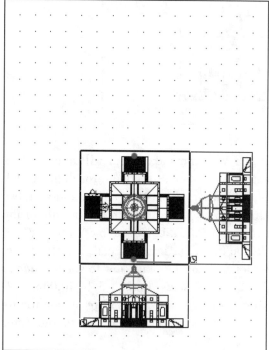

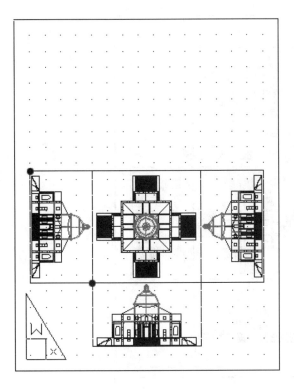

When the SOLVIEW command prompt reappears, enter U (the *Ucs* option) to create a viewport that will contain an axonometric view. Press *Enter* to select the *Current* option. Enter 0.002 as the *view scale.* Enter 4.25″,8.25″ [0.105,0.21] as coordinates of the *view center,* and press *Enter* to confirm its location. (AutoCAD will display a front elevation view sideways—you will set up an axonometric view later.) Set the viewport *clip corners* as shown in Figure 9.56i. Enter AXO as *view name.*

Enter X to exit the SOLVIEW command.

57 Next set up an axonometric view in the top viewport. First switch back to the model space. From the *View* menu choose *Model Space [Floating].*

58 From the *View* menu choose *3D Viewpoint,* then *Select* (R13 *Rotate*). Enter 300 as angle *from x axis,* and 60 as angle *from xy plane.* Zoom in so that the model fills the viewport (Figure 9.58).

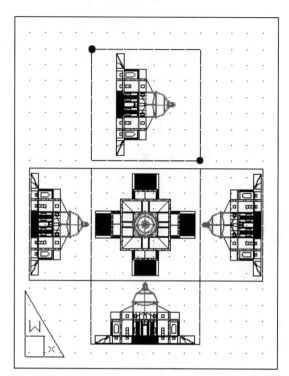

9.56i *Setting up clip corners of the floating viewport at the top of the drawing.*

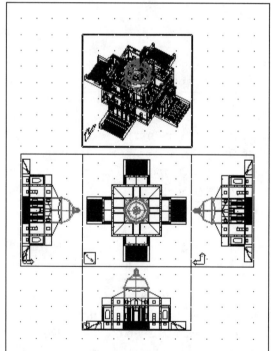

9.58 *Setting up an axonometric view in the top viewport.*

59 Switch back to paper space. From the *View* menu choose *Paper Space*.

60 Before you issue the SOLDRAW command, which will draw the profiles and sections in viewports, specify the cross-hatching pattern parameters. Enter the HPNAME command. Press *Enter* to select the currently active hatch style called ANSI31. Enter the HPSCALE command, and specify 100 [2.5] as the new value of the hatch pattern scaling factor.

61 Now generate the profiles and sections in each viewport. In R14, choose the *Setup Drawing* tool (Figure 9.61) on the *Solids* toolbar, or if you are using R13, enter the SOLDRAW command, and select all five viewports.

It will take several minutes for the SOLDRAW command to be completed. As already mentioned, the SOLDRAW command will generate profiles and sections in viewports created with SOLVIEW.

62 The SOLVIEW command creates layers that SOLDRAW uses to place visible lines, hidden lines, dimensions, and section hatching for each viewport. It uses the following naming convention:

Layer name	Object type it contains
View name-VIS	Visible lines
View name-HID	Hidden lines
View name-DIM	Dimensions
View name-HAT	Hatch patterns (for sections)

The *view name* is the name you gave to the view when you created it. Note that the information stored on these layers is deleted and updated when you run SOLDRAW; do not place permanent drawing information on these layers.

The SOLVIEW command places the viewport objects on the VPORTS layer; it will create this layer if it does not already exist. Freeze all layers that have the -HID or -DIM suffix. Only layers with the -VIS or -HAT suffix should be visible. Also freeze the layer VPORTS to make the viewport borders invisible. The paper space should look like Figure 9.62.

The HPANGLE command controls the angle of the hatch pattern.

9.61 The Setup Drawing *tool (SOLDRAW).*

When you apply SOLDRAW to a sectional view created with SOLVIEW, it creates a temporary copy of the solids and uses SLICE at a defined cutting plane. SOLDRAW then generates a profile of the visible half of the solids and discards the original copy. Next it sections the solids.

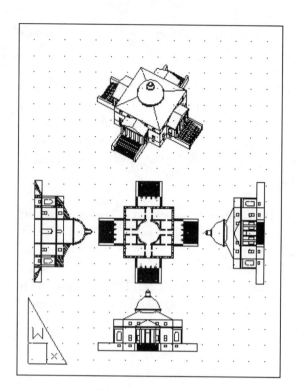

9.62 *The paper space after the views were set up and layers frozen.*

You can use both TrueType and Postscript fonts in AutoCAD drawings.

63 You will next add to this drawing the building's name (Villa Rotonda) as a text object. First create a new layer named TEXT, and set it up as the current layer.

64 Before you add the text, define a *text style* based on the *Times New Roman* TrueType font. From the *Format* (R13 *Data*) menu choose *Text Style*.

In R14, click *New*, and enter *Times* as the *new style name*. In the *Font Name* drop-down list choose the *Times New Roman* font. Click *Close* to continue.

In R13, enter *Times* in the first text box, and click *New*; the new style's name will appear in the list. In the *Font* section click *Browse*, and find the *Times New Roman* TrueType font file (with the .TTF extension). Click *Close* to continue.

65 Choose the *Text* tool (Figure 9.65a) on the *Draw* toolbar. Specify two opposite corners of the text box as shown in Figure 9.65b.

In R14, enter VILLA ROTONDA in the *Multiline Text Editor* dialog box, and enter 0.5″ [0.012] as the text's *height* (Figure

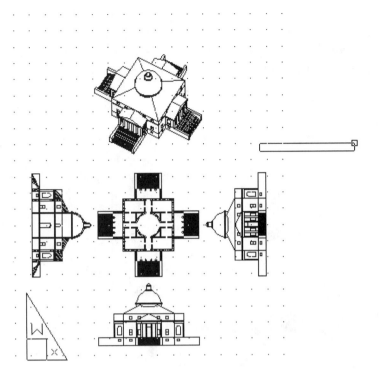

9.65a *The* Text *tool.*

9.65b *Specifying the corners of the text box.*

9.65c). Click on the *Properties* tab, click inside the *Rotation* text box, and enter 90 (Figure 9.65d) to rotate the text by 90 degrees once it is inserted into the drawing. Set *width* to *No Wrap*. Click *OK* to continue.

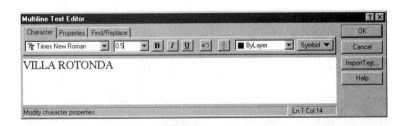

9.65c *The* Multiline Text Editor *(R14).*

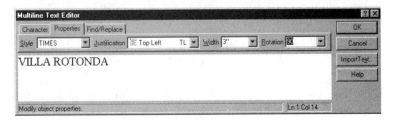

9.65d *Specifying additional text properties (R14).*

In R13, enter VILLA ROTONDA in the text box, and enter 0.5″ [0.012] as the text's *height*. Click *Properties*, click inside the *Rotation* text box, and enter 90 to rotate the text by 90 degrees once it is inserted into the drawing. Click *OK* to continue.

The text will be placed along the right edge (Figure 9.65e).

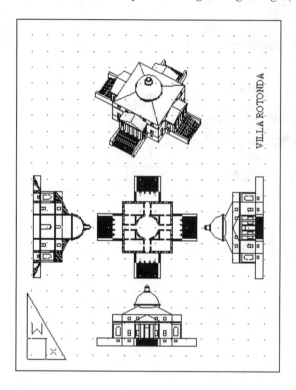

9.65e *The text is placed along the right edge.*

66 Switch to model space and delete lines that shouldn't be there, such as edges of the second-floor slab. When done, switch back to the paper space.

67 Finally, print the drawing. Do not *hide lines*—they are already hidden. Also, remove the check mark from the *Scale to Fit* box, and specify the correct scale: if you are using English units, enter 1 in the first box (*Plotted Inches*), or 1000 if you are using metric units. Enter 1 in the second box (*Drawing Units*). The printout should look like Figure 9.67.

68 You can also try to create a "digital" replica (Figure 9.68a) of Palladio's original drawing (Figure 9.68b) by clipping the ele-

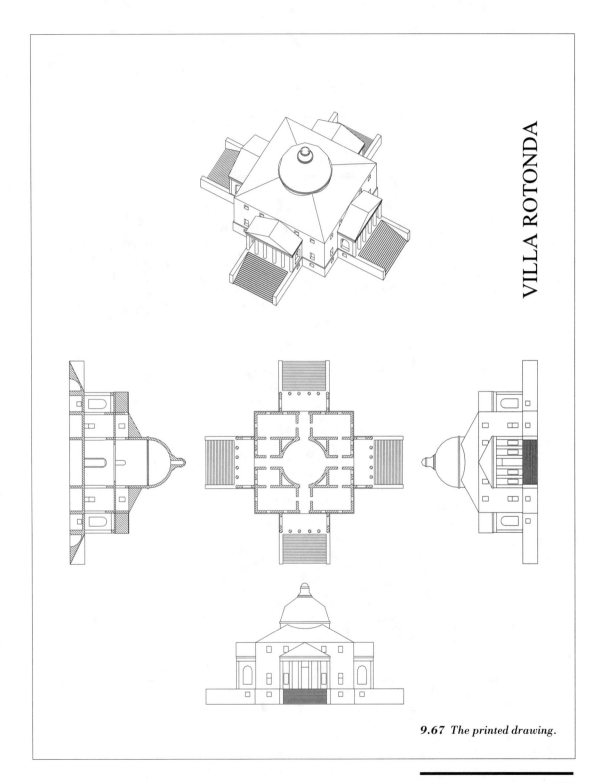

VILLA ROTONDA

9.67 *The printed drawing.*

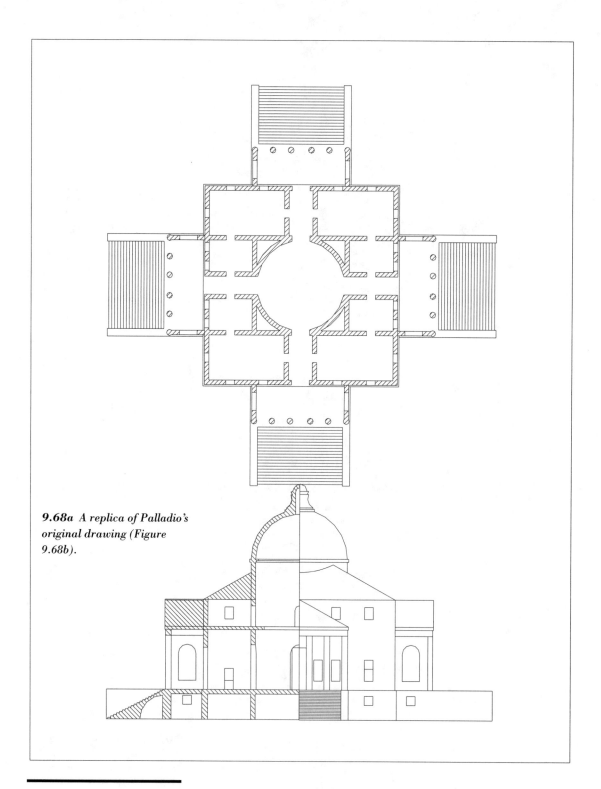

9.68a *A replica of Palladio's original drawing (Figure 9.68b).*

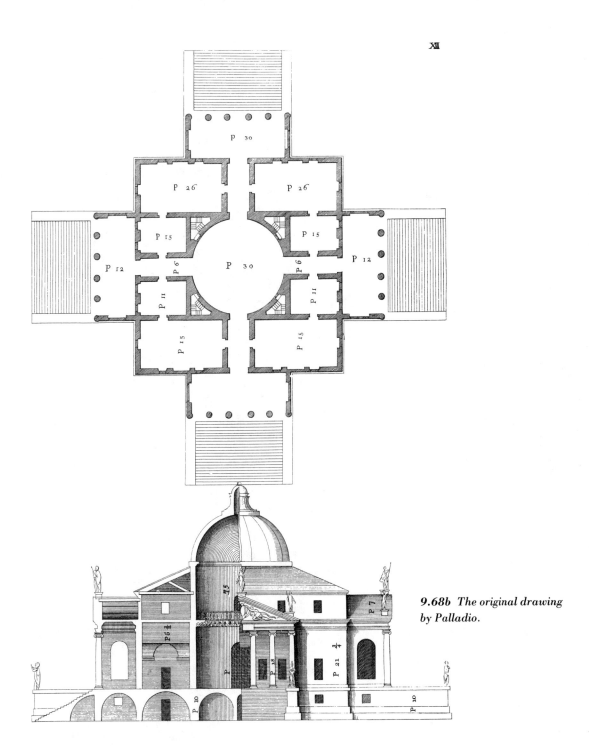

P 30

P 26   P 26

P 15   P 15

P 12   P 6 P 6   P 12

P 30

P 11   P 11

P 15   P 15

P 30

*9.68b The original drawing
by Palladio.*

P 7

P 6¼   P 21 ¾

P 18

P

P 10   P 10

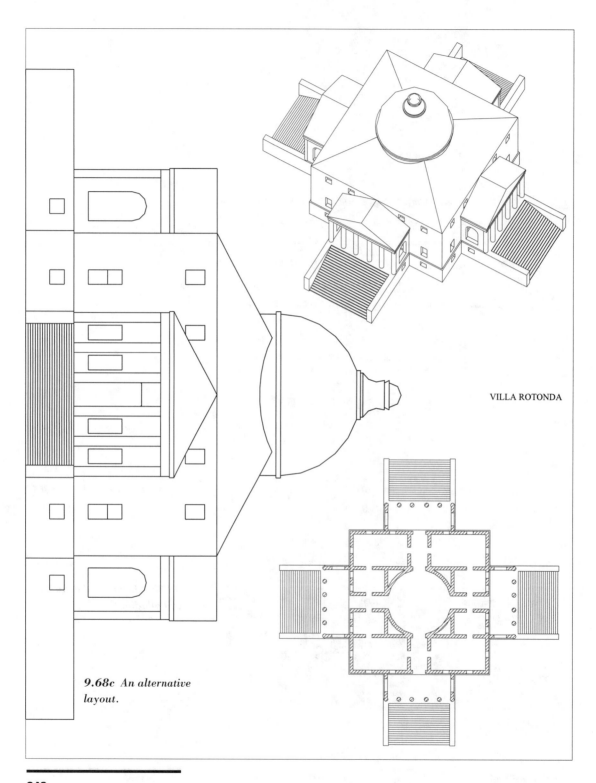

VILLA ROTONDA

9.68c *An alternative layout.*

vation and section viewports to show only one half of the building. You can also try alternative layouts (Figure 9.68c); note that viewports can *overlap* in paper space.

In this tutorial exercise, you have generated different representations of the villa's geometry using the SOLPROF, SOLVIEW, and SOLDRAW commands. You have also learned how to turn 3D hidden-line views into 2D drawings you can edit, how to create "exploded" views, and how to "section" and "slice" the 3D model.

The remaining part of the book covers the essential rendering concepts, such as lighting, material properties, and animation. The theoretical concepts will be introduced first, followed by the corresponding tutorial exercises.

BASIC CONCEPTS: RENDERING

Computer-rendered images with a high degree of realism are often called *photo-realistic* images.

AutoCAD R13 has only some basic rendering features as part of its standard package. Advanced rendering features, such as shadow casting and ray tracing, are provided in an Auto-CAD add-on program called *AutoVision,* which can be purchased separately from the basic R13 package (note that there are also some other third-party solutions, which are often better than AutoVision). Release 14, however, has *AutoVision* built in; it comes with both basic and advanced rendering software.

Colored pencils, crayons, inks, watercolors, and airbrush are used in traditional architectural rendering to create an image depicting an envisioned design. Often the intention is to *realistically* depict the "look and feel" of various *materials* applied in the building and capture the subtle effects of *transparency, reflectivity,* and *cast shadows* (Figure 10.1). To simulate such effects, computer rendering programs rely on *geometry, lighting,* and *surface material* information to *compute* rendered images.

With modeling software, you create 3D geometric models that consist of wire-frame, surface, and solid objects. As you create an object's 3D form, you work on wire-frame representation of its geometry, and from time to time generate hidden-line views to *visualize* and *verify* the results. To produce more realistic representations, you can generate *rendered images* by using rendering software, which computes *light intensities* at points on visible surfaces. In rendering programs, you place *lights* in 3D space and specify their properties, define *materials* and assign them to 3D objects, and use an appropriate *rendering technique* to generate an *image* representing the modeled object.

LIGHTING

Lighting, or illumination, is the single most important factor in creating computer renderings, just as important as in photography. Poorly lit models, no matter how carefully modeled, will

10.1 *A photo-realist computer rendering of Villa Emo by Robert Mayo.*

result in poor-quality images. Therefore, setting up lights of the appropriate type, color, and intensity, and in proper locations, is the most critical part of the rendering process.

In computer rendering, lights are defined as objects that can be described in terms of the following properties: *type of the light emission, color* and *intensity* of the emitted light, *rate of attenuation,* and *location* (Figure 10.2). Based on how the light is being emitted, light sources can be classified as *ambient,* which have no direction and illuminate a scene uniformly; *omni directional* (or *point*), which emit light rays in all directions (like a lightbulb); *directional* (or *spotlight*), which emit a directional cone of light *unidirectional* (or *distant*), with parallel light rays; *linear,* which emit light like a fluorescent tube; and *area (surface),* such as lighting panels or windowpanes.

In reality, the so-called *ambient light* fills the space, softening the shadows and reducing the contrast between light and dark areas; this effect is especially evident in interior spaces. The

AutoCAD (i.e., AutoVision) supports four types of light sources: *ambient, point, spot,* and *distant. Linear* and *area* lights are not supported.

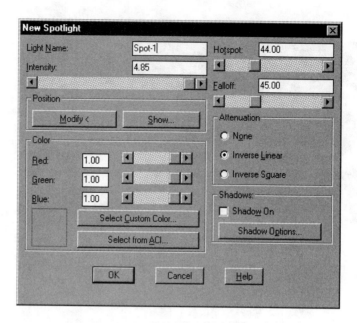

10.2 *Defining properties of a light source.*

ambient light provides constant, uniform illumination to every surface in the model; it comes from no particular source and has no direction.

The intensity of ambient light is often set on a scale from 0 to 1 (Figure 10.3). Setting the intensity to 0 is equivalent to turning the ambient light off and should be done when simulating a dark interior space or a scene at night. High settings, such as 0.7 and higher, can result in washed-out images and should be avoided; typically, the ambient light is set to low values, between 0.1 and 0.3. Note that ambient light by itself cannot be used to create rendered images—adjoining faces will be indistinguishable because all are equally illuminated (Figure 10.4). Ambient light should be used as "fill light" to illuminate surfaces in shadows, i.e., surfaces that are not directly illuminated.

Point light sources emit light in all directions (Figure 10.5); because of this property, they are often referred to as *omnidirectional lights*. The intensity of the emitted light can *attenuate* (diminish) with distance based on *inverse linear* or *inverse square* rate (see the description of light properties later in this section). Point lights are typically used to simulate light emitted by a lightbulb (Figure 10.6) or as an alternative to ambient light as "fill light."

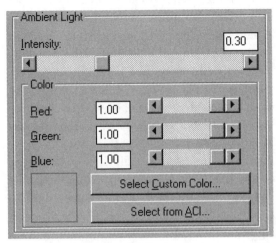

10.3

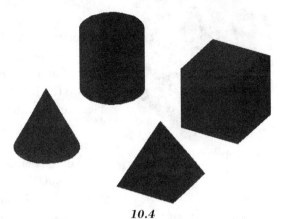

10.4

A *spotlight* emits a directional cone of light (Figure 10.7); when the light from a spotlight falls on a surface, it creates an area of maximum or full illumination (the *hot spot*), which is surrounded by an area of diminishing intensity (the *falloff*). Typically, the *direction* of the spotlight is specified by locating two points (the *target* and the *light*), and the size of the *light cone* is

10.3 *Setting the intensity of the ambient light.*

10.4 *Ambient light provides constant, uniform illumination to every surface in the model.*

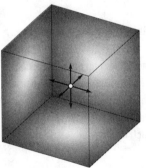

10.5 Point lights *emit light in all directions.*

10.6 *Illuminating Villa Rotonda's portico with a single point light source.*

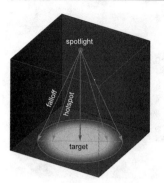

10.7 *A spotlight emits a directional cone of light.*

The intensity of spotlights can also attenuate over distance. Typically, you can choose *no attenuation,* or attenuation at *inverse linear* or *inverse square* rate. Note that light intensity diminishes much faster under inverse square than under inverse linear rate.

Although the sun is conceptually an omnidirectional, point light source, we can assume, because of its great distance from earth, that its light rays are parallel and unidirectional by the time they reach earth's surface.

10.8 *The illumination by a spotlight with the falloff angle greater than the hotspot angle.*

10.9 *The illumination by the same light with equal hot-spot and falloff angles.*

specified by *hot spot* and *falloff* angles (Figure 10.7). The hot spot cone angle, sometimes referred to as the *beam angle,* defines the brightest part of the light beam; the falloff cone angle, also called the *field angle,* defines the full cone of light. If the falloff angle is greater than the hot spot angle by more than 10 or 15 degrees, the edge of the light beam becomes fairly "soft" (Figure 10.8); if the falloff and hot spot angles are identical, the edge of the beam is sharp (Figure 10.9). Use spotlights as "key" lights, or for emphasis, i.e., to illuminate areas of special interest (Figure 10.10).

A *distant, unidirectional light* source emits light uniformly in one direction, as parallel light rays (Figure 10.11), and the intensity of the emitted light does not diminish over distance. Because of its emission properties, a distant light source is typically used to simulate the *sunlight.*

A simple and effective way to light architectural models then is to specify a single directional light source as the sun (Figure 10.12). In fact, many rendering programs provide a *sun angle calculator* (Figure 10.13) that can calculate the sun's position (its *azimuth* and *altitude* angles) based on the specified *time, date,* and *geographic location.*

Linear lights emit light in all directions along an imaginary line, much like a fluorescent tube (Figure 10.14). Conceptually, a linear light can be thought of as a string of point light sources, closely spaced and arranged in linear fashion.

Area lights are used to simulate surface light sources, such as a windowpane made of translucent glass or a light panel. Such light sources also emit light in all directions (Figure 10.15) and can often be approximated with a regular pattern of point light sources

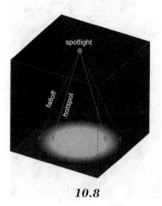

10.8

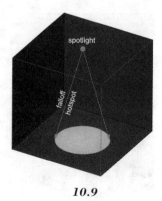

10.9

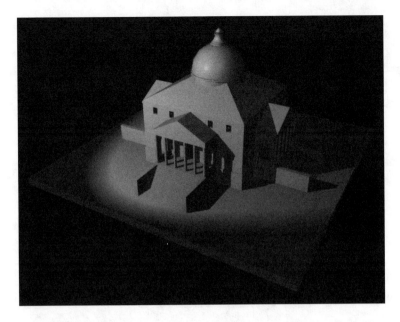

10.10 *A spotlight should be used as a "key" light, or for emphasis.*

(although that can be computationally very expensive). Both linear and area light sources are currently available only in advanced rendering programs and often require complex mathematical calculations to compute illumination levels within a scene.

Some rendering programs also feature *negative light sources,* which *subtract* light from the scene. Such lights have no physical

10.11 *A distant, unidirectional light emits light uniformly in one direction, as parallel light rays.*

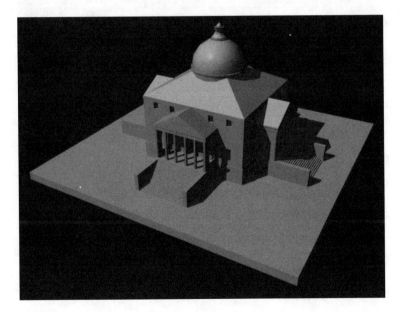

10.12 *Distant light sources are often used to light architectural models.*

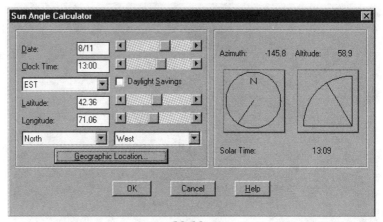

10.13a

Linear and area lights are typically provided by advanced rendering programs that support *radiosity*-rendering algorithm.

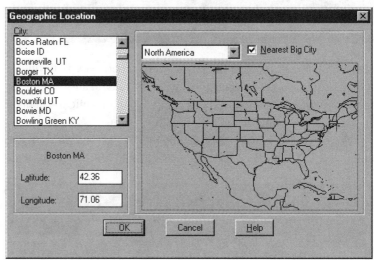

10.13b

10.13 *The* sun angle calculator.

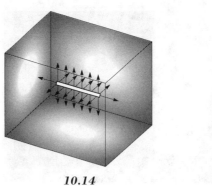

10.14

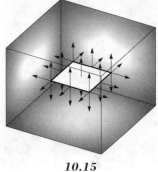

10.15

10.14 *A* linear light *source*.

10.15 *An* area light *source*.

counterpart and are often used to alter illumination levels within a scene to produce a desired lighting effect.

SHADOW CASTING

In reality, all light, regardless of how it is emitted, produces *shadows* when blocked by 3D objects, i.e., objects *cast shadows* when illuminated. Shadows provide important *visual* and *depth* clues that help us determine the shape and location of objects in space in relation to one another. Shadows are needed to make artificially created images realistic, but they are not always necessary or appropriate; they can often obscure an important detail or make certain areas of the rendering too dark.

A shadow is made of the so-called *umbra* and *penumbra*. The umbra is the part of the shadow that is very dark; the *penumbra* is a partial shadow, a fuzzy region between regions of complete shadow and complete illumination (Figure 10.16). It is possible to cast shadows without *penumbrae*. For example, a bright spotlight illuminating a dark interior space will cast shadows without penumbrae (Figure 10.17).

Determining cast shadows is a very time-consuming process if done by hand. What can take hours in traditional rendering takes minutes using rendering software and often involves nothing more than placing a check mark in the appropriate box (Figure 10.18).

In rendering software, cast shadows can be computed in several ways: as *volumetric shadows, shadow maps,* or *ray-traced shadows.*

The task of computing *volumetric shadows,* i.e., their shapes and locations, is very similar to producing a hidden-line perspec-

Note that in computer rendering, unlike in reality, a light source may or may not cast shadows; it is possible to specify light sources that penetrate all obstacles in the scene, regardless of their opacity. For example, in AutoCAD, *point* lights do not cast shadows. Because of that property, they are often used as "fill" lights, to illuminate parts of the model that are covered by shadows cast by other lights.

10.16 Cast shadows with both umbra *and* penumbra *regions.*

10.17 Cast shadows without penumbrae.

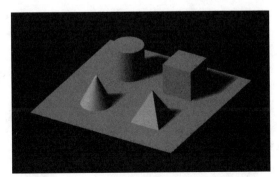

10.16

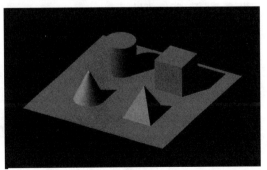

10.17

10.18 To cast shadows, place a check mark in the appropriate box.

The only way to produce "soft" shadows, i.e., shadows with penumbrae, in AutoCAD is to render shadows using the *shadow maps* technique (described later in this chapter).

The shadows will be cast *only* if light sources in the scene *do* cast shadows. In many rendering programs, you must explicitly specify this option when creating light sources.

AutoCAD (i.e., AutoVision) can cast shadows using *shadow maps* or *ray tracing* (described later in this chapter). Note that the AutoCAD R13 standard package (without AutoVision) cannot cast shadows.

tive. Surfaces that intercept light produce shadow volumes in a similar way that the surfaces visible to the eye produce occlusion volumes—the light source can't "see" the objects that are in the shadow; those surfaces that intersect or are completely within the shadow volumes will have shadows cast on them (Figure 10.19).

The *shadow maps* technique uses a slightly different strategy to compute the shadows. Instead of computing shadow volumes, this technique calculates an illumination or shadow map (also called a buffer) for each light in the scene. In some rendering programs, you can create soft-edged shadows (with penumbrae) using this technique (Figure 10.20). Note that if you use shadow maps, the transparent objects will not be shown in shadows.

Raytraced shadows are the most accurate of the three methods described so far. They are hard-edged, have accurate outlines, and can transmit color from transparent objects (Figure 10.21). (See the section on rendering techniques later in this chapter to find out how raytraced shadows are computed.)

Note that computing cast shadows can considerably increase the rendering time. For simple geometry, computing volumetric shadows is often quicker than calculating the raytraced shadows. However, if the geometry is fairly complex, i.e., if the number of faces is large, raytraced shadows are often computed faster than volumetric shadows. Shadow maps take longer to compute than either volumetric or raytraced shadows but are often the only way to generate soft-edged shadows.

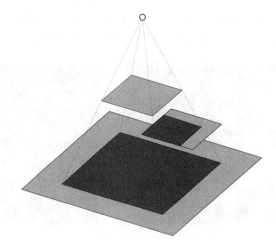

10.19 Volumetric shadows.

10.20 *Soft-edged shadows (with penumbrae) created using the* shadow maps *technique.*

Note that *transparency* is opposite from *shadow casting*. Where an opaque surface casts a shadow volume, a transparent surface casts a *light* volume, whereby the color of the light is a mixture of the color of the transparent surface and the color of the incoming light. The color of surfaces intersecting a light volume cast by a transparent object will be changed as a result of that spatial interaction.

In AutoCAD, you can specify the *size* of the shadow maps that will be generated. Larger shadow maps often produce better results but can take considerably longer to compute.

10.21 *Hard-edged* raytraced *shadows.*

OTHER LIGHT PROPERTIES

Each light source emits light of a specific *color* and *intensity*, which can *attenuate*, or diminish, with distance. If the intensity of the light emitted by the light source diminishes with distance, objects close to the light source will appear brighter than those that are farther away.

The rate at which light intensity decreases over distance is often referred to as the *rate of attenuation* or *falloff*. The intensity of the emitted light can attenuate with distance at the *inverse linear* or *inverse square* rate (Figure 10.22). In inverse linear attenuation, light intensity decreases in inverse proportion to the distance from the light source. Thus, if the intensity of the light is I at the distance of D, it will drop to 0.5I (I/2) at the distance of 2D, and to 0.25I (I/4) at the distance of 4D (Figure 10.24). In inverse square attenuation, light intensity decreases in inverse proportion to the *square* of the distance from the light source. If we assume, as in the previous example, that the intensity of light is I at the distance of D from the light source, the intensity will drop to 0.25I (I/2^2) at the distance of 2D, and to 0.0625I (I/4^2) at the distance of 4D (Figure 10.25). In short, surfaces become darker with distance much faster with inverse square than with inverse linear attenuation.

In rendering programs, the color of the emitted light is specified using the *RGB (red, green, blue) color model* based on *primary colors*, or the *HLS (hue, lightness, saturation) model.*

In the RGB color model, the light's color is determined based on the amount, or intensity, of each of the three component

Note that the light in reality attenuates at the inverse square rate, but in computer rendering, inverse linear attenuation often produces a more realistic effect for most applications.

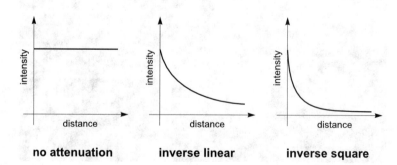

10.22 Rates of attenuation.

no attenuation   inverse linear   inverse square

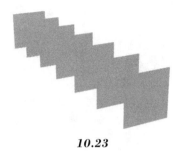

10.23

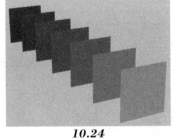

10.24

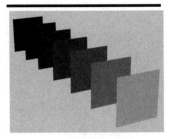

10.25

colors. The intensities of red, green, and blue are typically specified on a scale from 0 to 1, or 0 to 255 (Figure 10.26). Mixing two of the primary colors at full intensity produces *secondary* colors (Figure 10.27): to obtain *yellow*, red and green should be set to 1, i.e., full intensity, and blue to 0; to specify *cyan* (greenish blue), set green and blue to 1, and red to 0; for *magenta*, set red and blue to 1, and green to 0. *White* is produced by setting all primary colors to *full* intensity, and black by setting all primary colors to 0 intensity (no color). Various levels of gray can be produced by setting all three primary colors to the same intensity (Figure 10.28); for example, to produce a 50% gray, set all three colors to 0.5.

In the HLS color model, you first select the light's color from a range of *hues*, and then specify its *lightness* (brightness) and *saturation*, i.e., the amount of black contained in the hue (Figure 10.29).

SURFACE PROPERTIES

The appearance of an object depends largely on how it interacts with the light arriving at its surface—how much of the incoming

10.23 *Illumination with no attenuation.*

10.24 *Illumination based on inverse linear rate of attenuation.*

10.25 *Illumination based on inverse square rate of attenuation.*

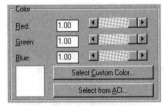

10.26 *Specifying the light's color using varying intensities of red, green, and blue.*

10.27 *Specifying secondary colors—yellow, cyan, and magenta.*

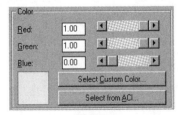

10.27a

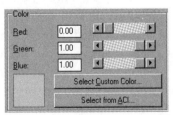

10.27b

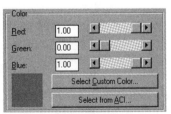

10.27c

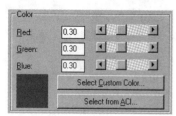

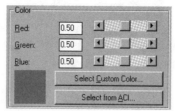

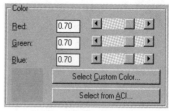

10.28a   10.28b   10.28c

10.28 *Producing various levels of gray using the RGB color model.*

Note that in some rendering programs, the *intensity* of the emitted light is specified by the light's color: white denotes full intensity, 50% gray is equivalent to half of the full intensity, and 75% gray is the same as a quarter of the full intensity.

In AutoCAD, the light's color can be specified using either the RGB or the HLS color model.

light is absorbed, how much of it is reflected, and how much of it is transmitted. It is also a function of other factors, such as properties of light reaching the surface (color, intensity), surface material properties (*color, reflectivity, specularity, transparency,* and *index of refraction*), the viewing direction, and surface-to-surface relationships.

The light can strike surfaces at different angles and with varying intensity (if it attenuates with distance). The intensity of the light at each surface then depends on the angle of the surface to the incoming light rays (the *angle of incidence*), and its distance from the light source if the light intensity attenuates with distance. Therefore, the more a surface inclines away from the incoming light rays, the darker it appears. The surface is brightest if it is perpendicular to the light rays; if the surface is parallel to the light rays, it will appear dark (Figure 10.30).

The computation of light intensities for each surface is based on Lambert's cosine law of optics. Johann Lambert, an eighteenth-century physicist and astronomer, discovered that the intensity of the light reflected from a surface is directly related to the angle at which the light is incident (Figure 10.31). Assuming that a surface has a dull matte finish and that the incoming light rays are unidirectional, the intensity of the reflected light (I_R) is directly proportional to the intensity of the incoming light (I_I) and the *cosine* of the angle of incidence ($\cos \alpha_I$), which is formed by the incoming light rays and the *surface normal,* the vector originating in the center of the surface and pointing perpendicularly outward toward

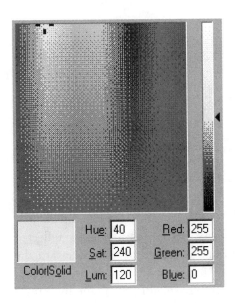

Hue: 40	Red: 255	
Sat: 240	Green: 255	
Color|Solid	Lum: 120	Blue: 0

10.29 *Specifying the light's color using the HLS (*hue, lightness, saturation*) color model.*

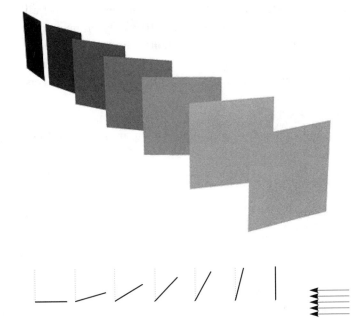

10.30 *The intensity of the light at each surface depends on the angle of the surface to the incoming light rays.*

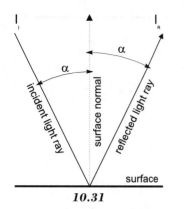

10.31

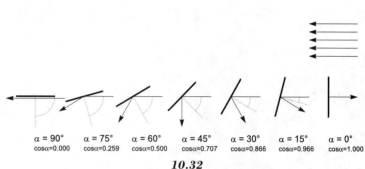

$\alpha = 90°$	$\alpha = 75°$	$\alpha = 60°$	$\alpha = 45°$	$\alpha = 30°$	$\alpha = 15°$	$\alpha = 0°$
$\cos\alpha = 0.000$	$\cos\alpha = 0.259$	$\cos\alpha = 0.500$	$\cos\alpha = 0.707$	$\cos\alpha = 0.866$	$\cos\alpha = 0.966$	$\cos\alpha = 1.000$

10.32

10.31 Lambert's cosine law of optics.

10.32 The surface's shade (its brightness) is directly proportional to the cosine of the angle of incidence.

Note that in some programs, mirror-like flat-plane reflections are computed by creating a copy of the geometric model about the mirror plane, and by projecting that copy in the same way as the original, nonreflected part of the model.

space; the formula $I_R = I_I * \cos \alpha_I$ cogently depicts this dependency. From this formula follows that the intensity of the reflected light decreases as the surface is tipped obliquely toward the incoming light rays (Figure 10.32). A surface with the normal parallel to the light rays (a surface perpendicular to the light rays) will have the highest intensity of the reflected light ($\alpha_I = 0° => \cos 0° = 1 => I_R = I_I$); a surface with the normal perpendicular to the light rays (a surface parallel to the light rays) will have zero intensity ($\alpha_I = 90° => \cos 90° = 0 => I_R = 0$), i.e., it will be dark.

How much of the arriving light is reflected will depend on the *reflective* properties of a surface, i.e., its material. Almost all surfaces exhibit *diffuse reflection* (Figure 10.33), whereby incoming light rays are dispersed in all directions. The *roughness* of the surface at the microscopic level determines the amount of light reflected by *diffusion*. For example, a matte-painted wall reflects almost all light by diffusion.

In *specular reflection*, on the other hand, light is reflected in a narrow cone (Figure 10.34). Highly specular surfaces reflect almost all incoming light.

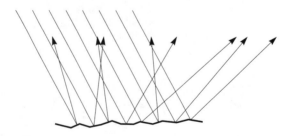

10.33 Diffuse reflection.

The tendency of a surface to exhibit specular reflection is known as its *specular reflectivity,* or *specularity.* In most rendering programs, specularity refers to the intensity and size of the *specular highlight,* i.e., the reflection of the light source on the surface (Figure 10.35). On highly reflective surfaces, such as a highly polished metal sphere, the intensity of the specular highlight is high, and its size fairly small. On less reflective surfaces, such as a sphere made of low-reflective plastic, specular highlights tend to be duller, fuzzier, and larger in size (Figure 10.36).

The size of the specular highlight is a factor of the material's roughness (Figure 10.37). Low roughness values thus produce intense, concentrated highlights on very shiny surfaces, and high roughness values result in almost imperceptible highlights on matte, dull surfaces. The greater the roughness, the larger the size of the highlight.

Note that specular highlights are viewpoint dependent—they move and change as the location of the viewer changes (Figure 10.38). The center of the highlight appears at the point where the angle of incidence equals the angle of reflection, which in turn coincides with the viewing angle, or direction.

It is also important to note that the color of a specular highlight can vary depending on the object's material (Figure 10.39). A specular highlight of the white light source on a highly pol-

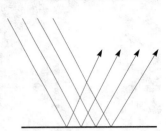

10.34 Specular reflection.

10.35 Specular highlight.

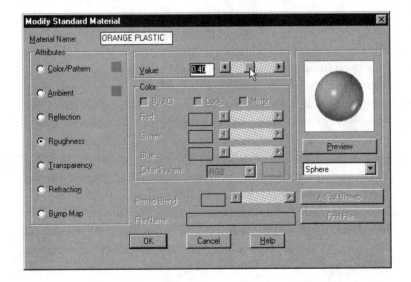

10.36 On less reflective surfaces, specular highlights tend to be fuzzier and larger.

10.37 The size of specular highlights is a factor of the material's roughness.

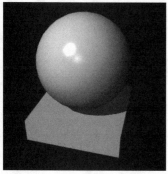

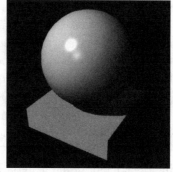

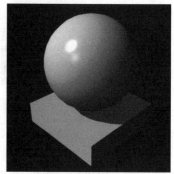

| 10.38a | 10.38b | 10.38c |

10.38 *Specular highlights are viewpoint dependent.*

In AutoCAD, the size of a specular highlight is controlled by the *Roughness* parameter.

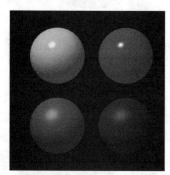

10.39 *The color of a specular highlight can vary depending on the object's material. On plastic spheres, shown in the top row, the highlight is white, i.e., it is the same as the color of the light source; on metallic spheres, shown in the bottom row, the color of the highlight shifts to reflect the color of the object.*

ished bluish metal sphere will be bluish in color, i.e., it will reflect the object's color; however, the specular highlight of the same light source on a shiny bluish plastic sphere will be white, i.e., the same as the color of the light source.

This change in color of the specularly reflected light is called *color shifting*. Often, the extent of color shifting must be explicitly specified (Figure 10.40). For plastic materials, there should be none—the color of the specularly reflected light is the same as the color of the incident light. For metal materials, the color shifting should be set to maximum value; the white light arriving onto the surface should be reflected with the color of the surface. Because plastic and metal materials are on opposite ends of the color-shifting scale, sometimes the color shifting is referred to as *metallic coefficient;* the plastic materials have a metallic coefficient of 0, while metallic materials have a coefficient of 1— all other materials are in between these two extremes.

In addition to being absorbed and reflected, light can also be *transmitted* through an object (Figure 10.41). An *opaque* object, such as a brick wall, does not transmit light: it absorbs most of it and reflects some. A *transparent* object, such as a glass window-pane, transmits most of the light that reaches it. By adjusting the material's degree of *transparency* (typically on a scale from 0 to 1), opaque, partially transparent, and fully transparent objects can be simulated in rendering programs (Figure 10.42).

As the light passes from one material to another (for example, from air to water), it *bends*, or is *refracted*. Figure 10.43 shows a cylindrical object in a prismatic glass container that is half filled with water. Note how the cylinder appears to be bent,

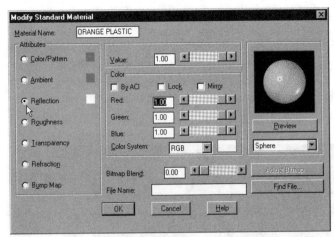

10.40a

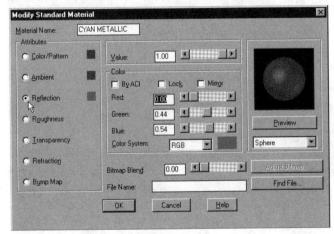

10.40b

10.40 *Often, the* color shifting *must be explicitly specified.*

because the light itself is bent to various degrees as it passes through air, water, and glass.

The ability of a material to bend light is determined by its *index of refraction* (Figure 10.44). The phenomenon of refraction has been thoroughly studied in physics, and over time, the indexes of refraction for various materials have been determined by experimentation.

While reflectivity and transparency (or opacity) determine how an object interacts with light, perhaps the single most important property that determines how an object looks when illumi-

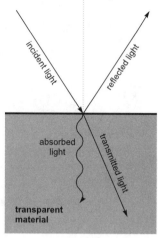

10.41

10.42

10.41 *Light can be absorbed, reflected, and transmitted.*

10.42 *Objects can have varying degrees of transparency.*

AutoCAD R13 (the standard package) supports only the material properties of color, reflectivity, and roughness—it does not support transparency (for that you need the AutoVision add-on). Note that R14 supports all the material properties mentioned in this section: color, reflectivity, specularity, transparency, and refraction.

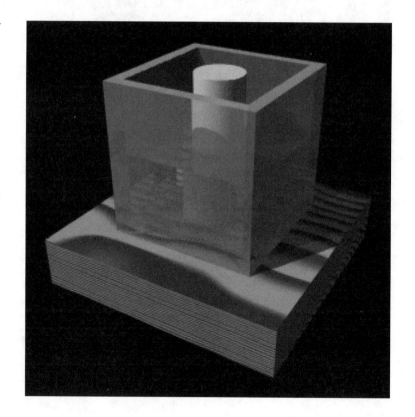

10.43 *Light bends, or is refracted, as it passes from one material to another.*

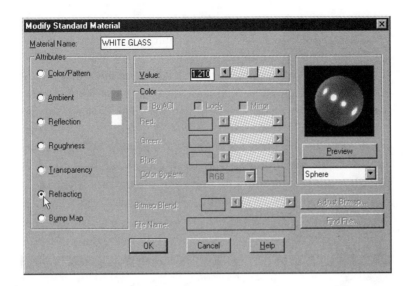

10.44 *The* index of refraction *can be explicitly specified for transparent materials.*

nated is its *color*. In reality, objects of the same color can appear to have different colors, depending on the geometry, reflection properties, and relative position of each object to the light sources. A cylindrical or spherical object will not have a uniform color that a prismatic one may exhibit: the side facing the light will be much brighter than the rest of the object, and the brightness will gradually change toward the sides (Figure 10.45). The part of the object in the shadow will be dark, depending on the

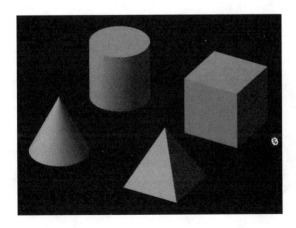

10.45 *The color of an object depends on its geometry, reflection properties, and relative position to the light sources.*

intensity and color of the ambient light. And if the object is highly reflective, the color of the specular highlight will be different from the rest of the object.

To account for these color variations, each material defined in rendering programs will typically have three associated color variables (Figure 10.46): *diffuse* color (the "main" color); *ambient* color, which will appear in the shaded parts; and *specular* or *reflection* color, which is the color of the specular highlight (Figure 10.47). In some programs, these variables can be defined as interdependent (or *locked*), so when any one of them is changed, the other two change accordingly.

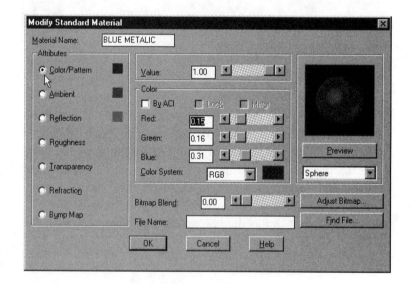

10.46 Defining the color variables in material definitions.

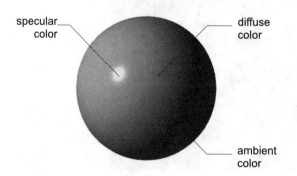

10.47 The diffuse, ambient, *and* specular *color.*

IMAGE MAPPING

In reality, surfaces rarely have uniform color or transparency. In fact, in most instances, changes in color are perceptible—consider, for example, a marble or a granite tile, a wood panel, or a painted vase. Even a brick wall, which can be rendered as a uniformly colored solid object at large scale, is composed of hundreds of bricks, each of which has a slightly different color in reality, and each of which is separated by a mortar joint. While it is possible to model each break and each mortar joint separately, such an approach is not only time-consuming but can result in large model files, with a rather large number of polygons to render and, consequently, very long rendering times.

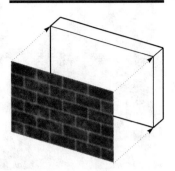

10.48 *Image mapping.*

In rendering systems, such subtleties in surface properties are simulated by *image mapping*, that is, by mapping or projecting two-dimensional digital images onto the surface of a three-dimensional object (Figure 10.48). An image is either scanned or selected from a digital image library, and its four corners are then mapped onto the surface.

Surface properties, such as color, reflectivity, opacity, and geometry, can be altered, respectively, by *color, reflection, opacity,* and *bump* image maps.

A *color* image map redefines the surface color, as if it were painted onto the surface. The image is simply projected onto the surface (Figure 10.48). Since color maps can be used very effectively to simulate the *texture* of a material, they are often referred to as *texture maps*. In some rendering programs color maps are called *diffuse color maps* because they specify the color of the light reflected by diffusion.

A *reflection* image map specifies an image that is reflected by shiny objects; it is often used to simulate reflection of objects that are not part of the model but that should be shown on reflective surfaces to achieve a convincing result (Figure 10.49). Because they are often used to simulate an object's environment, reflection maps are sometimes referred to as *environment maps*. For example, in photo-realistic renderings, an image of a desired environment (an image of a sunrise or sunset, or a mountain range on the opposite side of the building) is often used as an *environment map*.

Image mapping is not supported by the standard AutoCAD R13 package; R14 fully supports all mapping techniques described in this section.

10.49a

10.49b

10.49 *A reflection (or environment) image map applied to a spherical object.*

An *opacity* image map is a gray-scale image that defines opaque and transparent areas on a surface. When an opacity map is projected onto an object, the pure white pixels in the image define completely opaque areas, while black pixels specify fully transparent (hollow) areas, thus creating an effect of a solid surface with holes (Figure 10.50). Pixels with various gray levels define areas of varying transparency; areas on which dark gray pixels fall are more transparent than the light gray ones.

Opacity maps can be used to efficiently create desired geometry, with little or no modeling work. For example, applying an opacity image map that consists of a black square on a white background to a 3D object representing a wall will result in an image showing a square opening (hole) in the wall. You can very quickly create window mullions (Figure 10.51) or openings in building walls using this technique.

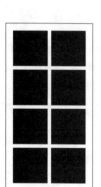

10.50 *An* opacity *image map.*

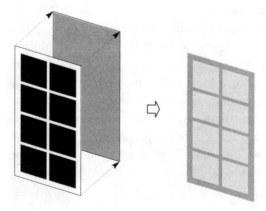

10.51 *Creating window mullions using an opacity map.*

Opacity maps can also be used to represent trees in renderings. An image of a tree on a black background can be applied as both the *color* and the *opacity* map onto a rectangular surface parallel to the viewing plane (Figure 10.52). The black pixels in the opacity map will render outer areas of the rectangle as fully transparent. The colored pixels will appear within the opaque area, perfectly matching its boundary. Sometimes two crossing rectangles with the corresponding color and opacity maps are used to represent trees (Figure 10.53), especially in situations when renderings from several viewing directions are needed.

A *bump* image map is used to create an embossed or bas-relief effect on the surface to which it is applied. When a bump map (Figure 10.54) is projected onto an object, the pure white areas in the image map appear raised (embossed) against the flat background in the rendered image (Figure 10.55); different gray-scale values in the image result in parts of the surface being raised to different heights.

10.52 Simulating trees using color and opacity maps.

10.53 An alternative technique for simulating trees.

10.52

10.53

10.54 A bump image map.

10.55 Applying a bump map onto a surface.

10.56 *Surface normals are perturbed depending on the gray-scale values in the bump map.*

To achieve the embossed effect, the rendering software perturbs the surface normals depending on individual pixels' level of gray at a particular point on the surface (Figure 10.56). For example, if you apply a bump map that consists of white text on a black background, the text will appear raised above the rest of the surface (Figure 10.55). You can easily create mortar joints in a brick wall by bump mapping an image that consists of thick black lines on a white background (Figure 10.57); you will also need to apply an appropriate color map to achieve a convincing effect (Figure 10.58). Note, however, that bump mapping cannot alter the rendition of an object's edges (Figure 10.59).

In addition to "surface" maps, many rendering programs support parametric *solid* or *procedural* materials (also known as *template* materials or *solid textures*). These material definitions generate at the rendering time a three-dimensional pattern, which is then applied to an object (Figure 10.60). Solid materials are especially useful in producing variant surface qualities over large areas or on solid objects; varying the associated parameter values (Figure 10.61) can change the generated pattern. A standard repertoire of parametric solid textures includes most commonly used materials, such as marble, granite, and wood.

In most renderers, attaching a material definition with image maps to an object involves specifying and assigning *mapping parameters*, such as *projection type, position, orientation, scale, blend value,* and *tiling* (Figure 10.62) so that the renderer can apply the image maps accordingly. In some renderers, this process is automatic, i.e., default values are used for mapping parameters; some require that mapping be explicitly specified before an image is rendered.

An image map can be applied onto an object in *planar, cubic, cylindrical,* or *spherical* projection. Planar projection applies an

10.57 *A bump map of a brick wall can be created by inverting a corresponding color map and converting it into a gray-scale image.*

10.57a

10.57b

10.58

10.59

image map to objects as if it were projected by a slide projector (Figure 10.63). In cubic projection, an image is projected separately onto each side of an imaginary cube (Figure 10.64), as if there were six slide projectors. In cylindrical projection, the image map is wrapped horizontally around the object (Figure 10.65), while in spherical projection, the image wraps around the object both horizontally and vertically, i.e., its top and bottom edges are compressed to a point (Figure 10.66).

Note that image maps can be applied to surfaces as *decals*, i.e., as single images at specific locations and scales (Figure 10.67), or they can be *tiled* as a pattern across the surface (Figure

10.58 Applying a color map and a bump map of a brick wall to achieve a realistic effect.

10.59 Bump mapping cannot alter the rendition of edges.

10.60 Solid or procedural textures (granite, marble, wood).

10.61 By varying the parameters of a solid texture, many different materials can be defined.

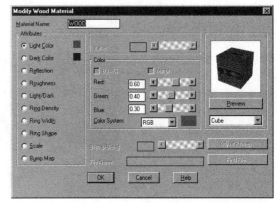

10.60

10.61

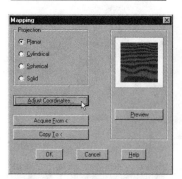

10.62a

AutoCAD (AutoVision) does not support *cubic* projection.

In general, the projection type should correspond to the object's geometry; otherwise you can produce illogical and confusing results. For example, use cylindrical projection when applying an image map to a cylindrical object, such as a column, and use spherical projection to apply an image map to a dome, etc.

10.62 Specifying mapping parameters.

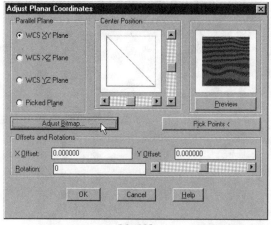

10.62b

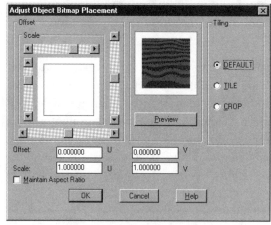

10.62c

10.63 A planar projection of an image map.

10.64 Cubic projection.

10.63

10.64

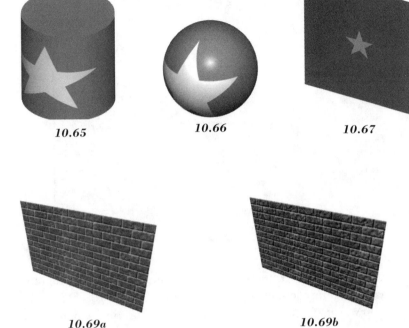

10.65

10.66

10.67

10.68

10.65 Cylindrical *projection.*

10.66 Spherical *projection.*

10.67 *Applying an image map as a* decal *onto a surface.*

10.68 *Tiling an image map across the surface.*

10.69 *The effect of image mapping can be varied by using different* blend *values.*

10.69a

10.69b

10.68). For example, you should apply an image map as a decal when you want to simulate a painting on a wall.

Note that all image maps can *blend* with the material's surface color. By lowering the blend value, the image map's effect can be reduced. For example, by varying the blend value, you can change the "depth" of the bump map's embossing effect (Figure 10.69).

Once you choose the appropriate projection and mapping type, you will have to position the image map relative to the object by specifying the *projection* or *UV coordinates* (Figure 10.70). The UV designation is used because these two-dimensional coordinates are independent from xy coordinates used to describe the model's geometry. By varying the UV coordinates you can change the placement of the image map on the object's surface.

Once the material properties and image mapping are specified, material definitions are *attached,* or *assigned* to objects in the model. Typically, a material is selected from the list and then objects to which the material will be applied are selected using

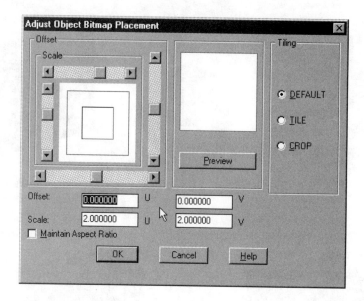

10.70 The UV coordinates determine the placement of the image map on the object's surface.

In AutoCAD (AutoVision) material definition can be attached to an object by object selection, or based on its color and layer.

standard object selection methods. Most rendering programs come with predefined *materials libraries* (Figure 10.71) and also allow users to create their own materials libraries, which can be reused.

In summary, using materials in rendering typically involves three steps. The first step is to *define* materials and specify *prop-*

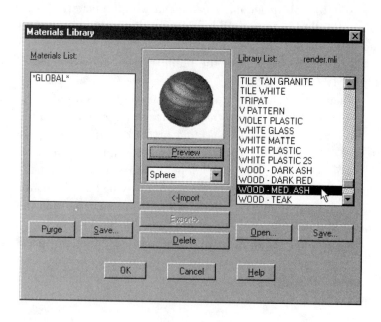

10.71 A materials library.

272

erties covered in this section: *color, reflectivity, specularity, transparency, and index of refraction.* The second step is to *attach,* or *assign,* material definitions to objects in the model. The third, optional step is to define *image mapping* for objects whose attached material definitions contain image maps.

Once the materials are attached, and mapping parameters specified, the model can be rendered using one of the several rendering techniques, which are described in the following section.

RENDERING TECHNIQUES

Generating a rendered image of a 3D model is a three-step process consisting of *projection, visible surface determination,* and *rendering.* First an appropriate projection method is applied to the model's geometry to create a desired orthographic, axonometric, or perspective view. Next visible surfaces are determined; those that are not visible, such as those at the back of the model, are discarded through a three-step procedure. In the first step, the rendering program computes the *surface normals,* that is, vectors originating in the center of each surface and pointing perpendicularly outward toward the space. The program then performs *back-face removal;* it searches for all normals that point away from the viewpoint and removes the associated surfaces from further computation (Figure 10.72). Using a technique called *Z-buffer,* the remaining faces are then compared according to their relative distance from the viewpoint along the line of sight (which becomes a temporary *z* axis—hence the term *Z-buffer*); those that would be hidden are removed. Finally an appropriate rendering algorithm is applied, and a *rendered image* is computed as light intensities at points on visible surfaces.

The most commonly used rendering algorithms are *flat shading, smooth shading* (*Gouraud* or *Phong*), *raytracing,* and *radiosity.*

Flat shading, also called *Lambert* or *cosine shading* because of Lambert's cosine law of optics, is the simplest rendering technique currently available (Figure 10.73). Once the correct projection is computed and visible surfaces determined, tonal, shading value is computed for each visible surface based on the angle that each *surface normal* forms with arriving *light rays* (Figure 10.74).

Note that flat shading renders each surface uniformly, i.e., there is no color variation across the surface, regardless of the

A rendering *algorithm* is a mathematical procedure of relating *geometry, lighting,* and *surface material* information.

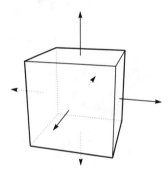

10.72 Back-face removal.

Note that sometimes you may not want to remove *back faces*—for example, if some objects are transparent, or if both the exterior and the interior of an object are visible.

AutoCAD R13 supports only flat and Gouraud smooth shading. Release R14 and AutoVision support all rendering techniques mentioned in this section except *radiosity.*

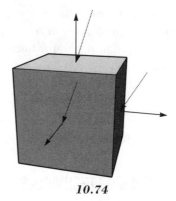

10.73 Flat shading.

10.74 *Computing the shading values based on Lambert's cosine law of optics.*

10.73   **10.74**

10.75 *Flat shading renders curved surfaces as faceted.*

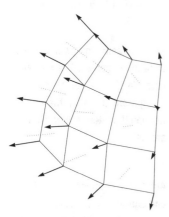

10.76 *In* Gouraud shading, *light intensities are computed at vertices instead of the centroid.*

light source that is used. Another limitation of flat shading becomes apparent in rendering faceted curved surfaces (Figure 10.75). If the facets are sufficiently small, the resulting image is reasonably satisfactory. However, increasing the number of facets increases the rendering time and makes the modeling work difficult in the wire-frame mode.

A better approach is to distribute intensities smoothly across the facets to avoid abrupt change at edges. Henry Gouraud, at the University of Utah, developed a simple three-step algorithm for *smooth tonal distribution (shade interpolation)*: first calculate surface normals at facet *vertices* instead of the center, taking into account the adjoining facets (Figure 10.76), then compute intensities for each vertex, and finally *linearly interpolate* computed intensities between vertices (Figure 10.77). The result is a smoothly shaded surface (Figure 10.78).

A parameter called a *smoothing angle* sets the angle between normals of adjacent surfaces at which the rendering algorithm interprets an *edge*. Typically, this angle is set to a value between 30 and 45 degrees. If the angle between the normals is less than a smoothing angle, the surfaces are smoothed; if it is greater, the surfaces are rendered as flat (Figure 10.79).

The shade-interpolation technique developed by Henry Gouraud is simple and computationally efficient, but it has one major shortcoming—in some situations, it can't render accurate specular highlights, i.e., the reflections of the light source on the object's surface (Figure 10.80). Bui-Tuong Phong further improved Gouraud's algorithm by using a more accurate interpolation technique. In contrast to Gouraud shading, which finds the

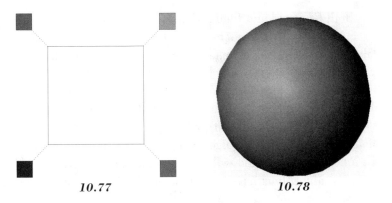

10.77

10.78

10.79

normal at each vertex, computes light intensities at vertices, and then interpolates the intensities across the surface, *Phong shading* finds the normal at each vertex, interpolates the *normals* instead of the intensities across the surface, and computes intensities at points that correspond to pixels in the rendered image. Phong's normal-interpolation algorithm is more complex and more computationally intensive than Gouraud's, but it is more accurate.

10.77 Linear interpolation of computed intensities (shade interpolation).

10.78 Smooth shading using Gouraud algorithm.

10.79 The smoothing angle is used to determine which surfaces should be rendered as smooth.

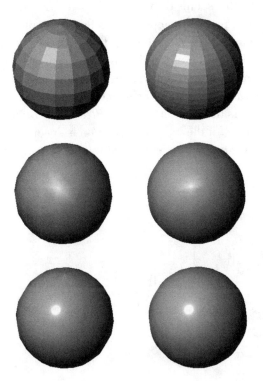

10.80 Smooth shaded surfaces using Gouraud *(middle row) and* Phong *shading (bottom row). Note how Gouraud shading cannot accurately render the specular highlights.*

Both Gouraud and Phong shading algorithms can produce inaccurate results in some instances. Figure 10.81 shows several polygons whose vertex normals point in the same direction, while surface normals at centroid clearly point in different directions. Since the vertex normals point in the same direction, Gouraud's algorithm will compute the same intensity for each normal (under a single unidirectional light), rendering all polygons with the same tonal value. Phong's algorithm, even though it uses a different interpolation method, will produce the same result. Several modified algorithms have appeared that address inaccuracies such as this one.

Ray tracing is a rendering technique that is mathematically more complex and therefore computationally more intensive than either Gouraud or Phong smooth shading. Because it traces light rays, as its name implies, it can accurately simulate intricate illumination effects of refraction and reflection on curved surfaces that neither Gouraud nor Phong algorithm can compute.

The ray-tracing algorithm splits the viewing plane into a fine, discrete grid of square picture elements (pixels) and back-traces a light ray into the scene through each pixel (Figure 10.82). The color of each pixel is computed in a fairly complex way. Each ray is traced to its first intersection with a surface; next a so-called *shadow ray* is fired toward each of the light sources to determine whether that point is in the shadow. If the surface is reflective, a *reflection ray* is fired into the scene at the angle of reflection. If the surface is transparent, a *transmitted ray* is fired into the scene, and *refracted* if the index of refraction is specified for the object. The newly spawned reflected and transmitted rays

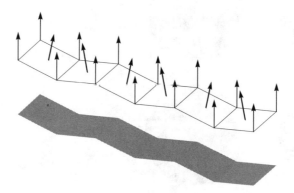

10.81 In some instances, both Gouraud and Phong shading can produce inaccurate results.

are traced to their corresponding intersections with surfaces, and the calculation goes through another iteration. The tracing of rays stops when there are no more rays to trace, or when the maximum *number of iterations* (also called the *sampling rate*) is reached. The color of the pixel (through which the initial ray is fired) is then determined based on the light intensity at the first intersection point, the light reflected from other objects (if the intersected surface is reflective), and the color of the objects seen through (if the intersected surface is transparent). Note that the computation time grows exponentially with the initial number of rays to trace and the maximum number of iterations needed to adequately render the cast shadows, reflections, and transparencies.

Raytracing is highly effective in rendering scenes that consist of point light sources, highly reflective surfaces, highlights, sharp shadows, and transparent objects with refraction (Figure 10.83). It is not very effective in rendering interior spaces with mostly matte surfaces, diffuse illumination and shading, and inter-reflection effects, such as "bleeding" of colors. In fact, these effects cannot be computed by raytracing—a rendering technique called *radiosity* should be used in such cases.

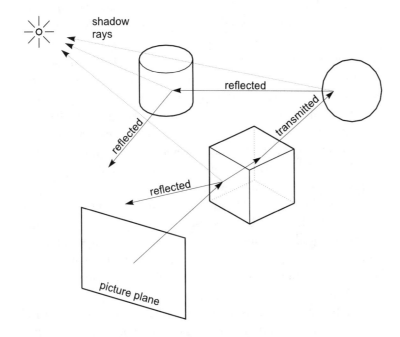

10.82 *Raytracing back-traces the light rays into the scene.*

10.83 A raytraced image.

The *radiosity* algorithm is based on *energy distribution,* or more precisely, on *radiant distribution of light energy.* The surfaces in the scene are divided into small patches, i.e., discrete elements, each of which can act as an emitter of light energy through reflection (Figure 10.84). The energy level of each patch is computed in iterative fashion. The first iteration determines the amount of light energy reaching each patch directly from light sources. Based on surface properties, the amounts of absorbed, transmitted, and reflected light energy are computed. The second iteration calculates the amount of light energy reaching each patch by reflection from other patches, and again computes the amounts of absorbed, transmitted, and reflected energy. The next iteration repeats this process, and so on, until some energy equilibrium is reached, or until the maximum number of iterations is completed. After several iterations, the amount of reflected energy becomes negligible, and the process stops.

The radiosity computation of energy distribution is computationally very intensive, but it is *view independent;* once the energy model is calculated, any view can very quickly be computed. Radiosity may not be the best technique to compute a single view, but it is very efficient for producing animations, which require a large number of rendered images.

Radiosity is best used in rendering interior spaces with matte and large brightly lit surfaces resulting in extensive *diffuse*

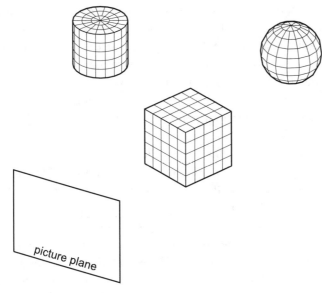

picture plane

10.84 *The radiosity algorithm divides each surface into small patches and computes energy levels for each patch in the scene.*

inter-reflections, and with diffuse area sources of light, such as panes of a window or ceiling light panels (Figure 10.85).

You should use raytracing to produce images of the building's exterior in sunlight with sharp shadows, or images of highly reflective interior spaces, such as building lobbies with mirrors, glass enclosures, and metal railings.

10.85 *A radiosity-rendered image (by Wai Man Cheung). Note the "soft" shadows and subtle changes in shading.*

RENDERING STRATEGIES

As abstractions, hidden-line views reveal limited information about an object's form—they show only outlines (profiles) of the elements making up the object's geometry. *Shaded* views (Figure 10.86), however, add considerably to our understanding of the object's geometry, because they show how it *interacts with light.* As Le Corbusier observed in *Vers une architecture,* "Our eyes are made to see forms in light; light and shade reveal these forms." Shading reveals the orientation of surfaces, clarifies their relationships, and reinforces the illusion of depth. Simple shading is therefore a very useful rendering technique for early design stages because it often clearly presents the essential spatial information, without irrelevant and distracting effects.

In some rendering programs, shaded and hidden-line views can be simultaneously displayed or overlaid (Figure 10.87), resulting in an image that defines both the shape and the orientation of surfaces. Use such images sparingly, because they can often dilute the viewer's attention—surface outlines are less emphasized than in hidden-line images, and similarly there is less emphasis on tone and volume than in shaded views alone.

Additional effects, such as *shadow casting, transparency,* and *reflectivity,* can often add a degree of realism to images created by computer-rendering software (Figure 10.88). To decide what type of image to create (hidden-line, shaded, or realistically rendered), you have to consider its intended purpose. If you just want to check the integrity of the created geometry, a hidden-line or shaded view is sufficient. For presentation purposes, however, you may want to add realistic effects, such as shadow casting and material properties. Use these realistic effects very carefully, since they can often distract both you and your audience from considering what is important. Design is an abstraction of

Although shadows are often needed to provide additional visual and depth cues, or to make artificially created images realistic, they are not always necessary or appropriate. Computation of cast shadows increases considerably the rendering time, and cast shadows can often obscure an important detail or make certain areas of the rendering too dark.

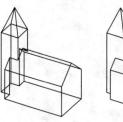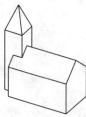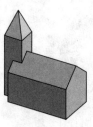

10.86 Wire-frame, hidden-line, and shaded views.

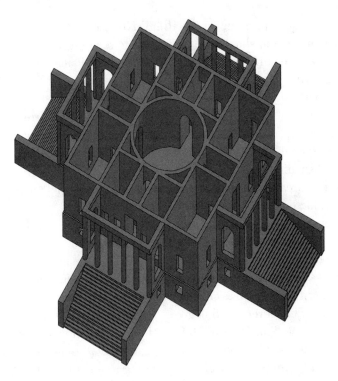

intended reality, and as such, its representation does not have to necessarily mimic the reality.

Among the several rendering techniques introduced in the previous section, *raytracing* and *radiosity* produce highly realistic images, which are often referred to as photo-realistic. Which of these two techniques you should use will depend on the amount of time and the computational resources that are avail-

The Radiosity is computationally much more intensive then raytracing, but, unlike raytracing, it is *view independent.* Once the energy model is generated, any view can very quickly be computed, which makes radiosity particularly suitable for producing animations (a large number of images).

10.88 Shadow casting and material properties can often add a sense of realism to rendered images (shown: an image of Villa Emo, rendered by Robert Mayo).

able, and most important, on the illumination effects that you want to achieve. You should use *raytracing* to render scenes with highly reflective surfaces, specular highlights, and sharp shadows; use raytracing to produce images of the building in bright sunlight, with sharp shadows (Figure 10.89), or to render highly reflective interior spaces, such as building lobbies with mirrors, glass enclosures, and metal railings. You should use *radiosity* to render interior spaces with mostly matte surfaces, diffuse illumination and shading, and inter-reflection effects (Figure 10.90).

As was already mentioned, correct lighting is the single most important factor in creating rendered images. Poorly lit models, no matter how carefully modeled, will result in poor-quality images. Therefore, carefully choose the type, color, and intensity of light sources, and carefully position them within the model.

Use a single *distant, unidirectional* light source to simulate the *sunlight*. A common architectural convention is to place a directional light source at 45 degrees horizontally and vertically from the line of sight (Figure 10.91). However, such a strategy may not always produce good results (Figure 10.92). In any case, make sure that there is sufficient difference in tonal intensities across the surfaces to make images sufficiently legible. Figure 10.93 shows an image with poor illumination and very little difference in shading levels. Figures 10.94 and 10.95 show lighting alternatives that result in much better image "readability."

If the building has an orthogonal plan layout, fairly good results can be achieved by placing the directional light source at

10.89 Raytracing can produce effective images of a building in bright sunlight, with sharp shadows.

10.90 Use radiosity to render images of spaces with diffuse illumination effects.

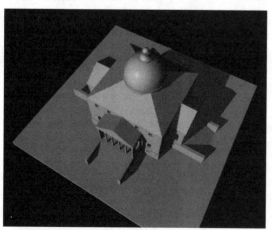

10.89

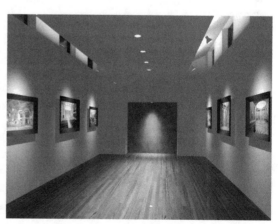

10.90

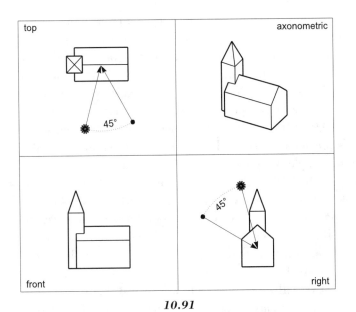

top

axonometric

45°

front

right

10.91

10.91 *A directional light source is typically set at 45 degrees from the line of sight.*

10.92 *Such a strategy may not always produce good results.*

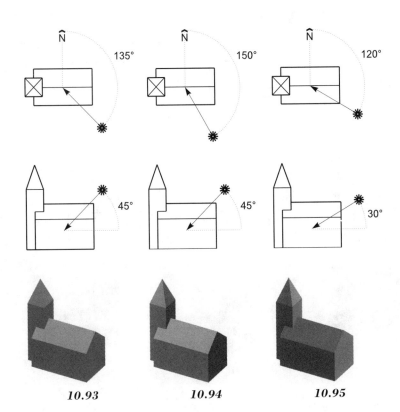

N̂   135°

N̂   150°

N̂   120°

45°

45°

30°

10.93

10.94

10.95

10.93 *A poorly illuminated scene.*

10.94 *The same scene, but with better lighting.*

10.95 *Another alternative.*

incidence angles of 30 degrees (in orthogonal projection) toward the side that will be the brightest, 60 degrees toward the side that will be rendered fairly dark, and 45 degrees toward the side that will be shaded in medium gray tones (Figure 10.96). If you want to have a higher shading contrast in the rendered image, use angles of 15, 75, and 60 degrees (in orthogonal projection), respectively. Figures 10.97–99 show rendered images with the lighting setup that was previously described. Notice how a different side of the building is emphasized in each of the three images.

Note that if the angle of incidence is exactly the same for each of the three sides of a building, all surfaces will be uniformly shaded—you will see only the building's outline (Figure 10.100). If the lighting direction bisects the angle between two surfaces, i.e., if the angle of incidence is identical for both surfaces, they will be shaded with the same tonal value, and the "edge" that visually separates them will be lost (Figure 10.101). To avoid such problems, adjust the lighting direction, display surface outlines, or change the material properties (such as color) of affected surfaces.

10.96 Illuminating the model with projected incidence angles of 30, 45, and 60 degrees.

10.97 Emphasizing the front side . . .

10.98 . . . the right side . . .

10.99 . . . and the top side using projected incidence angles of 15, 75, and 60 (or 30) degrees.

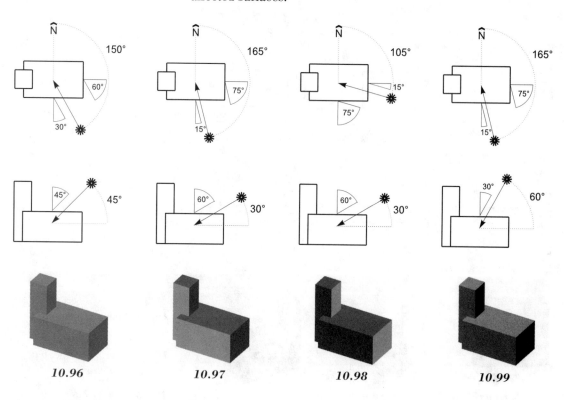

10.96   *10.97*   *10.98*   *10.99*

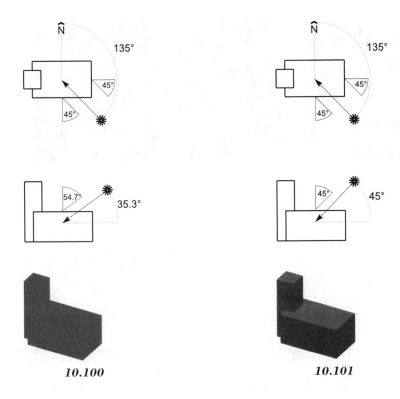

10.100

10.101

10.100 If the angle of incidence is identical for all three
sides, all surfaces will be uniformly shaded.

10.101 Two surfaces will be
identically shaded if the lighting direction bisects the angle
between them.

10.102 Under unidirectional
illumination, the parallel surfaces are shaded with the same
intensity, which can often
make it hard to visually distinguish their edges.

10.103 Such illumination
problems are especially evident in rendered elevation
images.

Another common problem with unidirectional illumination is
that the *parallel* surfaces are shaded with the same intensity.
Often, depending on the viewing direction, edges that separate
different but parallel surfaces are completely lost, thus making
the resulting images difficult to "read" (Figure 10.102). This
problem is particularly evident in plan and elevation projections,
or in one-point perspectives (Figure 10.103). Therefore, the view-

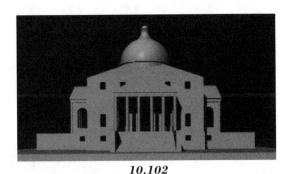

10.102

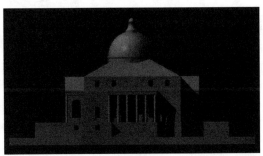

10.103

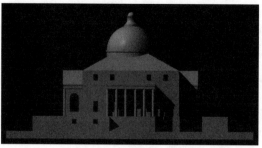

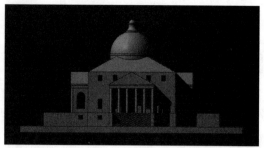

10.104   10.105

10.104 *To correct such problems, either display the surface outlines too . . .*

10.105 *. . . or add a point or spotlight source to introduce some variation in the shading of the affected surfaces.*

ing direction should be carefully selected to avoid visual overlapping of parallel surfaces. If that is not possible, you should either display the surface outlines too (Figure 10.104) or add a point or spotlight source to introduce some variation in the shading of affected surfaces (Figure 10.105).

If you are using more than one light source to illuminate the scene, determine which light will be the primary source of illumination (the so-called key light), and then set up one or more "fill" lights of low intensity to brighten and soften the shadows. In architectural photography, when taking pictures of scale models, the "key" and "fill" lights are typically placed on opposite sides (Figure 10.106) or across from each other (Figure 10.107). Which of the two methods you should use will depend on the desired illumination qualities, such as reflection on glazed areas or

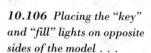

10.106 *Placing the "key" and "fill" lights on opposite sides of the model . . .*

10.107 *. . . or across from each other.*

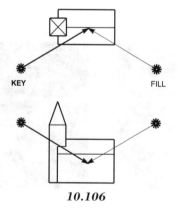

10.106

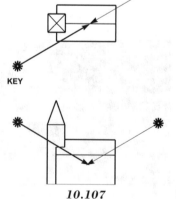

10.107

lighter shadows. Typically, *spotlights* are used as "key" lights, and *point* light sources as "fill" lights.

Another common convention from architectural photography is to render the model against a *black* background to emphasize light surfaces and their profiles (Figure 10.108). If the image background is white, the opposite visual effect occurs—the dark surfaces become emphasized (Figure 10.109). Another common alternative is to render the building against a three-color gradu-ated background, whereby a white color is typically specified at the horizon level (Figure 10.110).

Note that for most presentation purposes, a gray-scale image can be as effective as (and often more effective than) a color ver-sion. If you decide to use color, deploy it very carefully. Note that bright, saturated colors will attract the attention of your audience. You can use bright colors for visual emphasis, but if you apply them carelessly, note that you risk *distracting* the viewers. If you must use color, select soft tones, and apply them judiciously. As

10.108

10.109

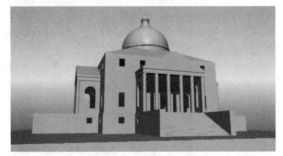

10.110

10.108 A black background emphasizes light surfaces and their profiles.

10.109 A white background emphasizes dark surfaces.

10.110 Another alternative is to use a three-color graduated background.

was already stated, design is an abstraction of intended reality, and, as such, its representation does not have to necessarily mimic the reality.

Image mapping should also be used very cautiously. It can produce very effective results, especially in studying whether the selected materials create desired spatial effects. It is particularly effective in studying interior spaces of considerable importance, such as entry lobbies or boardrooms in corporate buildings, or for detailed facade studies. Great care must be exercised to avoid typical problems, such as perceptible repetition of image maps (Figure 10.111), and illogical, unconvincing mapping to nonrectangular and curved surfaces (Figure 10.112).

Image map alignment is perhaps the most common problem in image mapping. Suppose that you are applying a marble image map onto sides of a cube, as in cubic projection. The rendered image will not look convincing, because the marble veins do not flow smoothly from one side to the other (Figure 10.113). In situations such as this one, project the image map at an angle (typically 45 degrees) using planar projection (Figure 10.114), or apply a *solid texture* of the same material (Figure 10.115).

Note that when the viewpoint is too close to the image-mapped object, most rendering programs perform automatic smoothing of image maps to eliminate *jagged* (*stepped*) *edges* and *pixelation* in rendered images.

Because digital images are composed of discrete square picture elements called *pixels*, straight and curved edges often

10.111 *Avoid perceptible repetition of image maps . . .*

10.112 *. . . and illogical, unconvincing mapping.*

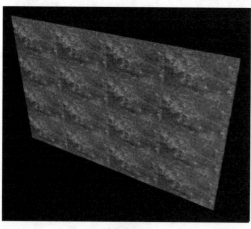

10.111

10.112

10.113

10.114a

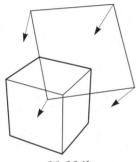

10.114b

10.115

10.113 *Image map alignment is a common problem in image mapping.*

10.114 *Image maps can be projected at an angle to achieve convincing results.*

10.115 *Solid textures often provide the best solution for texture mapping of 3D objects.*

appear in renderings as *jagged* or *stepped* (Figure 10.116). In computer graphics, this effect is referred to as *aliasing* and can be corrected by a technique called *anti-aliasing*, which computes and averages the intensity values of adjacent pixels by *adaptive sampling* (Figure 10.117). A sample of 4, 9, or 16 pixels is used

Note that while anti-aliasing improves the quality of the rendered image, it entails additional calculation. AutoCAD can automatically anti-alias rendered images.

AutoCAD (AutoVision) supports atmospheric effects.

10.116

10.117

10.116 *Jagged edges.*

10.117 *Anti-aliasing of jagged edges.*

10.118 *An image rendered with the "fog" effect.*

10.119 *The same scene rendered with the "falling darkness" effect.*

to compute intensities, which are then averaged to compute the intensity at a single pixel; the higher the sample, the longer it takes to *anti-alias* an image.

Finally, note that most rendering programs can simulate the *atmospheric effects* of fog, haze, and mist, which can often add a

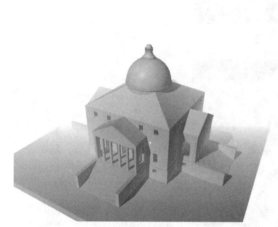

10.118a

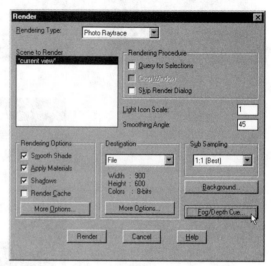

10.118b

10.119a

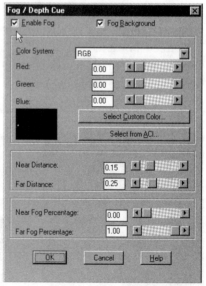

10.119b

heightened sense of depth. Such effects are generated by adding a selected color to surface colors based on a distance from the viewing plane. For example, adding white will produce fog (Figure 10.118), and adding black will produce falling darkness (Figure 10.119). In either case, the image will gain in "depth."

DIGITAL REPRESENTATION OF IMAGES

In the world of computer graphics, pictures are stored and encoded as bitmap images, as a raster grid of square elements called *pixels* (for "*picture elements*") (Figure 10.120). Each pixel has light intensities associated with it that are encoded as binary numbers, i.e., as strings of bits, 0's, and 1's (Figure 10.121); hence the name bitmap (map of bits) images. The number of pixels measured horizontally and vertically is called *image resolution* (Figure 10.122). Until a few years ago, image resolution of 640 pixels horizontally and 480 pixels vertically was considered standard. Today images with resolution of 800×600 and $1{,}024 \times 768$ pixels are becoming common. Higher resolutions are used

Image resolution is expressed as *number of pixels per inch* when image size is measured in inches.

10.120 Pixels (picture elements).

10.120a

10.120b

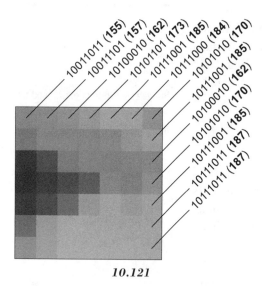

10011011 (**155**)
10011101 (**157**)
10100010 (**162**)
10101101 (**173**)
10111001 (**185**)
10111000 (**184**)
10101010 (**170**)
10111001 (**185**)
10100010 (**162**)
10101010 (**170**)
10101101 (**185**)
10111001 (**187**)
10111011 (**187**)
10111011 (**187**)

10.121

10.122a: 400 x 400 pixels

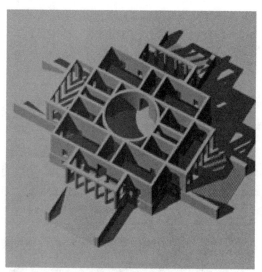

10.122b: 200 x 200 pixels

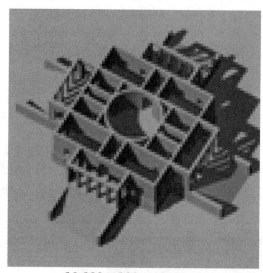

10.122c: 100 x 100 pixels

10.121 *Each pixel has a light intensity, encoded as a binary number.*

10.122 *Images of higher resolution contain more image data.*

when images are printed at paper sizes larger then 10 inches (25 cm) to avoid perceptible *pixelation*.

The number of bits used to describe the intensity of each pixel determines the *bit depth* (or *color depth*) of an image. By using one bit per pixel, a pixel can have either no intensity (black—0) or full intensity (white—1); thus, *black and white (b&w) images* (Figure

10.123a

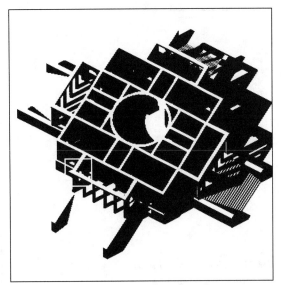

10.123b

10.123 *Black and white images contain only black or white pixels.*

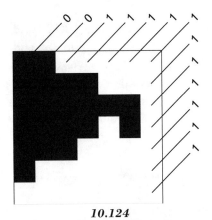

10.124

10.124 *Black and white images require only one bit of information per pixel.*

10.123) are often referred to as *one-bit* images, since they require one bit of information per pixel (Figure 10.124).

By using 8 bits per pixel, 256 ($2^8 = 256$) different intensities can be associated with each pixel, from none, or 0 (00000000), to full, or 255 (11111111 in binary representation, the highest value that can be represented with an 8-bit number). In this fashion, 256 different intensities of gray color can be represented from none (black) to full (white), which is more than sufficient to represent different shades of gray visible to the human eye (Figure

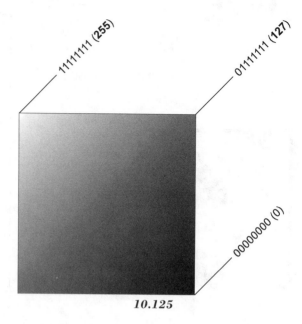

11111111 (**255**)

01111111 (**127**)

00000000 (**0**)

10.125

10.125 *256 different intensities can be represented using 8-bit numbers.*

10.125). The so-called *gray-scale* images (Figures 10.120 and 10.121) contain pixels whose intensities vary from 0 to 255 and therefore have the bit depth of 8 bits per pixel. This type of image is most often used when printing on black-and-white printers.

Color images are encoded as a combination of different intensities of red, green, and blue, whereby each color can have 256 intensities. In this fashion a total of more than 16 million colors

10.126 *16.7 million colors can be produced as a combination of different intensities of red, green, and blue.*

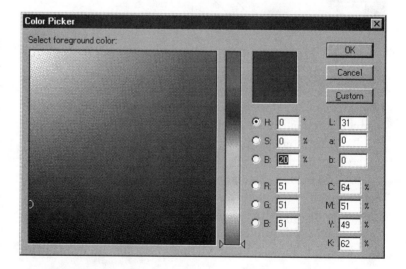

$(256 \times 256 \times 256 = 16,777,216)$ can be displayed (Figure 10.126). Each pixel in color images requires the total of 24 bits— 8 bits for each of the three primary colors (8 for red, 8 for green, and 8 for blue). In the RGB color model, specifying full intensity for two of the three primary colors and no intensity for the remaining color produces secondary colors, such as yellow, cyan, and magenta. For example, yellow color is composed of 100% red (at full intensity of 255), 100% green (255), and 0% blue (0). White is composed of all three colors at full intensity, and black (or no color) requires that the intensity of all three component colors be zero. Various shades of gray are produced as equal intensities of all three colors; for example, 80% gray (dark gray) is produced by setting each of the three intensities to 20%, or 51 (Figure 10.126).

Because of their ability to represent a rather large number of colors, 24-bit color images are also called *true-color* or *RGB images*. Humans, however, can distinguish approximately 4,000 different colors on average, which is far less than the 16.7 million that can be represented by "true-color," 24-bit images. As a result, images with lower bit depth are sometimes used. Fairly common are *16-bit* images, where 5 bits are used for each of the primary colors; the last, sixteenth bit is used as a control bit. The number of colors that 16-bit images can represent is 32,768 (2^5), far less than 24-bit images but far more than the 4,000 colors an average human can perceive.

Another type of digital images commonly used are the so-called *indexed color images*, which use 8 bits to represent 256 indexes, from 0 to 255, which point to a color table (also called a *color palette*) containing only 256 colors from the range of 16.7 million displayable colors (Figure 10.127). For example, index 0 (00000000) can point to a color whose RGB intensities are R = 255, G = 108, and B = 178, and index 69 (01000101) can point to color whose RGB values are R = 234, G = 204, and B = 098. Note that indexed color images are 8-bit images, i.e., they have the bit depth of 8 bits per pixel.

Digital images require a considerable amount of storage; each pixel in a 24-bit color image requires 24 bits of information, which equals 3 bytes (one byte of information has 8 bits). An RGB image with the resolution of 800 by 600 pixels has a total of $800 \times 600 = 480,000$ pixels, which will require $480,000 \times 3 = 1,440,000$ bytes of storage space, which corresponds to the maxi-

The actual image file size is slightly larger, due to some non-graphical data stored with the image, such as image resolution, a version number, the text of a copyright notice, or the compression method used.

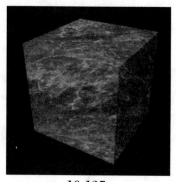

10.127a

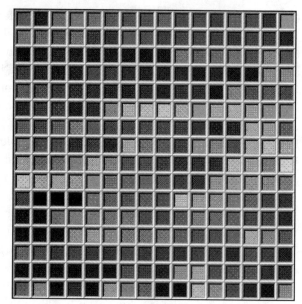

10.127b

10.127 *An 8-bit indexed color image and its color table (palette).*

mum storage capacity of a 3.5″ high-density diskette. The amount of storage space required by an image with the resolution of x by y pixels can be computed according to the following formula:

$$\text{number of bytes needed} = \text{total number of pixels} (X * Y) * \text{bit depth} / 8$$

According to this formula, a gray-scale image with the resolution of $1{,}024 \times 768$ pixels will require $(1{,}024 * 768) * 8 / 8 = 786{,}432$ bytes. For comparison, you can store within the same space a file containing text from a book with almost 400 pages (at 2,000 characters per page, i.e., 2,000 bytes per page)!

Since the storage requirements for digital images are rather high, a number of *image compression* and *decompression* techniques have been developed. A popular compression technique is *run-length encoding* (also known by its acronym—RLE). It exploits the fact that many digital images have adjacent pixels with the same intensity values. It counts these pixels in each row and replaces the successive, identical pixels by a number followed by the pixel's intensity. For example, a row of 12 8-bit pixels whose intensity values are, successively,

007 007 214 214 214 187 187 187 187 187 187 057

can be recorded using run-length encoding as

2 007 3 214 6 187 057

The compressed version contains 7 numbers and will require 7 bytes, compared with 12 8-bit numbers (12 bytes) in the uncompressed version. In this example, a savings of 42% in storage space can result by using RLE image compression.

Lempel-Ziv-Wenzel (or LZW) is another commonly used image-compression algorithm. Both RLE and LZW image compression are *lossless*—in other words, there is no information loss after decompression of the image information. While these two techniques can often produce considerable storage savings for images that contain large areas of the same color (such as computer renderings), they result in much smaller compression ratios for images in which color differs considerably from pixel to pixel (such as computer renderings with texture maps and image backgrounds, and most scanned images). To achieve higher compression ratios (1:10 to 1:50), *lossy* compression algorithms can be used, such as the one used in JPEG image format (see the next paragraph). While lossy compression techniques can often produce high compression ratios, the quality of the compressed image is often degraded, because some intensity values are altered in the process (the original values are *lost*). Lower compression ratios (1:10 and less) often produce satisfactory results. In summary, *lossless* image compression results in smaller file sizes, without image degradation; *lossy* image compression can produce very small files, but some image data is *lost* (hence the name *lossy* compression).

Image data can be encoded in different ways or *formats*. Each image format describes the graphical and nongraphical data associated with an image. The graphical data describes the color of each pixel, while the nongraphical data describes the image resolution, number of bits per pixel, and some other information, such as a version number, the text of a copyright notice, and the compression method used. The most commonly used image formats are TIFF—Tagged Image File Format (filename extension .tif), GIF—Graphics Interchange Format (.gif), Targa (.tga), Win-

The basic idea behind the JPEG compression method is to segregate image information based on importance, and then discard less important information to reduce the total amount of data associated with an image. JPEG image compression divides an image into small blocks of pixels, whose intensity values are processed using a *discrete cosine transformation*. A matrix of intensity values is transformed into a matrix of amplitude values corresponding to different cosine-wave frequencies; the high-frequency information is then discarded and replaced with zero values. When the image data is decompressed for display or output purposes, the inverse discrete cosine transformation computes the intensity values, which are very close to the original ones. Because of approximate intensity values, some blurring and discoloration are often evident in images.

10.128 *Painting and retouching tools in* Adobe Photoshop.

dows bitmap format (.bmp), JPEG—Joint Photographic Experts Group format (.jpg), and EPS—Encapsulated PostScript (.eps). Of all these formats, JPEG (pronounced *jay-peg*) is the only format with *lossy* compression.

In summary, the key characteristics of digital images are their *resolution,* measured in pixels horizontally and vertically, the *bit depth,* or the number of bits per pixel, the *compression method* used, and the image data *format.*

IMAGE PROCESSING AND COMPOSITION

Sometimes a rendered image will contain a perceptible error, such as a wrong material definition applied to some surface, a part of the model that isn't correctly modeled, or incorrect overall contrast, brightness, or tonal range. While each of the erroneous images can be re-rendered, it is often faster to use an *image processing and painting* program, such as *Adobe Photoshop,* and apply some of the painting and retouching tools (Figure 10.128) to achieve a desired result. Specific areas of an image can be selected, cut, copied, and pasted; painted over; and transformed in many different ways. The overall contrast, brightness, and tonal range can easily be adjusted

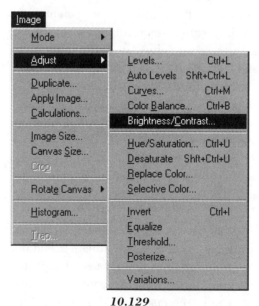

10.129 *The* Adjust *submenu options in* Adobe Photoshop.

10.129

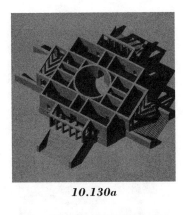

10.130a

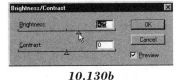

10.130b

10.130c

10.131a

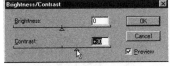

10.131b

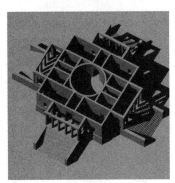

10.131c

(Figure 10.129). If the image is too dark, it can be brightened, and vice versa (Figure 10.130). If the image is blurry, it can be sharpened; if it is too crisp, it can be blurred to simulate the softening effect of the photographic filters. If the contrast is too low or too high, it can be interactively adjusted (Figure 10.131). If the image is reddish, the color range can be adjusted. The digital images can be manipulated in many ways.

More interesting, a computer-rendered image can be transformed through *filtering* into an image that looks like a watercolor painting, a graphic pen sketch, or a chalk and charcoal drawing, thus giving it a softer, handmade look (Figures 10.132–5). Many other transformations are possible (Figures 10.136–9). Generating an image altered by a filtering transformation is often a one-step process that involves selecting an appropriate option from one of the pull-down menus (Figure

10.130 *Adjusting the brightness of an image.*

10.131 *Adjusting the contrast of an image.*

10.132

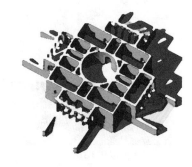

10.133a

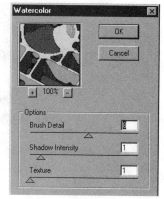

10.133b

10.132 The original image.

10.133 A watercolor filtering transformation of the original image.

10.134a

10.134b

10.134 A graphic pen sketch filtering transformation.

10.135a

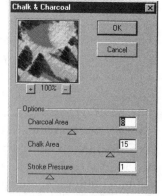

10.135b

10.135 A chalk and charcoal drawing.

10.136

10.137

10.138

10.139

10.136 *The original image.*

10.137 Negative clouds *transformation (brightness and contrast adjusted).*

10.138 Photocopy *transformation (brightness and contrast adjusted).*

10.139 High pass *transformation (brightness and contrast adjusted).*

Image filtering is accomplished by applying a *convolution matrix* transformation to each pixel in the image. The color value of each pixel and its surrounding pixels is multiplied by the corresponding coefficients in the convolution matrix, and new color value is computed by adding the resulting numbers. The coefficients of the convolution matrix determine the outcome of the filtering transformation. For example, the coefficients in the *blurring* convolution matrix have values smaller than one, with the total sum that equals one, meaning that every pixel will absorb some color of the adjacent pixels, but that the overall image brightness will remain the same. All coefficients in the *embossing* convolution matrix are zeros, except two in opposite corners of the matrix, which are set to 1 and −1. By varying the values in the convolution matrix, very different and often useful filtering transformations can be produced.

10.140) and specifying parameters of the transformation. Moreover, a rendered image can be used as an underlay in paint programs to sketch and paint over; new sketches can be saved on separate layers, which can then be shown simultaneously as a set, much like the sketches on tracing paper overlaid on top of one another.

In most renderers, the image of the rendered image can be superimposed over some background image at the end of the rendering process. A digital image of the building's site, a landscape, or a sky scene can be used as a background underlay for the rendered image (Figure 10.141).

Placing a rendered image of a building into a digitized image of the context requires careful matching of the viewing and lighting parameters. Typically, the location from which a photograph, a slide, or a digital image is taken is carefully recorded. Then a matching perspective view of the model is created using the same viewing parameters, such as the location of camera and target points, and the lens length. A rendered image

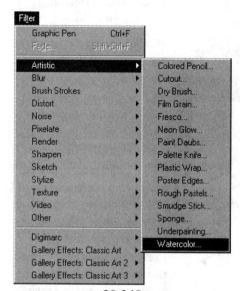

10.140a

10.140b

10.140 The menu of possible filtering transformations is fairly large.

is then computed using the same sun location, i.e., the same north direction and date and time when the site picture was taken. If the data when the picture was taken is not available, the image should be carefully analyzed to determine these parameters. First the *horizon* line should be located in the background image—typically, it is in the middle—but if the image is

10.141 Superimposing a rendering over a background image (images by Robert Mayo).

10.141a

10.141b

10.142

10.143

cropped, it might be in a different location (Figure 10.142). Then shadows should be analyzed in the background image to determine where the sun is located, and its angle from the horizontal plane (Figure 10.143).

In addition to viewing and lighting parameters, other elements will require attention to achieve a convincing result. Often there will be some objects in the background image that should remain in the foreground even after the rendering is overlaid on top. Such foreground fragments can be cut and pasted into the synthesized, composite image by using some image-processing software. Additional entourage elements, such as people, cars, shrubs, and trees, can be added as well. Finally, hard edges of the rendered image and pasted elements should be blended into the background using a "smudge" or "smoothing brush" tool.

Image composition is a powerful technique that allows rendered objects to be shown in the real context. It often requires careful placement of the rendered image and meticulous editing of the resulting composite image to achieve convincing results.

DIGITIZING IMAGES

Scanning is the process of digitizing an image, whereby the image itself (a photo or a slide) is divided into an imaginary grid of

10.142 Finding the horizon line.

10.143 Determining the sun location by analyzing the shadows.

Note that sometimes you may need to adjust the contrast and brightness of the rendering so that it matches the tonal values of the background image.

In most scanning devices, a beam of light traverses the surface of an image. The intensities of the reflected light are converted by light-sensitive cells into voltage levels, which are then converted into 8-bit numbers by analog-to-digital converter (ADC).

square elements called *pixels,* and whereby analog signals representing various intensities of light across the image are converted into their digital counterparts—binary numbers, which are then associated with the corresponding pixels.

Scanners are hardware devices used to perform the process of scanning. Flatbed scanners (Figure 10.144) are used to digitize photographs or other flat material, while slide scanners (Figure 10.145), as their name implies, are used to scan slides. Other devices, such as video-frame grabbers, are used to capture still video images, and digital cameras (Figure 10.146), like their analog counterparts, capture pictures that are stored as digital images on a miniature hard disk or some other storage device, instead of film.

One of the most important parameters of the scanners is *optical resolution,* which refers to the maximum number of pixels (horizontally and vertically) that the scanner can capture. An associated parameter is the maximum *interpolated resolution;* some scanners can further enlarge the resolution of the scanned images by interpolating intensity values between adjacent pixels. Scanners' *bit depth* determines the maximum number of bits used to encode light intensities; 24-bit, 30-bit, and 36-bit scanners are the most common nowadays. Another important parameter is how many passes the scanner needs to digitize an image. A single-pass scanner can detect intensities of red, green, and blue colors in one sweep across the image surface, while a three-pass scanner performs separate passes for each of the primary colors.

When scanning images that will be used for rough design studies, a low-image resolution, such as 640 by 480 pixels, is

Note that there is a direct relationship between the resolution of the scanned images and the quality of the printed output (which largely depends on the printer's resolution). This relationship is described in detail in the next section.

10.144 Flatbed *scanner.*

10.145 Slide *scanner.*

10.146 Digital *camera.*

10.144   *10.145*   *10.146*

often sufficient. If the scanned image is intended for image composition or for other presentation purposes, higher resolutions, such as $1,024 \times 768$ pixels and up, should be used.

PRINTING IMAGES

The most effective way to present computer renderings is to project them onto a white background at a size large enough that extends to the edges of the audience's viewing field. The images can be projected using a *video projector* (Figure 10.147) directly from the computer, or as slides, once the images are recorded on slide film using an output device called a *digital film recorder* (Figure 10.148).

For most presentation purposes, computer renderings are printed as gray-scale (black-and-white) or color images on *paper*. Using *black-and-white ink-jet* and *laser printers*, inexpensive hard-copy output can easily be produced. For best results, color images should first be converted to gray scale, and then printed. Sometimes you may have to adjust the image's contrast and brightness to achieve a desired result—you can either perform this adjustment in the image-processing software or use the printer's driver software to specify how graphics should be printed.

Another common printing problem is perceptible *banding* in the printed image, which results from the printer's limited ability to produce many levels of gray (Figure 10.149). The printer's resolution, the number of dots it can print per inch (*dpi—dots per inch*), determines the number of gray tones that can be printed: a 300 dpi printer can typically generate between

10.147 *Video projector.*

10.148 *Digital film recorder.*

10.149 *Perceptible bending can result in printed output from low-resolution printers.*

10.147

10.148

10.149

10.150 A dithered *image.*

10.151 A halftone *image.*

10.150

10.151

Matching colors **from the RGB to the CMYK system is not a very accurate process; not all RGB colors can be reproduced using the CMYK system. There are some color standards, such as** *PANTONE* **by Letraset, Inc., which attempt to alleviate the common color-matching problems.**

50 and 60 gray levels, while a 600 dpi printer can generate more than 100 (note that this is much less than a full spectrum of 255 different shades of gray that gray-scale images can contain). There is a direct relationship between the printer's resolution and the number of gray levels it can produce: the higher the resolution of the output device, the higher the number of tonal values it can generate.

Note that for the best results, you should use the correct image resolution. Use 75 pixels per inch image resolution for 300 dpi printers. Set the image resolution to 150 pixels per inch for 600 dpi printers, and use 300 pixels per inch for 1,200 dpi image setters. For most practical purposes, a gray-scale image with a resolution of 1,000 by 750 pixels will produce acceptable results.

You can print computer renderings as either *dithered* or *halftone* images. *Dithering* is a printing technique that randomly places the dots of the same size at different densities to achieve different tonal values (Figure 10.150). In *halftoning,* different intensities are represented by dots of varying size placed in a regular grid (Figure 10.151); the distance between dots and the size of the dots depend on the printer's resolution.

It is often difficult to achieve satisfactory color output of rendered images. The problems in color printing essentially stem from two different models of color representation. In computer graphics, colors are represented using different intensities of red, green, and blue (the *RGB color model*). The printing industry, on the other hand, uses a different color system, based on cyan, magenta, yellow, and black pigment colors (the so-called *CMYK color model*). Whereby the mixing of red, green, and blue produces white in the RGB color system, the same colors would yield black in the CMYK system.

To further aggravate the printing problem, different color printing technologies produce output of varying quality. While *ink-jet* technology produces satisfactory results, *dye-sublimation* printers can achieve the best, near photographic quality.

11

RENDERING TUTORIAL 1: LIGHTING

As mentioned in the previous chapter, *lighting,* or *illumination,* is the single most important factor in creating computer renderings. In this exercise you will learn how to define and place *lights* in 3D space, and how to apply different *rendering techniques* to generate *rendered images* of Villa Rotonda's 3D geometric model. You will also learn how to manipulate light properties, such as *position, type of light emission, color,* and *intensity,* to create well-lit *scenes.* Note that poorly lit models, no matter how carefully modeled, will result in poor-quality images.

MODIFYING THE MODEL

1 Before you place lights around the model and create rendered images, you will first delete model elements that are no longer needed, such as grid lines created at the very beginning. You will also "purge" unused layers, and assign white color to all objects by changing the layer colors.

Start AutoCAD, and open the previously saved drawing (Rotonda.dwg). If you are continuing from the last exercise, skip this step.

2 To delete the grid lines, turn on and set the layer GRID as the current layer, and turn off all other layers. You should see only the construction lines of the layer GRID. Make the plan viewport active, and choose the *Zoom All* tool to display the drawing in its entirety, i.e., within its limits; then choose the *Erase* tool, and use the *crossing* option to select all the construction lines; press the *Return* key to complete the object selection and the ERASE command.

3 Turn on all layers, and set the layer 0 (zero, i.e., the first layer in the list) as the current layer.

4 Enter PURGE at the command prompt, and enter LA (the *LAyer* option) to delete all unused layers. In R14, press *Enter* when asked for *names to purge* to choose all layers for inspection by AutoCAD (skip this step if you are using R13). Press *Enter* again to *verify each name to be purged* (skip this step if you are using R13). When prompted, enter Y to purge layers 0-OPENINGS, 0-STAIRS, 1-OPENINGS, 2-OPENINGS, and GRID. These layers will be purged since there aren't any objects on them. 3D objects on these layers were deleted either explicitly (construction lines on layer GRID), or in Boolean operations (layers containing solid objects representing stairs and openings).

5 Next click on the *Layers* button on the *Object Properties* toolbar. In R14, place the cursor inside the layers list, and press the right mouse button (or the *Return* button on your pointing device) and choose *Select All* from the pop-up list. In R13, click on the *Select All* button. All the layer names will be highlighted.

To change the color assigned to the selected layers, in R14 click on any square color swatch in the list or on the *Color (C . . .)* button; in R13 click on the *Set Color* button. Choose white color in the *Select Color* dialog box, and click on *OK*. Note that all the layers in the list are now assigned white color. Click on the *OK* button. All objects will now have white color.

6 Save the modified model file under a different name, such as Render.dwg.

FLAT AND SMOOTH SHADING

7 When architectural scale models are photographed, they are often placed against a black background, typically on a black, light-absorbing fabric. A similar convention is often used in architectural computer graphics, whereby models are rendered against a black background.

If the graphic window background is white, change it to black in the following way: from the *Tools* (R13 *Options*) menu choose *Preferences,* and in the resulting dialog box, click on the *Display* (R13 *System*) tab (Figure 11.7a), then click on the *Colors* (R13 *Color*) button. Select the *graphics window background* as the *window element* to change, and click on the black color swatch (Figure 11.7b). Click on the *OK* button to continue.

11.7a *Changing AutoCAD* display *preferences in R14 and R13.*

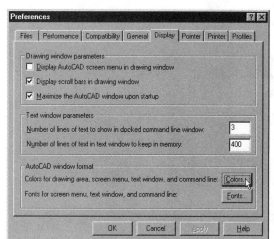

11.7a1

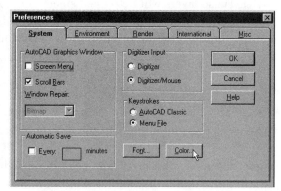

11.7a2

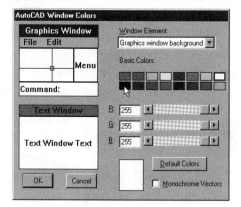

11.7b *Changing the graphics window background color to black.*

8 Flat shading is the simplest rendering technique supported by AutoCAD. To create a flat-shaded image of the Villa Rotonda 3D model, first make the axonometric view active. Turn off the display of the UCS icon: in R14, from the *View* menu choose *Display*, then *UCS Icon*, and then *On* to remove the check mark displayed next to it; in R13, from the *Options* menu choose *UCS*, then *Icon*.

Next, in R14, from the *View* menu choose *Shade*, then *256 Color;* in R13, enter SHADEDGE at the command prompt, set this system variable to 0, and then enter the SHADE command to create a shaded view. The result is a flat-shaded image displayed in the axonometric viewport (Figure 11.8).

The SHADEDGE system variable determines how the SHADE command generates the shaded images. When SHADEDGE is set to 0, a 256-color shaded image is created; faces are shaded, and edges are not highlighted. A setting of 1 produces a 256-color shaded image with surface edges drawn in background color. A setting of 2 produces a hidden-line image with edges drawn in object color. Finally, a setting of 3 (the default setting) creates shaded images, whereby surfaces are shaded uniformly, in object color, with edges drawn in background color. AutoCAD also uses the percentage of diffuse reflection and ambient light set by the SHADEDIF system variable.

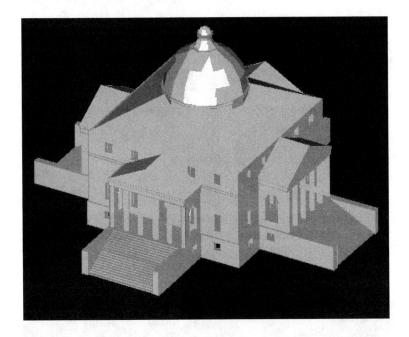

11.8 The flat-shaded image of Villa Rotonda.

In this shading mode, AutoCAD uses an imaginary directional light source placed directly behind the "eye" (the camera), with light rays parallel to the viewing direction. AutoCAD shades the surfaces in the image based on the angle that each surface forms with the lighting, i.e., viewing direction. (If you recall from the previous chapter, in flat or cosine shading, the tonal shading values are computed based on the angle that each *surface normal* forms with the arriving *light rays*.) Note that flat shading renders each surface uniformly; there is no color variation across the surface.

9 In flat shading, the curved surfaces are approximated by a number of small four-sided or triangular surface patches or facets, and are rendered as faceted (note how the dome is rendered in Figure 11.8). If the facets are sufficiently small, i.e., if the approximation is sufficiently fine, the resulting image is often satisfactory (Figure 11.9). Increasing the number of facets, however, increases the rendering time.

In AutoCAD, the number of facets in curved surfaces is controlled by the FACETRES system variable. To increase the number of facets, enter FACETRES at the command prompt, and enter 2 as the new value; then create another shaded view of the model. Note how the approximation is much finer this time (Figure 11.9); also note that it takes much longer to compute the shaded image.

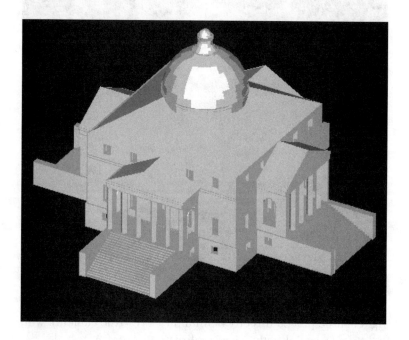

11.9 Curved surfaces can be shaded more accurately by increasing the number of facets.

10 Flat shading is most often used during modeling to verify the results of the various operations and transformations because it is the fastest rendering algorithm available in AutoCAD. To increase visual clarity and readability of flat-shaded images, they are often rendered with visible surface edges (Figure 11.10a). To render such images in AutoCAD, in R14, from the *View* menu choose *Shade,* then *256 Color Edge Highlight;* in R13, set the SHADEDGE system variable to 1, and enter the SHADE command to create a shaded view with edges.

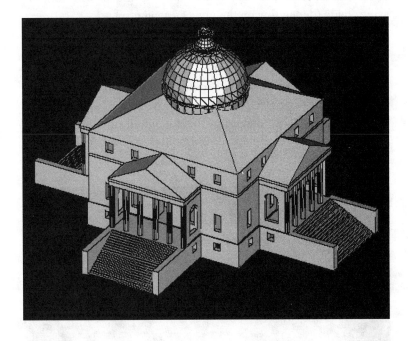

11.10a Displaying edges in flat-shaded images.

This shading mode is almost a necessity in rendering facades or plan views. To see the difference, make the plan viewport active, and create shaded images without edges (Figure 11.10b) and with edges (Figure 11.10c). Note how the shaded view without edges is almost completely illegible.

11.10b

11.10c

11.10b Shaded plan view without edges.

11.10c Shaded plan view with edges.

11 Another common problem with flat-shaded views is that under certain viewing (lighting) conditions, perpendicular surfaces can be rendered with the same tonal value. For example, if you shade an isometric view, almost all the surfaces will have the same shade (depending on the object's geometry).

Make the axonometric viewport active, and set up an isometric view: from the *View* menu choose *3D Viewpoint* (R13 *3D Viewpoint Presets*), then *SE Isometric*. In R14, from the *View* menu choose *Shade,* then *256 Color* to create a flat-shaded image; in R13, first set the SHADEDGE system variable to 0, and then enter the SHADE command at the command prompt. Note the uniform shading on almost all horizontal and vertical surfaces (Figure 11.11).

11.11 If you shade an isometric view, almost all the horizontal and vertical surfaces will have the same shading values.

In this case, the horizontal surfaces and vertical surfaces parallel to the front and the right side of the building will have the same shading values because their surface normals form the same angle with the lighting (viewing) direction.

12 Restore the previous axonometric view. From the *View* menu choose *Named Views.* Select the view named STANDARD_AXO in the list, click on the *Restore* button, and click on *OK.*

13 Smooth-shaded views are created using the RENDER command. In R14, from the *View* menu choose *Render,* and then *Render* again; in R13, choose *Render* from the *AutoVis* menu, or enter RENDER at the command prompt. Alternatively, you can select the *Render* tool (Figure 11.13a) on the *Render* (R13 *AutoVis*) toolbar (Figures 11.13b and c).

11.13a The Render tool.

11.13b The Render toolbar in R14.

11.13c The AutoVis toolbar in R13.

In the resulting *Render* dialog box (Figure 11.13d), make sure that the *Smooth Shade* option is checked in the *Rendering Options* section, that the *Rendering Type* is set to *Render* (R13 *AutoCAD Render*), and that the *Destination* is set to *Viewport;* then click on the *Render* button to create a smooth-shaded rendering (Figure 11.13e).

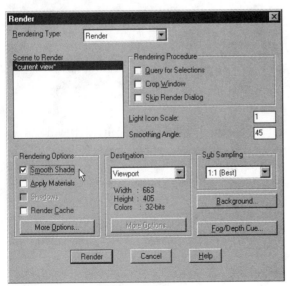

11.13d1

11.13d The Render dialog box in R14 and R13.

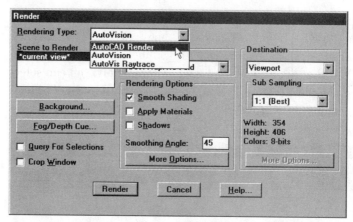

11.13d2

11.13e *The smooth-shaded rendering of Villa Rotonda.*

Since no light source has been defined, AutoCAD will use an imaginary directional light source placed directly behind the "eye," with light rays parallel to the viewing direction (as in previous examples).

14 You can apply either *Gouraud* or *Phong* rendering algorithm to create smooth-shaded views. AutoCAD uses Gouraud algorithm by default. To use Phong algorithm, select the *Render* tool, and click on the *More Options* button. In the *Render Options* dialog box (Figure 11.14a) select the *Phong* option, and click on *OK*.

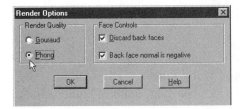

11.14a The Render Options *dialog box.*

Although there is no apparent difference between smooth-shaded renderings created by Gouraud and Phong algorithms, note that Gouraud algorithm often renders inaccurately the *specular highlights* on curved surfaces (such as the villa's dome); Phong algorithm computes much more accurate renderings (Figure 11.14b). Also note that Gouraud algorithm is slightly faster than Phong.

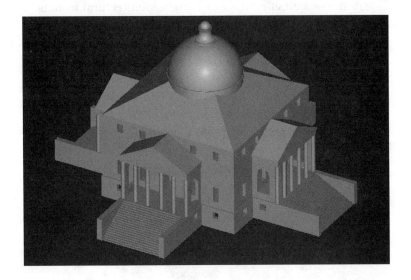

11.14b The smooth-shaded rendering created using Phong algorithm.

15 Flat-shaded views can also be created using the RENDER command. Simply remove the check mark from the *Smooth Shade* option in the *Render* dialog box (Figure 11.13d), and click on *OK* to create a flat-shaded view.

16 Save the model file as Render.dwg.

DISTANT LIGHTS

17 AutoCAD (i.e., AutoVision) supports four types of light sources: *ambient, point, spot,* and *distant.*

The *ambient* light provides constant, uniform illumination to every surface in the model; it comes from no particular source and has no direction—it is omnipresent. *Point light* sources emit light in all directions and are often referred to as *omnidirectional lights* because of this property. Point lights are typically used to simulate light emitted by a lightbulb, or as an alternative to ambient light as "fill light." *Spotlights* emit a directional cone of light and are most often used as "key" lights or to illuminate areas of special interest. *Distant* light sources are unidirectional—they emit light uniformly in one direction, as parallel light rays. Because of its emission properties, a distant light source is typically used to simulate the *sunlight.*

A simple and effective way to light architectural models in AutoCAD is to specify a single *distant* light source as the "sun." To create a distant light source, in R14, from the *View* menu choose *Render,* then *Light;* in R13, from the *AutoVis* menu choose *Lights.* Alternatively, you can select the *Lights* tool (Figure 11.17a) on the *Render* (R13 *AutoVis*) toolbar. In the resulting *Lights* dialog box (Figure 11.17b), select *Distant Light* from the drop-down list, and click on the *New* button.

11.17a The Lights *tool in R14 and R13.*

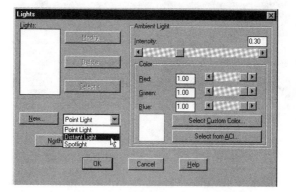

11.17b The Lights *dialog box.*

In the *New Distant Light* dialog box (Figure 11.17c), name this new light source SUN, and enter −150 as its *azimuth;* note that its *altitude* is 30 degrees. Click on *OK* to continue. The name of the newly created light source will appear in the list. Click on *OK* to place this light source in the model space.

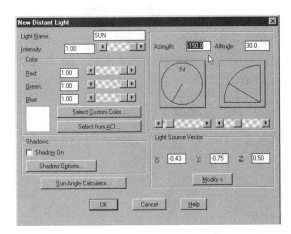

11.17c The New Distant Light *dialog box.*

18 Now create a smooth-shaded rendering of the axonometric view. In R14, enter 100 [1] as the *Light Icon Scale* before you click on the *Render* button in the *Render* dialog box (skip this step if you are using R13). Notice how the right side of the building is dark (Figure 11.18) because it is in the shadow—it doesn't receive any light from the "sun." Also notice the location of the specular highlight on the dome.

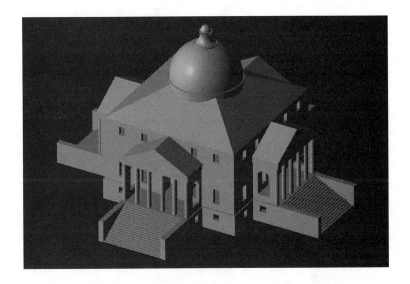

11.18 A rendered image of the model illuminated by a single distant light source.

19 When you create a light source, AutoCAD inserts a *block* object ("icon") into the model, which indicates the position, type, and name of the light source. It uses different icons to represent point, spot-, and distant light sources (Figure 11.19a). To see the icon representing the previously created light source (SUN), make the plan view active, and select the *Zoom All* tool. Notice the small icon in the lower left corner (Figure 11.19b); zoom in to that area to get a better look at the icon (Figure 11.19c), then select the *Zoom Previous* tool to display the previous view.

11.19a AutoCAD uses differ-
ent icons to represent point,
spot-, and distant light
sources.

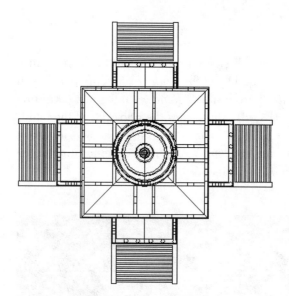

11.19b The SUN light source
icon in the model space.

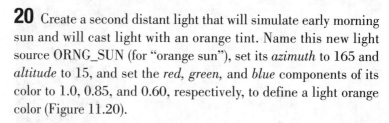

11.19c The SUN icon.

20 Create a second distant light that will simulate early morning sun and will cast light with an orange tint. Name this new light source ORNG_SUN (for "orange sun"), set its *azimuth* to 165 and *altitude* to 15, and set the *red*, *green*, and *blue* components of its color to 1.0, 0.85, and 0.60, respectively, to define a light orange color (Figure 11.20).

21 There are now two light sources in the model space. If you render the axonometric view, there will be too much light in the

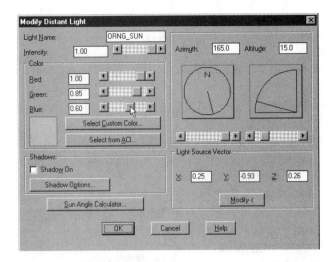

11.20 Defining a distant light source that will simulate early morning sun.

"scene" (Figure 11.21a), i.e., the image will appear too bright in some areas.

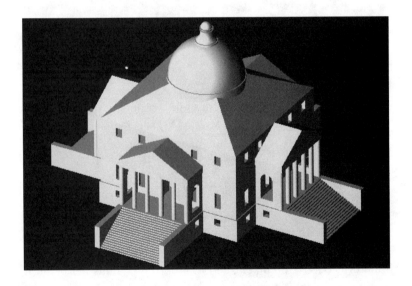

11.21a A rendered image with too much light.

In AutoCAD (and AutoVision in R13) you can specify the light sources that should be used to compute rendered images by using the "scene" concept. A scene is defined based on a selected view of the model and one or more light sources selected from the list of already created lights. You can define an unlimited number of scenes.

11.21b *The* Scenes *tool.*

To define a scene with only one light source, the "orange sun" (ORNG_SUN), in R14, from the *View* menu choose *Render,* then *Scene;* in R13, from the *AutoVis* menu choose *Scenes.* Alternatively, you can select the *Scenes* tool (Figure 11.21b) on the *Render* (R13 *AutoVis*) toolbar, or enter SCENE at the command prompt. In the resulting *Scenes* dialog box click on the *New* button (Figure 11.21c). Enter MORNING as the *scene name* in the *New Scene* dialog box, and select the ORNG_SUN light and the CURRENT view in the corresponding lists (Figure 11.21d). Click on *OK* to continue.

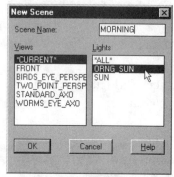

11.21c *The* Scenes *dialog box.*

11.21d *Defining a new scene.*

11.21c

11.21d

22 Now make the axonometric viewport active and render an image using the newly defined MORNING scene. Select the *Render* tool, enter RENDER at the command prompt, or choose *Render* from one of the pull-down menus. Select MORNING as the *Scene to Render,* check *Smooth Shade* in the *Rendering Options,* choose *Render Window* in the drop-down list as the *Destination* (Figure 11.22a), and click on the *Render* button to display the rendered image in a separate "render" window (Figure 11.22b).

Note that the *resolution* of the image displayed in the render window is 640 × 480 pixels, and its *bit depth* is 8 bits per pixel. If you want to create a higher resolution image, or an image with larger bit depth, i.e., with a larger range of displayable colors, such as 24 bit, choose *Options* from the *File* menu, and in the resulting dialog box select the desired options (Figure 11.22c). If you are rendering color images, you should use the 24-bit option. Note that you can specify any image resolution by selecting the *User* option and entering the desired horizontal and vertical resolution in pixels.

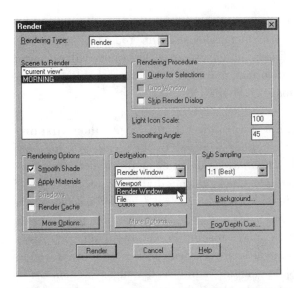

11.22a Selecting a scene to be rendered.

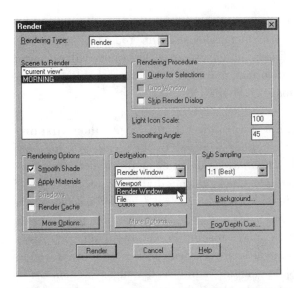

11.22b The "render" window.

Close the previously rendered image by clicking on the *close* button in the upper right corner (the icon with an X inside). From the *File* menu in the render window choose *Options*, and select the *24-bit color depth*. Use the *Alt-Tab* key combination to switch back to the AutoCAD main window, or just click on AutoCAD's window title bar. Then re-render the axonometric view. Notice that the newly rendered image will have 24-bit color depth, as displayed in the top part of the window.

If you recall from the previous chapter, 8-bit images can display only 256 different colors; 24-bit images can display more than 16 million colors, but they also take more disk space.

11.22c The render window options.

You can print the rendered image displayed in the render window: from the *File* menu choose *Print*. You can also save the image: from the *File* menu choose *Save*. The image will be saved in *Windows bitmap* format, and the file will have the .BMP extension. Save this image as MORNING.BMP.

23 You can render images directly to a file, without first displaying them in a render window. In the *Render* dialog box, choose *File* as the *Destination*, and click on the *More Options* button. In the *File Output Configuration* dialog box (Figure 11.23), select *TIFF* as the *File Type*, and select *User Defined* resolution from the corresponding drop-down lists. Enter 600 and 400 as x and y values for the image resolution, i.e., the number of pixels horizontally (x) and vertically (y). Select *8 Bits (256 Grayscale)* in the *Colors* section to generate a gray-scale image. Click on *OK* to continue, and click on the *Render* button to create the image file.

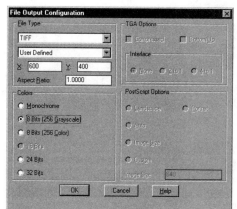

11.23a

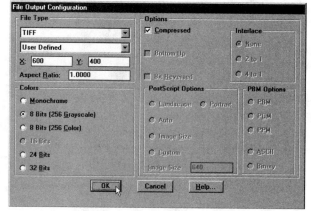

11.23b

11.23 The File Output Configuration *dialog box in R14 and R13.*

You can also save images that are rendered in graphic window viewports. From the *Tools* menu choose *Display Image*, then *Save*.

Save this image file as MORNING.TIF.

24 You can view the rendered image files in AutoCAD. From the *Tools* menu choose *Display Image* (R13 *Image*), then *View*. In the *Replay* dialog box choose the TIFF image file type, and then select the previously saved image file (MORNING.TIF). Click on *OK* in the *Image Specifications* dialog box (Figure 11.24).

The image will be partially displayed in the viewport that is currently active. To view another part of the image, redisplay the

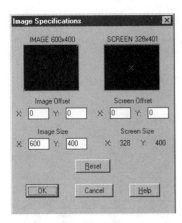

11.24 The Image Specifications *dialog box.*

image file, and specify the desired image offset in the *Image Specifications* dialog box. Often a better alternative is to display a single viewport in the graphics window (from the *View* menu choose *Tiled Viewports*, then *1 Viewport*), and then redisplay the image file. To redisplay the wire-frame view in the viewport, select the *Redraw* tool on the *Standard* toolbar, or enter R at the command prompt. You can restore the previous viewport configuration by entering the U (single undo) command several times, or by restoring the RIGHT_THREE viewport configuration saved in one of the previous exercises.

25 Save the model file as Render.dwg.

SHADOWS

26 In AutoCAD, when defining lights, you must explicitly specify whether the light source can cast shadows. You can also specify how the shadows are computed for the selected light, as *shadow maps, shadow volumes,* or *raytraced shadows.*

If you recall, when the SUN light source was defined, the shadows option wasn't selected. To enable this light source to cast shadows, you must *modify* its definition. Select the *Lights* tool, or enter LIGHT at the command prompt, and in the list of the defined lights, select SUN, and click on the *Modify* button. In the *Modify Distant Light* dialog box, place the check mark in the *Shadow On* dialog box (Figure 11.26a). Click on the *Shadow*

Options button, and verify that the *Shadow Volumes/Ray Traced Shadows* option is selected (Figure 11.26b). Click on *OK* to continue.

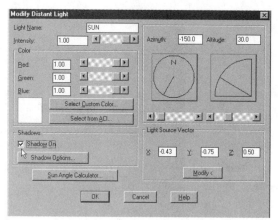

11.26a

11.26b

11.26a Enabling shadow casting for a distant light source.

11.26b Specify the method for computing the cast shadows.

27 Create a scene definition that will contain the current view and the distant light SUN. Select the *Scenes* tool, or enter SCENE at the command prompt, and click on the *New* button. Enter SUNLIGHT as the *scene name* in the *New Scene* dialog box, and select SUN light and CURRENT view in the corresponding lists. Click on *OK* to continue.

28 Make the axonometric viewport active, and select the *Render* tool, or enter RENDER at the command prompt, to render an image with cast shadows. (You can also choose *Render* from a pull-down menu.) In the *Render* dialog box (Figure 11.28a), select *Photo Real* (R13 *AutoVision*) from the drop-down list as the *Rendering Type*, place check marks in the *Smooth Shade* and *Shadows* check boxes, and select *Viewport* as the *Destination*. Click on *More Options*, and in the *Photo Real Render Options* (R13 *AutoVision Render Options*) dialog box (Figure 11.28b), place the check mark in the *Discard Back Faces* box, to instruct AutoCAD to disregard the invisible back faces during computation and therefore to speed up the rendering. Click on *OK*, and finally click on the *Render* button to create the rendered image with cast shadows (Figure 11.28c).

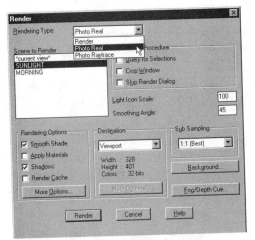

11.28a1

11.28a2

11.28a *Specifying the rendering options for shadow casting in R14 and R13.*

11.28b *The* Photo Real Render Options *dialog box.*

11.28c *The rendered image of the villa with cast shadows.*

29 Often architectural models are placed on a base. In this step, you will add one to the existing model of Villa Rotonda.

Create a new layer and name it BASE, assign white color to it, and make it the current layer.

On the *Solids* toolbar select the *Box* tool, or enter BOX at the command prompt, and enter the following coordinates for the *corner* points: −84′,−84′ [−25.2,−25.2] and 84′,84′ (25.2,25.2); enter −10′ [−3] for the box *height*.

30 Make each of the three viewports active and select the *Zoom All* tool to display the base box in each of them.

31 Set the layer 0 (zero) as the current layer. Note that this is the layer on which we have placed the *block* objects (icons) representing light sources; you can create a separate layer (for example, named LIGHTS) for this purpose. AutoCAD stores additional information about lights on a locked layer named ASHADE; do not modify this layer in any way.

32 In the right viewport, define an axonometric view with the angle from the *x* axis set to 300, and the angle from the *xy* plane set to 60 so that the view shows more of the villa's roof and the model base. From the *View* menu choose *3D Viewpoint,* and then *Select* (R13 *Rotate*), and enter the new angle values in the resulting *Viewpoint Presets* dialog box.

33 Zoom in to the area around the villa, as shown in Figure 11.33, and then issue the REGEN command at the command prompt to regenerate the model's display in the axonometric viewport. If you do not issue the REGEN command, AutoCAD will use the previous view boundaries (before the zoom command) to compute the rendered image.

34 In the next rendered image, you will simulate the shading effects for a specific location, date, and time. AutoCAD (i.e., AutoVision in R13) provides a *sun angle calculator* (Figure 11.34a) that can calculate the sun's position (its *azimuth* and *altitude* angles) based on the specified *time, date,* and a *geographic location.*

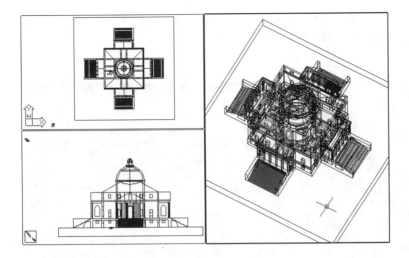

11.33 *The villa's model with the base box.*

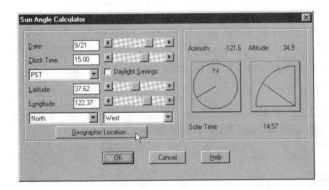

11.34a *The* Sun Angle Calculator *dialog box.*

Select the *Lights* tool, or enter LIGHT at the command prompt. In the list of lights, select SUN, and click on the *Modify* button. In the *Modify Distant Light* dialog box, click on the *Sun Angle Calculator* button.

In the resulting dialog box (Figure 11.34a) click on the *Geographic Location* button. Select *Europe* as the continent in the drop-down list (Figure 11.34b). In the list of the cities, scroll to the bottom, and look for Vicenza, the commune in Italy where Villa Rotonda is located. You will discover that Vicenza is not listed; the closest listed city is Venice, Italy (Figure 11.34c). Click on it, and notice its geographic *latitude*, 45.25 (north), and *longitude*, −12.18 (east). Vicenza's latitude is 45.33 (slightly more to the north than Venice), and its longitude is −11.33 (slightly less to the east). Remove the check mark in the box

Always modify lights' parameters using the LIGHT command (the *Lights* **tool). Do not use standard AutoCAD commands such as MOVE or ROTATE to change the lights' location and orientation.**

labeled *Nearest Big City,* and enter these values for Vicenza's latitude and longitude. Click on *OK* to continue.

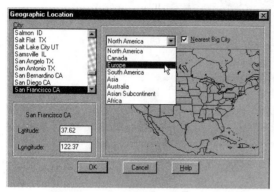

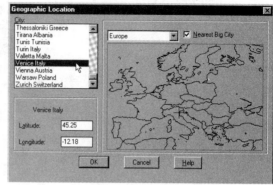

11.34b

11.34c

11.34b *Selecting the continent to specify the geographic location.*

11.34c *The geographic latitude and* longitude *of Venice, Italy.*

Next set the *date, time,* and *time zone* (Figure 11.34d). Set the date to September 21; enter 9/21. Set the time to 13:00 (1:00 P.M.), and select MET, i.e., the Middle-European time zone. Click on *OK* to continue.

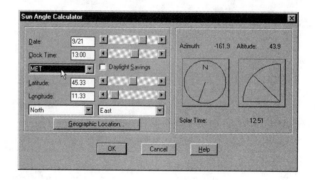

11.34d *Setting the* date, time, *and* time zone.

Note that you can also specify the *north direction* in the *Lights* dialog box. In this tutorial, we will assume that the north is located in the direction of the positive *y* axis, i.e., at 0 degree.

35 Re-render the axonometric view. Select the *Photo Real* (R13 *AutoVision*) rendering type, choose SUNLIGHT as the *scene to render,* and make sure that the *Smooth Shade* and *Shadows* options are checked and that the *destination* is set to *viewport.* The shadows will be precisely cast over the building's elements and the model base (Figure 11.35), simulating the natural sunlight conditions on September 21, at 13:00 MET, in Vicenza, Italy (assuming that the north is in the direction of the positive *y* axis).

Note that the shadow studies, such as the one you just did, are very useful in studying the impact of a proposed building on its surroundings. They are typically done for extreme sunlight conditions, such as the winter (22 December) and summer solstice (21 June). Typically, shadow impact studies are done for early morning hours (such as 9:00), noon, and late afternoon (16:00 or 17:00); the specific times will of course vary depending on the geographic location.

11.35 Simulating the natural sunlight conditions on September 21, at 13:00 MET, in Vicenza, Italy.

36 Notice the sharp edges of shadows in Figure 11.35; the change from shaded to lit areas is very abrupt. Also notice that the lighting isn't particularly good: the vertical surfaces on the front facade and the horizontal "ground" plane have almost identical shading tonal values.

The sharp-edged shadows result from using the *shadow volumes* method to compute cast shadows. Using *ray-traced shadows* will produce identical results but will result in longer rendering times; this method is used by AutoCAD when *Photo Raytrace* (R13 *AutoVis Raytrace*) rendering algorithm is selected.

AutoCAD can also compute rendered images with soft-edged shadows, which are created using the *shadow maps* method. Select the *Lights* tool, choose the SUN light source in the list, and click on the *Modify* button. Click on the *Shadow Options* button in the *Modify Distant Light* dialog box. In the *Shadow Options* dialog box (Figure 11.36), remove the check mark from the box labeled *Shadow Volumes/Ray Traced Shadows* to enable *shadow maps* for this light; when this option is selected, the *Photo Real* renderer produces volumetric shadows, and the *Photo Raytrace* renderer

The size of the shadow map should roughly correspond to the size of the rendered image; if you are rendering an image with a resolution of 1,024 × 768 pixels, then set the size of the shadow map to 1,024. Also, if you use higher values for *shadow softness,* use a larger shadow map.

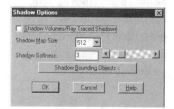

11.36 The Shadow Options *dialog box.*

11.37 Soft-edged cast shadows produced using the shadow maps *method.*

produces ray-traced shadows for this light. Select 512 from the drop-down list as the *Shadow Map Size,* which controls the size of the shadow map in pixels. Note that you can set a value between 64 and 4,096; the larger the map size, the more accurate, i.e., the sharper the shadows, and the longer it takes to compute the map. Set the *Shadow Softness* to 3; this parameter controls, as its name implies, the softness or fuzziness of shadow-mapped shadows, as the number of pixels at the edge of the shadow that are blended into the underlying image. Its value can range from 1 to 10; higher values tend to produce shadows that appear detached from the objects that are casting them. Click on *OK* to continue.

37 Render another image of the axonometric view with cast shadows. Notice how the edges of the cast shadows appear soft and fuzzy (Figure 11.37); also note how the shadows appear detached from the objects.

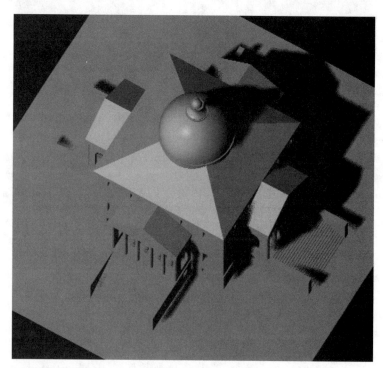

38 Modify the SUN light's definition, and set the shadows back to *Shadow Volumes/Ray Traced Shadows,* i.e., check this option in the *Shadow Options* dialog box (Figure 11.36).

39 Save the model file as Render.dwg.

"KEY" AND "FILL" LIGHTS

40 In all the images that were previously rendered with cast shadows (Figures 11.28c, 35, and 37), the areas in the shadow were rendered with a dark, uniform tonal value; those areas were not completely black, because they too were receiving some light, referred to as *ambient* light.

In reality, the *ambient light* fills the space, softening the shadows and reducing the contrast between light and dark areas; these effects are especially evident in interior spaces.

As described in the previous chapter, the ambient light provides constant, uniform illumination to every surface in the model. It is often used as "fill" light to illuminate surfaces in shadows, i.e., surfaces that are not directly illuminated. It comes from no particular source and has no direction.

In AutoCAD, the intensity of ambient light is set on a scale from 0 to 1 and is specified in the *Lights* dialog box (Figure 11.17b). Setting the intensity to 0 is equivalent to turning the ambient light off and should be used when simulating a dark interior space or a scene at night. High settings, such as 0.7 or higher, should be avoided because they can result in washed-out images. The default value of 0.3 often produces good results.

Because the ambient light provides *constant, uniform* illumination to every surface in the model, surfaces that are in the shadow will have the same shading tonal value regardless of their position or orientation in space. It is very difficult to read the model's geometry in the shaded areas. To bring some definition of the model's geometry in those areas, you should define a low-intensity "fill" light on the opposite side or across from the main "key" light; the primary role of the "fill" light then is to illuminate the areas in the shadow.

You will most often use the ambient light to control the contrast between areas that are lit and those that are in shadow.

To create the "fill" light, select the *Lights* tool, or enter LIGHT at the command prompt. Choose *Distant Light* from the drop-down list and click on the *New* button. Name this light SUN_FILL, and set its intensity to 0.25. Its azimuth should be set to 150 and altitude to 60 degrees, which corresponds to the current viewing direction. Click on *OK* to create this light. Note that this fill light will not cast the shadows.

Note that the more lights you use to illuminate the model, the longer it takes to render an image. Typically, using one "key" and one "fill" light is sufficient to illuminate the model. More than two lights are typically used for rendering interior images.

11.41 *Modifying the scene definition.*

When the *Render Cache* option is selected in the *Render* dialog box, AutoCAD will write the rendering information to a *cache* file on the hard disk. As long as the drawing geometry or view is unchanged, the cached file will be used for subsequent renderings, thus saving time and speeding up the rendering process.

41 Next you should add the newly created SUN_FILL light to the SUNLIGHT scene. Select the *Scenes* tool, or enter SCENE at the command prompt. Select SUNLIGHT in the list, and click on the *Modify* button. When the *Modify Scene* dialog box appears, hold down the *Ctrl* (control) key, and click on SUN_FILL light in the list to add it to the scene's definition. Both SUN and SUN_FILL lights should be highlighted in the list (Figure 11.41). Click on *OK* to continue.

42 Re-render the axonometric view. Select the *Render* tool, or enter RENDER at the command prompt. Select the *Photo Real* (R13 *AutoVision*) renderer, check the *Smooth Shade* and *Shadows* options, and set the *Destination* to *Viewport*. Notice that now you can better understand the geometry of the areas in the shadow because they are not uniformly shaded (Figure 11.42). Also note how the overall quality of the image has improved. There is a greater difference in shading between vertical surfaces on the front facade and the horizontal surfaces.

11.42 *The rendered view of the model illuminated by a "key" and a "fill" light.*

43 Once the lighting is set up, you can render different views of the model. You can, for example, show the layout of the villa's main level with cast shadows (Figure 11.43). Turn off layers DOME, ROOF, 2-WALLS, and 2-SLAB, and create another rendering.

11.43 *A rendered image of the villa's main level with cast shadows.*

44 You can also examine the effects of shadow casting from different viewpoints. Turn on layers you have previously turned off, and restore the view named TWO_POINT_PERSPECTIVE in the right viewport. From the *View* menu choose *Named Views*, select the desired view in the list, and click on the *Restore* button. Click on *OK* to continue.

45 Render the newly restored perspective view. In the *Render* dialog box, select the *Crop Window* option to render only a part of the viewport. The rest of the settings should be the same as in step 42. After you click on the *Render* button, AutoCAD will prompt you to pick a crop window. Select the area around the building so that the rendered image looks like Figure 11.45.

The quality of the rendered image is acceptable if you are just examining the effects of shadow casting (Figure 11.45). However, if your intention is to create a presentation-quality rendered

11.45 *A rendered two-point perspective of the villa.*

image, then the illumination must be improved: the roof surfaces are too bright, and the right side of the building is almost completely dark.

46 A possible improvement of the rendered image shown in Figure 11.45 is to make the front facade surfaces brighter and to illuminate the areas of the right facade in the shadow. That requires a lower key light and a brighter fill light.

Select the *Lights* tool, and select SUN light source from the list. Click on the *Modify* button, enter 0.7 as the light's new intensity, and enter 20 as its new *altitude*. Click on *OK* to continue. Next select the SUN_FILL light and change its intensity to 0.4, and set its altitude to 30 degrees. Click on *OK* to continue.

47 Re-render the two-point perspective (Figure 11.47). This time deselect the *Crop Window* option; all the other settings should be as in step 42.

Save the image rendered in the viewport: from the *Tools* menu choose *Display Image* (R13 *Image*), then *Save.* Save the rendered image as a TIFF file; enter *Persp.tif* as the image file name, and click *OK* to save the file.

48 Notice the stepped, *aliased* appearance of the building edges in previous renderings. As explained in the previous chapter,

11.47 *The same two-point perspective, but with different illumination.*

straight and curved edges often appear *jagged* or *stepped* in renderings because digital images are composed of discrete square picture elements called *pixels.* That effect is referred to as *aliasing* in computer graphics and can be corrected by a technique called *anti-aliasing,* which computes and averages the intensity values of the adjacent pixels by *adaptive sampling*—a sample of 4, 9, or 16 pixels is used to compute intensities, which are then averaged to compute the intensity at a single pixel; the higher the sample, the longer it takes to anti-alias an image.

In AutoCAD, you can specify as one of the rendering options that the rendered image be *anti-aliased,* that is, that the jagged edges be rendered without aliasing. Select the *Render* tool, or enter RENDER at the command prompt. In the *Render* dialog box, select options as in step 42, and then click on the *More Options* button in the *Rendering Options* section. In the resulting dialog box, select the *High* option in the *Anti-aliasing* section (Figure 11.48a). Click on *OK* to continue, and click on the *Render* button to create an anti-aliased image (Figure 11.48b).

Note that it takes considerably longer to compute an anti-aliased image. Use *anti-aliasing* only when rendering final versions of images.

49 Save the model file as Render.dwg.

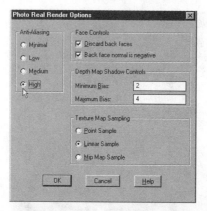

11.48a Specifying anti-aliasing for rendered images.

11.48b An anti-aliased rendering.

POINT LIGHTS

50 A *point* light source emits light in all directions and is typically used to simulate omnidirectional interior lighting. Point lights are sometimes used as "fill" lights because of their ability to render surfaces unevenly.

To create a *point light*, select the *Lights* tool, or enter LIGHT at the command prompt. In the resulting dialog box, select *Point Light* as the light type, and click on the *New* button. In the *New Point Light* dialog box, enter POINT as the light's name (Figure 11.50). Set the light's intensity to 1500 [37.5], and select the

Shadows option. Next click on the *Modify* button to specify its *position*, that is, its location in space. Enter 0,0,100′ [0,0,30] as the light's coordinates—the light will be located right above the villa's dome. Note that you can also graphically *pick* the light's location.

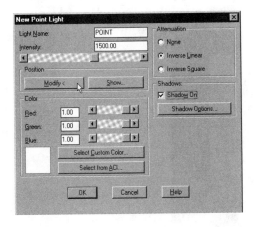

11.50 Specifying a new point *light source.*

51 You will use this newly created point light source to render a "top" perspective view of the villa's main level. As in step 43, turn off layers DOME, ROOF, 2-WALLS, and 2-SLAB.

52 Make the plan viewport (the upper left viewport) active. From the *View* menu choose *Tiled Viewports*, then *1 Viewport*.

53 Select the *Zoom Center* tool, or enter Z (*ZOOM*) at the command prompt, followed by C (*Center*). Enter 0,0 as the view's center point, and press *Return* to accept the default value for *height* or *magnification*. The model should be centered in the viewport.

54 Next set up a perspective view. From the *View* menu, select *3D Dynamic View*, or enter DVIEW at the command prompt. Select all the objects, and at the command prompt, enter D (*Distance*) to create a perspective view; enter 150′ [45] as the *new camera/target distance*. Next enter Z (*Zoom*) to specify a wide-angle perspective. Enter 18 as the lens length—the model should fill the window. Press *Return* (or *Enter*) to *exit* the perspective setup command.

55 Create a new scene named POINT that will contain the current view and the newly created point light source.

56 Render this top perspective view. Select the *Render* tool, select the newly created POINT scene as the scene to render, and specify *Photo Real* (R13 *AutoVision*) as the *Rendering Type*. Select *Smooth Shade* and *Shadows* options, and choose *Viewport* as the *Destination*. Click on *Render* to create a rendered image (Figure 11.56).

11.56 A top perspective view of the model, illuminated by a single point light source.

Note how the point light source emits light in all directions.

57 The intensity of the emitted light can *attenuate* (diminish) with distance based on *inverse linear* or *inverse square* rate (see the description of light properties in the previous chapter). The rendering produced in the previous step was created using a single point light source whose intensity attenuated at the inverse linear rate.

The maximum intensity value is determined based on the selected rate of attenuation and the model's extents. If there is no attenuation, the maximum intensity value is 1. For *inverse linear* rate of attenuation, the maximum intensity is the distance between the extents' lower left and upper right corners. If attenuation is *inverse square,* the maximum intensity is the square of the extents' distance.

Re-render the previous scene, but with the inverse square rate of attenuation for the point light source. Select the *Lights* tool, choose the POINT light in the list, and click on the *Modify* button. Select the *Inverse Square* option in the *Attenuation* section, set the intensity to 1800000 [1125], and click on *OK*. Re-render the POINT scene using the same settings as in the previous step. Note how the intensity of the light at the edges of the model base is lower than in the previous image (Figure 11.57).

58 Save the model file as Render.dwg.

SPOTLIGHTS

59 The *spotlight* emits a directional cone of light. As described in the previous chapter, when the light from a spotlight falls on a surface, it creates an area of maximum illumination called the *hotspot,* which is surrounded by an area of diminishing intensity called the *falloff.* Spotlights are primarily used for visual emphasis in renderings. Like point light sources, they are sometimes used as "fill" lights because of their ability to render surfaces unevenly.

The *direction* of the spotlight's *cone* is specified by locating two points (the *target* and the *light*), and its size is defined by *hotspot* and *falloff* angles. The hotspot cone angle defines the brightest part of the light beam; the falloff cone angle defines the full cone of light. If the falloff angle is greater than the hotspot angle by more than 10 or 15 degrees, the edge of the light beam becomes fairly "soft"; if the falloff and hotspot angles are identical, the edge of the beam is sharp.

To create a *spotlight,* select the *Lights* tool, or enter LIGHT at the command prompt. In the resulting dialog box, select *Spotlight* as the light type, and click on the *New* button. In the *New Spotlight Light* dialog box, enter SPOT as the light's name (Figure 11.59). Set the light's intensity to 1800 [45], and select the *Shad-*

ows option. Set the *hotspot* angle to 30 degrees, and set the falloff to 60. Next click on the *Modify* button to specify its *position,* that is, the location of its light and target points in space. Enter 0,0 as the coordinates of the light's *target;* enter 80′,−120′,60′ [24, −36,18] as the coordinates of the light's *location.* The spotlight will be located close to the lower right corner of the model. Note that you can also graphically *pick* the light's location.

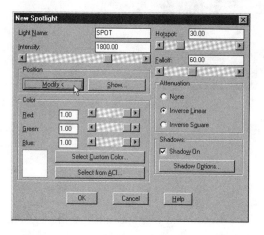

11.59 *Specifying a new* spot-light *light source.*

60 You will use the newly created spotlight to render a "two-point" perspective view of the villa. Before you set up a perspective view, turn on layers DOME, ROOF, 2-WALLS, and 2-SLAB.

61 Restore the "two-point" perspective view. From the *View* menu choose *Named Views;* select TWO_POINT_PERSPEC-TIVE, click on the *Restore* button, and click on *OK* to continue.

62 Note how the villa's dome is clipped by the top edge of the graphics window. To adjust the perspective, select *3D Dynamic View* from the *View* menu, or enter DVIEW at the command prompt. Select all the objects, and at the command prompt, enter PA (*Pan*) and move the line of sight higher so that the villa is centered in the view. Next enter D (*Distance*) to move the camera closer so that the villa fills the viewport's frame (Figure 11.62). Press *Return* (or *Enter*) to *exit* the perspective setup command.

63 Create a new scene named SPOT that will contain the *current view* and the newly created spotlight source.

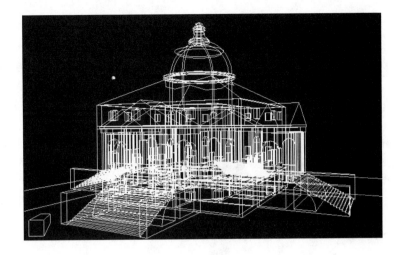

11.62 Modified "two-point" perspective view of the villa.

64 Render the newly created perspective view. Select the *Render* tool, select the newly created SPOT scene as the scene to render, and specify *Photo Real* (R13 *AutoVision*) as the *Rendering Type*. Select *Smooth Shade* and *Shadows* options, and choose *Viewport* as the *Destination*. Click on *Render* to create a rendered image (Figure 11.64).

11.64 A "two-point" perspective view of the villa, illuminated by a spotlight light source.

65 Experiment with hot-spot and falloff angle settings. For example, set both hot-spot and falloff angles to 30 degrees, and re-render the scene; the result will be a brightly lit area of the model (the villa's corner). Restore the hot-spot and falloff settings to 30 and 60 degrees, respectively.

66 Save the model file as Render.dwg.

If you do not want to continue at this point, choose *Exit* from the *File* menu to exit AutoCAD.

In this exercise you have learned how to define and place *lights* in 3D space, and how to manipulate light properties, such as *position, type of light emission, color,* and *intensity,* to create well-lit *scenes.* In the next tutorial exercise, you will learn how to define and assign *material properties,* such as *color, transparency, reflectivity,* and *texture,* to the model's components.

12

RENDERING TUTORIAL 2: MATERIALS

In this tutorial exercise you will learn how to define various *materials* and assign them to solid objects in the villa's model. You will learn how to manipulate material properties, such as *color*, *reflectivity*, and *transparency*, to create convincing results. You will also learn how to apply *image mapping*, that is, how to project (map) two-dimensional digital images onto the surface of a three-dimensional object to simulate the subtleties in surface properties.

DELETING THE SCENES AND LIGHTS

1 You will first delete some of the *scenes* and *lights* created in the previous tutorial that are no longer needed.

Start AutoCAD, and open the previously saved model file (Render.dwg). If you are continuing from the last exercise, skip this step.

2 Select the *Scenes* tool, or enter SCENE at the command prompt. In the *Scenes* dialog box, delete the scenes MORNING and POINT; after you select each of these two scenes in the list, click on the *Delete* button, and confirm the deletion. Click on *OK* to continue when done.

Always delete the lights using the *Lights* tool (or the LIGHT command). Do not use the *Erase* tool to delete lights!

3 Select the *Lights* tool, or enter LIGHT at the command prompt. In the *Lights* dialog box, delete the lights ORNG_SUN and POINT; select each of these two lights in the list, and click on the *Delete* button; confirm the deletion when prompted. When done, click on *OK* to continue.

4 Save the displayed two-point perspective view. From the *View* menu, choose *Named Views*. In the *View Control* dialog box, click on the *New* button. In the *Define New View* dialog box, enter HIGH_TWO_POINT_PERSP as the view's name, and click on the *Save View* button to continue. Then click on BIRDS_EYE_PERSPECTIVE, and click on the *Restore* button to restore that view. Click on *OK* to continue. A new perspective view will be displayed in the graphics window (Figure 12.4).

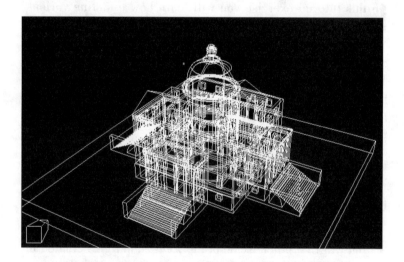

12.4 The bird's-eye-view perspective.

5 If the graphics window background is not black, change it to black in the following way: From the *Tools* (R13 *Options*) menu choose *Preferences*, and in the resulting dialog box, click on the *Display* (R13 *System*) tab, then click on the *Colors* (R13 *Color*) button. Select the *graphic window background* as the *window element* to change, and click on the black color swatch. Click on the *OK* button to continue.

6 Save the model file as Render.dwg.

DEFINING AND ATTACHING MATERIALS

7 In AutoCAD, materials are defined using the *Materials* tool (Figure 12.7a) on the *Render* (R13 *AutoVis*) toolbar, or by entering the RMAT command at the command prompt. In R14, you can also choose *Render* from the *View* menu, and then *Materials;* in R13, select *Materials* from the *AutoVis* menu.

12.7a The Materials *tool.*

Select the *Materials* tool. In the *Materials* dialog box (Figure 12.7b), click on the *New* button to define a new material (make sure that *Standard* is selected in the drop-down menu under the *New* button). The *New Standard Material* dialog box will appear (Figure 12.7c). Enter BASE as the *Material Name,* and select the *Color/Pattern* attribute if it isn't already selected.

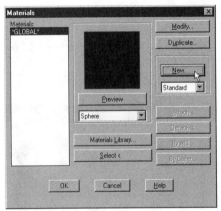

12.7b

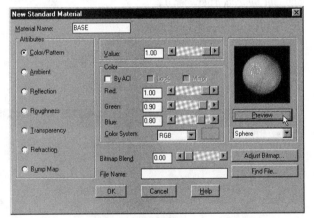

12.7c

Note that *color* is probably the single most important property that determines how an object looks when illuminated. The side of an object facing the light will be much brighter than the side that isn't illuminated, and if the object is highly reflective, the color of the specular highlight will be different from the rest of the object. To account for these color variations, each material defined in AutoCAD (or in AutoVision in R13) will have three associated color variables (Figure 12.7c): the object's *main* (diffuse) color, its *ambient* color, which will appear in the shaded parts, and the *reflection* color, which is the color of the specular highlight. These color variables can be defined as interdependent

12.7b The Materials *dialog box.*

12.7c The New Standard Material *dialog box.*

You can set the color of each attribute by using the RGB (red, green, and blue) or HLS (hue, lightness, and saturation) slider bars, the color wheel, or the AutoCAD Color Index (ACI) number of the object itself.

For a dull, matte surface finish, set the value for *Color* between 0.7 and 0.8, and set the value for *Reflection* between 0.2 and 0.3. For a shiny surface finish, set the value for *Reflection* between 0.7 and 0.8, and set the value for *Color* between 0.3 and 0.4.

or *locked;* when any one of them is changed, the other two change accordingly.

To define the material's *main* color, make sure that the *Color/Pattern* attribute is selected, and then, in the *Color* section, remove the check mark from the option labeled *By ACI* (when this option is turned on, the color of an object with this material will match the object's AutoCAD color). Make sure that the RGB color system is selected, and set the red, green, and blue components to 1.0, 0.9, and 0.8, respectively, to create a very light orange color. Next set the *Value* (above the *Color* section) to 1.0. Click on the *Preview* button to examine what has been defined so far.

Next define the *ambient* color for the BASE material. Select the *Ambient* attribute option. Make sure that the *Lock* option is selected in the *Color* section, and set the *Value* to 0.8 so that the *ambient* color is only 80% as bright as the main color (Figure 12.7d). Then define the *reflection* color. Select the *Reflection* attribute, make sure that the *Lock* option is selected in the *Color* section, and set the *Value* to 0.0, i.e., no reflection (Figure 12.7e).

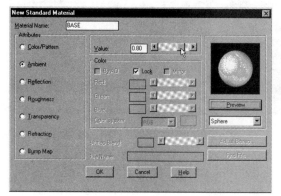

12.7d

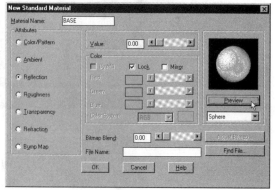

12.7e

12.7d *Defining the* ambient *color.*

12.7e *Defining the* reflection *color.*

Since the base will be made of a matte material, set the *roughness* to 1.0. Select the *Roughness* attribute, and set the *Value* to 1.0 (Figure 12.7f). Click on the *Preview* button to examine how this material will appear when rendered.

Click on *OK* to continue. The new material named BASE will be added to the list of defined materials (Figure 12.7g).

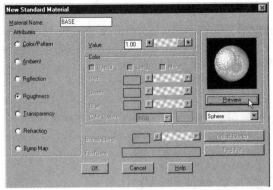

12.7f

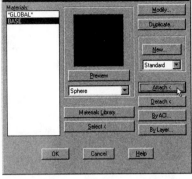

12.7g

Once the material has been defined, it can be *attached* to objects in the model. Click on the *Attach* button (Figure 12.7g); AutoCAD will ask you to *select objects to attach "BASE" to*. Select an edge of the solid representing the model's base; the solid will become highlighted. Press *Enter* (or *Return*), or press the right mouse button (or the *Return* button on your pointing device) to end object selection. When AutoCAD completes updating the drawing, the *Materials* dialog box will reappear—the material BASE has been attached. Click on *OK* to continue.

8 Render the perspective view to see the change. Select the *Render* tool, or enter RENDER at the command prompt. In the *Render* dialog box (Figure 12.8a) select *Photo Real* (R13 *AutoVision*) *rendering type,* and select SUNLIGHT as the *scene to render.* In the *Rendering Options* section, check options *Smooth Shade, Apply Materials,* and *Render Cache* (to speed up the subsequent renderings); make sure that the *Shadows* option is deselected. Click on the *More Options* button, and set the *Anti-Aliasing* to *Minimal;* click on *OK*. Finally, set the *Destination* to *Viewport,* and click on the *Render* button. The model's base will be rendered in a different color (Figure 12.8b).

9 Next define a material for the building itself. Select the *Materials* tool, and click on the *New* button. Enter WHITE MATTE as the material's name. Set the *main* color to white, i.e., set all three RGB values to 1.0, and set the *value* parameter to 0.8. Lock the *ambient* color to the main color, and set its value to 0.8. Lock the

12.7f Defining the roughness.

12.7g The new material will appear in the list of defined materials.

The value of the *roughness* attribute controls the size of the specular reflection. The greater the roughness, the larger the size of the highlight. *Roughness* values have no effect unless you enter a value for *Reflection.*

If the *Apply Materials* option is not selected, all objects in the model assume the attribute values defined for the *GLOBAL* material.

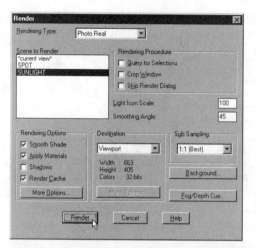

12.8a The Render *dialog box.*

12.8b The rendered image
with a material definition
applied to the model's base.

reflection color to the main color, and set its value to 0.0 (no reflection). Finally, set the *roughness* to 1.0, since this material is *matte*. Click on *OK* to complete the material's definition. The material WHITE MATTE will be added to the list.

Attach this material to the model's objects using the *by layer* method. Click on the *By Layer* button, and in the *Attach by Layer* dialog box (Figure 12.9a), hold down the *Shift* key, and select layers 0-WALLS, 1-WALLS, 2-WALLS, and 2-SLAB in the list on the right, then click on the *Attach* button. The material's name, WHITE MATTE, will be listed next to the layers' names (Figure 12.9b). Click on *OK* to continue.

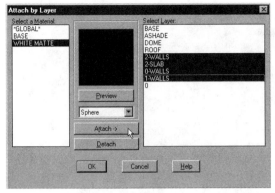

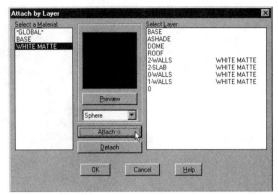

12.9a

12.9b

10 Define a new material for the villa's roof. You will define another matte, i.e., nonreflective, material, with a light reddish color. Click on the *New* button, and enter ROOF as the material's name. Set the *main* color to light red, i.e., set the RGB component values to 0.70, 0.60, 0.55, and set the *value* parameter to 0.8. Lock the *ambient* color to the main color, and set its value to 0.6. Lock the *reflection* color to the main color, and set its value to 0.0 (no reflection). Finally, set the *roughness* to 1.0, since this material is *matte*. Click on *OK* to complete the material's definition. The material ROOF will be added to the list.

Attach this material to the model's roof objects *by layer*. Click on the *By Layer* button, and in the *Attach by Layer* dialog box, select the layer ROOF in the list on the right, then click on the *Attach->* button. The material's name, ROOF, will be listed next to the layer's name. Click on *OK* to continue.

11 Re-render the perspective view to see the changes. Use the same rendering parameters as in step 8. The model's three levels and the roof will be rendered in different colors (Figure 12.11). The only remaining object without any material definition is the dome.

12 For the dome object you will use the COPPER material definition in the materials library that comes with AutoCAD software (AutoVision in R13). Select the *Materials* tool, and in the *Materials* dialog box (Figure 12.7b) click on the *Materials Library* button. In the resulting dialog box (Figure 12.12) select COPPER in

12.9a *The* Attach by Layer *dialog box.*

12.9b *Attaching the material to layers.*

You can *attach* materials to individual objects, to all objects with a specific AutoCAD Color Index (ACI) number, or to layers. To *detach* a material attached to an object, choose *Detach* in the *Materials* dialog box. To detach a material attached by ACI, choose *Detach* in the *Attach by AutoCAD Color Index* dialog box. To detach a material attached by layer, choose *Detach* in the *Attach by Layer* dialog box.

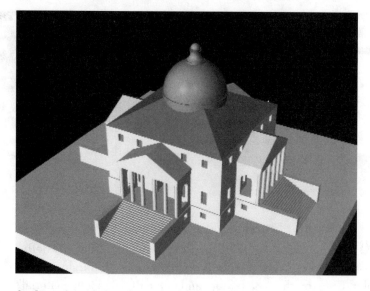

12.11 *The rendering with material definitions applied to the villa's three levels and the roof.*

AutoCAD saves the materials libraries as files with the *.mli* extension. The standard AutoCAD materials library file is called *render.mli.* Note that you can use *3D Studio* material libraries in AutoCAD, and AutoCAD materials libraries in 3D Studio.

the list of predefined materials in the standard library, and click on the *Preview* button to see how this particular material renders. Click on the *Import* button to copy this material definition into the model. The COPPER material will be added to the list on the left. Click on *OK* to continue.

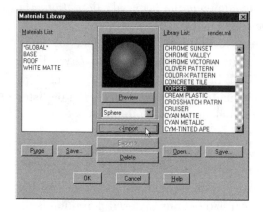

12.12 *The* Materials Library *dialog box.*

In the *Materials* dialog box, select COPPER in the list on the left, and click on the *Modify* button to examine its properties. Notice how the color and roughness attributes are set. When done, click on the *Cancel* button to continue.

In the *Materials* dialog box, select COPPER in the list of materials on the left, click on the *By Layer* button, and attach COPPER to the DOME layer. Click on the *OK* button to continue.

13 Re-render the perspective view. Use the same rendering parameters as in step 8. Note that the rendered image (Figure 12.13) is not particularly good—the dome stands out in the image, i.e., its color is too strong. Also note the *specular highlight*, i.e., the light's reflection, on the dome's surface.

12.13 The rendering of the villa with the copper material applied to the dome.

14 Modify the definition of the COPPER material. Select the *Materials* tool, select COPPER in the list of the materials on the left, and click on the *Modify* button. Set the RGB components of the *main* color to 0.63, 0.46, and 0.42. Set the RGB components of the *ambient* color to 0.67, 0.45, and 0.39, and set the RGB components of the *reflection* color to 1.00, 0.68, and 0.52. Click on *OK* to continue.

Then modify the definitions of the materials ROOF and WHITE MATTE. Select ROOF in the list of the materials and click on *Modify*. Set the *Value* parameter for the *main* and *ambient* colors to 1.00. Click on *OK* to continue.

Select WHITE MATTE in the list and click on the *Modify* button. Set the *Value* parameter for the *main* and *ambient* colors to 1.00. Click on *OK* to continue.

Click on the *OK* button to complete the material editing.

15 Re-render the perspective view. Use the same rendering parameters as in step 8. Note that the rendered image (Figure

Color can be highly distracting and should be used very carefully in renderings. Note that gray-scale images are often much more satisfactory than color ones. You can either save the rendered image as a gray-scale image or convert a color rendered image into a gray-scale one using image-processing software such as Adobe Photoshop.

12.15) is much better this time—there is less difference in tonal values between colors, and the dome doesn't stand out as much as it did in the previous rendering.

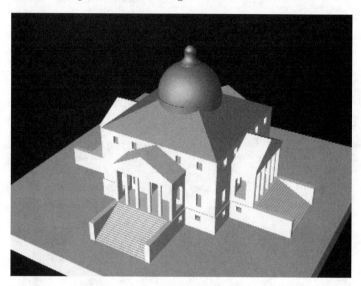

12.15 The rendering with the redefined materials.

16 Re-render the perspective view, but this time with shadows and *high* anti-aliasing. Save the rendered image (Figure 12.16) in TIFF format as *Image1.tif*. From the *Tools* menu choose *Display Image* (R13 *Image*), then *Save*. Select TIFF file format; enter *Image1.tif* as the image file name, and click *OK* to save the file.

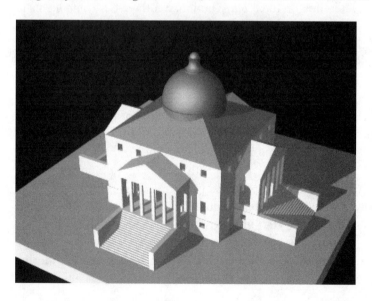

12.16 The rendering of the villa with applied materials and cast shadows.

17 Save the model file as Render.dwg.

REFLECTIVITY AND TRANSPARENCY

18 The light striking a surface can be absorbed, reflected, and transmitted. Highly reflective objects, such as mirrors, reflect the light almost totally. Very rough materials, such as concrete, absorb a significant amount of light. The extent to which a certain material reflects light is controlled in AutoCAD by an attribute called *roughness*. For example, the COPPER material used in the previous section has a roughness of 0.72.

Reflective materials defined in AutoCAD can also have the mirrorlike property of high reflectance. You will create a mirrorlike material and assign it to a base solid.

Select the *Materials* tool. In the *Materials* dialog box, click on the BASE material in the list on the right, and then click on the *Duplicate* button to create a copy of its material definition. Enter BASE MIRROR as the name of this new material. Select the *Reflection* attribute, select the *Mirror* option in the *Color* section of the dialog box, and set the *value* to 1.00 (Figure 12.18). Next select the *Roughness* attribute, and set its *value* to 0.00 for full reflectivity. To make this mirrorlike material more realistic, select the *Color/Pattern* attribute, and set its value to 0.80; then select the *Ambient* attribute, and set its value to 0.20. Click on *OK* to add this new material to the list of the defined materials. In the *Materials* dialog box click on the *By Layer* button, and attach this new material to the BASE layer. Click on *OK* to continue.

12.18 Specifying the mirror-like reflection in a material definition.

19 Select the *Render* tool and create yet another rendering, but this time without shadows and with minimal anti-aliasing. Specify SUNLIGHT as the scene to render, select *Photo Raytrace* (R13 *AutoVis Raytrace*) as the *rendering type*, and choose *viewport* as

The *Back Face Normal is Negative* option controls which faces AutoCAD considers as back faces. The back faces have negative normal vectors that point away from the viewer.

the *destination*. Click on the *More Options* button, and in the *Face Controls* section select the *Discard back faces* option to eliminate the invisible faces from the calculation.

Note the reflected image of the building on the surface of the base (Figure 12.19).

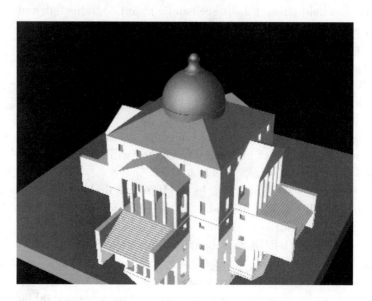

12.19 *The mirrorlike reflectivity of the base solid.*

20 Reattach the BASE material definition to the base solid. Select the *Materials* tool, select the BASE material in the list on the left, click on the *Attach* button, and pick the base solid. Click on *OK* to continue.

21 Next you will create a rendering of the villa's main level with the upper-level solids rendered as transparent. To do that, you should first turn off layers containing the roof and dome solids, and then define a transparent material, and assign it to the upper- (second-) level solids.

Turn off the layers ROOF and DOME, and issue the REGEN command to regenerate the graphics window display.

22 You will import an existing transparent material definition from the standard materials library (render.mli). Select the *Materials* tool, and click on the *Materials Library* button in the *Materials* dialog box.

In the *Library List* on the right, select GLASS, and click on the *Preview* button. A transparent sphere will be rendered in the preview window (Figure 12.22). Next click on the *Import* button to import this material definition into the model. Click on *OK* to continue.

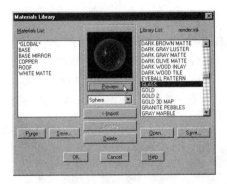

In the *Materials* dialog box, click on the *By Layer* button, and attach the GLASS material to the layers 2-WALLS and 2-SLAB. Click on *OK* to continue.

23 Select the *Render* tool and create yet another rendering, using the same parameters as in step 19. The second-level solids will be rendered as transparent (Figure 12.23).

Note that transparency increases rendering time.

12.23 *A rendering with transparent objects.*

24 Note, however, that the transparency in the previously rendered image (Figure 12.23) is not very convincing. The "back" faces, i.e., those faces that are invisible in solid objects, are not rendered—if you remember, in step 19, you have specified that the "back" faces should be discarded during rendering. When rendering transparent objects, however, you should disable this option. Select the *Render* tool, and click on *More Options* in the *Rendering Options* section. Deselect the *Discard back faces* option in the *Face Controls* section (the *Back face normal is negative* option should be selected). Click on the *OK* button to continue, and click on the *Render* button to create another rendering with transparent objects (Figure 12.24).

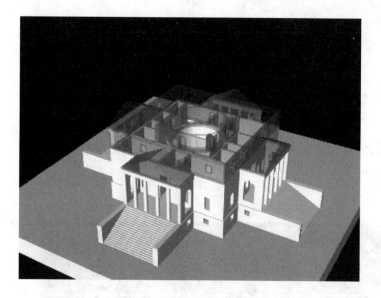

12.24 A more accurate rendering of transparent objects.

25 To make the previously rendered image (Figure 12.24) more readable, you will increase the transparency of the second-level solids.

Select the *Materials* tool, select the GLASS material in the list on the left, and click on the *Modify* button. Click on the various attributes associated with this material and notice how the various parameters are set. Select the *Transparency* attribute, and set its value to 0.99 (if you set it to 1.00, the objects will become invisible). Click on *OK* to modify the material's definition, and then click on *OK* again to continue.

Note that the transparency tends to fall off near the edges of objects or when the surface normal is perpendicular to the line of sight.

26 Re-render the perspective view using the same rendering parameters as in step 24. Notice how the second-level solids are now more transparent (Figure 12.26).

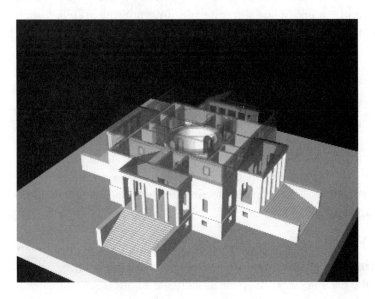

12.26 Another rendering with more-transparent objects.

27 Create another rendering with cast shadows. Note how the transparent objects cast shadows (Figure 12.27).

28 Save the model file as Render.dwg.

12.27 Shadow casting by transparent objects.

IMAGE MAPPING

AutoCAD renderers support *color*, *reflection*, *opacity*, and *bump* maps.

29 In reality, surfaces rarely have uniform color—consider, for example, a marble or a granite tile. In rendering systems, such subtleties in surface properties are simulated by *image mapping*, that is, by mapping or projecting two-dimensional digital images onto surfaces.

In this section you will attach materials with image maps to the parts of the villa's model, and you will adjust the mapping of images to create convincing simulations.

Begin by setting up an axonometric view. From the *View* menu, choose *Named Views*, select STANDARD_AXO in the list, and click on the *Restore* button to restore that view. Click on *OK* to continue. A new, axonometric view will be displayed in the graphics window.

30 Select one of the *zoom* tools, and zoom in to the upper left corner of the portico on the left side of the axonometric view so that what you see corresponds roughly to Figure 12.30. Once you set up the view correctly, issue the REGEN command to regenerate the graphics window display.

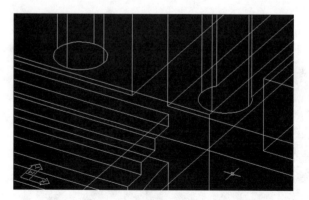

12.30 Zooming in to the portico area.

31 Next import an image-mapped material from the materials library, such as granite or marble, and attach it to the portico solids. Select the *Materials* tool, and click on the *Materials Library* button. Select MARBLE - PALE in the *Library List*, and click on the *Preview* button. Notice how the sphere is rendered as if it were made of marble (Figure 12.31a). Click on the *Import* button to import this material definition, and click on *OK* to continue.

The MARBLE - PALE material will be listed among the model's materials. Click on the *Modify* button to examine this material's definition. Notice that the *Color/Pattern* attribute has an image file named MARBPALE.TGA associated with it (Figure 12.31b). Click on *OK* to continue.

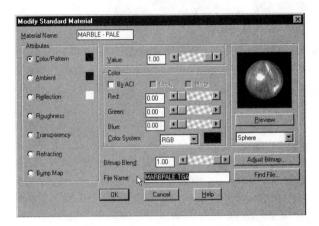

Attach this material using the *by layer* method to the layer 0-WALLS (the villa's base). Click on the *OK* button to continue.

32 Render the displayed view of the model. Select *Photo Raytrace* (R13 *AutoVis Raytrace*) as the *rendering type,* and SUN-LIGHT as the scene to render; choose the *Smooth Shade, Apply Materials,* and *Render Cache* rendering options (make sure that *Shadows* are deselected), and select *Viewport* as the *destination.* Click on *More Options* in the *Rendering Options* section, check *Discard back faces* in the *Face Controls* section, and set *Aliasing* to *Minimal.* Click on *OK* to continue, and click on *Render* to create a rendering with image mapping (Figure 12.32).

33 Notice the "streaks" generated on the vertical faces of the villa's portico, especially on the right side. These are generated because the image map is *projected* in a *planar* fashion onto the *xy* plane, as if it were pushed from the top down (along the *z* axis). To avoid such "streaking," image maps should be projected at an angle, that is, the projection should not be parallel to the *xy, yz,* or *xz* plane.

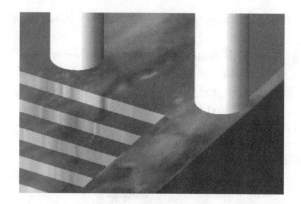

12.32 *A rendering with image mapping.*

12.33a *The* Mapping *tool.*

12.33b *The* Mapping *dialog box.*

12.33c *The* Adjust Planar Coordinates *dialog box.*

To adjust image mapping, select the *Mapping* tool (Figure 12.33a), or enter SETUV at the command prompt. When prompted to select objects, pick the villa's portico by clicking at an edge of its steps. The *Mapping* dialog box (Figure 12.33b) will appear; click on the *Adjust Coordinates* button. In the *Adjust Planar Coordinates* dialog box (Figure 12.33c), select the *Picked Plane* option in the *Parallel Plane* section to specify the mapping plane. When prompted to *place the lower left corner of the mapping plane,* enter 0,0,0; enter 400,400,0 [10,10,0] as the coordinates of the *lower right corner,* and enter −400,400,400 [−10,10,10] as the coordinates of the *upper left corner.* As a result, the projection plane will be tilted toward each of the coordinate system planes, as shown in the dialog box (Figure 12.33d). Note that the value of 400 [10] stems from the largest dimension of the bounding box for the portico's base: its dimensions are 29′ × 33′ × 10′ [8.7 × 9.9 × 3.0], or

12.33b

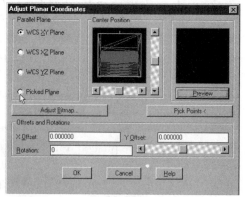

12.33c

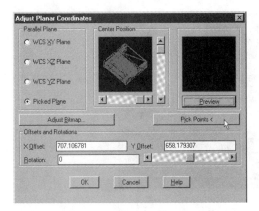

12.33d Tilting the projection plane.

in inches $348'' \times 396'' \times 120''$. Use the largest dimension if you want the image map to cover the entire object.

When you specified the corners of the projection plane, you defined not only the size and orientation of the image map, but also its *offset* from the object. To place the image map exactly over the portico solid, enter 0 for *x* and *y Offset* in the *Offsets and Rotations* section (Figure 12.33e). The green rectangle representing the relative size of the image map will appear in the *Center Position* window. Click on *Preview* to examine the results (Figure 12.33e). Click on the *OK* button to continue.

Image maps are applied by default in a 1:1 relationship to the selected geometry.

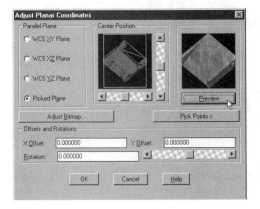

12.33e Adjusting the offset of the image map.

34 Create another rendering (Figure 12.34) using the same parameters as in step 32.

35 Even though the "streaks" are eliminated, the image is still not convincing, because the image is too large. To adjust the rela-

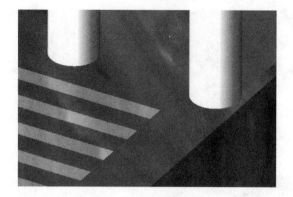

12.34 A rendering with a tilted image map.

tive size of the image map, select the *Mapping* tool, pick the solid object representing the portico's base, and click on the *Adjust Coordinates* button. In the *Adjust Planar Coordinates* dialog box, click on the *Adjust Bitmap* button. In the *Adjust Object Bitmap Placement* dialog box enter 5 as the *U* and *V Scale* (*u* and *v* are analogous to *x* and *y* directions) to shrink the relative size of the bit map five times (Figure 12.35). Click on *Preview* to see the result. Click on the *OK* button to continue.

When you project an image map onto an object, you can choose to create either a *tiled* or a *cropped* ("*decal*") effect if the image is scaled smaller than the object. If the scale of the image map to the object is less than 1:1, *tiling* repeats the image or pattern until the entire object is covered. With *cropping,* you can place an image in a single location on an object. The rest of the object is rendered with the colors of the material.

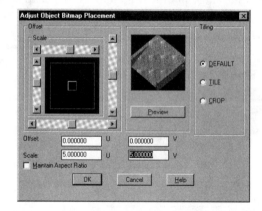

12.35 Adjusting the relative size of the bit map.

36 Create yet another rendering (Figure 12.36) using the same parameters as in step 32.

37 Notice the abrupt change in the continuity of the projected image near the bottom of the rendering (Figure 12.36) created in the previous step.

By default, AutoCAD *tiles* image maps across the objects, and if the image map is not seamless, the "seams" become per-

12.36 *A rendering with the adjusted size of the image map.*

ceptible in the renderings. To avoid such perceptible tiling of image maps, either resize the image map or modify the map itself in one of the image-processing programs. Since image mapping is often applied in close-up views, another alternative in such cases is to *offset* the image map so that its edges are outside of the graphics window.

Select the *Mapping* tool, and select the portico's base. Click on the *Adjust Coordinates* button, and enter 20 [0.5] as *X Offset* and −30 [0.75] as *Y Offset*. Click on the *OK* button to continue.

38 Re-render the scene. Notice how the image map is rendered this time without perceptible seams (Figure 12.38).

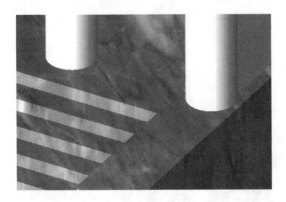

12.38 *A rendering without "seams."*

39 Next attach the MARBLE - PALE material to the column. Select the *Materials* tool, choose MARBLE - PALE in the list on the left, click on the *Attach* button, and pick the column on the left in the graphics window. (If necessary, select the *Redraw* tool to redisplay the wire-frame view.) Click on *OK* to continue.

Great care must be exercised to avoid typical problems when using image mapping, such as perceptible repetition of image maps and illogical, unconvincing mapping to nonrectangular and curved surfaces.

12.40a A planar projection of an image map onto a cylindrical object.

12.40b The Adjust Cylindrical Coordinates *dialog box.*

40 If you were to render the scene now, the column would appear with vertical "streaks" (Figure 12.40a) because the image map is projected parallel to the *xy* plane by default. Since the column's geometry is cylindrical, you should apply the *cylindrical* instead of *planar* mapping.

Select the *Mapping* tool, and select the column. Choose the *Cylindrical* option in the *Projection* section, and click on the *Adjust Coordinates* button. In the *Adjust Cylindrical Coordinates* dialog box (Figure 12.40b), select *WCS Z Axis* as the *Parallel Axis,* and click on *Preview;* notice how edges of the image map are "stitched" at the top of the column. Click on the *OK* button to continue.

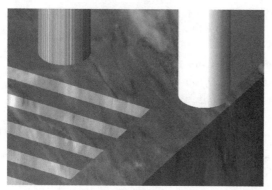

12.40a

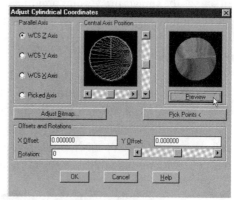

12.40b

41 Create another rendering. Note how the image map appears "wrapped" around the column (Figure 12.41).

12.41 The rendering with an image mapped in a cylindrical projection to a column.

42 So far you have used image mapping to simulate color changes on surfaces. By using *solid* materials, however, you can avoid numerous mapping adjustments and achieve more convincing results, because solid material definitions generate at the rendering time a three-dimensional pattern that is then applied to objects.

To create a solid material definition of marble, select the *Materials* tool, or enter RMAT at the command prompt. In the drop-down list below the *New* button, select *Granite* (Figure 12.42a), and click on *New*. In the *New Granite Material* dialog box (Figure 12.42b), enter GRANITE as the *material name*. Note the various attributes (parameters) associated with this material definition, such as four different *colors* of the granite pebbles, their *sharpness*, and their *scale*. Choose the *Scale* attribute and set its value to 3.0 [0.01]. Click on the *Preview* button to see how this material renders, and then click on *OK* to add this material definition to the model file.

Note that you cannot export procedural materials to other applications, such as *3D Studio*.

12.42a Selecting a solid material definition (granite).

12.42b The New Granite Material *dialog box.*

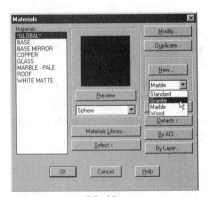

12.42a

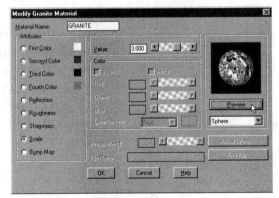

12.42b

Attach this new material to all objects visible in the graphics window. When done, click *OK* to continue.

43 Next adjust the mapping parameters for the visible objects. Select the *Mapping* tool, or enter SETUV at the command prompt, and select all visible objects. In the *Mapping* dialog box, select the *Solid* option in the *Projection* section, and click on the *OK* button.

44 Select the *Render* tool and create a rendering with the newly attached solid material. Notice how all the solid objects are textured uniformly regardless of their geometry (Figure 12.44).

12.44 A rendered image of a solid material attached to solid objects.

45 Save the model file as Render.dwg.

If you do not want to continue at this point, choose *Exit* from the *File* menu to exit AutoCAD.

In this tutorial exercise you have learned how to define various *materials* and attach them to solid objects in the model. You have also learned how to manipulate various material properties, such as *color, reflectivity,* and *transparency,* and how to simulate the subtleties in surface properties using *image mapping.* In the next section you will learn the basic concepts associated with animation and virtual reality.

BASIC CONCEPTS: ANIMATION AND VIRTUAL REALITY

The model's geometry, viewing parameters, lighting, and surface material properties can change over *time*, thus adding a fourth dimension to the model. 3D objects can be translated, rotated, scaled, skewed, or transformed in other ways. Cameras that define perspective views can change their location and lens length. Lights can change their position, orientation, intensity, and color. And surface materials can change, too.

ANIMATION

The model changes its states in incremental fashion as transformations take place over time. The specific moment of time when some change begins or is completed is called a *keyframe*. The intermediate states between keyframes can be computed by *interpolation* and rendered automatically by the software—that's a key idea behind computer animation.

Consider, for example, a camera object in some hypothetical building model that moves from one corner of the building to another over a period of three seconds. The first keyframe at 00:00:00 (*minutes:seconds:frames*) defines the model's state before the camera begins to move (Figure 13.1). The second keyframe, at 00:03:00 (three seconds later), defines the model's state after the camera has moved to the other corner (Figure 13.2). All the intermediate states (frames) are then interpolated—in each successive frame the camera moves a little bit, in precise, incremental steps (Figure 13.3).

AutoCAD (AutoVision) offers limited animation features, which are sufficient for most purposes in architectural design.

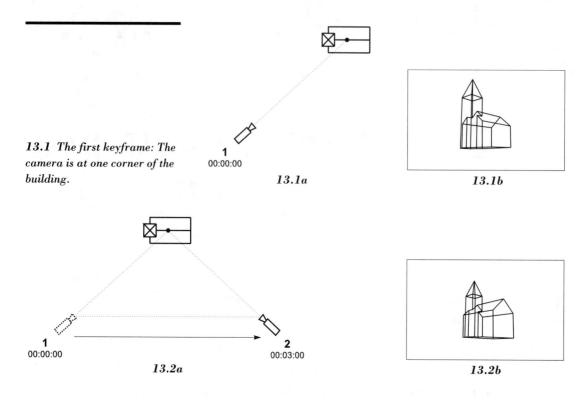

13.1 *The first keyframe: The camera is at one corner of the building.*

1
00:00:00

13.1a

13.1b

1
00:00:00

2
00:03:00

13.2a

13.2b

13.2 *The second keyframe: The camera is at the opposite corner.*

The number of steps needed to complete the transformation will be determined based on the desired number of *frames* per second (or between keyframes). At a rate of 25 frames per second, the sequence showing the previously described movement of the camera will contain 76 frames, that is, the beginning keyframe at 00:00:00, and 25 frames for each successive second. Since the beginning and end states are known, there will be 74 remaining frames to compute by interpolation.

After the keyframes are defined, the animation software computes each frame as a *rendered image*. At the end, a number of images are created, which if shown at an appropriate *display rate* and in fixed *temporal sequence,* will visually depict the model's transformation over time.

This sequence of rendered images, rapidly shown on the screen, is called *animation*. The rate at which images are shown is known as *display rate* and is measured by the number of images, that is, *frames per second* (fps). Low display rates result in jerky motion. To achieve the illusion of smooth motion, animation frames must be shown at a rate faster than 24 frames per second,

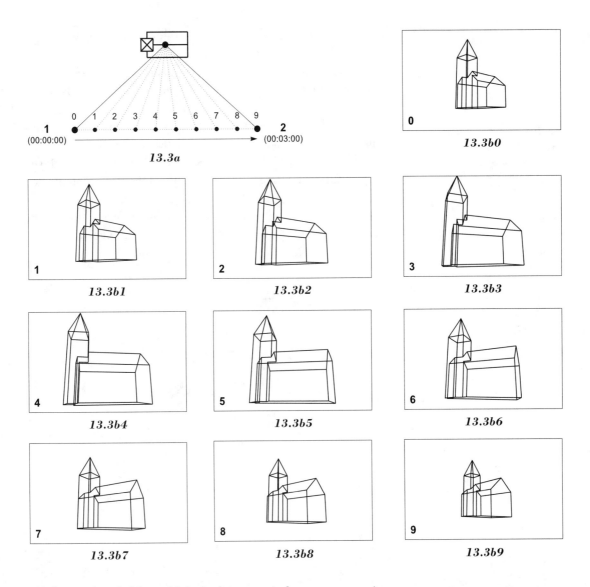

13.3a

0

13.3b0

1

13.3b1

2

13.3b2

3

13.3b3

4

13.3b4

5

13.3b5

6

13.3b6

7

13.3b7

8

13.3b8

9

13.3b9

which is a threshold at which the human mind stops to perceive individual frames and begins to see the smooth motion instead. If the sequence is shown rapidly enough, the illusion of a "moving picture" is created.

As 3D objects, cameras, and lights change their position and orientation over time, they define the so-called *motion paths*, swept during the transformation by some characteristic point (Figure 13.4). As graphic records of the change, motion paths also show the keyframes, that is, the key states in an object's

13.3 The intermediate steps can be computed by interpolation over time.

The motion picture film is shown at 24 fps (frames per second), and videotape at 30 fps in the United States and Japan, or at 25 fps in Europe and the rest of the world.

transformation, as well as intermediate states, known as *in-between frames* (states between keyframes).

If the intervals between frames, shown along the motion path, are of equal length, the transformation will take place at a uniform rate. However, if the intervals are unequal, the transformation will be faster or slower, depending on whether the intervals are longer or shorter, respectively (Figure 13.5).

The rate at which the change takes place can be displayed graphically by plotting a desired variable (position, rotation, etc.) against the time (Figure 13.6). In fact, some animation programs display the rate of change in this fashion, allowing the user to make adjustments by changing the shape of the corresponding curves.

13.4 *A camera motion path swept as it moves from one position to another.*

13.5 *Longer intervals between frames mean a faster pace of change, and shorter intervals mean a slower pace of change.*

13.6 *The rate of change can also be displayed graphically.*

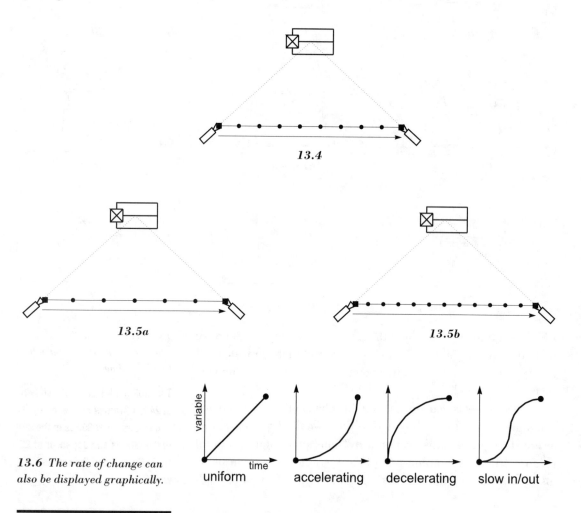

13.4

13.5a   13.5b

uniform   accelerating   decelerating   slow in/out

ANIMATION STRATEGIES

Several standard types of animations can be produced by simply varying the viewing parameters. A *"fly-by"* or *"drive-by"* animation can be produced by moving both the camera and the target point uniformly along a linear path, either above the building or at eye level above ground (Figure 13.7).

An often used alternative is to move the camera and keep the target fixed (Figure 13.8); the resulting effect resembles that of filming a building from a passing car while constantly keeping the building within the picture frame.

13.7 A "drive-by" animation: Both the camera and the target point move along a linear path.

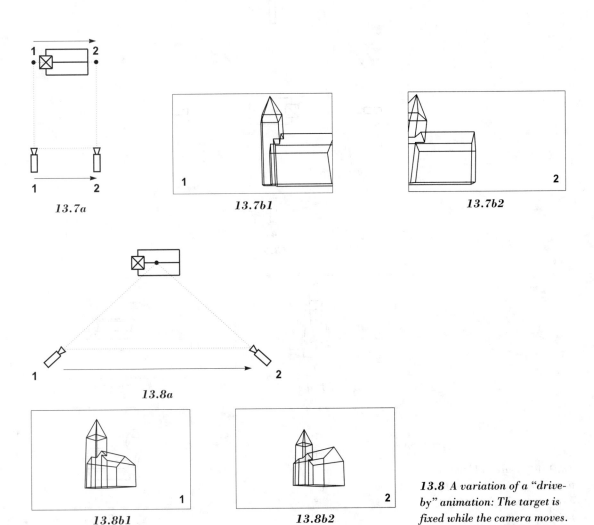

13.7a

13.7b1

13.7b2

13.8a

13.8b1

13.8b2

13.8 A variation of a "drive-by" animation: The target is fixed while the camera moves.

In a "*fly-around*" or "*drive-around*" animation the camera rotates full circle (360 degrees) around a fixed target point (Figure 13.9). Note that this type of animation can be *looped,* that is, shown repeatedly, for a longer-lasting effect.

The most commonly used animation technique in architecture is "*walk-through,*" whereby both the camera and the target move along complex and often separate paths (Figure 13.10). It is often the most difficult type of animation to set up, because the

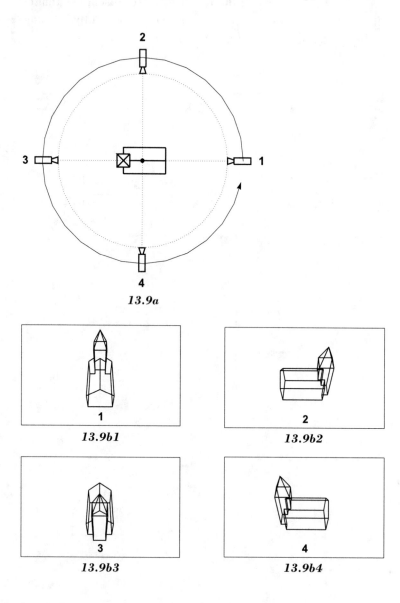

13.9a

13.9 A "fly-around" animation: The camera rotates full circle around a fixed target point.

13.9b1

13.9b2

13.9b3

13.9b4

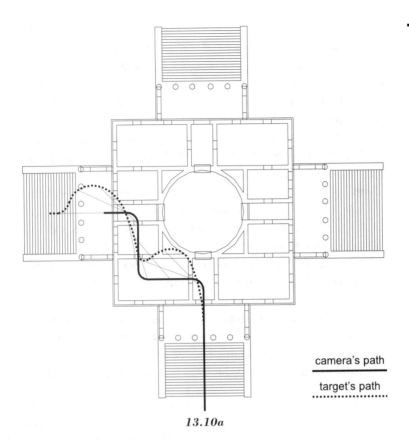

camera's path
—————————

target's path
....

13.10a

13.10 A "walk-through" ani-mation: Notice the complex motion paths for camera and target points.

13.10b1

13.10b2

13.10b3

13.10b4

13.10b5

motion paths can often be complex, with many keyframes, while the pace of animation (the rate of change) must be fairly uniform.

Panning animation is produced by keeping the camera at a fixed position and moving the target point along a linear path (Figure 13.11). This technique is often used to show a facade of a long horizontal building or a tall skyscraper.

Another commonly used technique is *zooming*, which involves a simple change of the lens length (Figure 13.12): to *zoom in*, change the lens length from smaller to higher values (for example, from 35 mm to 70 mm); to *zoom out*, do the opposite (for example, change the lens length from 50 mm to 25 mm). Either of the zooming techniques offers an effective way to show a detail within some larger context.

Another technique, although rarely used in architectural animation, is *tilting*, whereby the camera is rotated at its location (Figure 13.13).

These animation techniques are based on varying viewing parameters—the model's geometry and illumination are left unchanged. Interesting animations can be produced by moving the lights within or around the model while the camera remains

13.11 A panning *animation: The camera remains fixed while the target moves along a linear path.*

13.12 A zooming *animation: The camera's lens length changes between two keyframes.*

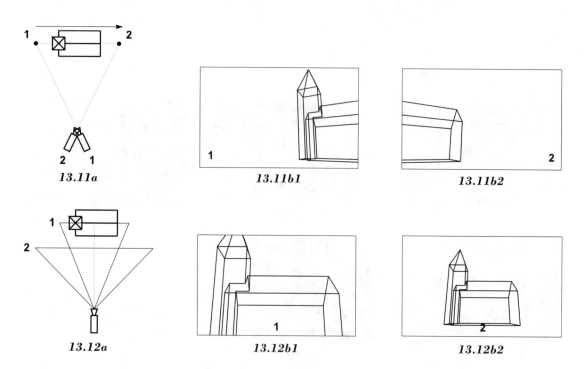

13.11a

13.11b1

13.11b2

13.12a

13.12b1

13.12b2

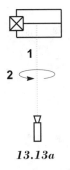
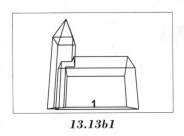

13.13a 13.13b1

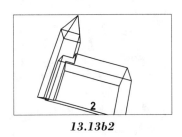

13.13b2

fixed. Cast shadows can be studied by moving the directional light source representing the "sun" along its imaginary path from "east" to "west" (Figure 13.14). By simultaneously changing the intensity and the color of the "sunlight," the sunrise and sunset lighting effects can be simulated.

Other types of animations can be produced by translating and by rotating 3D objects in the model while keeping both the camera and the lighting fixed. The so-called *assembly* animations can be generated in this fashion (Figure 13.15).

Note that an animation can feature *simultaneous* changes to the model's geometry, lighting, and viewing. For example, a cam-

13.13 A tilting *animation: The camera is rotated about the line of sight.*

13.14 *Lights can be animated, too: in this example, a directional light source moves from one side of the building to another (from "east" to "west").*

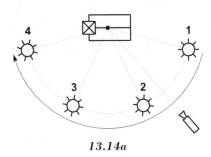

13.14a

13.14b1

13.14b2

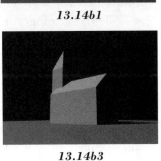

13.14b3

13.14b4

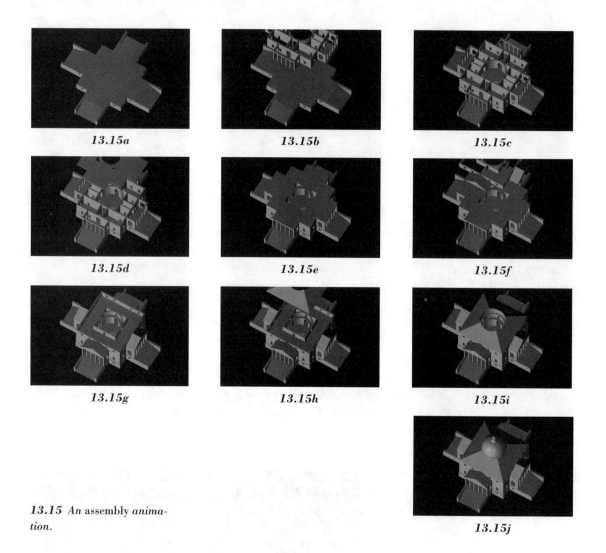

13.15a

13.15b

13.15c

13.15d

13.15e

13.15f

13.15g

13.15h

13.15i

13.15j

13.15 An assembly *animation.*

era with a spotlight attached to it can be moving toward a door that is slowly opening. An object representing a glazed elevator can move simultaneously with the camera to show the building's lobby.

The secret to creating successful architectural animations lies in *simple* motion paths and a fairly *slow* rate of change. Complex motion paths combined with fast-paced changes can make the audience dizzy and distracted by too much motion. In architectural animation, it is not the *motion* that matters, but the *spatial, experiential* qualities of space that you are trying to convey.

COMPUTATIONAL STRATEGIES

Generating animation sequences is a process that can take a considerable amount of time to complete, depending on the complexity of the model and the selected rendering algorithm. Powerful graphic workstations, with a fast processor, or several processors, plenty of working memory (RAM), high storage capacity, and special hardware for rendering acceleration are often used to shorten the time it takes to compute an animation sequence.

Animation sequences are computed *frame by frame*, i.e., *image by image*. Since a typical 10-second animation at 30 frames per second will require 300 images to render, various computational strategies need to be employed to shorten the rendering time. In other words, the animation process must be organized very carefully to achieve optimal results within the constraints of time and computational resources. There are several strategies animators use to optimize the animation process. First, motion and other spatial changes within the model are typically *previewed* in wire-frame mode, often at low resolution (160 × 120 or 320 × 240). Any perceptible jerkiness in motion can easily be corrected and reexamined at this point. Next, every fifth or tenth frame of the animation (depending on the total number of frames) is computed to verify that the lighting and material properties are rendered properly. Finally, when motion, lighting, and surface properties have been carefully examined, a lengthy process of rendering each animation frame can begin.

Note that 3D geometric models built for rendering animation sequences require *less detail* than ones developed for still images, because the motion through the model, if it is not too slow, leaves little time for examining the details. Thus, animation models can often be simplified to reduce the amount of time it takes to render individual frames.

If you have limited computation resources, you will have to carefully balance the level of detail in the model that will be rendered, the rendering technique that will be applied, and the total length of the animation, that is, the total number of frames that will be rendered. For example, Phong shading requires less time than ray tracing, which in turn requires less time than radiosity.

With sufficient computing power, animation frames can be computed "on the fly," that is, at rates of 25 to 30 frames per second, and shown on-screen in "real time." If "real-time" animation

Note that if there are no changes in the model's geometry, a walk-through animation of interior spaces can often be generated faster using radiosity than ray-tracing—in fact, once the lengthy computation of energy transfer paths is completed, you can instantly generate any walk-through animation in *real time*.

is not feasible, individual animation frames can be stored on hard disk or some other fast storage device while the images are being rendered, and retrieved for "real-time" playback once the rendering is complete. Such "real-time" playback requires very fast, high-capacity storage and often involves lossy image compression to reduce the individual image sizes and, consequently, the retrieval time.

VIDEO POST-PROCESSING

Another commonly used approach is to save individual frames onto hard disk, and then transfer (record) them, frame by frame, to videotape, which is then played back. This requires a video card that can translate digital image data into analog video output in NTSC (the so called "American") or PAL ("European") format, and a *frame-accurate* video recorder that will perform the actual recording onto a videotape.

Note that certain highly saturated colors (for example, bright red) cannot be displayed accurately, because of the limited color range. Many animation programs have video filters that can check and correct the image colors to fit within a displayable color range. You should avoid areas of high contrast in images, such as thin dark lines against a bright background, because they can often cause perceptible *flicker*. Use *anti-aliasing* when rendering to avoid flicker that can result from jagged edges.

Just as a rendered image of a building can be superimposed over a scanned site picture, a rendered animation can be superimposed over video footage of the site using *video editing equipment* or using *digital video editing systems* (Figure 13.16). Both types of equipment are fairly expensive. Superimposing animation over video is a particularly difficult task—the motion of the animated camera must be coordinated perfectly with the motion path of the "live" camera that is used to record the video footage. You can greatly simplify this difficult task by using a fixed camera position or by moving the camera along a simple linear or circular path.

A particularly simple strategy to add a higher degree of realism to presentations is to superimpose a *still* image of the proposed building over *still* live video footage (i.e., shot with a still camera), with people and cars moving by. Such superimposition of a computer rendering over a video sequence can be accom-

Digital video (DVD) is already replacing analog video; soon there will be no need to record computer animation onto videotape.

NTSC is a video standard used mainly in the United States and Japan, while PAL is a standard used in most of the European countries and the rest of the world. The key difference between these two standards is the rate and resolution at which they display images. NTSC uses 30 fps, and PAL a 25 fps display rate.

For best results, use video cards that can generate the so-called S-video or YC component video signal, with SMPTE time code for frame-accurate recording. You should, of course, also use a video recorder that accepts S-video or YC component video signal as input, and that supports remote control by computer for *frame-accurate* recording.

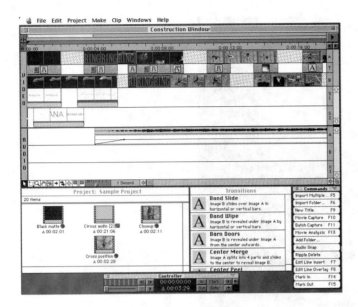

13.16 *The software for digital video editing (Adobe Premiere).*

plished by *chroma-keying*, whereby a selected color within the rendered image is defined as transparent, and, therefore, all pixels that have that chroma-key color are replaced with video data.

VIRTUAL REALITY

Unlike animation systems, which produce carefully scripted sequences of spatial experiences, virtual reality (VR) systems allow the viewer to interact with the "virtual" space. They provide *immersive, real-time stereoscopic* interaction with the artificial 3D environment that is so visually and spatially convincing and enveloping that your mind begins to perceive it as *reality*.

A typical VR system consists of a very powerful graphic workstation, a *headset* that projects *images* and *sounds* generated by the computer, and a *data glove* or *joystick* used for interaction with the virtual environment (Figure 13.17).

The headset (or a pair of "eyeglasses" and headphones) has two small displays, each showing a slightly different view of the model to each eye (Figure 13.18) to produce a stereoscopic visual effect, an illusion, of the "true" three-dimensional space.

The viewer navigates through the model by using a joystick, or by simply moving the head or eyes. Some headsets have sensory equipment that can translate head or eye motion into a corre-

BASIC CONCEPTS: ANIMATION AND VIRTUAL REALITY   381

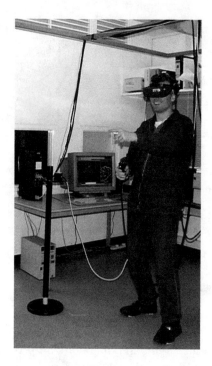

13.17 *A typical* virtual reality system.

13.18 *In VR systems, each eye sees a slightly different image.*

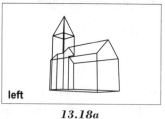

left

13.18a

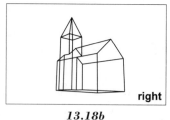

right

13.18b

sponding "virtual" camera movement within the model. Based on sensed motion parameters, the VR system can determine the viewer's position and the viewing direction, and can then compute the correct animated sequences of images for each eye. Some systems can also simulate the sound reverberations through space, and through headphones, present slightly different sounds to the left and right ear to yield a stereo effect, thus reinforcing the illusion. Further extensions are also possible; if the viewer wears a *data glove* on his or her hand, objects within a 3D scene can be "grasped," "carried," or transformed in some other fashion. For example, you could enter a "virtual" house by "grasping" the "door handle" or by "turning" the "doorknob"; you could turn the lights on by "touching" the "light switch."

To achieve convincing results, a virtual reality system must be *immersive* and *interactive*. It should *immerse* you in its artificial environment so convincingly that you believe you are *in it*. It should allow you to *interact* with that environment using bodily gestures, such as moving your eyes, head, or hand. Try to imagine an environment where images are not displayed in front of you but are *all around you;* where instead of using a keyboard and a mouse to navigate through 3D space, you simply extend your hand or point in some direction with a finger; where you simply move your head to see a different part of the scene.

THE VR SURROGATES

At present, any software that simulates the temporal phenomenon of moving through "virtual" 3D space has the VR suffix or prefix in its name, even though it doesn't provide the stereoscopic effect necessary for the illusion of depth, or immersiveness. For example, Apple Computer, Inc. has devised an elegant way of interacting with and navigating through 3D space called QuickTime VR. The *authoring* software first generates a static 360-degree panoramic view of the scene from a number of real or rendered images, which are taken in precise increments (Figure 13.19). The visual information in the panoramic view is then compressed and transformed in real time by *viewing* software into a correct perspective projection (Figure 13.20). The viewer can also zoom in or zoom out, and the software will perform the interpolation of pixels to approximate the real effect of getting closer to or farther away from a particular area of the scene.

The QuickTime VR software also offers the ability to create a spherical projection of an object so that it can be viewed from any direction, as if you were holding it in hand and turning it around.

QuickTime VR has many advantages. The resulting "movie" files are fairly small in size and can be viewed on inexpensive computer systems. Its main drawback is a relatively low resolution (160×120 or 310×240) of the displayed image, which is required for real-time interaction on most systems. (Of course, if the panorama is viewed on a powerful workstation, the resolution and consequently the level of detail can be higher.)

HOLOGRAPHY

An animated sequence of images can be recorded on a holographic plate, which if viewed under appropriate lighting conditions, can reproduce the effect of a 3D object "floating in space."

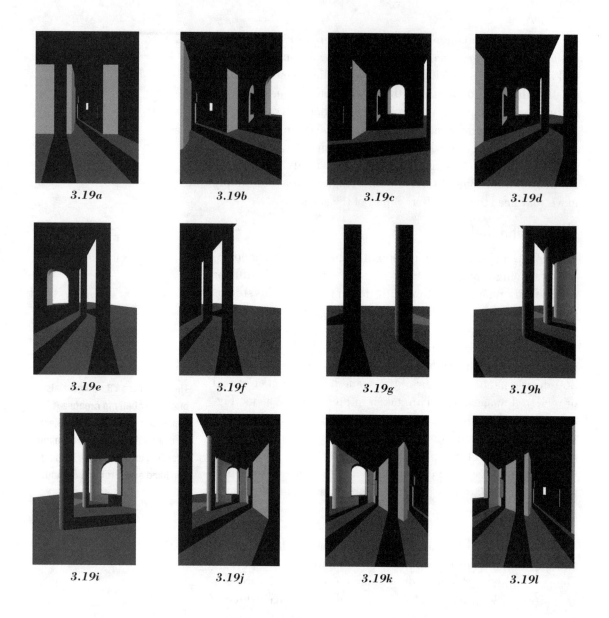

3.19a   3.19b   3.19c   3.19d

3.19e   3.19f   3.19g   3.19h

3.19i   3.19j   3.19k   3.19l

13.19 Creating a panoramic view by "stitching" a sequence of images.

The technology needed to create such holographic images is fairly simple. To produce the correct *parallax* effect, an animation sequence must first be created in which the camera and the corresponding target point are translated at precise increments in front of the model (Figure 13.21). The corresponding images are then rendered and recorded on film. Using red laser light, each

3.19m

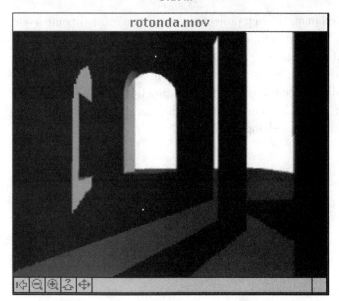

13.20 *The panoramic view is transformed by the viewing software into a correct perspective view of the scene.*

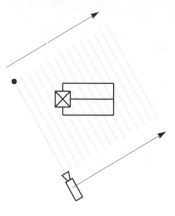

13.21 *The camera and target points are translated at precise increments to create a correct animation sequence of images.*

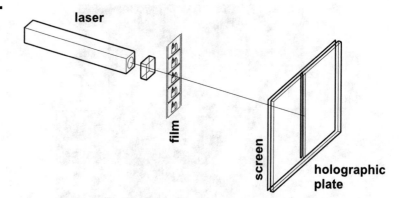

laser

film

screen

holographic
plate

*13.22 Using red laser light,
each rendered image is projected through a narrow slit
onto a holographic plate.*

**Even though crude prototypes of
holographic printers have been
developed and demonstrated,
this promising technology is still
not available commercially.**

rendered image is then projected through a narrow slit onto a corresponding part of the holographic plate (Figure 13.22).

After processing, the holographic plate, if viewed under appropriate lighting and at a specific angle, will reproduce a three-dimensional image of the building floating in space. As the viewer moves his head left or right, parallel to the plate, the "floating" image changes accordingly.

ANIMATION TUTORIAL: ANIMATING CAMERA AND LIGHT

In this tutorial exercise you will learn how to define and render various *animations*. You will create drive-by, panning, fly-around, and walk-through animations. You will also learn how to create sun and shadow studies by animating lights.

In AutoCAD R13, the AutoVision add-on software lets you set up and render animations of 3D models. You can specify camera and light movements over time. After you specify motion paths for a camera, target, or light, AutoVision creates a script file that renders a series of still images, which you can later compile into an animation file (a "movie") using the FLCREATE utility supplied with the software. You will use the Autodesk Animation Player software to view the animation files.

Note that AutoCAD R14 does not support animation. If you have AutoVision software for AutoCAD R13, however, you can enable R14 to render animations by simply copying some of the AutoVision files into the *Support* directory for R14, and by making a simple modification to one of those files (anim.lsp) in a word-processing program (such as Microsoft Word).

To enable R14 to render animations, copy the following AutoVision files into the *Support* directory for R14:

from the AVIS_SUP directory:

anim.lsp
api_anim.lsp
dlg_anim.lsp

walk.lsp
animdcl.dcl
flcreate.exe
rtm.exe

from the AVWIN directory:

aawin.exe
aaplay.dll
aavga.dll
aawin.hlp

After the files are copied, start some word processing program (such as Microsoft Word), and open the copied file *anim.lsp,* located in R14's *Support* directory. Find the following line in the file:

```
(if (/= (type c:render) `EXRXSUBR) (arxload
;|MSGO|;"autovis.arx")) ; arxload AutoVision if it's
not already loaded
```

and delete it. (This AutoLISP code instructs AutoCAD to load AutoVision software if it isn't already loaded; since the AutoCAD R14 program file contains AutoVision code, this code is unnecessary and can be removed.) After the deletion, save the file under the same name (in the *Text Only* [*.txt*] format), and exit the word processing program.

To load the animation program code in AutoCAD R14, enter at the command prompt the following AutoLISP instruction (including the parentheses and the quotation marks):

```
(load "anim")
```

If the execution was successful, you will see the message "Animation loaded" displayed in the command window. You can now proceed with the rest of this tutorial exercise.

DELETING THE MATERIAL DEFINITIONS

1 You will first undo some of the changes made to the model in the previous tutorial exercise. You will redisplay all the building layers and will delete the material definitions previously defined and attached to objects.

Start AutoCAD, and open the previously saved model file (Render.dwg). If you are continuing from the last exercise, skip this step.

2 Display the entire model within the graphics window. From the *View* menu select *Named Views*. In the resulting dialog box, select STANDARD_AXO in the list, click on the *Restore* button to restore that view, and then click on *OK* to continue.

3 Display all the building layers. Turn on the layers DOME and ROOF, and turn off the layer BASE.

4 Select the *Materials* tool on the *Render* (R13 *AutoVision*) toolbar, or enter RMAT at the command prompt. Click on the *Materials Library* button. Select all of the previously defined materials in the *Materials List* on the left (except *GLOBAL*), and then click on the *Delete* button. A number of warnings, such as "Warning: material BASE is currently attached," will be displayed; click on *OK* to dismiss them. Once the materials are deleted, click on the *OK* button in the *Materials* dialog box to continue.

5 Next delete the SPOT scene. Select the *Scenes* tool, or enter SCENE at the command prompt. In the *Scenes* dialog box, select the SPOT scene, click on the *Delete* button, and confirm the deletion. Click on *OK* to continue when done.

6 Also delete some of the lights that are no longer needed. Select the *Lights* tool, or enter LIGHT at the command prompt. In the *Lights* dialog box, select the SPOT light, click on the *Delete* button, and confirm the deletion when prompted. When done, click on *OK* to continue.

7 Save the model file as Render.dwg.

DRIVE-BY ANIMATION

8 In this section you will learn how to set up a "drive-by" animation. If you recall from the previous chapter, a "drive-by" animation is created by moving both the camera and target points uniformly along a linear path, either above the building or at eye level above ground.

Begin by displaying a plan view of the model. Enter PLAN at the command prompt, and press *Enter* to select the *current UCS* (which is the World Coordinate System).

9 Animation in AutoVision is based on defining *polyline* or *spline* paths along which camera and target should move. Create a layer named ANIMATION_PATHS, assign red color to it, and make it the current layer.

10 Draw the polyline paths for the camera and the target.

First draw the target's polyline path. Select the *3D Polyline* tool, or enter 3DPOLY at the command prompt. Enter 70′,0 [21,0] as the first point, and −70′,0 [−21,0] as the second point of the target's linear path. (Press *Enter* to complete the polyline.)

Next draw the camera's polyline path. Enter 70,−220 [21, −66] as the first point, and −70′,−220′ [−21,−66] as the second point of the camera's linear path.

The two paths should be parallel to each other (Figure 14.10).

11 Note that the two polyline paths are located at "ground" plane, that is, they are located at the "zero" height. You will move both of them up in space, that is, along the *z* axis. The target's path will be placed higher in space, at 40′ [12] above the ground, so that the building fits within the camera's "frame." The camera's path will be placed at the standard 5′6 [1.65] above the "ground."

Select the *Move* tool, or enter MOVE at the command prompt. Pick the target's polyline, and enter 0,0,40′ [0,0,12] as *displacement*. (Press *Enter* when prompted for the *second point of displacement*.) Reselect the *Move* tool, pick the camera's polyline, and enter 0,0,5′6 [0,0,1.65] as displacement.

12 You will use in R13 the *Animation* tool (in R14 the ANIMATE command) to define a new animation and to specify the drawn polylines as camera and target motion paths.

In R13 select the *Animation* tool (Figure 14.12a) on the *AutoVision* toolbar, or if you are using R14, enter ANIMATE at

Always use the *3D Polyline* tool (3DPOLY command) to draw motion paths.

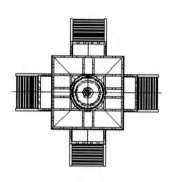

14.10 The motion paths for the camera and the target.

the command prompt. In the *Animation* dialog box (Figure 14.12b), click on the *New* button. Enter DRIVE_BY as the animation name, and click on *OK* in the *Animation Name* dialog box (Figure 14.12c). The newly created animation will be displayed in the *animation* list.

14.12a The Animation *tool.*

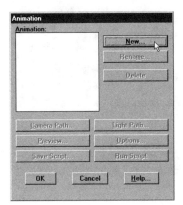

14.12b

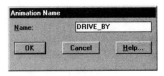

14.12c

14.12b The Animation *dialog box.*

14.12c Entering the animation name.

Next click on the *Camera Path* button to specify the previously created polylines as camera and target paths. In the resulting *Camera Path* dialog box (Figure 14.12d), click on the *Insert Movement* button. The dialog box will disappear, and the *camera movement* prompt will be displayed in the command window; press *Enter* to select the default option (*Path*), i.e., to pick polyline paths. When prompted, pick the *camera path polyline*. After you pick the camera path, the *target movement* options will be displayed in the command window; press *Enter* again to select the default option (*Path*). When prompted, pick the *target path polyline*. After you select the path polylines, the *Camera Path* dialog box will reappear. Notice that the *Movement Number* box shows 1.

Before you click on *OK* to continue, you should also set up the duration of the animation, that is, the *animation time*. Enter 2 (two seconds) in the box labeled *Current Movement* in the *Animation Time* section (Figure 14.12e). Click on *OK* to continue. Click on *OK* again to return to the *Animation* dialog box.

The *Animation* dialog box will reappear. Click on the *Preview* button to preview the animation in the active viewport. In the *Animation Preview* dialog box (Figure 14.12f), deselect the *Pause Between Frames* option, make sure that the *Camera* option is

The animation will be composed of 61 frames, or still images. The animation time is two seconds, and since the default rate is 30 frames per second, the animation will have $1 + 2 \times 30 = 61$ frames.

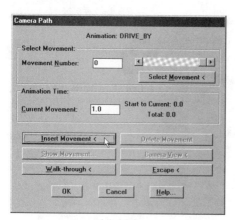

14.12d

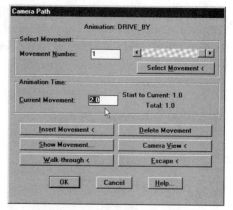

14.12e

14.12f

14.12d *The* Camera Path *dialog box.*

14.12e *Specifying the duration of the animation.*

14.12f *The* Animation Preview *dialog box.*

Note that you can specify at which frame in the animation to start and end the preview, by using the slide bars to define the *start* and *finish* times.

selected in the *View* section, and click on *OK*. The animation preview will be shown in the wire-frame mode in the active viewport.

Click on *OK* to continue.

13 In AutoVision, animation frames are rendered using current rendering options. Before you render the animation (that is, *run the animation script*), you should select the *Render* tool, and set the desired rendering options. This will often require creating a "dummy" rendering.

You will render your first animation at the low resolution of 320×240 pixels, with the fastest rendering algorithm. Once you are satisfied with the results, you can render a final animation at the higher resolution, using ray tracing, and with shadows, anti-aliasing, and materials. This way you will not waste time waiting for a lengthy computation to take place before you can preview the animation to verify that the camera motion or lighting is correctly set up.

Select the *Render* tool, or enter RENDER at the command prompt. Choose *Render* (R13 *AutoCAD Render*) as the *rendering type.* Select SUNLIGHT as the scene to render (this way, you will specify that lights associated with this scene should be used to render the animation). Choose *File* as the rendering *destination,* and then click on the *More Options* button. Choose *TGA* (TrueVision's *Targa* format) from the pop-up list as the *file type.* Select *User Defined* resolution from the pop-up list below, and enter 320 and 240 as *x* and *y* values, respectively (that is, the number of pixels horizontally and vertically in the rendered image). Select the *24 Bits* option in the *Colors* section. In the *Options* section, remove the check mark next to *Compressed* (i.e., no image compression), and choose *None* in the *Interlace* section. Click on *OK* to continue. Finally, click on *Render,* and enter *temp.tga* as the image file name, and save it in a directory for temporary files (typically, the TEMP directory) so that you can delete it later.

To compile still image files into an animation file (a "movie"), make sure that the file type is 24-bit, noninterlaced Targa (TGA). Note that if you intend to record your animation to a videotape, you should use 640 × 480 image resolution. Also, make sure that you choose high anti-aliasing for final rendering to avoid often perceptible "flicker" at objects' edges.

14 Select the *Animation* tool (or enter ANIMATE at the command prompt) again to render the animation. In AutoVision, to render the animation, you *run the animation script;* notice the *Run Script* button in the dialog box (Figure 14.12b). Before you do that, click on the *Options* button to specify the name prefix for image files and the directory where the images will be saved. In the *Animation Options* dialog box (Figure 14.14a) enter DRBYXXXX as the *Image File Name Template,* and enter the absolute path of the *Image File Directory* (C:/TEMP/, for example). The *Image File Name Template* determines the file names created by the animation script. For example, the value you entered (DRBYXXXX) will result in image file names starting with DRBY0001.tga through DRBY0061.tga (this animation has 61 frames and will be rendered in TGA file format). Notice that you can also specify the number of *frames per second* and the camera's *lens length* in this dialog box. Click on *OK* to continue.

Next save the animation script. You have specified the camera's path, set the rendering options, and specified the animation options, and are ready to render the animation. Click on the *Save Script* button, and in the resulting file specification dialog box (Figure 14.14b), enter DRIVE_BY.scr (if it is not already there), select the directory where the script should be saved, and click on *OK.*

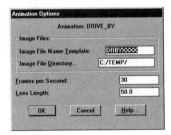

14.14a The Animation Options *dialog box.*

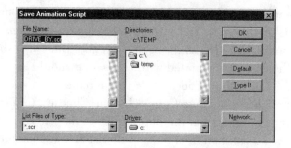

14.14b Saving the animation script file.

Note that image files take up disk space. Make sure that you have plenty of available storage space before running an animation script.

Finally, click on the *Run Script* button to run the animation script, that is, to render the animation. It will take several minutes for AutoCAD (AutoVision) to render 61 still images that make up the "drive-by" animation.

15 Save the model file as Render.dwg.

COMPILING AN ANIMATION

16 After the animation script is run, the result is a series of TGA still-image files, named DRBY0001.TGA to DRBY0061.TGA. To compile these into an animation file (an *.flc* or *.fli* "movie" file), you must run the FLCREATE utility supplied with the AutoVision software.

To run FLCREATE, open a DOS command window (an "operating system shell"), and change the directory (using the CD command) to locate the FLCREATE command file. If you are using R13, enter

```
CD C:\AutoVisionDirectory\ANIM_SUP
```

at the command prompt (replace *AutoVisionDirectory* with the name of the directory where AutoVision is installed [for example, AV]. If you are using R14, enter

```
CD "C:\Program Files\AutoCAD R14\Support"
```

assuming that you have installed R14 in the "Program Files\AutoCAD R14" directory on the C: hard disk.

To execute the FLCREATE command, enter the following at the command prompt (assuming that the image files are stored in the C:\TEMP directory and that you want the final animation file to be named DRBY.FLC and stored in the same C:\TEMP directory):

```
FLCREATE C:\TEMP\DRBY*.TGA /OC:\TEMP\DRBY.FLC
```

Note that DRBY*.TGA stands for all 61 previously created TGA files; the /O option is used to specify the desired location and the name of the output animation file, in this case C:\TEMP\ DRBY.FLC. A number of messages will be displayed in the command window as FLCREATE processes the rendered TGA image files. Once the FLCREATE command is completed, a "movie" file named DRBY.FLC will be created.

The syntax for the FLCREATE command is FLCREATE *filenames* *options.* **Typically, the** *filenames* **is the list of still-image files. Commonly used options are /O** *name,* **to specify output file name, and /B24, to create a 24-bit "flic" file.**

PLAYING AN ANIMATION

17 To play the previously created DRBY.FLC "flic" file, use the *Autodesk Animation Player for Windows.* Locate this file in the AVWIN directory if you are using R13, or in Support directory if you are using R14, and double-click its icon (Figure 14.17a).

The introductory screen will appear for a second, and the Player's (AAPlay) application window will appear (Figure 14.17b). Notice the play controls in the menu bar.

14.17a The Autodesk Animation Player for Windows program icon.

14.17b The Player's application window.

14.18 The first frame of the animation.

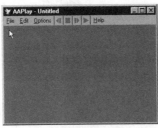

Aawin.exe
14.17a   *14.17b*

14.18

18 Choose *Open Animation* from the *File* menu, and locate and open the DRBY.FLC flic file that was previously created. The first frame of the animation will be displayed in the Player's window (Figure 14.18).

19 Click on the *Play* button (Figure 14.19a) to play the animation. Notice how the building quickly "zooms" from left to right, as if you were driving by (Figure 14.19b).

14.19a *The* Play *button.*

14.19a

14.19b1

14.19b2

14.19b3

14.19b4

14.19b5

14.19b6

14.19b7

14.19b8

14.19b9

14.19b10

14.19b11

14.19b12

14.19b *Every fifth frame
from the "drive-by" animation.*

14.19b13

20 You can change the animation playback speed. Click on the *Stop* button (Figure 14.20a) to stop the animation playback, then select *Anim Settings* from the *File* menu. In the *Animation Settings* dialog box (Figure 14.20b), select the *Frames per Second* option to set the playback speed, and enter 30 as the desired *fps* (*frames per second*) speed, which corresponds to the number of frames set before the animation script was run. Click on *OK* to continue. Click on the *Play* button again. Notice how the animation is playing much slower now—its total duration is now very close to 2 seconds, which was set up in AutoCAD before the animation was rendered.

14.20a The Stop *button.*

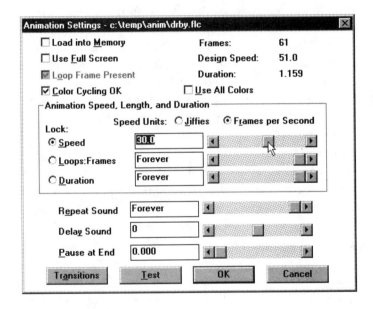

14.20b The Animation Settings *dialog box.*

21 You can also advance through the animation in a frame-by-frame fashion. Click on the *Stop* button, and then click on the *Forward* button (Figure 14.21a). You can also step through the animation by clicking on the *Backward* button (Figure 14.21b).

14.21a   *14.21b*

14.21a The Forward *button.*

14.21b The Backward *button.*

22 Switch back to AutoCAD. Leave the Player open, because you will need it to view the animation files that will be created in the remaining part of this tutorial.

PANNING ANIMATION

23 In this section you will set up and render the so-called panning animation. This type of animation is produced by keeping the camera at a fixed position and moving the target point along a linear path. This animation technique is often used to show a facade of a long horizontal building or a tall skyscraper. In R13 select the *Animation* tool, or if you are using R14, enter ANIMATE at the command prompt. In the *Animation* dialog box, click on the *New* button. Enter PANNING as the animation name, and click on *OK*. The newly created animation will be displayed in the *animation* list; click on it to make it active (Figure 14.23a).

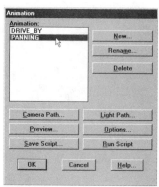

14.23a Selecting the "active" animation.

Next click on the *Camera Path* button to specify the camera and target paths. In the resulting *Camera Path* dialog box, click on the *Insert Movement* button. The dialog box will disappear, and the *camera movement* prompt will be displayed in the command window. Enter PO (*POint*) to select the point at which the camera will be located (the camera's location will be fixed). Enter 0, −180′,5′6 [0,−54,1.65] to specify the camera location on the villa's central axis. After you specify the camera's location, the *target movement* options will be displayed in the command window; press *Enter* to select the default option (*Path*). When prompted, pick the same *target path polyline* you used in the "drive-by" animation. The *Camera Path* dialog box will reappear.

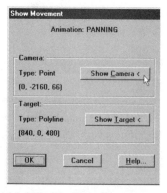

14.23b The Show Movement *dialog box.*

Click on the *Show Movement* button to examine the selected location of the camera and the selected motion path for the target. In the resulting dialog box (Figure 14.23b), click on the *Show Camera* button. The camera's location will be indicated by an X in the plan view (Figure 14.23c). Hit any key to continue. Click on the *Show Target* button. The target's motion path polyline will be also indicated by an X (Figure 14.23d). Hit any key to return to the dialog box, and click on *OK* to continue.

In the *Camera Path* dialog box, click on the *Camera View* button to display a wire-frame preview of the model from the camera position at the beginning of the current camera movement (Figure 14.23e). Hit any key to return to the dialog box.

Next set up the duration of the animation before you continue. Enter 4 (four seconds) in the box labeled *Current Movement* in the *Animation Time* section. Click on *OK* to continue. Click on *OK* again to return to the *Animation* dialog box.

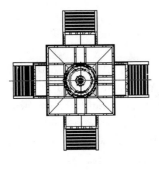

14.23c

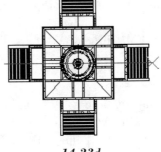

14.23d

14.23e

In the *Animation* dialog box, click on the *Preview* button to preview the animation in the active viewport. In the *Animation Preview* dialog box, deselect the *Pause Between Frames* option, make sure that the *Camera* option is selected in the *View* section, and click on *OK*. The animation preview will be shown in the wire-frame mode in the active viewport. Notice how the top and the bottom part of the villa are "clipped." To show the entire villa, from the top of the dome to the bottom of the portico stairs, increase the camera lens length. Click on the *Options* button, and set the lens length to 35 mm (Figure 14.23f). Click again on the *Preview* button to see the change; the villa's top and bottom are no longer clipped.

The animation is now almost set up. The only remaining part is to specify the image file names and the location where the files will be stored. Click on the *Options* button again, and set the *image file name template* to PANXXXX and the *image file directory* to C:/TEMP/ (or some other directory). Click on *OK* to continue.

Save the animation script: Click on the *Save Script* button, and save the script as PANNING.scr. Click on *Run Script* to render this animation; note that the rendering parameters will be the same as in the previous animation (320 × 240 resolution, TGA image file format, with no compression and no interlacing).

14.23c The camera's location, indicated by an X.

14.23d The target's motion path.

14.23e The first frame of the current camera movement.

14.23f Adjusting the camera's lens length.

24 After the rendering is completed, save the model file as Render.dwg.

25 Compile the image files using the FLCREATE utility, as described in step 16. To run FLCREATE, switch to a DOS command window you have opened in step 16, and enter the following command at the system prompt (assuming that the image files are stored in the C:\TEMP directory and that you want the final animation file to be named PAN.FLC and stored in the same C:\TEMP directory):

```
FLCREATE C:\TEMP\PAN*.TGA /OC:\TEMP\PAN.FLC
```

A number of messages will be displayed in the command window as FLCREATE processes 121 (4 seconds * 30 frames/second + 1) rendered TGA image files. Once the FLCREATE command is completed, a "movie" file named PAN.FLC is created.

26 Switch to the *Autodesk Animation Player for Windows*, which you opened in step 17. Choose *Open Animation* from the *File* menu, and locate and open the PAN.FLC flic file. Adjust the playback speed to 30 frames per second, and click on the *Play* button. Notice how the motion is much slower now (Figure 14.26), because it takes place over a longer period of time.

27 Stop the animation playback, and switch back to AutoCAD. (Leave the *Player* open.)

FLY-AROUND ANIMATION

Often the best way to render an architectural animation is to use simple motion paths and specify long animation time.

28 In a "fly-around" (or "drive-around") animation, the camera rotates full circle (360 degrees) around a fixed target point. This animation technique is often used to show a building in its context from an aerial perspective.

To create a "fly-around" animation, first create a circular motion path for the camera. Since AutoVision recognizes only polylines as the motion paths, you will have to create a curve-fitted polyline that has a circular shape. You will first draw a square polyline, and then apply the *Edit Polyline* tool (the PEDIT command) to fit a curve to that polyline.

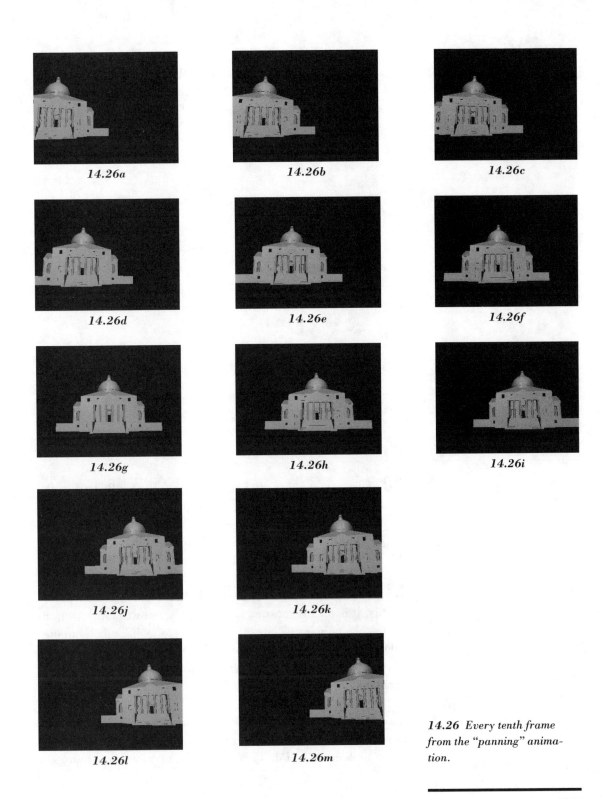

14.26a

14.26b

14.26c

14.26d

14.26e

14.26f

14.26g

14.26h

14.26i

14.26j

14.26k

14.26l

14.26m

14.26 Every tenth frame from the "panning" animation.

Select the *Polyline* tool, or enter PLINE at the command prompt, and enter 0,–220′ [0,–66] for the first point, 220′,0 [66,0] for the second point, 0,220′ [0,66] for the third point, –220′,0 [–66,0] for the fourth point, and then C (close) to close the polyline shape (Figure 14.28).

14.28 The square polyline that will be curve-fitted to create a circular motion path for the camera.

29 Select the *Zoom All* tool to see the entire polyline shape.

30 Next select the *Edit Polyline* tool, or enter PEDIT at the command prompt. Select the previously created polyline. At the command prompt, enter F to select the *Fit* option. The square polyline will instantly be turned into a circular shape (Figure 14.30). Enter X to exit the PEDIT command.

31 Note that this circular path is located on a "ground" plane, that is, it is located at the "zero" height. You will move it up in space, along the *z* axis, by 80′ [24]. Select the *Move* tool, or enter MOVE at the command prompt. Pick the circular polyline, and enter 0,0,80′ [0,0,24] as *displacement*. (Press *Enter* when prompted for the *second point of displacement*.)

32 Now that the path is placed at the correct height, set up a new animation. In R13 select the *Animation* tool, or if you are using R14, enter ANIMATE at the command prompt, and create a

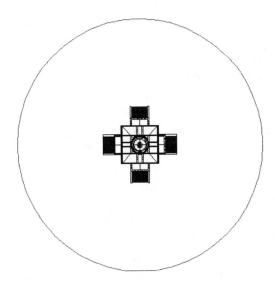

new animation called FLY_AROUND. The newly created animation will be displayed in the *animation* list; click on it to make it active.

Next click on the *Camera Path* button in the *Animation* dialog box to specify the camera and target paths. In the resulting *Camera Path* dialog box, click on the *Insert Movement* button. The dialog box will disappear, and the *camera movement* prompt will be displayed in the command window; press *Enter* to select the default option (*Path*). When prompted, pick the *circular polyline*. After you specify the camera's path, the *target movement* options will be displayed in the command window. Enter PO (*POint*) to select the point at which the target will be located (the target's location will be fixed). Enter 0,0,20′ [0,0,6] to specify the target's location on the villa's vertical axis. The *Camera Path* dialog box will reappear. Click on *OK* to continue.

Next set up the duration of the animation. Enter 4 (four seconds) in the box labeled *Current Movement* in the *Animation Time* section. Click on *OK* to continue. Click on *OK* again to return to the *Animation* dialog box.

In the *Animation* dialog box, click on the *Options* button, and set the lens length to 35 mm.

Click on the *Preview* button to preview the animation in the active viewport. In the *Animation Preview* dialog box, deselect the *Pause Between Frames* option, make sure that the *Camera* option

Note that you can insert more than one movement associated with a camera path. This feature is often useful in setting up walk-through animations.

is selected in the *View* section, and click on *OK*. The animation preview will be shown in the wire-frame mode in the active viewport. Notice how the building "rotates" in the viewport (actually, the camera rotates around the building).

The fly-around animation is now almost set up. The only remaining part is to specify the image file names and the location where they will be stored. Click on the *Options* button again, and set the *image file name template* to FLYXXXX and the *image file directory* to C:/TEMP/ (or some other directory). Click on *OK* to continue.

Save the animation script: Click on the *Save Script* button, and save the script as FLY_ARND.scr. Click on *Run Script* to render this animation; note that the rendering parameters will be the same as in the previous animation (320 × 240 resolution, TGA image file format, with no compression and no interlacing).

33 After the rendering is completed, save the model file as Render.dwg.

34 Compile the image files using the FLCREATE utility, as described in step 16. To run FLCREATE, switch to a DOS command window you have opened in step 16, and enter the following command at the system prompt (assuming that the image files are stored in the C:\TEMP directory and that you want the final animation file to be named FLY.FLC and stored in the same C:\TEMP directory):

```
FLCREATE C:\TEMP\FLY*.TGA /OC:\TEMP\FLY.FLC
```

A number of messages will be displayed in the command window as FLCREATE processes 121 (4 seconds * 30 frames/second + 1) rendered TGA image files. Once the FLCREATE command is completed, a "movie" file named FLY.FLC is created.

35 Switch to the *Autodesk Animation Player for Windows*, which you opened in step 17. Choose *Open Animation* from the *File* menu, and locate and open the FLY.FLC flic file. Adjust the playback speed to 30 frames per second, and click on the *Play* button. Notice how the back of the building in this animation (Figure 14.35) has a uniform dark color—that's because it doesn't receive

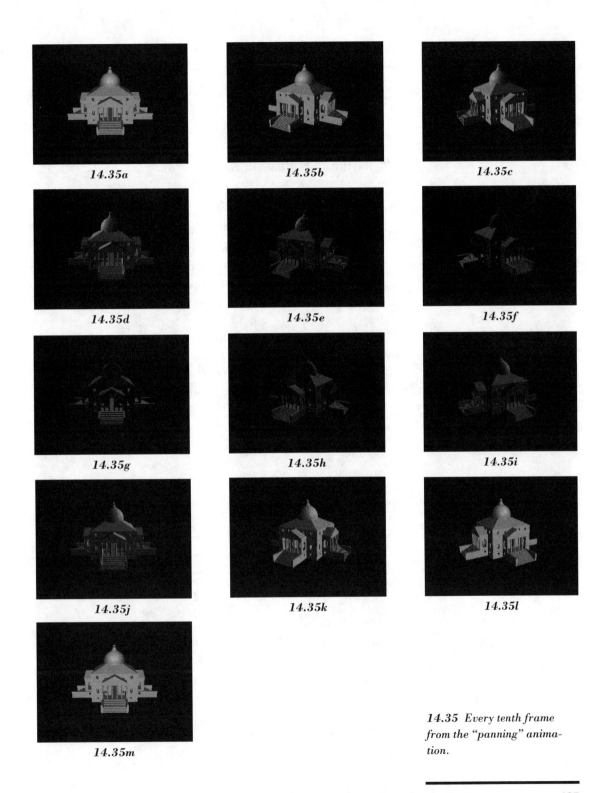

14.35a

14.35b

14.35c

14.35d

14.35e

14.35f

14.35g

14.35h

14.35i

14.35j

14.35k

14.35l

14.35m

14.35 Every tenth frame from the "panning" animation.

any light. When lighting a model for a fly-around animation, you should always place the "fill" light opposite the "key" light.

36 Stop the animation playback, and switch back to AutoCAD. (Leave the *Player* open.)

WALK-THROUGH ANIMATION

37 The most commonly used animation technique in architecture is "*walk-through*," whereby both the camera and the target move along complex and often separate paths. As described in the previous chapter, it is often the most difficult type of animation to set up because the motion paths can often be complex, with many keyframes, while the pace of animation (the rate of change) must be fairly uniform.

To create a walk-through animation of the villa, first create separate motion paths for the camera and the target. Select the *3D Polyline* tool, or enter 3DPOLY at the command prompt, and enter the following coordinates to define the camera's motion path polyline:

1	0,–46′	[0,–13.8]
2	0,–28′	[0,–8.4]
3	0,–26′	[0,–7.8]
4	–2′,–24′	[–0.6,–7.2]
5	–4′,–24′	[–1.2,–7.2]
6	–18′,–24′	[–5.4,–7.2]
7	–20′,–24′	[–6,–7.2]
8	–24′,–20′	[–7.2,–6]
9	–24′,–18′	[–7.2,–5.4]
10	–24′,–4′	[–7.2,–1.2]
11	–24′,–2′	[–7.2,–0.6]
12	–26′,0′	[–7.8,0]
13	–28′,0′	[–8.4,0]
14	–38′,0′	[–11.4,0]

The camera's polyline path should look like Figure 14.37a.

Next draw the target's motion path polyline. Enter the following coordinates for its points:

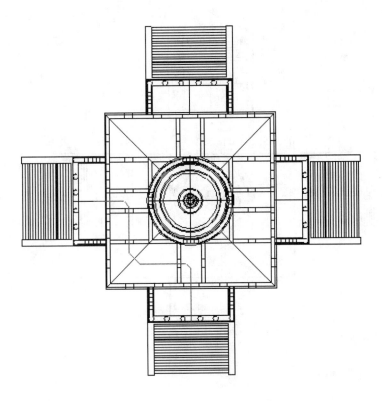

14.37a *The camera's path for a walk-through animation.*

1	0,−34′	[0,−10.2]
2	0,−28′	[0,−8.4]
3	−2′,−22′	[−0.6,−6.6]
4	−4′,−20′	[−1.2,−6]
5	−10′,−17′	[−3,−5.1]
6	−16′,−17′	[−4.8,−5.1]
7	−21′,−17′	[−6.3,−5.1]
8	−24′,−15′	[−7.2,−4.5]
9	−26′,−8′	[−7.8,−2.4]
10	−28′,0	[−8.4,0]
11	−36′,−3′	[−10.8,−0.9]
12	−45′,0′	[−13.5,0]
13	−60′,0′	[−18,0]
14	−70′,0′	[−21,0]

The target's polyline path should look like Figure 14.37b.

38 Next select the *Edit Polyline* tool, or enter PEDIT at the command prompt. Select the previously created polyline path for

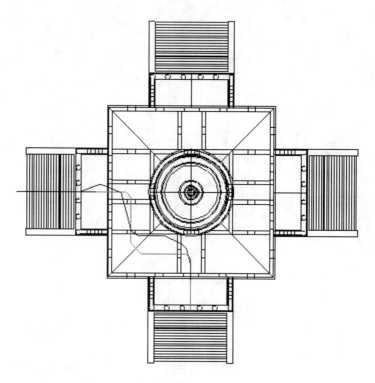

14.37b *The target's path for a walk-through animation.*

the camera. At the command prompt, enter S to select the Spline option and to turn the polyline path composed of linear segments into a smooth, curved path (Figure 14.38). Enter X to exit the PEDIT command.

39 Select the *Edit Polyline* tool again, and select the polyline path for the target. At the command prompt, enter S to select the Spline option and to turn that polyline into a smooth, curved path (Figure 14.39). Enter X to exit the PEDIT command.

40 Move both curved paths up in space, that is, along the *z* axis, by 15′6 [4.65], (10′ + 5′6, i.e., 3.0 + 1.65). Select the *Move* tool, or enter MOVE at the command prompt. Pick both paths, and enter 0,0,15′6 [0,0,4.65] as *displacement*. (Press *Enter* when prompted for the *second point of displacement*.)

41 Now that the paths are correctly placed, set up a new animation called WALK_THROUGH. Make sure that the newly created animation is selected (highlighted) in the *animation* list.

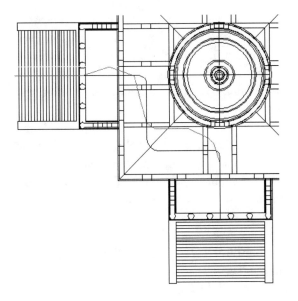

14.38 *The curved motion path for the camera.*

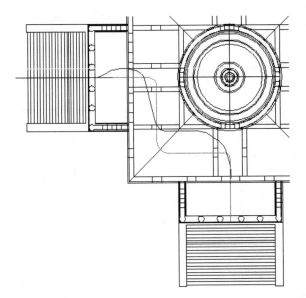

14.39 *The curved motion path for the target.*

Click on the *Camera Path* button in the *Animation* dialog box, then click on the *Insert Movement* button, and select the two curved paths, one for the camera, and the other one for the target motion. The *Camera Path* dialog box will reappear. Click on *OK* to continue.

Next set up the duration of the animation. Enter 4 (four seconds) in the box labeled *Current Movement* in the *Animation Time* section. Click on *OK* to continue. Click on *OK* again to return to the *Animation* dialog box.

In the *Animation* dialog box, click on the *Options* button, and set the lens length to 35 mm.

Click on the *Preview* button to preview the animation in the active viewport. In the *Animation Preview* dialog box, deselect the *Pause Between Frames* option, make sure that the *Camera* option is selected in the *View* section, and click on *OK*. The animation preview will be shown in the wire-frame mode in the active viewport.

Click on the *Options* button again, and set the *image file name template* to WALKXXXX and the *image file directory* to C:/TEMP/ (or some other directory). Click on *OK* to continue.

Save the animation script: Click on the *Save Script* button, and save the script as WALKTHRU.scr. Click on *Run Script* to render this animation; note that the rendering parameters will be the same as in the previous animation (320 × 240 resolution, TGA image file format, with no compression and no interlacing).

42 After the rendering is completed, save the model file as Render.dwg.

43 Compile the image files using the FLCREATE utility, as described in step 16. In the DOS command window, enter the following command at the system prompt (assuming that the image files are stored in the C:\TEMP directory and that you want the final animation file to be named WALK.FLC and stored in the same C:\TEMP directory):

```
FLCREATE C:\TEMP\WALK*.TGA /OC:\TEMP\WALK.FLC
```

44 Switch to the *Autodesk Animation Player for Windows*, choose *Open Animation* from the *File* menu, and locate and open the WALK.FLC flic file. Adjust the playback speed to 30 frames per second, and click on the *Play* button. You will move very quickly through the villa's interior (Figure 14.44).

45 Stop the animation playback, and switch back to AutoCAD. (Leave the *Player* open.)

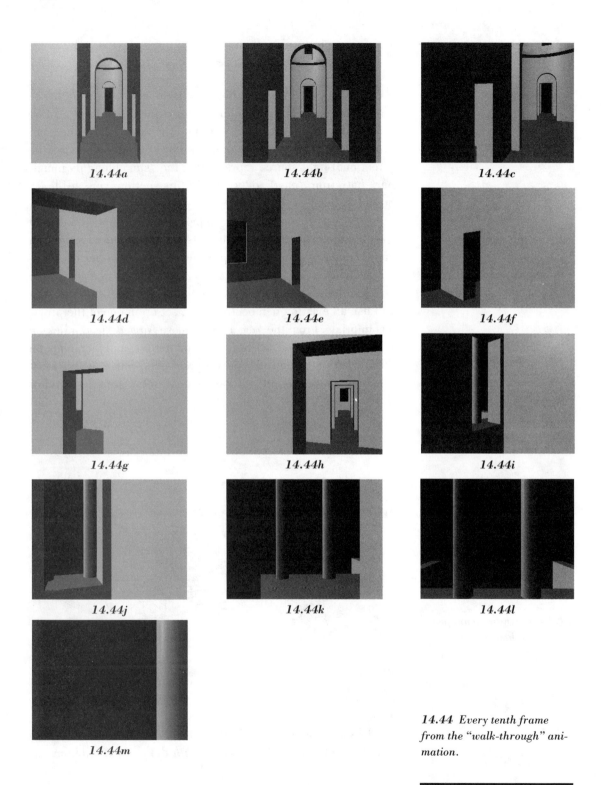

14.44a   14.44b   14.44c

14.44d   14.44e   14.44f

14.44g   14.44h   14.44i

14.44j   14.44k   14.44l

14.44m

14.44 Every tenth frame from the "walk-through" animation.

ANIMATING LIGHTS

46 All the animation techniques introduced so far were based on varying viewing parameters. Interesting animations can be produced by moving the lights around the model while the camera remains fixed. Cast shadows can be studied by moving the directional light source representing the "sun" along its imaginary path from "east" to "west." In this section, you will learn how to do that.

The AutoVision software can modify the position of a distant light source over time, including its *sun angle calculation*. You can animate a light source representing the sun either over certain hours during a single day or over certain days in a year.

Begin by setting up a fixed camera and target points. You will use an existing perspective view, set up in one of the previous tutorials. From the *View* menu choose *Named Views*, click on HIGH_TWO_POINT_PERSP, click on *Restore*, and then click on the *OK* button to continue. A two-point perspective, with a sight line high above ground, will be restored in the graphics window (Figure 14.46).

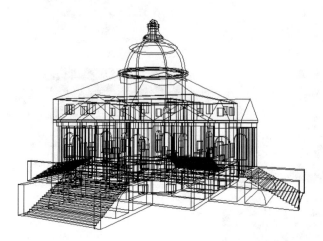

14.46 A high two-point perspective of the villa.

47 Now that the desired perspective view is set, create a new animation called SUN_STUDY. Make sure that the newly created animation is selected (highlighted) in the *animation* list.

Click on the *Camera Path* button in the *Animation* dialog box, and in the resulting *Camera Path* dialog box, click on the

Insert Movement button. The dialog box will disappear, and the *camera movement* prompt will be displayed in the command window. Enter C to select the *current camera position*. After you specify the camera's position, the *target movement* options will be displayed in the command window. Enter C to select the *current target position*. The *Camera Path* dialog box will reappear. Click on *OK* to continue.

Enter 2 (two seconds) in the box labeled *Current Movement* in the *Animation Time* section. Click on *OK* to continue. Click on *OK* again to return to the *Animation* dialog box.

In the *Animation* dialog box, click on the *Options* button, and set the lens length to 35 mm.

Next click on the *Light Path* button to define the distant light ("sun") path. In the *Light Path* dialog box (Figure 14.47a) select SUN distant light in the list, and select *Time* in the pop-up list as the light animation type. Click on the *Start/End Time* button, and set the *start time* to 9:00 and the *end time* to 15:00 (Figure 14.47b). Click on the *OK* button. Then click on the *Start/End Date*, and set both the *start* and *finish dates* to 6/21, i.e., June 21 (Figure 14.47c). Click on *OK*, and then click on *OK* in the *Light Path* dialog box to continue.

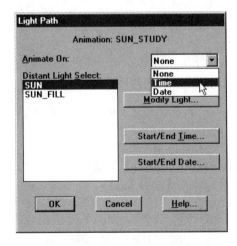

14.47a *The* Light Path *dialog box.*

Click on the *Options* button again, and set the *image file name template* to SUNXXXX and the *image file directory* to C:/TEMP/ (or some other directory). Click on *OK* to continue.

Save the animation script: Click on the *Save Script* button, and save the script as SUNSTUDY.scr. Click on *OK* to continue.

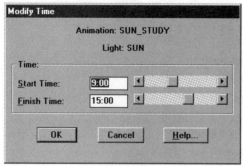

14.47b

14.47c

48 As mentioned previously, in AutoVision, animation frames are rendered using current rendering options. Before you render the sun-study animation (that is, *run animation script*), select the *Render* tool. In the *Render* dialog box, select *PhotoReal* (R13 *AutoVision*) as the rendering type, choose SUNLIGHT as the scene to render, select the *shadow* option, click on *More Options*, set *anti-aliasing* to *minimal*, and then create a "dummy" rendering in TGA file format.

49 After the rendering of a "dummy" image is completed, select the *Animation* tool again (or enter ANIMATE at the command prompt), and click on *Run Script* to render the sun-study animation.

50 After the rendering is completed, save the model file as Render.dwg.

51 Compile the image files using the FLCREATE utility, as described in step 16. In the DOS command window, enter the following command at the system prompt (assuming that the image files are stored in the C:\TEMP directory and that you want the final animation file to be named SUNSTUDY.FLC and stored in the same C:\TEMP directory):

```
FLCREATE C:\TEMP\SUN*.TGA /OC:\TEMP\SUNSTUDY.FLC
```

After the animation is compiled, close the command window.

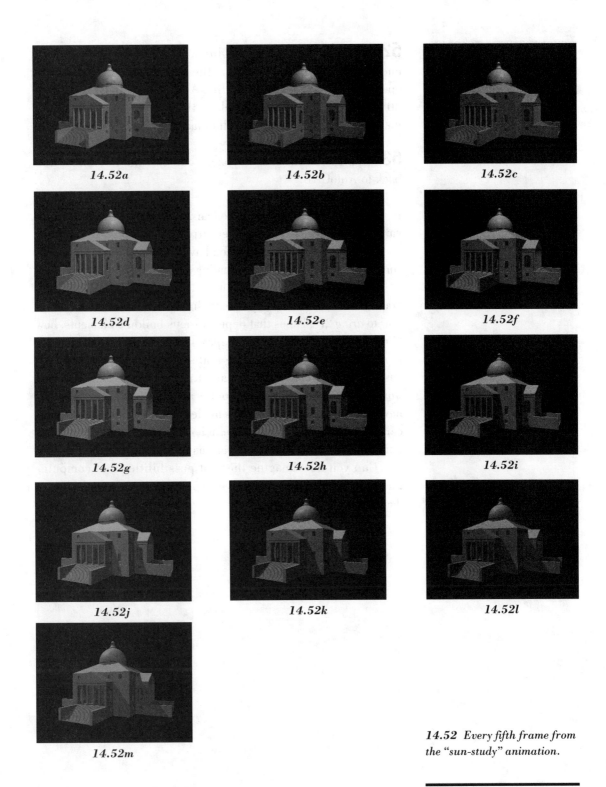

14.52a

14.52b

14.52c

14.52d

14.52e

14.52f

14.52g

14.52h

14.52i

14.52j

14.52k

14.52l

14.52m

14.52 *Every fifth frame from the "sun-study" animation.*

52 Switch to the *Autodesk Animation Player for Windows,* choose *Open Ani 9-mation* from the *File* menu, and locate and open the SUNSTUDY.FLC flic file. Adjust the playback speed to 30 frames per second, and click on the *Play* button. Notice how the shadows move across the villa's facade (Figure 14.52).

53 Stop the animation playback, and exit the *Player.* Switch back to AutoCAD.

In this tutorial exercise you have learned how to define and render various *animations.* You created drive-by, panning, fly-around, and walk-through animations. You have also learned how to create sun and shadow studies by animating distant lights.

This chapter concludes the introduction to 3D computer graphics in AutoCAD. As you read through this book, you learned how to *draw* 2D shapes that depict various building elements, how to *model* 3D objects from 2D shapes, how to illuminate 3D objects to *render* images that simulate realistic effects such as shadow casting and material textures, and finally, how to create *animations,* moving pictures of computer models. In the process you have also seen how AutoCAD's modeling and rendering features can be used to effectively and efficiently explore and represent a building's geometry, form, and various spatial qualities.

Can you now imagine the vast possibilities that computer graphics offers for the creative exploration and expression of design ideas?

The enclosed CD-ROM contains files for each of the seven tutorial exercises, so that you can start almost at any point. The files are also provided in case you make a mistake that you can't correct. In order to use the files on the CD-ROM, you must have AutoCAD R13 or AutoCAD R14 installed on your computer.

On the CD-ROM, files are divided into two folders: one contains files for AutoCAD R13, the other one for R14. Each of them has two sub-folders that contain files with either English or metric units. Finally, the files are organized into seven folders, each folder corresponding to one of the tutorial exercises (Draw-1, Draw-2, Model-1, Model-2, etc.). Within each of these folders, files are numbered according to the tutorial step in which they should be used. For example, file named MT3-27.DWG indicates an AutoCAD file that should be used in Modeling Tutorial 3, starting with step number 27.

USER ASSISTANCE

If you have basic questions about using the CD-ROM, contact Wiley Technical Support at:

Phone: (212) 850-6753
Fax: (212) 850-6800 (Attention: Wiley Technical Support)
E-mail: techhelp@wiley.com

To place additional orders or to request information about other Wiley products, please call (800) 225-5945.

A

scaling, 33, 105
stretch, 34, 105
trim, 33–34, 105
Translation, 33
Transparency, 254, 258,
    355–357
Trim, 33–34

U

UCS,
    definition (see Coordinate
        system)
    setup, 155–157, 159, 168,
        183
UCSICON system variable,
    159
Umbra (see Shadow)
Undo, 55
Union (see Boolean operations)
Units, 39, 40, 56
User interface, 8, 44–50

V

Viewing,
    operations, 34–36
    methods (see Projection)
    pyramid (see Cone of vision)
Viewports,
    description, 125, 126
    floating, 205
    printing, 150–152
    saving, 189

setup, 137–139
tiled, 125, 126
Video,
    editing, 378
    projector, 303
    post-processing, 378–379
Villa Rotonda, 16–18
Virtual reality, 379–381
Visual Aids, 28–32

W

WCS,
    description (see Coordinate
        system)
    setup, 164
Windows,
    bitmap format (BMP), 322
    interface, 8

X

Xline, 32, 62

Y

Yessios, Chris, 5
YC component video, 378

Z

Z-buffer, 271
Zooming, 35, 53–54

Branko Kolarevic is an architect with the Doctor of Design degree from Harvard University Graduate School of Design. Over the past eight years, he has taught computer-aided design courses at universities in Boston, Los Angeles, Miami, and Hong Kong. Presently he teaches design studio and CAD courses as assistant professor at the University of Hong Kong Department of Architecture. He is also the president of Association for Computer Aided Design in Architecture (ACADIA).

For information about the disk, refer to the Appendix on page 417.

WILEY
Publishers Since 1807